D0343381

HANDICAPPING SPEED:

The Thoroughbred and Quarter Horse Sprinters

HANDICAPPING SPEED:

The Thoroughbred
and Quarter Horse Sprinters

Charles H. Carroll

The Lyons Press

For my sons,
Cristopher and Cody

Copyright © 1991 by Charles Carroll

ALL RIGHTS RESERVED. No part of this book may be reproduced in any manner without the express written consent of the publisher, except in the case of brief excerpts in critical reviews and articles. All inquiries should be addressed to: The Lyons Press, 123 West 18 Street, New York, New York 10011.

Printed in the United States of America

10 9 8 7 6 5 4 3   (paperback edition)

Design by Heidi Haeuser

All excerpts from the *Daily Racing Form*
are reprinted with the kind permission of the copyright owner:
Copyright © 1990 by News America Publications, Inc.

Library of Congress Cataloging-in-Publication Data

Carroll, Charles H.
  Handicapping speed : the thoroughbred and quarter
horse sprinters / Charles H. Carroll.
        p.   cm.
  Includes index.
  ISBN 1-55821-497-6
  1. Horse race betting.   2. Quarter racing—
Betting.
I. Title.
SF331.C317   1991
798.401—dc20   91-29189
                                                CIP

CONTENTS

Introduction   1

Introduction to The *Daily Racing Form*   5

Part One   The Changing World of Horse Racing

1   Handicapping the Horse Players   17

2   Odd Dynamics   31

3   The Sprints—Faster Horses, Shorter Races   43

Part Two   The Noise of Time

4   Class in Races and Horses   65

5   The Mechanics of Time   79

6   Chaos—Why There Are Horse Races   107

Part Three   The Elements of Speed

7   Top Speed   123

8   Parallel Speed   140

9   Computing Speed   153

10 Handicapping Speed   169

11 Betting in the Money   210

    Bibliography   211

    Acknowledgments   213

    Appendix   214
        Speed Handicapper™ Program

    Index   221

Gambling is a disease of barbarians superficially civilized.

—DEAN INGE,
Wit and Wisdom of Dean Inge

But on the other hand . . .

INTRODUCTION

*M*ore than any other form of gambling, horse racing has a dream to fit every imagination. From the great Thoroughbred farms of Kentucky to the backyard breeders across the country, and from the $2 bettors on the rail to the exclusive glass booths in the grandstand canopy, each mind is filled with hope. The dreams are so varied that they often have little in common except that they have horses at their center.

In the dreamlike darkness of morning, before the sun gives color, dark shapes of horses move in and out of shadows with only occasional animal noise. Exercise riders—too young, too old, too big of bone to be race riders—stand bent in the stirrups, seeing each other only in the edges of their vision as they let their colts loosen their muscles before they begin work. In the barns, out of sight, other horses walk in mechanical circles led by an iron arm and try to stop and look out at some new shape as shadows grow. The arm tugs and they walk on. A stallion screams as a trainer opens the halfdoor of his stall. The routine is broken and he knows he will run today. Other stallions, overflowing with energy but with no one yet to complain to, answer, with only a little less fury.

A car pulls quietly into the almost empty horseman's area and an owner, unable to sleep since three o'clock, walks quickly through the barn rows to be with the baby who was helped to stand only two years before and today will run alone amid tough jockeys and roaring crowds. Her husband will join her later.

Miles away, in cities, towns, and isolated farms and ranches out of sight of the nearest neighbors, a few lights are on and college professors, auto mechanics, office workers, and cattlemen turn pages in copies of the *Daily Racing Form* less than twenty-four hours old and already worn to the softness of an old flannel shirt.

The dream-filled world that began in New York and Florida a few hours before crosses Illinois and Oklahoma to the mountains of New Mexico and Arizona and, without slowing, moves on to the Pacific coast. In a few hours, buzzers and bells will ring, pent-up muscles and heart will burst into action, thousands of voices will call out at once, and then, in the aftermath rumble, as the jockeys stand again in the stirrups, one or two voices will shriek in victory or curses, while many more will smile quietly to themselves or shake their heads and look back into the rumpled *Form*.

Among the many differences between horse racing and casino gambling is the fact that owners and trainers bet too. You probably won't see the manager of a casino in Las Vegas or Atlantic City down at the crap table, rattling the dice with the serious intention of winning. You *will* see horse owners and trainers, or their representatives, at the betting windows with intentions as serious as anyone's. If you are not familiar with the rules of racing, you may be a bit surprised to learn that a jockey can bet—but only on the horse he is riding. Owners, trainers, and jockeys have the obvious handicapping advantage of being in the midst of the action. They have the closest knowledge of anyone of their own horse and the competition. They may have even owned or ridden one or more of the other horses. And they *do* talk. They know the condition of the track up to the minute, the assistant starters, and their own intentions—all of the natural and unnatural factors that make a horse race. And yet they can still lose.

The more you know, the more you win. That is the allure of horse race handicapping. Like other forms of gambling, horse racing requires a basic knowledge of the rules to avoid random and foolish losses. But unlike other forms of gambling, knowledge not only minimizes mistakes, it actually alters the odds of winning.

No matter how much you know about the rules and practice of placing bets on a roulette wheel, each drop of the ball is a random occurrence with fixed and unfavorable odds. Skill and knowledge in roulette can do nothing to predict which number will win—and they can do nothing to eliminate even *one* of the possibilities.

Knowledge in horse race handicapping can frequently eliminate over half the possibilities almost immediately and focus on the horses in real contention. Speed handicapping can frequently step beyond this to predict not only which horse will win, but how all three in-the-money horses will finish—up to and including the distance and time between them.

In a world as wide and varied as the racetrack and the aspects of business, horse breeding, training, marketing, and betting that compose it, full knowledge can take a lifetime to accumulate. Even those who spend their lives within it may still see it in a narrow view. If front gate handicappers knew what trainers know about a specific race, they would greatly increase their winnings. If *trainers* knew what a few of the grandstand handicappers know, they might be unbeatable, whether their own horse wins or loses.

Often the way to understand more about something is to look at it from a different vantage point. In this book, we will look at horse racing from a number of different perspectives. Throughout, we will consider quarter horse racing, which is seldom viewed from a handicapping perspective. We will consider it both as a way to investigate what goes on in the early stages of a Thoroughbred sprint and as a handicapping arena of its own. We will compare and contrast it with Thoroughbred racing, and new ideas for handicapping both breeds should emerge.

Part One focuses on the underlying framework of horse racing from a handicapping perspective, which must be understood before intelligent bets can be made. The odds of horse racing are not fixed by the track; they are the dynamic result of the actual bets placed by your neighbors in the grandstand. In chapter 1, Handicapping the Horse Players, we will survey several of the most prominent schools of handicapping to see how and why other people place bets that directly affect the odds.

Since the odds are dynamic in horse racing, chapter 2 covers how they work and how the bets of the crowd—and your own bets—affect both the payback and the risk of betting.

Chapter 3 discusses the types of sprint races and the horses that run them, where speed handicapping has greatest success.

Part Two covers some of the elements of chaos that can enter into the logical analysis of speed, from the elusive phenomenon of class through the mechanical properties of clocks, racing surfaces, and wind. Chaos itself is then examined in chapter 6 as an introduction to a shift in paradigm toward speed handicapping and away from the traditional measurement of time.

In Part Three we will complete the shift away from time to speed. If you are already a knowledgeable handicapper and are aware of the various schools—of trip, pace, and others—a different perspective may shed light on some areas of speed you hadn't considered. If you are new to handicapping—unlike some other schools, which must virtually become a way of life—speed can become the foundation of a handicapping strategy that can improve your betting experiences, even if you only occasionally visit the track.

Speed is a valuable tool in Thoroughbred handicapping, but it is paramount in quarter horses. There are still many other factors to consider, but there is no pace in a 350-yard dash. The horses run flat out and most jockeys couldn't stop them if they tried. Because of the nature of the races and the absence of pace, quarter horses tend to run more consistently up to their individual potential for speed than Thoroughbreds. In recognition of this fact, the *Daily Racing Form* now publishes finish times for quarter horse non-winners in the past performances. Thoroughbred non-winner times are still left to mystery. We will see how to unravel it.

With all the new information published by the *Form* there is still the greatest mystery of all: how to compare horses' past performances at different distances. Generations of handicappers have tabulated millions of races by hand and with computers in search of some truth in the form of parallel speed charts. The quest is for *consistency* of comparison. In chapter 8 we will isolate a natural mathematical root of comparison that is not dependent upon the quality of last year's horses or the fact that there was a month of rain during last year's meet. In practice you won't need a chart. The figure calculates itself.

You will need a hand calculator, at the least, to manage the figures. In chapter 9, Computing Speed, we will arrange the calculations in logical steps for personal computers to be as simple or as sophisticated as you want. You can buy a serviceable personal computer for about the amount of one good or bad day at the races. Either one might prompt you to take the plunge to organize your data and your handicapping.

Chapter 11 shows how this process of analysis can be utilized in the most critical phase of all: laying down your money. Betting in the Money is offered as an approach for developing bets from the results of handicapping, rather than beginning with a betting objective such as winning a trifecta and forcing the results to fit.

Every science has its benchmarks. In modern horse race handicapping, it was Andrew Beyer's 1978 book, *Picking Winners: A Horseplayer's Guide.* Mr. Beyer brought a whole new public to the track by taking handicapping out of the sleeve-garter realm of tipsters and systems and into the light of logic. Even then, before his conversion to trip handicapping, when he saw speed as "truth and light," Beyer warned that blind adherence to speed was the path to ruin. Nevertheless, his book changed tote board odds across the nation. All of a sudden, speed, hidden behind several losing lengths in past performances, emerged as a deserving 3/2 favorite instead of a 5-to-1 insider bet. The purpose here is to refine speed to regain its power in Thoroughbred sprint handicapping and to understand it as the dominant factor available to handicappers in the realm of chaos of a quarter horse race.

In horse racing, any *realistic* dream is a little more attainable. The realistic dreams are those in the middle of the spectrum. Pick-Six bets and picking a Kentucky Derby winner out of a pen of yearlings are off opposite ends of the scale. For serious handicappers and serious horse owners, racing provides attainable goals. Both are in search of speed. As we look at each factor, from the industry in general to the finest details of the mathematics of time, it will be for the purpose of finding what adds and detracts from speed.

INTRODUCTION TO THE
DAILY RACING FORM

Finding Speed

Every handicapper has some core theory underlying the method he or she uses in evaluating a race. Unless the method is purely mindless entry of data into a computer, there is a thought process that begins with the first glance at the *Daily Racing Form* and continues through factors that the handicapper believes are usually secondary, balancing and mentally testing them to determine whether they should emerge to primary status.

Speed handicapping can achieve moderate success almost blindly with a computer. But in order to break beyond the average of the crowd—which is *losing*—you need not only to be able to make numbers, but to be able to choose the right data, interpret the results in view of secondary factors, and then place bets that make best use of your conclusions.

The first thing to know is where to find the information.

Several changes have occurred in the *Daily Racing Form* since the excerpts used in this book were selected, perhaps the biggest of which has been the adoption of Beyer Speed Figures for Thoroughbreds.

The Beyer Figures have not put an end to comprehensive handicapping. On the contrary, along with other refinements, such as the improved narratives of *Form* writers, the Beyer Figures seem to have made the crowd more complacent, which is great for handicappers who are willing to work for a living. (Some Beyer admirers believe that making the figures public was a strategy to reverse the dip in the odds.) Certain types of false favorites, based on superficial handicapping, are more common today than they were five years ago, when a greater percentage of the crowd understood the method, and took the time to make their own figures. The work required to distinguish between sham favorites and true contenders pays at least as well today—often better—than it did in the past. (For handicapping information available through online computer services see * page 13.)

The *Daily Racing Form*

No other sport and, for that matter, no other business has a publication like the *Form*. Only the *Wall Street Journal* would be remotely close in the data and facts presented and its impact upon monetary decisions made by its readers. But even the *Wall Street Journal* is far removed from the sheer quantity of data presented each day by the *Form*.

Daily editions of the *Form* are published for specific regions and sometimes even for small, individual tracks. Handicapping could not exist without the *Daily Racing Form*—even though the primary goal of handicapping has always been to beat the *Form*'s analyses, which are available to the rest of the crowd.

The East Coast edition is a full-size newspaper with the heft of a big-city daily. Other editions are tabloid size and may range from a half-inch thick to just a couple of pages. The major editions carry a greater number of in-depth articles, many more "comment lines" within the data, and vastly more advertising for handicapping and tips, but in all cases the essential information is there. The two key sets of information are the past performances and the charts.

Each race day's information begins with a table of "Experts' Selections." This table consists of columns of the top three picks of five "handicappers" in each race and then the consensus of their choices. (The quotes around "handicappers" is not prejudicial. At large tracks, some or all of these may be real handicappers; at smaller tracks, only "Trackman" is likely to be a breathing person—the rest are generated by computer.) "Handicap," "Ana-

---

Racing Form — AMERICA'S TURF AUTHORITY

Experts' Selections

Consensus Points: 5 for 1st (today's best 7), 2 for 2nd, 1 for 3rd. Today's Best in Bold Type.

GOLDEN GATE FIELDS   Selections Made for Fast Track

	TRACKMAN	HANDICAP	ANALYST	HERMIS	SWEEP	CONSENSUS	
1	WINGS AND RINGS SPIN SUM GOLD GIA	WINGS AND RINGS FULL OF MISCHIEF GARDEN VIEW	WINGS AND RINGS GARDEN VIEW GIA	FULL OF MISCHIEF WINGS AND RINGS GARDEN VIEW	FULL OF MISCHIEF WINGS AND RINGS GARDEN VIEW	WINGS AND RINGS FULL OF MISCHIEF GARDEN VIEW	19 12 5
2	FORCE D'ORO TAWNY TINA LITERATO	LILLIE'S FAKER NIKI'S BEST SECRET JULIES RAINBOW	FORCE D'ORO WITHOUT A NET TAWNY TINA	ANNA MARIE FORCE D'ORO TAWNY TINA	LILLIE'S FAKER NIKI'S BEST SECRET JULIES RAINBOW	FORCE D'ORO LILLIE'S FAKER ANNA MARIE	12 10 5
3	WYOMING KNIGHTS BET KESHKA	CONVIVIAL MISS SPRING STEAM BELLA'S NOSTALGIA	WYOMING KESHKA KNIGHTS BET	KNIGHTS BET WYOMING KESHKA	CONVIVIAL MISS SPRING STEAM BRAZEN IRISH	WYOMING CONVIVIAL MISS KNIGHTS BET	12 12 8
4	RASCALIOUS ICE THE GAME RENEE DANCER	PRIMMIE NUNCA FALLO ICE THE GAME	LAST WHALE PRIMMIE RENEE DANCER	LAST WHALE RENEE DANCER CLASSIC CANDY	PRIMMIE NUNCA FALLO A. YOUNG KISS	PRIMMIE LAST WHALE RASCALIOUS	12 10 5
5	SEEYOUATTHETENT MISTED FATHER SEAMUS	JACK QUACKER IMPERIAL TROPIC SEEYOUATTHETENT	JACK QUACKER MISTED SEEYOUATTHETENT	**SEEYOUATTHETENT** HONEY'S BART JACK QUACKER	KING JUDGE IMPERIAL TROPIC JACK QUACKER	SEEYOUATTHETENT JACK QUACKER KING JUDGE	14 12 5
6	JESTIC MR. INEVITABLE ROUND TWO	JESTIC I CAN DO THAT MR. INEVITABLE	MR. INEVITABLE ENDURING SPORT ROUND TWO	JESTIC NO EQUAL MR. INEVITABLE	I CAN DO THAT GOLD RAPTURE NO EQUAL	JESTIC MR. INEVITABLE I CAN DO THAT	15 9 7
7	YOUR CHEATIN HEART ZHA ZHANA TOOTIE	YOUR CHEATIN HEART MERRY CATCH STORM RYDER	ZHA ZHANA YOUR CHEATIN HEART TOOTIE	YOUR CHEATIN HEART ZHA ZHANA TOOTIE	YOUR CHEATIN HEART TOOTIE ZHA ZHANA	YOUR CHEATIN HEART ZHA ZHANA TOOTIE	24 10 5
8	LOVELY RULER TRINITY BELLE HONEYMOON TOAST	RETROGRADE LOVELY RULER COAX CLASSIC	COAX CLASSIC LOVELY RULER DOT'S L'NATURAL	COAX CLASSIC LOVELY RULER MEGASTAR	COAX CLASSIC RETROGRADE MEGASTAR	COAX CLASSIC LOVELY RULER RETROGRADE	16 11 7
9	**RUNNING HEART** SCARE GOTTA COPY	NAIROBI EXPRESS STANSTAR SCARE	**RUNNING HEART** SCARE LADY JOAN	SCARE NAIROBI EXPRESS RUNNING HEART	STANSTAR RUNNING HEART MAGGIE'S MAIDEN	RUNNING HEART SCARE NAIROBI EXPRESS	17 10 7

---

lyst," "Hermis," "Sweep" each take a different approach to selection, such as speed or class, and "Today's Best" is highlighted in bold print.

The "Experts' Selections" are followed by the "Graded Handicaps," a larger group of tables, this time listing all of the horses in each race with their morning-line odds. Note that this is not post position order. The post position is listed in the left column, and may correspond to the horse's number in the race, or may not, depending on whether horses are coupled or scratched. Horses are "coupled" in an "entry" when two or more horses are entered in the same race by the same owner, and are run under the same betting number (such as 1 and 1a). The rules of coupling vary to cover several possibilities of owner and trainer combinations, but the bet pays, as long as one of the horses in the entry meets it.

In some editions the offtrack-betting code is included next to the post position. For betting numbers at the track, you need the track program.

THIRD RACE   *Probable Post, 1:50*
6 FURLONGS. 3 & 4–Year–Olds. Maidens Claiming ($8,500). Purse $6,200.

8	CHARLEY'S PENSION	Rocco J	115	Can hang on here	3-1
5	MASTERFUL SEARCH	Johnston M T	5110	Good try debut	4-1
12	BE CAREFUL	Johnston M T	5110	Rallied local bow	5-1
2	MAHVELOUS MATT	Delgado A	115	Dropping absentee	6-1
1	SIR FRANCIS	Johnston M T	5110	Speed first two	8-1
3	LENAPE'S DAY	No Rider	115	Recent disappointment	8-1
19	A JOYFUL CHARGE	Pino M G	115	Improved latest	10-1
18	MASTER WHITE OAK	Rocco J	115	Chance if he goes	10-1
6	BREAK THE CODE	Forrest C W	115	J-bred; for tag	10-1
15	THE GRAZER	Castaneda K	115	Fair at AC	12-1
4	EGGS HERO	Rocco J	115	First timer	10-1
10	I LIGHT UP	Wallace J L II	115	Must better last	15-1
9	ROUGH PET	Ladner C J III	115	Dull return	15-1
13	DI JIM	No Rider	115	Begins career	10-1
17	MAX EDISON	Delacruz V	115	Outrun; comes down	20-1
7	PASSAMBER	Ladner C J III	115	Had many chances	20-1
16	HASTY'S ACE	Hutton M W	122	Hasn't been close	30-1
14	NOW YOU'VE DONE IT	Roverson B A	5110	Stopped comeback	30-1
11	RACHEL'S HUSH	No Rider	115	Nothing yet	30-1

Other information in the table are the horse's name, jockey's name, weight that the horse will carry (all of which are shown in larger print in the past performances), and the *probable* odds. The latter is known as the "morning-line." In some editions there is also a comment line, which can range from useful to hopelessly cryptic.

Most handicappers place little weight on the experts' selections or morning-line odds. In fact, it is just as well not to even look at them until after you have finished your own work. If any of the published selections or morning-line odds were consistently correct, no one else would need to handicap.

Depending upon the edition and/or the daily layout, other pieces of interesting information are tucked in and around the past performances. You will find jockey and trainer standings and their percentages of wins and in-the-money races, "Beaten Favorites" racing today, "Winning Post Positions," and various other regular and special features, perhaps including picks by handicappers with real names and more detailed comments on the fields for each race. Also published on different days are various tables of reference facts, glossaries of racing terms, and more detailed information on how to read and interpret different portions of the *Form*.

In most editions, the first race of the day includes a chart demonstrating how to read the past performance columns (if not in this exact position, it will be found somewhere in the pages), followed by the conditions of the race, then the "Past Performances" of the individual horses. The past performances are the front-line handicapping data.

In this large table, the "PP's" are in preliminary post-position order. Again, post positions do not necessarily correspond to betting numbers and sometimes change before race time for a variety of reasons—which is important to keep in mind so you can check them against the track program before placing a bet.

Thoroughbred and quarter horse past performances are listed in slightly different formats, the primary difference being the method of recording time. The Thoroughbred format is shown on page 9.

Notice that between the explanatory chart and the first line of a past race, there is a considerable amount of information. This is the first race at Hollywood Park, and it is for one and one-sixteenth miles. The diagram of the track shows how it will be run, around two turns, but over less than the full oval. The short paragraph beside it sets the conditions for horses entered in the race.

This horse is "Sir Hon," and since he is listed first, he should be running in the rail position from Gate 1. If he had shown the ability to run in the mud, an asterisk or other symbol shown above would go next to his name. Under his name is his jockey's, C. A. Black, and under that his owners'. (Some editions of the *Form* do not list the jockey's name here, but in the Graded Handicaps.) To the right you can see that he will be carrying 115 pounds. He is a dark bay or brown gelding, four-years-old; his sire is He's Our Native, and his dam, Tracton's Valley, a daughter of Gunter. The breeder and trainer are listed, as are his annual, turf, and lifetime racing records of starts, firsts, seconds and thirds, with his earnings. He has started in nineteen races, won one, placed in two, and showed in three, with earnings of $29,675. In slightly larger print is his claiming price of $12,500, so his trainer and owners have not accepted the 2-pound inducement that they could have under the conditions of the race, if they were willing to chance losing him for a claiming price of $10,500. (His light weight of 115 pounds is based on other allowances.) We will be talking about "claiming," "allowance," and other categories and classes of races in some detail later, but in a "claiming" race, each horse is vulnerable to be purchased by any trainer or qualified owner at the track at the stated claiming price by placing a sealed "claim" in the track stewards' box before the race. The objective is to balance competition by ensuring that high-quality horses are not dropped into lesser races to run away with the purses. Horses that regularly run in these classes of races are referred to as "claimers." If claimed, the horse becomes the property of the new owner when the starting gate opens, but the previous owner receives any purse money won. Ordinarily, no one would know about the "claim" except the new owner, until immediately after the

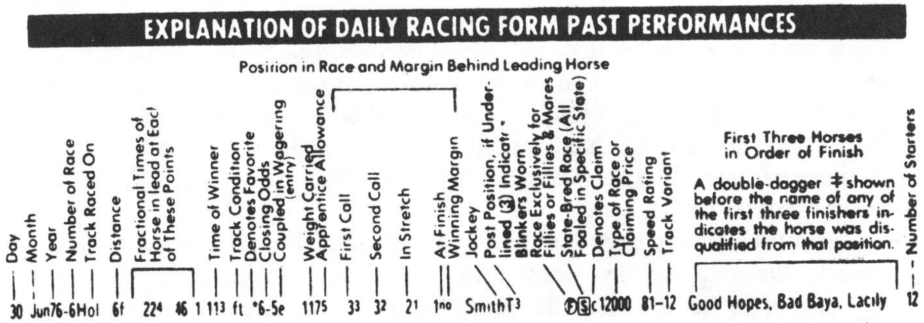

EXPLANATION OF DAILY RACING FORM PAST PERFORMANCES
Position in Race and Margin Behind Leading Horse
Day
Month
Year
Number of Race
Track Raced On
Distance
Fractional Times of Horse in lead at Each of These Points
Time of Winner
Track Condition
Denotes Favorite
Closing Odds
Coupled in Wagering (entry)
Weight Carried
Apprentice Allowance
First Call
Second Call
In Stretch
At Finish
Winning Margin
Jockey
Post Position, if Underlined (3) Indicates Blinkers Worn
Race Exclusively for Fillies or Fillies & Mares
State-Bred Race (All Foaled in Specific State)
Denotes Claim
Type of Race or Claiming Price
Speed Rating
Track Variant
First Three Horses in Order of Finish
A double-dagger ‡ shown before the name of any of the first three finishers indicates the horse was disqualified from that position.
Number of Starters
30 Jun76-6Hol 6f 22⁴ 46 1 11³ ft *6-5e 117⁵ 3³ 3² 2¹ 1no SmithT3 Ⓕ Ⓢ c12000 81-12 Good Hopes, Bad Baya, Lacily 12

Note In past performances the position in the race for "first call" is as follows: In races less than 5 furlongs the first call is the start; at 5 furlongs the first call is the three-sixteenths; from 5½ to 7½ furlongs the first call is the quarter mile; at 1 mile or more the first call is the half.

✻ Fair Mud Runner **× Good Mud Runner** **⊗ Superior Mud Runner**

Past Performances Listed According to Post Position

1st Hollywood

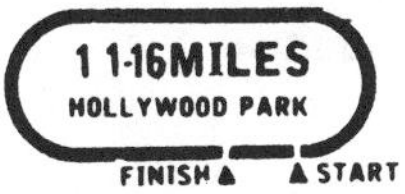

1 1-16 MILES
HOLLYWOOD PARK
FINISH
START

1 1/16 MILES. (1.40) CLAIMING. Purse $13,000. 4-year-olds and upward. Bred in California. Weight, 121 lbs. Non-winners of two races at a mile or over since April 1 allowed 3 lbs.; such a race since then, 6 lbs. Claiming price $12,500; if for $10,500 allowed 2 lbs. (Races when entered for $10,000 or less not considered.)

Sir Hon — **Dk. b. or br. g. 4, by He's Our Native—Tractons Valley, by Gunter**

BLACK C A **115**

Br.—Dyer B & Joan L (Cal) — 1990 6 0 1 1 $7,625

Tr.—Copland Jeffrey **$12,500** — 1989 10 0 0 2 $11,100

Own.—Accardy Jr–Nadel–Snyder — Lifetime 19 1 2 3 $29,675 — Turf 2 0 0 0 $1,275

2May90-3Hol	7f	:22^2	:45^2	1:23^{2}ft	2¼	116	3^{3½}	4^{3½}	3^{1½}	3^{2½}	Black C A 2	Ⓢ 10000	85-13	Somerst'sTurn,MusclBound,SirHon	6
21Apr90-7SA	7f	:22^4	:45^2	1:23^{4}ft	9½	116	8^{4¾}	8^8	9^{16}	9^{13¾}	Flores D R 10	Ⓢ 20000	70-17	Flor'em Jak,PapaStan,WickedIdea	10
21Apr90—Wide into stretch															
25Mar90-1SA	6½f	:22^1	:45^4	1:17 ft	5	116	5^{5½}	4^5	4^4	2^{3½}	Davis R G 3	Ⓢ c16000	81-15	Cracksman, Sir Hon, Just Encores	6
25Mar90—Steadied 3 1/2															
8Mar90-5SA	7f	:22^4	:45^2	1:23^{1}ft	22	116	10^{8¾}	10^{8½}	8^{9½}	5^6	Baze R A 2	20000	81-16	Lark'sLegacy,RumboSeat,Eratone	11
8Mar90—Broke slowly															
18Feb90-7GG	1	:46^2	1:10^4	1:37 gd	6	114^5	6^{7½}	6^6	6^7	5^{8½}	Diaz I G 5	Aw20000	71-29	SpeakJosh,Halogrlo,WoodsideFlsh	10
27Jan90-6GG	1⅛	:46	1:10^1	1:48^{4}ft	9	119	2^{1½}	2^2	2^{1½}	4^{1¼}	GonzalezRM 6	Aw21000	80-16	FlyingOver,LeSuccessor,HeadTable	8
27Jan90—Bumped start															
23Dec89-6BM	1	:45^3	1:10^1	1:35^{3}ft	13	117	8^{7¼}	6^{4¼}	4^3	4^{2½}	Loseth C 8	25000	91-15	LSuccssor,HookumHnk,RdMyMind	8
23Dec89—Broke in a tangle															
8Dec89-6BM	1	:47^1	1:11^1	1:36^{3}ft	6½	117	3^1	2^1	4^{1½}	6^{4¼}	Gonzalez R M 7	32000	85-07	GoldImpression,QunMry'sBoy,Tgus	7
25Nov89-6BM	6f	:21^4	:44^3	1:10^{3}sy	7¾	112^5	8^{11}	8^{13}	8^{9¼}	6^5	Diaz I G 4	Aw16000	84-11	HavenDrive,Pukkaraki,Perpendiculr	9
8Nov89-3BM	6f	:22	:45	1:10^{1}ft	5½	112^5	5^{8½}	5^{5½}	4^{2½}	4^{1¼}	Diaz I G 2	32000	90-12	Vote, Greek Equalizer, Haven Drive	6
8Nov89—Lacked room 1/16															

Speed Index: Last Race: 0.0 3–Race Avg.: +0.6 4–Race Avg.: –1.5 Overall Avg.: –3.1

Apr 15 SA 4f ft :51 H Apr 9 SA 4f ft :50^1 H Apr 3 SA 4f ft :49^4 H

race, when the stewards' box is opened and the horse is ordered to be led to its new barn.

Sir Hons' past races follow, beginning with the most recent. Like many horses, he has moved back and forth between routes (longer distance races) and sprints.

On May 2, 1990, he ran at Hollywood Park, in a seven-furlong sprint. Then, reading across, begins a series of times and call positions. As can be seen in the fine print of the explanation, the first call position for a seven-furlong race is at the quarter mile; the other call positions (also referred to as the "splits") are not explained, but are for the half-mile, stretch, and finish. In longer races, such as his mile races below, the calls are for the half, three-quarter, stretch, and finish.

In Thoroughbred past performances, all of the published times are for the *leader* at the splits and the *winner* at the finish. None of the times listed for the splits in his last ten races, therefore, are Sir Hon's, since he was never in the lead at those points. The smallest division of time in Thoroughbred races is one-fifth of a second, and the times for the leaders in his last race were 22 2/5 seconds at the quarter; 45 2/5 at the half; and 1 minute 23 and 2/5 seconds at the finish. Immediately after the finish time is the abbreviation "ft," which indicates that the track was officially "fast." In two of his previous races, you will see that one was listed as "gd" (good), and one as "sy" (sloppy). Next are the actual crowd's odds (not the morning-line) that he went off at, which was a pretty surprising $2.25 to $1; an asterisk next to the odds would mean that he was the favorite in the race.

This is followed by the weight that he carried, then a series of positions that he held at the splits. Notice that there is one more position than call time, since they add a stretch position call. The larger type represents Sir Hon's position in the field—the smaller, his lengths back from the leader. So he was third by three and a half lengths at the quarter, fourth by three and a half lengths at the half, and so forth. He had the same rider, C. A. Black, and the small superscript number is his post position, which in this case was 2, and underlined, indicating that he wore blinkers. The S in the box indicates it was a race limited to "state-bred" horses (California horses in this case, eligible for special races and purses supplemented by a state association). Then come his claiming price, speed index, track variant, and names of the top three finishers, with his own name in the third position. The final number indicates that there were six horses in the race.

If you glance down the rest of Sir Hon's past races, you will notice a number of changes. He started out in 1989 at Bay Meadows, moved to Golden Gate Fields, then Santa Anita before coming to Hollywood Park. Four of his races drew trip note comments, such as "Wide into stretch." Such notes are standard at some tracks and absent at others.

As you go back through Sir Hon's career, the distances change, the jockeys change, the value of his races change significantly, but one of the biggest changes is found in the tiny "c" next to the 16,000 in his third-to-last race. This indicates that he was claimed (bought) by another owner. The only thing that did not change with the new ownership was Sir Hon's ability to lose at any distance or price.

Quarter horse past performances are listed almost identically, except for the time format and splits. They provide a few less data points, but one that outweighs them all. After the date, track, and distance, they list the winner's time to hundredths of a second. Then the odds, call position (times are not given), jockey's name, race conditions, and the same miscellaneous symbols and codes—*THEN:* the actual, electronically clocked time of *this horse*.

For those of us who had pretty accurate methods of figuring this out on our own, this new gift from the *Form* was like getting a gorilla for your birthday. Luckily, this did not make handicapping obsolete; the crowd's picks improved only slightly.

Explanation of Daily Racing Form Quarter Horse Past Performances

9Jan88-5LA	350	:17.77 ft	*9-5 e	122	2hd	1hd	1hd	Adair R³	Ⓕ	Ⓢ	c10000	:17.77	96	Jane Doe, Mary D, Ruth J	9

MARTIN J D
Merganser   Life 21 13 2 2 $1,372,427

Ch. h. 4, by Duck Dance Tb—Hug Tiny, by Tiny's Gay
Br.—McKinnerney-Deering-Shaw (Fla)   1990   1 0 0 0
Own.—Shalz & Wells   120   Tr.—Brooks Jack W   1989   7 3 1 1 $40,258

7Jly90-7RP	400	:20.29 ft hw	9½	120	5½	82¾114½	MartinJ 1	Rem PtChp2:21.00	73	TeeRoyReb,ClssyCommnt,CsdyKing	12
10Oct89-9RP	400	:20.02 ft hw	*1	120	6½	72¼	Martin J 10	Dby :20.38	92	Rime, Andy Sixes, First A Rose	11
26Sep89-3RP	400	:20.28 ft		120	3nk	31	Martin J 4	ⒷDby Trl :20.45	90	Alota Effort, Plum Pie, Merganser	6
16Aug89-7Rui	440	:21.92 ft cw	*1-3	120	2hd	1no	Martin J D 5	Dby Trl :21.92	85	Merganser,ImAPepperBug,WinFame	10
2Jly89-11Rui	440	:21.55 ft	*3-2	120	31	1hd	Martin J D 4	Dby Con :21.55	95	Merganser, Reeboks,MiteyEasyDash	10
22Jun89-6Rui	440	:21.45 ft tw	*1-5	120	2½	2no	Martin J D 4	Dby Trl :21.46	97	Wicked Wind, Merganser, Faithfully	8
20May89-13Rui	400	:19.81 ft hw	6-5	120	71	51½	Martin J D 3	KanDby1 :19.97	93	FloydDeGret,MyDsh,OnNightWithYou	9
14May89-9Rui	400	:20.34 ft hw	*2-5	120	42	1nk	Martin J D 2	Dby Trl :20.34	84	Mrgnsr,OnNightWithYou,HvnlySmsh	10
13Oct88-13BRD	400	:20.27 ft cw	*1-3	120	6	72	31	Martin J6	ⒷFut Trl :20.45	81	Sids Bullet, Runnin John, Merganser	9
5Sep88-11Rui	440	:21.69 ft tw	4½	120	41	1hd	Mrtin.JD 4A	AmcnFut1 :21.69	90	Merganser, See Me Do It, Sky Fire	10

Another important addition to quarter horse past performances, which is not found in Thoroughbreds' (since it is not manageable, except on a straightaway), is wind direction. Note that after the winner's time in Merganser's two most recent races, a head wind was noted ("hw"). At tracks like Ruidoso, where winds can often be strong and changeable, the direction is a significant factor in determining final times. At other quarter horse tracks, such as Los Alamitos, wind is rarely listed.

The racing "charts" are the other major data set published by the *Form*. These are found on various pages in different editions of the *Form*, and present a more detailed account of each past race. In some editions they are timed a week before the current day's past performances, so that if you are reading Saturday's *Form*, the charts are for Saturday of the previous week; in the larger editions they are published two or three days after the race. The notations are similar to the past performances and include a column giving each horse's odds and the actual payoff of the mutuel pools and all exotic bets.

There is one major and often confusing difference in the charts and past performance notations: the call position listed in the chart is the horse's position in relation to the horse immediately *behind* it—not to the leader.

SECOND RACE
Penn Nat.
MARCH 20, 1990

6 FURLONGS. (1.08⅘) CLAIMING. Purse $3,000. 4-year-olds and upward which have not won two races since September 20. Weight, 122 lbs. Non-winners of a race since February 20, allowed 3 lbs. A race since January 20, 6 lbs. Claiming Price $3,200; if for $3,000, allowed 3 lbs. (Races where entered for $2,500 or less not considered in estimating eligibility or allowances).

Value of race $3,000; value to winner $1,800; second $600; third $330; fourth $180; fifth $90. Mutuel pool $11,143. Exacta Pool $15,710

Last Raced	Horse	Eqt.A.Wt	PP	St	¼	½	Str	Fin	Jockey	Cl'g Pr	Odds $1
11Mar90 ^{1}Pen^2	Rudy's Wiggle	b 7 109	3	4	4^4	1^{hd}	$1^{\frac{1}{2}}$	1^2	Roberson B A^7	3200	2.40
10Mar90 ^{6}Pen^4	Hai Philadelphia	b 5 119	2	3	1^{hd}	$2^{1\frac{1}{2}}$	2^3	$2^{2\frac{1}{4}}$	B[illegible]er C J	3200	2.50
3Mar90 ^{2}Pen^4	Pocket Saber	7 115	5	1	3^{hd}	3^{hd}	3^2	$3^{\frac{1}{2}}$	Rojas E E	3000	5.30
10Feb90 ^{3}Pen^2	Drat Foot	b 9 113	1	5	5	5	5	$4^{3\frac{1}{2}}$	Valdes R A	3000	11.10
7Mar90 ^{8}Pen^4	My Last Dollar	b 5 116	4	2	$2^{2\frac{1}{2}}$	4^5	4^{hd}	5	Deibler C E III	3200	1.50

OFF AT 7:55 Start good, Won driving. Time, :22⅕, :46⅕, :59⅗, 1:13⅕ Track good.

$2 Mutuel Prices:			
3-RUDY'S WIGGLE	6.80	3.80	2.60
2-HAI PHILADELPHIA		3.60	2.40
6-POCKET SABER			2.60

$2 EXACTA 3-2 PAID $25.80

Dk. b. or br. g, by Restive Minority—Susan's Bolero, by Sam Bolero. Trainer Horvath Sandor. Bred by Blanken R & S (Md).

RUDY'S WIGGLE, rallied along the rail on the turn, challenged HAI PHILADELPHIA for command and drew clear late. The latter, set or forced the pace and held on well. POCKET SABER, up close early, steadied slightly nearing the stretch then lacked a further bid MY LAST DOLLAR, stopped.

Owners— 1, Horvath S; 2, Cinemod Stable; 3, Pappagallo Stable; 4, Pizzurro J; 5, Dellapasca R.

Trainers— 1, Horvath Sandor; 2, Mick Stephen R; 3, Henry Billy J; 4, Pizzurro Joe; 5, Beattie Dennis M.

Overweight: Pocket Saber 2 pounds.

Scratched—Rare Coinage (14Mar90 ^{1}CT^2); Jack's Goldrunner (10Mar90 ^{9}Pen^5).

Rudy's Wiggle won the race, but was fourth by about three lengths at the quarter. The superscript "4" next to his position at the quarter is not four lengths behind the leader but *ahead* of Drat Foot, who was fifth at the call. The Wiggle's own lengths back at the quarter are composed of the distances ahead of him: a head, two and a half lengths, and a head, or a little under three lengths. Hai Philadelphia led My Last Dollar by a head in a quick first quarter (22:1), but slowed down to a 46:1 half, where Rudy's Wiggle put a head in front, and My Last Dollar faded. The leaders battled side by side through the stretch, with the Wiggle a half-length ahead, until he pulled away, or Hai tired, to finish two lengths behind. Pocket Saber, who ran third throughout, finished four and a quarter lengths behind the Wiggle (2 + 2 1/4) and four lengths ahead of the trailer (1/2 + 3 1/2).

This method of recording positions can appear confusing at first—and can be confusing in fact, if you forget to shift gears when you read it. It does, however, give a broader picture of the race than the previous method.

This particular chart gives a short narrative of the events and changes in the race. Many times this narrative is more detailed; sometimes it is absent. Without it, the chart method of position calls can still give a fair picture of how the race developed.

Charts are an important information source for handicapping, but usually at a seriously time-consuming level. In order for them to be an immediate handicapping tool—where they are used as a substitute for self-devised trip notes (which will be discussed in the following chapter)—you must have a complete set, not the hit-or-miss collection you might accumulate on the days you attend the races.

Complete sets can be purchased as back issues of the *National Charts Weekly* of the *Daily Racing Form*, or as digital files through several computer services. The latter are a huge time-saver if your interests lean toward statistical analyses. Conversely, there is a lot to be said for what is learned during the pure drudgery of inputting race data by hand. In order to understand the output of computer statistical analyses, whether you conduct them yourself as described later in this book, or purchase any of the numerous commercial summaries now available (see Gamblers' Book Club for current offerings), it is a good idea to know what the data meant before it became abstract numbers—when it was still horses, jockeys, wind, dirt, and sweat.

*Some of these are simply electronic tout-sheets; others provide "read only" templates resembling the paper version of the *Daily Racing Form*; still others offer actual past performance files that can be down-loaded. Many of the services also offer some attractive booby traps, such as "filters" and black-box handicapping routines, which should be used with caution. I am very enthusiastic about computers in handicapping and I use some of these sources to greatly reduce the work of feeding data into my programs. I still find, however, that nothing compares to the *Form* for being able to intuitively find information in a hurry in the last minutes before post time—or for rolling up and whacking when a jockey needs instructions on riding techniques in the stretch.

PART ONE

The Changing World of Horse Racing

1

HANDICAPPING
THE HORSE PLAYERS

If He plays, being young and unskillful,
for shekels of silver and gold,
Take His money, my son, praising Allah.
The kid was ordained to be sold.

—RUDYARD KIPLING,
"Certain Maxims of Hafiz,"
Departmental Ditties and Other Verses

*E*ach time a horse race is run, hundreds of handicapping strategies are confirmed. No two handicappers decide on horses in precisely the same manner. Even if they are of the same school, their methods of turning selections into bets are almost certain to differ. As the losers tear up their tickets and the winners move toward the cashiers' windows, it is confirmed that *for this race* the correct strategy was to

- Bet on a horse that bore out in its last trip but is running with blinkers for the first time today
- Bet on a horse with sun dapples, because they are an indicator of good condition
- Bet against a favorite wearing wraps on the front legs for the first time
- Stay up all night making pace figures
- Box a quinella on three horses recently claimed by better trainers

And so on, up to the number of bets cashed. Of course, in the next race the dappled horse loses, the leg wraps are for decoration (or the medication worked), and the horse bore out again in spite of the blinkers. A new set of handicappers goes to the pay windows and just as many equal and opposite strategies are proven. For one race.

But among those who go to the cashiers' windows for the second race will be a small percentage who were also there the first time—or the last time they bet. If you see them there regularly, you can be certain that they know something. The strange thing is that what they know can be almost as varied as the crowd at large. Every conceivable method of picking winners works

Horseplayers at Belmont Park, New York. Everyone wins on Cap Day—until the races start. *Photo by Bob Coglianese*

sometimes. Methods that work more regularly are usually in direct proportion to the intensity of study of some aspect of the game. This has been the fascination of horse racing for centuries.

From the beginning, and until perhaps a generation or two before us, horse races were handicapped on fundamentals. People knew horses and were willing to put money on their opinions. In many parts of the world, including hidden crossroads and brush tracks across our own country, bets remain between individuals and the bet is basic: my judgment of horse flesh is better than yours. Winning inflates both the pocketbook and the ego.

Since Colonial times, both Thoroughbreds and "short horses," the predecessors of quarter horses, have been run, one-on-one in match races for purses put up by the owners with side bets for all comers. This is generally viewed as disappearing about fifty years ago, when quarter horse racing was brought in off the dusty back roads. Quarter horse racing was organized by The American Quarter Horse Association in 1940 and, in pari-mutuel states, operates under the same governmental scrutiny (and taxation) as Thoroughbred racing, which has been governed in the U.S. by The Jockey Club since 1894.

But especially across the South and Southwest, hundreds of quarter horse and Thoroughbred sprinters still break out of two-hole gates every Sunday, with crowds of ten to a few hundred watching, testing the fundamentals of handicapping. Some of the horses are slipped off the track, "for a rest," and will show up again on the program in a few weeks, missing one or two interesting past performances. Others will never see the inside of a pari-mutuel racetrack grounds—some because they would be marginal as bottom-of-the-line, $2,500 claimers; others, because they are making more money at less expense than allowance horses at Los Alamitos. A shoe store owner and a rancher may go head-to-head with their horses on a $50,000 bet, winner take all. No second- and third-place money, no track "takeout" or "breakage," no $30-a-day trainer's fees. The bystanders may bet with the owners or among themselves. The handicapping is as fundamental as it was in ancient Rome—what they know about the horses from personal observation or word of mouth, how the two horses are built, how each one looks today, whether the jockeys are dirty or clean.

Trip Handicapping

On pari-mutuel tracks, where the horses number in the thousands instead of the dozen or so that may run in the neighborhood, there are still a certain number of insiders who practice the fundamentals. For the most part, they are trainers, owners, racetrack personnel, and the tiny handful of sportswriters and broadcasters whose *job* it is to know horses. They were *trip handicappers* before there was a convenient name for it. They are, however, a special grade of trip handicapper, with access to the backside—the barns and stable area—where firsthand information abounds.

Some trainers are almost astonishingly open about problems with their horses. Every trainer, jockey, groom, and security guard on the grounds may know that so-and-so is blatantly trying to dump a horse by dropping it into a cheap claiming race, praying that the tendon doesn't bow out of the wraps before the gates open. Everyone outside the barn area can only guess as they read the *Form*. The funny thing is, the horse *still* might be claimed, by someone who didn't get the word or by a trainer who thinks he can handle the horse better—or by one not above taking his owners for a ride. If a trainer is the stoic type, the condition of his horses can still rarely be kept a secret. Each morning at the workouts dozens of trained eyes watch, and even if it can't be seen, the jockeys and exercise riders feel it, and the tiniest missed step can start the word of a shin buck.

For the rest of the world, without access to the workouts and backside information, trip handicapping is the closest thing to the fundamentals. Trip handicappers outside the inner circle must base their knowledge on the races they watch. And, they must watch every race. They must know if a horse hesitated in the gates, if it was bumped or pinched back in the first strides, how it or the jockey set up for the corner, whether it was forced to run wide in traffic, whether it ran against a strong track bias in its lane in the stretch—every bump and bobble, real or imagined, of its trip around the racetrack and down the straightaway. Trip handicapping is just as effective in an eighteen-second quarter horse race as it is in a nine-furlong Thoroughbred route.

The theory of trip handicapping is fairly simple; the practice and application is high art. Trip handicappers must know something about speed, whether it is from the speed indexes printed in the *Daily Racing Form* or from self-devised methods, to determine the *potential* of each horse in the race. In practice, it works like this: if two horses stand out in a field of eight based on the times of past races, and one horse was bumped hard at the start, then taken wide into the turn by an inept jockey, and stumbled on the lead change coming into the stretch, while the other in its past race jumped to the lead, ran in the inside lane of its choice, and was never seriously challenged—and yet both horses posted approximately the same time—then, all things being equal, the horse with the bad past trip should beat the horse with the perfect one. The flaw, of course, is in the phrase "all things being equal." But trip handicapping works—*more* than just occasionally. Trip handicapping *combined* with speed handicapping and careful bet placement may be the most powerful strategy available to dedicated, noninsider handicappers.

However, aside from the "all things being equal" factor, which will be discussed further in chapter 6, the next key word is *dedication.* In some parts of the country, each day's races are taped and played back on public-access or commercial cable TV channels; in many other areas, they are not. Without taped replays, a trip handicapper must be *present* and undistracted during every race he hopes to use for future handicapping. Making trip observations and notes on each individual in a ten-horse race while the race is in progress takes the concentration of a black belt yogi.

Assessing past trips is only the first step. The next is to apply the detailed notes of a whole field of horses' diverse past races to the race at hand to determine who should be the winner—and *then* to make betting decisions based on them. Each of the three steps takes about an equal exercise of mental gymnastics.

There are two serious drawbacks to trip handicapping. The first is that the majority of us hold other jobs. Trip handicapping is a time-consuming avocation if you follow your home track and maybe one other that horses move between; it is a life study if you try more than that. But among the diverse handicapping strategies and schemes, it is high art; it is traditional, fundamental handicapping moved into the video era.

The second drawback, which is the same for all of the higher handicapping forms, is that the past, no matter how artfully or scientifically analyzed, can only be an *indicator* of the future; it cannot *predict* it. A skillful trip handicapper may have keen observations of every step of each of the past races of the ten horses who are going to meet today. He or she also may be a master of the second level of analysis, which is where the true art comes in: the mental simulation of today's race based upon reams of information. Each horse is reanalyzed in view of the conditions it faces today: a different or similar post position; the same or different jockey—perhaps a dozen other factors—and then in concert with the other horses.

Will the strong finisher, placed close to an early speed horse in the post, be drawn along to stay within striking distance for its final kick, or will it lose heart and fade before the turn? We will be talking about computers in some detail later, but this is where the finest computer known—the human mind— really shines. The mental simulation phase of trip handicapping is directly analogous to computer simulation, but far more personal and subjective.

As in the examples at the beginning of this chapter, a horse that veered badly in its previous race may do so again. A horse that has never acted up in the gates may be sore today and flip over backward and go down under them, kicking its neighbor in the next gate in the process, as Piebyeu did to Valid Proposal in the $394,000 1990 Kansas Futurity, putting the two morning-line favorites dead last.

If Piebyeu had been loaded a little later, if he hadn't seen another horse rear slightly, if the gates had opened a moment sooner, both he and Valid Proposal would have stood an excellent chance of placing or winning the race—sore or not. In chaos theory this is called "sensitive dependence on initial conditions," and whether they know it or not, trip handicappers apply it in their mental simulations. Without it, trip handicapping contains a deadly flaw.

Some trip handicappers go to extraordinary lengths to study and analyze each step of each horse's past races and apply a wide variety of plus and minus factors to arrive at a value for that horse. This is actually an intuitive form of speed handicapping. For example, if a horse ran a previous race from an inside post position on a track or at a distance where this is an advantage, some factor is subtracted from its overall score. If, on the other hand, a horse had to overcome some disadvantage, such as being forced wide on a turn by traffic, then a factor is added to its score. The theory and objective is to determine a value for what each horse *would* have run if there had been no advantages and no disadvantages, then compare the value of each horse to determine the finish of the upcoming race. In its simplest form, trip handicapping stops right there. If one horse earns a 98 and the other a 92 on whatever scale the handicapper has devised, the 98 horse is bet.

Clearly, trip handicapping *without* the phase two mental simulations is folly, because, to paraphrase the popular saying, "Chaos happens." But some people do it, and like every other form of handicapping, *it works*—some of the time.

Hundreds of thousands of people go to horse races each day around the world; of these, probably only a few hundred are fully accomplished trip handicappers. The reason is not that it is hopelessly complicated; anyone with a keen interest in horses and racing could probably become a functional trip handicapper. The reason is, it is hopelessly *time consuming.* If you live in an area where the entire day's card is televised so you can tape it on your

VCR, then trip handicapping can be your second full-time job. It beats working in a gas station and has the potential of paying a *lot* better. If you do not have access to taped replays, then you had better be independently wealthy or have a job at the track—because you are going to have to be there every single race day—*and* have ten-power eyes and lightning reflexes in order to make your trip notes at the full speed of the race and during the immediate on-track replays. It is no accident that the best trip handicappers *do* have jobs at the track; they are sportswriters, television journalists, and members of track management staffs who do not hold positions that prohibit them from betting, and the tiny handful of professional gamblers who were already good enough at some other form of handicapping to adopt trip-handicapping techniques.

I once asked an accomplished trip handicapper, who also happens to be the marketing director for a major racetrack, how normal humans, with regular jobs—who make up 99 percent of the paying attendance—could hope to handicap and win. For a minute I thought he was going to void my press pass. This, you understand, is the guy responsible for getting the 99 percent in the gate. *"The Weekend Warriors?"* He stared at me for a moment in disbelief "They don't stand a chance!" Then he smiled, thinking I was kidding. "Of course . . . we *need* them."

We need them to form the money pool to pay the tiny fraction of real winners. Unfortunately, *we* are *them*. On any given day at the races, only about 30 percent of the crowd does better than break even. From the track's point of view, it needs to be a *different* 30 percent next time, or there would be nobody in the grandstands but pigeons. Only a handful will repeat as winners the next time they attend, whether it is the next day, the next week, or the next month. Why do the rest go back? Dozens of graduate degrees in psychology have been based on analysis of this phenomenon, but the answer is really very simple: because it is fun. Defining *fun* will get you the advanced degree.

Since winning, or *the hope of winning,* is central to the fun, the rest of us, at the least, have to figure out ways to avoid being fodder for the big winners, whether they are consistent, accomplished handicappers or one-time-lucky grandmothers who knock down a single twin trifecta for enough to set up the kids for life.

For the 99 percent of horse race fans who either don't have jobs that require them to be at the track or aren't professional gamblers, there has always been a middle ground. Somewhere between picking horses because of the jockey's silk colors and the fanatical pursuit of trip handicapping lie a thousand schemes, "systems," and serious handicapping studies.

Tom Ainslie and Andrew Beyer are two of the most widely read writers on horse racing, and their methods, therefore, have had considerable influence in shaping how crowds bet. In one of Ainslie's early books, *Ainslie's Complete Guide to Thoroughbred Racing,* he offers *seventy-some-odd* systems for betting that work some of the time. Systems, whether they come out of Ainslie's books or a pamphlet purchased through the mail at an exorbitant price from a post office box, may involve a little handicapping, but are usually focused on some curiosity of the horses, jockeys, trainers, or toteboard odds that occurs occasionally, and if you bet *only* when it occurs, maybe you'll win, maybe you won't. Ainslie, of course, is not a system player, but a first-rate handicapper and a mentor for virtually all of us who write about handicapping today.

Pace Handicapping

Pace handicapping is based on the premise that changes in speed and levels of effort within a race affect the outcome. Every race has not just a primary pace, but numerous paces—often as many as there are horses. Since the *Daily Racing Form* provides intermediate times at known distances for the leaders, it is possible to get an idea of the primary pace of a race by simply glancing across a string of fractional times in a past performance or chart:

Distance:	1/4	1/2	5/8	finish
Time:	22	44	56	1:08

The primary pace of this 6 furlong race is *quick*. A general gauge for thoroughbred races is 12 seconds per furlong, so you can see that the first 2 furlongs (1/4) were run in an average of 11 seconds per furlong. The same for the next 2 furlongs (to the 1/2), then at 12 seconds per furlong to both the 5/8s pole and the finish.

A list of fractional times like the one above represents the primary pace of a race, but it would only be representative of a particular horse's rate of speed if the corresponding position calls were all "1s," for example:

$$1^{hd} \qquad 1^2 \qquad 1^1 \qquad 1^2$$

This type of race, with a front runner loose on the lead, producing both the primary pace of the race and an individual pace is fairly common, with numerous implications that are widely discussed in the literature (including later chapters). It is also easy to imagine a hypothetical opposite, in which a field of horses averages an identical primary pace—yet where each fraction is set by a different horse running one blazing furlong, then fading back. The primary pace then would not reflect the actual performance of *any* horse in the race. Between the two possibilities lie an infinite range of patterns that can occur in racing.

The ability to categorize and compare patterns of internal racing speeds is a very useful handicapping tool, yet many early forms of pace handicapping tended to obscure the patterning rather than reveal it. In 1983, however, Huey Mahl quietly published a brilliant and brief set of clues called *The Race Is Pace* (recently reissued by Gamblers' Book Club). In 1991, Mahl's theoretical foundation was turned into a revolution when Tom Brohamer published *Modern Pace Handicapping* and almost simultaneously, Tom Hambleton, Dick Schmidt, Mike Pizzolla, and Dr. Howard Sartin went public with *Pace Makes the Race: An Introduction to the Sartin Methodology*.

Possibly because of its beginnings in a therapy group for compulsive gamblers, the "Sartin Methodology" for some years was portrayed as something of a mysterious personality cult. The slightly less colorful, but equally interesting story of Dr. Sartin has been widely told (Quinn 1987, pp. 224–237; Beyer 1993, pp. 138–141).

A unique aspect of the Sartin methodology was that it evolved through a process that is uncommon in horse race handicapping: a relatively small group of advanced players actively taught a much larger group of less experienced players in an organized, team approach to developing handicapping theory. When this happened in a sport that had historically been practiced by loners, the predictable result was an explosion of new ideas.

Pace is often portrayed as complex and frustrating for beginners, but it can be fairly straightforward—and it is extremely useful in envisioning how a race will develop. I use my own approach to pace routinely in handicapping Thoroughbreds in both sprints and routes. In later chapters you will find all of the raw materials to develop an advanced approach to pace if you are willing to invest some work and thought. It is great fun to pick a winner at the finish line and speed will help you do that—but it is a *real* kick when an entire race unfolds just as your pace analyses predicted.

Speed Handicapping

Here's this guy with longish hair combed over a balding dome on top, looking up from a rumpled *Racing Form* like a graduate student in physics stumped on some problem—and *bugged* that you interrupted—but wondering if maybe *you* have the answer.

That was the cover of Andrew Beyer's first book, *Picking Winners*. No trench coat, no green visor or sleeve garters.

I could identify with this guy, and so could a new freshman class of handicappers then in their twenties and thirties. But *Picking Winners* was a lot more than a catchy title and cover picture. It was (and is) a short, enthusiastic little book that covered the basics and a *logical,* thinking-man's approach to handicapping Thoroughbred racehorses. *And* it worked—a *lot* of the time.

A number of other books on speed handicapping have been written and Andrew Beyer didn't invent the concept, but he gave it life and put it in the grandstands.

The basic premises of speed handicapping are: *Horses that can run the fastest most often win races;* and *The final time of a race is the primary measure of speed.*

In Thoroughbred races the times published in the *Daily Racing Form* are for the leader at the "splits" (intermediate distance calls) and the *winner* at the finish. A speed handicapper wants to know how fast each horse ran in its past races, whether it won or not. With a little crude mathematics, and the notion that one length is equal to one-fifth of a second (handy, since Thoroughbred races are timed in minutes, seconds, and fifths of a second), you can calculate the approximate finish times of horses that did *not* win their past races. For example, if the winner's time was 1:12:2, and the horse you are studying came in behind him by two lengths, then this horse's time was 1:12:2 + 0:00:2, or 1:12:4.

Simple. And powerful. Add to this some thoughtful handicapping, and even a tad of the mental simulations of trip handicapping, and you were in a position to find strong bets, sometimes at stupendous odds. You could find classic speed handicapper bets on horses that had consistently run three to five lengths faster than any of their competitions' best races and yet were clouded behind several losing lengths or other vagaries and were going off at fifteen-to-one. The crowd was betting against the losing lengths, in favor of past winners or better finishers, no matter how pathetic their times. At that time (the B.B. years and *early* A.B. years—before and after Beyer) the speed indexes and other hints provided by the *Daily Racing Form* were murky at best, and you actually had a tool that the great majority of the crowd did not share. *Eureka!* Then along came Andrew. By about 1983, prime speed bets were going off at even money. Picking winners, as a sole pursuit, was no longer a paying proposition. *Everybody* could do it—not only those willing to stay up half the night before the races with a calculator. There was so much interest in speed handicapping that the *Form* started refining its speed indexes to the point that lazy blokes could pick up a *Form* at the front gate and make two or three decent selections while they were walking to the beer counter (see next page).

The problem with speed handicapping is not that it doesn't work, but that it works too well, too often. In 1980 the crowd, to the extent that they paid attention to speed at all, could look down the past performances and see that a horse trailered in from Arlington Park for today's one-mile handicap had a *Form* speed index of 86 against tough local horses that regularly scored in the low 90s. What they didn't seem to know—although it was usually noted somewhere in the *Form,* so perhaps they just didn't know how to take it into account—was the fact that the speed index was calculated by subtracting increments from the track *record* time, which was set at 100.

In the case of the Arlington horse, this was based on Dr. Fager's fabulous time for a mile, set on August 24, 1968, of 1:32:1—which was not only the

Bugsy — B. g. 6, by First Albert—Bug Off, by Golden Ruler

Own.—Korszloski W — **$7,500** Br.—Rosslara Farm (Fla) — Tr.—Preciado Guadalupe — **116**

Lifetime		1990	1	0	0	0	
48 6 7 8		1989	19	1	3	5	$19,680
$46,886		Turf	10	1	3	1	$12,512

19Jan90- 7Pha	fst	6f		:22⅕	:46⅕	1:12⅖		Clm 7500	10	1	8^{6}	$7^{5\frac{1}{2}}$	7^{11}	$8^{13\frac{1}{2}}$	Romero J A		116	*2.60	66-27	Flint Steel $116^{1\frac{1}{2}}$ Orange Lake Boy $122^{1\frac{1}{2}}$ Torvill $109^{2\frac{1}{2}}$	Wide	10
14Dec89- 9Pha	fst	6f		:22⅕	:45⅗	1:10⅘	3↑	Clm 14000	10	1	$6^{4\frac{1}{2}}$	$10^{9\frac{3}{4}}$	9^{17}	$9^{21\frac{1}{4}}$	Romero J A		116	6.90	67-18	Deansgate $114^{1\frac{3}{4}}$ Jumpin John $116^{1\frac{1}{2}}$ Grand Cross $116\frac{1}{2}$	Outrun	10
2Dec89- 1Med	fst	$1\frac{1}{16}$		:47	1:11⅕	1:43	3↑	Alw 16500	1	2	2^{1}	$4^{3\frac{1}{4}}$	$5^{6\frac{1}{2}}$	5^{10}	Romero J A		116	6.90	82-07	Sand Devil $113^{5\frac{1}{2}}$ King Luigi $113^{1\frac{1}{4}}$ Sir Salima 113^{nk}	Tired	7
14Nov89- 9Lrl	yl	6f	Ⓣ	:23	:47⅕	1:12⅗	3↑	Alw 18000	4	3	6^{6}	$7^{7\frac{1}{4}}$	$6^{3\frac{1}{4}}$	$6^{1\frac{3}{4}}$	Stacy A T		117	17.10	77-21	What He Duz 108no Bail Denied$115\frac{1}{2}$RacingSplendor$115\frac{1}{2}$	Checked	13
3Nov89- 1Med	fst	6f		:22⅖	:45⅘	1:10	3↑	Clm 12500	1	3	$2\frac{1}{2}$	3^{1}	3^{3}	2^{5}	Romero J A		119	7.70	87-17	Will Cojack 116^{5} Bugsy $119^{3\frac{1}{2}}$ Dirty Delbert $119^{2\frac{1}{2}}$	2nd best	7
22Oct89- 6Pha	fst	7f		:22⅗	:46⅕	1:24⅖	3↑	Clm 14000	8	3	$6^{2\frac{3}{4}}$	$7^{3\frac{3}{4}}$	$4\frac{3}{4}$	$3^{5\frac{1}{2}}$	Romero J A		116	5.90	79-15	Packy's Prospect $116^{5\frac{1}{2}}$ Lumumba 112^{hd} Bugsy 116^{hd}	Hung	9
12Oct89- 5Pha	fst	6f		:22	:45	1:11⅖	3↑	Clm 11000	2	3	2^{2}	2^{1}	2^{2}	1^{hd}	Romero J A		116	3.80	84-19	Bugsy 116^{hd} Community Hall 113^{nk} RoyalGoodTime$116^{1\frac{1}{2}}$	Driving	9
4Oct89- 2Pha	fst	7f		:22⅗	:46⅘	1:25⅗	3↑	Clm 18000	5	4	$4^{2\frac{3}{4}}$	$3^{2\frac{1}{2}}$	3^{2}	$3^{3\frac{3}{4}}$	Romero J A	b	116	3.70	75-21	Icy Stare $116^{2\frac{1}{2}}$ Arctic Energy $122^{1\frac{1}{4}}$ Bugsy 116^{12}	Hung	8
22Sep89- 7Med	fst	1^{70}		:46	1:11⅕	1:42	3↑	Clm 16000	8	4	$3\frac{1}{2}$	$2\frac{1}{2}$	4^{6}	4^{8}	Desormeaux KJ	b	115	17.60	78-21	BraveDiplomt$115^{1\frac{1}{4}}$BustinRoos111^{1}GoldenChief$115^{5\frac{3}{4}}$	Forced wide	10
31Aug89- 6Atl	fm	5½f	Ⓣ	:21⅘	:46⅕	1:03⅘	3↑	Clm 17500	4	6	$7^{3\frac{1}{4}}$	$8^{3\frac{1}{4}}$	$6^{7\frac{1}{2}}$	$8^{9\frac{1}{4}}$	Romero J A	b	117	*3.10	85-07	Purrmont 117^{3} Halo Sheila 115^{3} Our Duke $114^{1\frac{1}{2}}$	Checked	11

→ **Speed Index: Last Race: –7.0 3–Race Avg.: –6.0 6–Race Avg.: –4.1 Overall Avg.: –4.7**

track record, but still stands as the *world* record for the distance. (Dr. Fager was carrying 134 pounds!) At tracks with more earthbound records, the Arlington-86 horse was going to eat the locals alive. Now, sadly, the *Daily Racing Form,* in improving its services to its readership, bases its speed indexes on the fastest time of the previous three years for each distance at each track. Not only that. It throws in some fancy figures in bold print for the horse's speed index in its last race under the same conditions (notice, not necessarily *last* race), the average for its last three races at the same conditions, the average for all races (up to twelve) at the same conditions, and the average for all starts (up to twelve), no matter what the conditions.

And that's not the worst of it. Look what they've done to the true bastion of speed handicapping: quarter horse racing. They publish the actual finish time, to hundredths of a second, for *nonwinners!* Nothing is sacred. Few people bet on quarter horse racing, because it is one of the mysteries of the universe that bites back. If you apply standard Thoroughbred-handicapping theories to quarter horse racing you will be disheartened, destroyed, cast out. The old handicapping axiom "One length equals one-fifth of a second," is wrong for Thoroughbred racing; it is hilarious in quarter horse racing. There are probably at least a few high-rolling East Coast gamblers who came west to fleece the yokel tracks now pushing shopping carts in the back alleys of L.A. and El Paso.

With all the changes in the *Daily Racing Form,* the horse-racing industry, and the composition of crowds at the track, speed remains at the core of most successful handicapping strategies. Trip handicapping, in all its variations, requires some concept of speed, whether it is intuitive or highly mathematical. Pace handicapping applies speed methodology to various portions of races. But even with the advances of the *Form,* blind speed handicapping remains no better than the average success of the crowd at large, except that the payback odds have been *lowered.*

So what is left for the fan who loves the races, the horses, the crowd, the betting—and is willing to spend a few hours handicapping—but isn't ready or has more sense than to quit his or her job and become a full-time gambler? What is left is a closer look at speed, in ways that the *Daily Racing*

Form doesn't publish, and a closer look at alternatives to the traditional "win" bet.

Such a look would not hurt the established trip handicapper, either—nor the odds player, whom we will talk about next.

Odds "Handicapping"

I saw my first true odds player when I visited Caliente Race Track in Tijuana on Kentucky Derby day in 1982. I had several days between meetings in San Diego, and while my colleagues went to the beach, I went to Mexico and the racetrack. It was heaven. They were showing the Derby on simulcast TV in the otherwise old-fashioned, chalkboard, open-air, offtrack-betting veranda. There was a fairly good ontrack race card with some of the excellent horses that travel the West Coast circuit. I made one bet on an allowance race, based on a handicapping strategy that I may never admit, and paid for most of my out-of-pocket expenses for the week. But that was just in a stolen moment; the rest of the time, I was spellbound.

Not by the Derby. Gato Del Sol won, and I didn't even know it until the next day. I don't remember much about the other races, because I didn't watch them. I was standing on the fringes of the grandstands in awe. Among the milling crowds and blowing papers were a dozen or so Mexican men, of every age and dress, standing with their eyes locked on the tote board and with double handfuls of wrinkled money held at their chests, calling odds to all comers, while they took bets and made change. At first, I was a little shocked. *Bookies—right at the track.* I looked around quickly to see if policemen were going to burst through the crowd and hustle them away to waiting paddy wagons. No one was paying any attention, except the circle of bettors around each man, calling out when they heard odds they accepted and waiting their turn to exchange money.

Now my Spanish is not very good—then, it was nonexistent—but I watched for hours, moving my eyes back and forth from the bookies to the tote board, which their eyes never left. At the time, I would have been thrilled to meet gurus Andrew Beyer or Tom Ainslie; here I felt I had accidently walked into the presence of twelve bodhisattvas. Some of them, at least—and I can't say for sure all—were giving fixed odds, based on and a little better than the tote board odds, which changed every couple of minutes, accepting bets and making change like Las Vegas crap table captains, never looking beyond the hands that placed the bets, eyes only on the money and the board.

It has always amazed me that Las Vegas dealers can keep straight who made what bet, but they have a big advantage. On a gambling table, there are chips for evidence and the odds for each type of bet are known and fixed. These guys were taking verbal bets on eight to twelve horses at varying odds, and when the race was over, not only wasn't anyone killed, I didn't even see a dispute. Moreover, not one of the bookies folded and went home, which at first, I expected to see at any moment. If ever there was a place where natural selection would be instantaneous, it would be among ontrack bookies.

Although bookies, ontrack or not, must be masters of odds and odds theory, they may or may not be pure odds players. In traditional bookmaking, the bookie, to some extent, handicaps. Whether he is expert in one of the schools or gets his information from some other source, he probably has some personal idea of what the outcome of the race should be. Other bookies, perhaps just as traditionally (since the onset of pari-mutuel wagering), may be pure odds players, using information as basic as the morning line or as complex as the changing tote board. In either case—handicapper or odds maker—the bookie must have *some* expectation of each horse's probability of winning. He then juggles the odds in a dozen mind boggling ways to either overbalance fixed-rate bets on likely and unlikely horses or acts like a pari-mutuel bank himself by extracting a "takeout" for himself at some rate less than the track or otherwise acceptable to his clients.

In legal pari-mutuel wagering in North America and Mexico, odds can be played by individual bettors in a way that is approximately opposite that of the pure, odds-maker bookie. The bookie stacks his bets and adjusts his odds so that his long shot/favorite accounts balance, and hopefully, for him, he will make a profit—*regardless* of the outcome of the race.

The pari-mutuel odds player analyzes the odds only and adjusts his bets to fit known or derivable probabilities to achieve long-term, mathematically predictable profits. In its purest form horse race odds playing involves no handicapping at all. It doesn't necessarily involve *horses*. It is claimed to work equally well with dog races, sulky races, or presumably duck races, so long as there are pari-mutuel odds and anything other than straight win bets.

The odds player lets the crowd do the handicapping, even though, with all of the various means we have discussed so far, the sum total of crowd favorites win only about 30-some-odd percent of the time. It doesn't matter. The odds player knows precisely how often they are right and all this is taken into account in complex calculations that determine *when, how,* and *how much* to bet. Some of these systems work and they appeal to some people. It is all in how you define *fun.*

In my first experience with the stock market, I was curious to see that there were a few stock market players who stood around the broker's office watching the minute-by-minute prices scroll across the ticker lights. They weren't big investors and this wasn't New York, Chicago, or L.A.; but, they were *active* players with their own bank rolls of a few thousand or tens of thousands. These players might find true *fun* in pure horse race odds betting.

I don't; and it is unlikely that anyone who has ever handicapped with even modest success could ever turn off the simple truths of horse racing to bet blindly in amounts dictated by the odds of the crowd, as if the race itself didn't exist. Some of these systems, including one of the most prominent, the *Dr. Z's Beat the Racetrack* system, by Drs. W.T. Ziemba and Donald B. Hausch, start from the premise that handicapping is an unfathomable mystery best left to "experts." Since they go on from this premise to make money, handicappers' ears should perk up.

I have not personally tested The Dr. Z System but believe that it would probably work—for the moment. Like other approaches that have become fairly widespread, the Dr. Z system and its allies are skewing their own odds. The Dr. Z system analyzes the win, place, and show pools, seeking place and show bets that are low risk, with modest returns. This is a highly sophisticated system, which takes into account how the planned bet will affect the odds and the payback. What it can't take into account is the other small but growing percentage of the crowd, among whom may be some heavy hitters, who are working the same or a similar system. Show pools seem to be changing. Whether the effect on the odds will be as profound as speed handicapping remains to be seen, but it may well be.

A classic odds-player bet occurred in the 1990 quarter horse Rainbow Futurity at Ruidoso Downs. Leading trainer Jack Brooks managed to qualify four outstanding horses and these were coupled in an "entry." With an entry, two or more horses of the same trainer or owner are coupled under a single bet. In this case, you not only got four chances for the price of one, you got *the four standout* selections of the race. It looked like a sure thing and it was; the Brooks entry came in 1-2-3-4. Along with half the crowd's $2 bets, someone up in the VIP booth laid down $2,500 to show. The $2,500 returned about $2,750, for a $250 profit.

Maybe there is some "fun" in risking $2,500 to make $250; perhaps *skydivers* do it on their days off.

On August 16, 1990, another classic odds-player bet appeared at Ruidoso Downs, again in a quarter horse race, and again courtesy of Jack Brooks. This time he rolled out Strawberry Silk, the magnificent gray daughter of the Thoroughbred Beduino, for a cakewalk through the pretenders in the time trials for the All-American Derby. "The Silk" had scorched the boys by one and a quarter lengths as a slim two-year-old in the All-American Futurity on the same track the year before. When she stalked onto the track in the post parade, a $1,235,166 winner, she seemed to be carrying two hundred pounds more—of pure, unladylike muscle. Looking straight down on her from the press box, no filly ever looked so huge, so *powerful*. By my speed figures, or anybody else's, she was ten points over her nearest contender any day of the week. In the box we watched the bets on her load, and the only question was what to couple her with to maybe pick up a *little* odds in an exacta. Dr. Z seemed to be at work, because the show pool was a whopping *six times* any other horse's. At one interval, as the tote board changed, someone clearly made another $2,500 to $3,000 odds-player show bet. Many others were in the show pool for $50 or $100.

As you have no doubt guessed, Strawberry Silk lost. She didn't win, she didn't place, she didn't show. No obvious excuses in her trip . . . she was looking a little too much at the outside 9 horse, as if she wanted to stop and talk, but there was no stumble, no foul. She just wasn't in the mood.

To me this is the unacceptable flaw of odds playing. Not just because the entire win, place, and show pools—plus all of the exotic bets tied to her—lost. I *handicapped* the race and I lost. The problem for me is that in order to turn a modest profit on very-low-odds show betting, you must make *substantial* bets—bets that hurt if you lose. The $2,500 bet to show on Strawberry Silk at $2.10 odds would have returned a $250 profit—the same amount returned by a $10 bet on the average *handicappable* $50 exacta. All loses hurt—$2,500 is wasteful.

Handicapping and odds playing can exist as if the other didn't, but they are far more frustrating that way. Odds players are in it for the money, handicappers for the glory. But there is only one way to measure glory at the racetrack, and that is in dollars and cents.

Show betting is a useful tool with handicapping, as well as with odds playing, and we will look further into it later. One of the imponderables of horse race betting is the *confidence* that inexplicably carries you forward. Cashing tickets at small but sometimes very decent odds in the place and show pools helps keep both a positive cash flow and a positive outlook—and it beats the hell out of losing. Two or three winning tickets in your pocket from the last race are a remarkable steadying factor as you make your final decisions on how to bet the next. One definition of *fun* is to never use cash again at the racetrack—to make your future bets with past winning tickets.

2

ODD DYNAMICS

Get your facts first, and then you can distort them as much as you please.

—MARK TWAIN,
letter to Rudyard Kipling in
From Sea to Sea

*M*any fine handicappers have given up the game in disgust or worse when they could not turn the romance of picking winners into the reality of winning bets. Everyone who has attempted handicapping has gone through a phase when they are picking a respectable percentage of winners, or horses in the money, yet are losing money hand over fist. On any given day, they may wisely sit out the first races or middle races, for which there are no strong bets under their methods. Then comes the first strong choice of the day: they bet to win, and their horse comes in second by a bob of the head to their second choice. If only they had boxed an exacta on their first two choices!

With their confidence shaken, they box a quinella to beat that bob of the head in the next race. The horse they had picked as a standout to win *does* win. Their second choice fades in the stretch and nobody knows where it finished—the quinella bet is lost. There is no bet in the next race and they never seriously tried to handicap it, but they make a bet anyway; the crowd's favorite is walking funny in the parade, and there's this well-bred, unraced . . . . . After losing that one, they box a trifecta, costing $54, and win . . . $49. If an experienced horse player tells you he has never done any of these things, take no more advice from him, he'll probably lie about that, too. Everyone who has lived through this stage and still goes to the races has had to learn something about pari-mutuel odds and placing bets.

In pari-mutuel racing the track is a passive player. The track keeps the grounds, paints the grandstands, provides stall space for trainers, sells hot dogs and beer or rents concession space to those who do, employs the racing officials who organize and sanction the races, and takes a percentage of the money bet to keep all this going and hopefully make a profit. The only thing that the track bets on is that you will show up. This is not always a winning bet; many small and a few fine old tracks have folded. But new tracks, like Remington Park, Prairie Meadows, and The Woodlands, are opening up and "the industry" is finding its way in changing times. None of the tracks, old or new, are your competitors at the betting window, except indirectly, in the percentage of takeout and "breakage."

Takeout is the straightforward deduction of a certain percentage of all money bet and is generally around 17 percent, plus or minus a couple. The *Daily Racing Form* publishes the takeout in the charts section for each track, and it varies not only from state to state, but depending upon the type of wagering.

A percentage of the percentage goes to purse money for the races, to state taxes, various benevolent funds, and to operating expenses and profits. Both the overall percentage and the internal split of the "take" have always been the subject of controversy. The overall percentage is settled in the political arena of racing commissions and state legislatures; the internal split is always in hot contention with horsemen's associations, pension funds, the track, and others, and tied back into politics. Although it is political, democracy has nothing to do with it. There is no association to represent the tax payers.

At some tracks, the takeout is fairly simple:

Mutuel take 18 3/4%. Exotic take 21% on Daily Double, Quinella, and Exacta and 25% on Trifecta, Twin Trifecta, and Triple.

Then there are tracks like Laurel:

Daily Double wagering on first and second races. No couplings permitted in Daily Double races & exacta wagering on all races. $3 Triple Wagering on 5th, 7th and last race. $3 Double Triple on 3rd and 5th races. $2 Pick Three on 8th, 9th and 10th races. Stable couplings are permitted in Exacta Races. Mutuel take 17% (state .50%, purses 7.70%, track, 7.45%, pension fund .25% Maryland Breeders' Fund 1.10%. Daily Double and Exacta take 19% (state .50%, purses 8.70%, track 8.45%, pension fund .25%, Maryland Fund 1.10%) and Triple take .25% (state .50%, purse $11.70%, track 11.45%, pension fund .25% and Maryland Fund 1.10%). Breakage Track 50 per cent, purses 45 per cent with 5 per cent to Maryland Fund. Superior figure following jockey's name indicates number of pounds apprentice or rider allowance claimed. Equipment: s-spurs, b-blinkers. NOTE: All riders are equipped with whips unless otherwise indicated in footnote below chart. "Lower" finish line, one sixteenth of a mile down the stretch from the regular finish line, is being used for the entire Laurel summer meeting.

There are exhaustive (and exhausting) studies that show how minor variations in takeout percentages affect both the money won by bettors and track attendance. Like any business, the question becomes whether to bank on high profit/low volume, or low profit/high volume, and it is settled differently from state to state.

The "breakage" is a little more insidious. Breakage is simply the rounding down of any odd cents after calculating the payoff for each bet. If, after subtracting the takeout and conducting the elaborate calculations required for some bets, the payoff on a winning ticket comes to $2.83, the actual amount paid is $2.80. No big deal. But, suppose the actual payoff calculates to $2.99? The amount paid is still $2.80, since tracks round in twenty-cent increments. Racetracks do not round up. This is called "ten cent" breakage in the same spirit that something purchased at $100 wholesale and sold at $200 is called a 50 percent markup in the retail sales business. Thus, a good portion of the time, the money taken out before the winning bets are paid can run around 19 to 20+ percent. In states like Texas, where pari-mutuel horse racing was recently legalized with a punitive sin tax, the internal state tax is 5 percent, vs. the 2 to 3 percent in other states, forcing either an exorbitantly high takeout or a major internal crunch, diminishing both purses and the tracks' operating margins.

No one can seriously resent a reasonable takeout, insofar as it goes to higher purses to attract better horses and finer competition; nor can one object to the portion that goes to keeping up the track grounds, salaries for high-quality officials, and a tidy profit for the investors; or even the tax off the top for the state. But in the push and pull between the three political bodies, the fourth body is usually forgotten. That is the disorganized crowd, which dutifully provides the cash flow that makes the system work.

Large takeouts make it harder to win over the long term. In that limited sense, every bettor has to beat the track. If a handicapper, through careful selection of horses and placement of bets, made a theoretical 20 percent profit over a year, he would actually win nothing. In order to show a true 20 percent profit over a year a handicapper must select horses and bets at a 40 percent return. This is a much harder task. When it comes to long-term handicapping profits, each 10 percent increase seems to result in a geometric increase in difficulty. So, just to *break even* at a 20 percent takeout, you have to have the skill of a better-than-average race fan . . . *squared.*

Pari-mutuel betting was devised in the last century by a French perfumer, but as brilliant as the system was—and as custom-made for taxation—it wasn't adopted in this country until it was legalized state by state. The governor of New York signed it into law for that state on April Fool's Day, 1940. Texas, Oklahoma, and Kansas waited almost another fifty years.

In pari-mutuel betting, each type of bet is held separately in a "pool." There are win, place, and show pools in every race (referred to collectively as the "mutuel pool"), as well as separate pools for whatever special bets are offered on a given race, or series of races. Thus, in addition to the mutuels, there may be a quinella pool, an exacta (perfecta) pool, and a trifecta or superfecta pool on a given race, plus one or more carry-over pools between races, such as the daily double, and other, more complicated bets, which often have different names at different tracks, such as twin trifectas, big T's, pick sixes, etc. Although the pools may be lumped as "mutuels" and "exotics," there is actually a separate pool for each type of bet. The basics of these bets are

- *Win*: pays if you pick the winner of the race

- *Place*: pays if your horse "places," by coming in second *or* by winning—therefore two chances

- *Show*: pays if your horse "shows," by coming in third, second, or first—three chances
- *Quinella*: pays for picking two horses who finish first and second, in either order
- *Exacta, or Perfecta*: pays for picking two horses who finish first and second, in exact order
- *Trifecta*: pays for picking three horses who finish first, second, and third, in exact order (called a "triple" at some tracks)
- *Superfecta*: pays for picking four horses who finish first, second, third, and fourth, in exact order
- *Daily Double*: pays for picking the winners of two successive races (naturally, before the first race starts)
- *Big T, Triple, Pick Six, etc.*: pay for picking the winners of a series of three or more races
- *Twin Trifecta*: Pick a trifecta in one race, collect the winning money plus an "exchange" ticket for the next race, in which you *again* pick a trifecta. The second half of twin trifectas, as well as other more complicated bets, are frequently not won on a given day and are carried over to the next, sometimes resulting in payoffs of several hundred thousand dollars.

The win, place, and show pools can be readily seen on the tote board, and are revised every 90 seconds as the betting progresses, until the last horse is in the gates and both the racing gates and the teller machines are locked. Each horse is shown by number, with the odds for a win bet and the dollar amount bet in each of the win, place, and show pools. Since the money wagered on each type of bet is held separately, the win odds do not necessarily reflect the odds of that horse in any other type of bet.

More and more tracks are moving toward showing the approximate dollar payoff on a $2 bet on the tote board rather than the traditional odds of 4-to-1, 8-to-5, etc. This is helpful to new players and will probably become universal over time, but right now it is confusing to old players or anyone who follows more than one track, where the methods differ. With so many betting systems based on odds, you will often see people staring in frustration at the board with lips moving and fingers counting, trying to figure out the odds equivalent of $2.80. The same information found on the tote board, and additional information on the special wagering pools, such as quinellas, exactas, etc., are generally shown on television screens throughout the racetrack.

After the takeout and breakage, the money that is redistributed to winning bettors is about 80 percent of the total (again, plus or minus a few percent depending upon the track). To simplify matters, suppose there are just three horses in a race. As the gates close and the teller machines lock, the crowd has bet a total of $200 to win on number 1, $500 to win on number 2, and $300 to win on number 3. The total win pool, therefore, is $1,000. If the track takeout is 20 percent, then $800 is left in the pool to pay winning tickets.

If number 1 wins, there are 100 winning $2 tickets that must be returned to the owners, so $600 is left to be divided among them. Each $2 bet returns $600 divided 100 ways, or $6. Since six is three times the original bet, the odds on horse number 1 would have shown on the tote board at closing as 3 (to one) or $8 (since the winners get their original $2 back).

If number 2 had won, there would be 250 winning $2 tickets and $500 in original bets to be returned. So the $800 after takeout diminishes to $300, and each winning ticket would pay $1.20 plus the original $2, or $3.20. The odds on the tote board would have shown $3.20, or 3/5.

Odds at less than even money are sometimes confusing. Even money would show on the tote board as 1, or $4. Which means the return would be the original $2 bet plus $2 in winnings. In any other business, this is called doubling your money and is an honorable pursuit. In horse race gambling it is often frowned on for a variety of reasons we will touch on later. Betting at less than even money might get cigar smoke blown in your direction, if any old-school handicappers are within earshot, *but every winning ticket beats a losing ticket, no matter how low the odds.*

Odds are simply a fraction. Odds higher than even money are often spoken as 2-to-1, 10-to-1, etc. This means the fraction is 2/1, 10/1—all of which come out to the number on top. So it is simply 1 times the original bet, 2 times the original bet, 10 times the original bet, and so on. Odds at less than even money are shown as 3/5 (3-to-5), 1/3 (1-to-3), and so forth. For 3/5 odds, the payoff is 3 *divided* by 5, which equals 0.6, *times* the original bet of $2, which equals $1.20. The original bet of $2 is returned, so the total payback is $3.20.

Odds and paybacks are usually calculated using $2 as the basic bet, but you can bet any amount in whole dollars that you like (although some tracks, and especially some offtrack facilities have limiting rules). A $5 bet returns 2.5 times the $2 standard; a $10 bet, 5 times. Some tracks have minimum $3 and $5 exactas on certain or all races.

You can have the same bet many, *many* times—which simply means that you wager more money. But, as can be seen with the hypothetical example above, a large bet dilutes the odds. For example, if you run to the teller window at the last second and place a $250 bet on number 1, and it wins, then, instead of 100 winning tickets, there are 225; the total win pool is now $1,250, of which $1,000 is available to be divided between the winners after the takeout. $450 comes out of the $1,000 base to return each $2 winning bet, leaving $550 to be divided now 225 ways. That comes to $2.44, which is rounded down through breakage to $2.40. So, with one substantial bet, you have lowered your own odds from 3-to-1 to 6-to-5, and the payback per winning $2 ticket from $6 to $4.40. Of course, you "have it" 125 times, so your return is $550, for a $300 profit, or 120 percent. There is clearly no shame in 6/5 odds—or any odds—that you *win*. The concern with low odds is that there is also a calculated risk, and many horse players, whether they are handicappers or odds players, have set odds that they will not bet below. In general, handicappers seem to set these higher than odds players, who, for the most part, are looking for modest but virtually risk-free "investments."

Occasionally, with an overwhelming favorite, such as Strawberry Silk, the betting is so heavy on one horse that the pool goes out of whack. This creates a "minus pool," and it usually occurs in show betting pools, as it did with The Silk. It can happen in win pools, though, and to continue the example, suppose that at the moment you slapped down your $250 on horse number 1 the owner of the horse and her mother each slapped down $5,000. Now the bet on number 1 is $10,450 and the total win pool is $11,250. The takeout is $2,250, leaving $9,000. There's a problem here. The track has collected $10,450 in winning bets that must be returned before dividing the winnings; instead of "winnings," there is a $1,450 deficit. That is a minus pool. By law, the track will have some fixed minimum payback that it must present on each winning ticket, usually at 1-to-10 or 1-to-20 odds, so that the full return on each $2 ticket is $2.10 or $2.20 (*including* the original $2; in other words, five to ten cents on the dollar). The track must make up this difference, and it is the only time the track ever loses.

In show pools, where this is most likely to happen, it is a little more complicated. As you recall from the list of bets above, one horse wins—but two horses place, and three horses show. Show pools must be divided among three sets of winning bettors, and in a minus pool *all three* horses drop to minimum odds.

At one time serious horse players scorned everything other than win bets. This was based on a little logic and a lot of ego. The logic was, and is, that there is considerable risk in making bets and that risk should be taken only if the rate of return is great enough to carry you over the losses that are certain to occur. The ego was that each type of progressively safer bet reflected a progressive decline in courage and conviction. Show bets were for the ladies. Now, of course, there are female bettors who would have some of those old handicappers for lunch.

The Exotics

Horse racing was the only major sport in the United States to be requested—in no uncertain terms—to suspend operations during World War Two, to conserve resources for the war effort. The order was quickly rescinded and the disruption was minor, but when the tracks reopened in 1945, racing boomed. There was a huge national sigh of relief that the war was over and we could get things more back to normal than "normal" ever was. Whether it was a cause or result, there were also superhorses who became national heros. Citation and Native Dancer were as widely known as Ted Williams and Joe DiMaggio. My friends and I knew in our cowboy games of the fifties that whoever got dibs on Native Dancer would be one tough hombre to catch. Those were great times for us, but they must have been even better for the old inner circle of handicappers, whose careers had begun in the Damon Runyon years of the twenties and thirties: thousands of fresh, new, *unskilled* bettors pouring record amounts of money into the mutuel pools for the taking. Whether it was a cause or result, too, the tracks introduced the first simple combination bets, daily doubles and perfectas (exactas). The older handicappers dubbed them "exotics," and the name stuck, although they don't seem very exotic today.

One measure of "exoticness" is the odds that they pay. Originally, old-school handicappers objected to them because it is hard to pick a winner, and the idea of risking money on picking two winners or the first and second horses in exact order for some inflated payback seemed a proposition for suckers, who would be better off in bingo parlors. The reason that the tracks introduced them, of course, was exactly that. To bring in lottery-type betting, where people who otherwise might bet single $2 show tickets would take eight or ten $2 "chances" on the daily double, in hopes of a $200 or $300 return. Old-school horse players considered this *gambling*.

Like every other aspect of pari-mutuel betting, the exotics have changed with the knowledge and skill of the crowd. Payoffs on the simpler exotic bets have dropped drastically because so many people have become adept at picking and betting them. They now often fluctuate radically, and the exacta in one race may pay $8.60, while in the next it pays $240. Skill in betting the exotics is at least equally as important as picking the horses that will fill the winning ticket.

Anyone can win every single exacta offered in a day of racing. All you have to do is "box" every single horse in every single race. "Boxing a bet" (sometimes called "baseball") means coupling one or more of the possible combinations. If you box the 1 and 2 horses in an exacta, you make two bets: 1-2 and 2-1. Boxing three horses gives you 1-2, 1-3, 2-1, 2-3, 3-1, 3-2. This is called a permutation, which is a function of factorials, written "*n!*" You don't have to know mathematics. Just look at the exclamation point, which is not mine but the actual math symbol, and the increase in possible combinations from two horses to three. The greater the number of horses boxed, the greater the possibility that the winning combination will produce low odds and a payback lower than the bet. And this is for an exacta, where there are only two possible combinations of winners.

In a trifecta, there are three possible finish combinations and the permutation of bets increases dramatically. Tracks that offer trifectas usually include information on boxing in the program. Without running through them all, if you select three horses, there are six possible combinations. A $2 bet on each possibility would cost $12. For an eight horse field, there are 336 possible combinations; a $672 bet. Boxing is an essential betting strategy, but since both exacta and trifecta odds vary wildly, it must be used with great care.

"Wheeling" is another betting method used in exotics that increases both the chances of winning and the amount at risk. It is used when there is a clear standout horse in the race. Like boxing, it is a useful method, if kept within reason. For example, if you love one horse, like two, and hate the rest, you can then wheel the two horses with the standout in a trifecta and there are only two possible combinations: 1-2-3 and 1-3-2. The bet costs you $4 instead of the $12 to box it.

We are talking in $2 increments, but if you are betting in multiples of $10, $20, or $100, these betting methods get expensive—fast.

You can also wheel horses around the first two positions, or the other positions by themselves, if you have a strong conviction that a particular horse is destined to finish second or third. If there ever was a case where it was a sound bet to pick a horse to come in second and wheel two horses *ahead* of it, I would love to hear the story.

To take a little of the edge off such bets—like *half*—many tracks allow $1 incremental bets on at least the most exotic propositions, such as trifectas or pick sixes. A $1 bet on a three-horse trifecta box costs $6 instead of $12. Of course, if you win, you collect half the $2 payoff.

Occasionally, usually once or twice a season, even at smaller tracks, the truly exotic bets, such as twin trifectas, reach astronomical carryovers. When the betting on them is heavy, but no one wins for several weeks or months, the carryover pool can grow to hundreds of thousands of dollars. This is when big-time gamblers and syndicate representatives get on jets in places like Chicago and L.A. and fly to places like Albuquerque. "Syndicate" isn't as ominous as it sounds; when word gets out that $380,000 is waiting to be won, it isn't all that uncommon for a group of auto workers in Detroit or uncles and cousins on Long Island to get together several thousand and a plane ticket for someone to head out to whup the locals. If you are ever offered this position, just be sure the ticket is round-trip.

To consider such bets a little further, suppose the twin trifecta is based on two eight-horse fields (which they usually are not—more often they will be ten- or twelve-horse fields of unraced two-year-olds, or horses that have never come within thirty-five lengths of a winner in their lives). A $380,000 payoff can call for some serious betting, so suppose you simply boxed all of the entries in both races? In the second race of a twin trifecta you don't bet money; you exchange winning tickets from the first race. So for an eight-horse second race, you would need 336 winning tickets from the first. In order to be sure of getting them from an eight-horse first race, you would have to bet each of the 336 combinations 336 times . . . 112,896 bets. At a $2 bet, that's $225,792. You will be *absolutely certain* of having the correct horses and the payoff is $154,208 *more* than your bet! There's only one problem (aside from the fact that they are rarely eight-horse fields, which raises the number of bets horrendously). Suppose the horses come in 8-2-5 in the first race and 1-3-7 in the second, and those happen to be the birth months of the grandchildren of a little blue-haired lady who paid $12 to box the first three in the first race and then hits the second with her one exchange ticket? She gets half the $380,000 and you lose $35,792. If someone else gets lucky, it splits three ways, and you lose $99,126. Every track that has carryover pools that rise to such heights also has stories of just such losses. Such huge pools exist only for two reasons: the races are unhandicappable, and people lose large amounts of money regularly and systematically. The $380,000 may be made up of a few large losing bets (which increase as the pool rises), but it is mostly made up of $50 and $100 $1 boxes and wheels contributed by the crowd at large.

Trifectas, and even twin trifectas, can occasionally be handicapped, and this is why the odds and payoffs fluctuate wildly. When the racing secretary, who organizes and cards the races, slips up and lets a handicappable race fall into the second twin-tri slot, somebody, and usually several people, are going to win. The carryover drops back to zero and the track secretary starts looking in backyards for retired race horses he might coax back to the track.

Trifectas have become popular both with the fans and the tracks. The fans like them because there is the potential for healthy payoffs, and the tracks love them because the takeout percentage is higher than the standard win, place, and show pools and, more importantly, people who otherwise would be placing single $2 bets now bet $12 or $24 in $1 boxes and wheels without batting an eye. Trifectas are now scattered throughout daily racing cards, and when they appear on races that can be handicapped, the odds are outrageously low. It has reached the point where a *winning* $2 box on three horses, costing $12, can *lose* money. Trifectas have theoretically paid as little as $4! If the old-school win bettors are not spinning in their graves, this would probably put them there. Picking three horses in exact order of finish for even money odds boggles the mind.

Four-dollar payoffs on trifectas don't happen, since tracks have minimum payoffs for exotic minus pools, but payoffs of $50 and less are not uncommon. It is because exacta and even trifecta payoffs have dropped into the range of the quinellas of ten years ago that tracks are adding ever more complex betting schemes. Superfectas (four horses in exact order) have been added to one race a day at some tracks, as trifectas originally were, and will probably follow the same pattern of acceptance. All of the exotics, from

SIXTH RACE **1 ⅝ MILES. (2.46⅖) STARTER HANDICAP. Purse $9,500. (Plus 35% Pa Bred Bonus). 3-year-olds and upward which have started for a claiming price of $5,000 or less in 1990. Weights Wedneaday, PM Declarations by Thursday 10:30 a.m. Highweight preferred.**

Phila Park

NOVEMBER 24, 1990

Value of race $9,500; value to winner $5,700; second $1,900; third $1,045; fourth $570; fifth $285. Mutuel pool $50,055. Exacta Pool $71,032

Last Raced	Horse	M/Eqt.A.Wt	PP	¼	½	1	1⅜	Str	Fin	Jockey	Odds $1
4Nov90^{11}Del^{1}	Verdian	L 4 114	3	10	10	8^{5}	4^{4}	3^{6}	1^{hd}	Piecuch M A	3.60
15Nov90 ^{6}Lrl^{7}	Frank Alford	Lb 4 117	1	2^{2}	$2^{1\frac{1}{2}}$	$2\frac{1}{2}$	1^{3}	2^{1}	$2^{6\frac{1}{2}}$	Pagano S R	.80
4Nov90^{11}Del^{3}	Rugged Emperor	Lb 5 111	7	$5^{2\frac{1}{2}}$	5^{5}	4^{5}	3^{3}	1^{hd}	$3\frac{3}{4}$	Vigliotti M J	11.90
10Nov90 ^{7}Pha^{4}	Master Of Arts	Lb 7 114	5	7^{4}	6^{2}	7^{hd}	6^{2}	4^{4}	4^{6}	Lukas M	37.00
10Nov90 ^{7}Pha^{6}	General Consent	L 4 110	10	4^{3}	4^{hd}	$6^{1\frac{1}{2}}$	5^{hd}	5^{2}	5^{5}	Moyers L	92.60
16Nov90 ^{2}Pha^{7}	Tangier	Lb 4 112	8	8^{3}	8^{3}	5^{hd}	7^{2}	$7^{1\frac{1}{2}}$	6^{nk}	Harvey B	14.90
10Nov90 ^{7}Pha^{5}	Diamond Joy	Lb 6 113	4	9^{2}	9^{2}	10	9^{5}	8^{6}	$7\frac{1}{2}$	Capanas S	31.00
10Nov90 ^{7}Pha^{10}	King Of Light	Lb 5 114	9	1^{4}	1^{3}	$1^{1\frac{1}{2}}$	2^{2}	6^{3}	8^{4}	Lloyd J S	6.80
10Nov90 ^{7}Pha^{8}	Balzac's Quill	b 5 110	2	6^{hd}	7^{hd}	9^{hd}	10	9^{15}	9^{29}	Collins D M	76.50
16Nov90 ^{4}Med^{5}	Steak Dinner	Lb 6 114	6	3^{1}	3^{3}	3^{5}	8^{2}	10	10	Nied D	10.10

OFF AT 2:41 Start good Won driving Time, :23$\frac{4}{5}$, :48$\frac{2}{5}$, 1:41$\frac{2}{5}$, 2:09$\frac{2}{5}$, 2:38$\frac{2}{5}$, 2:53$\frac{2}{5}$, Track fast.

$2 Mutuel Prices:

3–VERDIAN	9.20	3.60	3.20
1–FRANK ALFORD		2.60	2.40
7–RUGGED EMPEROR			4.40

1ST HALF TWIN TRIFECTA 3–1–7 PAID $12.20 $2 EXACTA 3–1 PAID $21.20

quinellas to twin trifectas, offer a whole new range of opportunities for good handicappers to *lose* money while *winning* bets (see next page).

There is no predictable relationship between the tote board odds on the mutuels (win, place, and show) and the odds on any of the exotic bets. A rule of thumb, however, is that if the win and place pools are bet *in proportion* to the same two horses in an exacta, then the exacta payoff should be the payoff of the win horse *times* the payoff of the place horse. So, if the win horse pays $5 and the place horse pays $5, the exacta should be $25 (allowing for differences in takeout). At large tracks with large handles, mutuels and exactas often balance toward this rule. This rule has its basis in the laws of compound probability and holds for trifectas as well in which the payoff should equal the win odds times the place odds, times the show odds. (There is a lot more room for variation in trifecta pools, so perfect balances are rare.) The Sixth at Belmont shows the rule in action.

Just as often, exactas and other exotics may vary wildly from the expected. Exactas can pay much less, if there are one or two heavy bets made that are not reflected in the win and place pools. Since fewer people watch the exotic odds on the screens than on the tote board, the exotics retain some opportunity for old-style betting finesses. Exactas can also sometimes pay much higher odds than the expected—when, for example, a drastic long shot is bet in the place and show pools by the $2 bettors looking for odds alone, and not backed in the exacta, since no one would dream the horse would actually win (See B.B. Power, Second at Playfair, next page).

There are two ways to avoid being a *losing winner* in exotic betting. One is to ignore the odds and keep your bets low and recreational, so if you bet $24

SIXTH RACE
Belmont
SEPTEMBER 10, 1990

6 FURLONGS. (1.07⅘) CLAIMING. Purse $29,000. 3-year-olds and upward. Weight: 3-year-olds 118 lbs. Older 122 lbs. Claiming Price $100,000; for each $5,000 to $75,000, 2 lbs.

Value of race $29,000; value to winner $17,400; second $6,380; third $3,480; fourth $1,740. Mutuel pool $195,473. Exacta Pool $413,001

Last Raced	Horse	M/Eqt.	A.	Wt	PP	St	¼	½	Str	Fin	Jockey	Cl'g Pr	Odds $1
26Aug90 ^{3}Sar^{2}	True and Blue	b	5	116	5	4	$4\frac{1}{2}$	3^{2}	1^{hd}	1^{nk}	Santos J A	85000	1.50
2Sep90 ^{5}Bel^{3}	Happiano		4	112	6	5	7	7	5^{hd}	$2^{1\frac{1}{2}}$	Chavez J F	75000	7.20
12Aug90 ^{4}Sar^{4}	Your Hope		5	111	3	2	$2^{1\frac{1}{2}}$	2^{hd}	2^{hd}	3^{hd}	Smith M E	80000	10.90
25Aug90 ^{1}Sar^{4}	Diamond Anchor	b	5	112	4	7	$5\frac{1}{2}$	$6\frac{1}{2}$	6^{3}	$4^{1\frac{1}{2}}$	Rojas R I	75000	18.10
19Aug90 ^{9}Rkm^{2}	Race 'N Brace		6	122	1	3	3^{hd}	4^{hd}	4^{hd}	5^{hd}	Migliore R	100000	2.60
6Sep90 ^{4}Bel^{3}	Bravely Bold	b	4	116	2	1	$1\frac{1}{2}$	1^{hd}	3^{2}	6^{6}	Maple E	85000	3.20
22Apr90 ^{7}Aqu^{3}	Henuda		3	106	7	6	6^{2}	$5\frac{1}{2}$	7	7	VelazquezJR^{5}	80000	18.90

OFF AT 3:31 Start Good, Won driving. Time, :22⅗, :45⅗, 1:09⅗ Track fast.

$2 Mutuel Prices:				
	5-(E)-TRUE AND BLUE	5.00	2.40	2.40
	6-(F)-HAPPIANO		5.20	3.00
	3-(C)-YOUR HOPE			3.20

→ **$2 EXACTA 5–6 PAID $25.60**

SECOND RACE
Playfair
AUGUST 26, 1990

6 FURLONGS. (1.09⅗) CLAIMING. Purse $1,500. 3-, 4- and 5-year-ods. Non-winners of two races. Weights, 3-year-olds, 117 lbs.; older, 120 lbs. Claiming price $2,500.

Value of race $1,500; value to winner $825; second $300; third $195; fourth $120; fifth $60. Mutuel pool $4,786. Exacta Pool $3,328.

Last Raced	Horse	M/Eqt.	A.	Wt	PP	St	¼	½	Str	Fin	Jockey	Cl'g Pr	Odds $1
10Aug90 ^{2}Boi^{5}	B. B. Power	B	3	117	10	2	$1^{1\frac{1}{2}}$	$1^{1\frac{1}{2}}$	$1^{1\frac{1}{2}}$	1^{3}	Kato A	2500	68.90
19Aug90 ^{10}Pla^{2}	Sneaken Holme	B	5	122	1	1	2^{2}	$2\frac{1}{2}$	$3\frac{1}{2}$	2^{2}	Obrist R	2500	5.30
15Aug90 ^{10}Pla^{3}	Sherlock's Dynasty	B	5	122	3	8	$4\frac{1}{2}$	3^{hd}	4^{2}	$3\frac{1}{2}$	Garcia R Jr	2500	6.00
15Aug90 ^{5}Pla^{4}	Blazing Jake	LBb	3	118	4	9	$5^{1\frac{1}{2}}$	4^{5}	2^{hd}	4^{2}	Wilson J P	2500	7.30
11Aug90 ^{7}Boi^{1}	Nipper O.	Bb	5	122	9	10	8^{hd}	5^{2}	5^{5}	5^{4}	Rennaker L	2500	3.80
1Aug90 ^{7}Pla^{9}	Sambal	LBb	4	122	5	7	6^{1}	6^{2}	6^{hd}	6^{hd}	Pierce B T	2500	63.90
11Aug90 ^{9}Pla^{6}	Defiant Love	LB	3	117	6	5	9^{1}	$8\frac{1}{2}$	$7^{1\frac{1}{2}}$	7^{6}	Mitchell G V	2500	3.70
19Aug90 ^{1}Pla^{1}	Revved Up Tsuba	B	4	122	8	6	10	9^{3}	8^{8}	8^{8}	Ward V M	2500	2.40
12Aug90 ^{7}Boi^{8}	Cousin Brandon	B	4	122	2	4	7^{1}	10	9	9	Utecht K	2500	57.60
6May90 ^{3}SuD	Polachee	b	5	117	7	3	$3^{1\frac{1}{2}}$	7^{hd}	—	—	Kingrey R D	2500	68.90

Polachee, Eased.

OFF AT 1:54. Start good. Won driving. Time, :23⅗, :47, :59⅗, 1:12⅗ Track fast.

$2 Mutuel Prices:				
	10–B. B. POWER	139.80	123.40	12.80 ←
	1–SNEAKEN HOLME		6.80	3.60
	3–SHERLOCK'S DYNASTY			4.20

→ **$2 EXACTA 10–1 PAID $2,612.40.**

and the payoff is $18, you don't lose your entire perspective on life. The other is to watch the minute-by-minute odds changes on your planned bet on the TV monitors scattered throughout the grandstands.

With falling exotic prices, as soon as your intention is to go past about $20, especially in a straight bet, but also in wheeling and boxing, it is essential to follow the odds on the screen in the last minutes before the race.

It is a time-honored tradition, as well as an economic axiom, that big bets go in last. It is always attributed to the "smart money." The oldest, nonhandicapping system of all is to simply watch the tote board in the last moments before the teller machines are locked, and when a big drop in odds suddenly occurs, run—don't walk—and bet the farm on whichever horse took the drop. The reasoning is that the smart money—the owners, trainers, jockeys, heavyweight gamblers—*know* something, and you go along for the profits. The big bettors do in fact hold back until the last moment. As we saw earlier, a $2,000 bet can drastically alter the odds, and although a big bettor knows that his own bet will do this, he also knows that the crowd will follow and, instead of a drop to even money, which he might be willing to accept, it could well drop below the value for the risk.*

I know virtually nothing about dog racing, but a visit to the Juárez greyhound track once provided quick instructions on both odds and smart money. One thing I did pick up on quickly is that almost nobody bets in the mutuel pool; the betting is all in exotics. I was winning minuscule amounts betting place and show, using "condition" as a sole factor. It had been incredibly hot all week in El Paso/Juárez, with daytime temperatures in the low hundred-and-teens, and it was still 96 degrees at ten o'clock at night. If a dog wasn't panting, I bet him. I was doing so well, winning almost every bet (for a total profit of about $17), that I thought I would take the big plunge and bet one to win.

There was a dog in the next race who actually looked pretty good. I read the dog *Form* about as well as I read Bulgarian, but on paper he looked like one of the two or three contenders. Not only that—he wasn't panting. I watched the odds on the tote board until about three minutes before post time (perhaps it's "box time"—you see, they put these dogs in boxes . . .) and My Dog was standing at 99-to-1! It was time to throw caution to the wind and bet the big one: $2 to win.

I turned around from the teller and glanced back for my odds as the lights rippled across the tote board—and they had dropped to *17-to-1!* There was a wave of excitement—I had hit the Smart Money Dog without knowing it. The lights flowed across the next row and I waited to see what heavy hitter had nailed the bet, too. When it passed My Dog, there was a big 2 under the odds. *I* was the smart money. It wasn't exactly a stampede, but in the one minute left before lock-up, half a dozen smart money players caught the drastic drop and got their bets in, just in time. The dog went off at 2/1, with a total of $14 bet on it. I made four bucks, feeling pretty smug.

---

*Dick Mitchell, Barry Meadow, Huey Mahl, and others have written extensively on betting strategies that take odds and their associated risks closely into account (see Bibliography). A complete understanding of these topics is essential if you intend to take handicapping beyond a profitable diversion into a business. An excellent place to begin is Mitchell's *Commonsense Betting* (1995).

3

THE SPRINTS—FASTER HORSES, SHORTER RACES

Breed the fastest horses to each other—you will get the conformation you need.

—Attributed to OTT ADAMS,
early breeder of running quarter horses

*E*very track has a place on the back ramp toward the barns where trainers, owners, breeders, and hangers-on gather to watch the morning workouts. If you stand and listen for more than a minute in late fall or early spring, as young horses are ponied onto the track for the first time, you will hear the same words spoken over and over again: "Maybe he'll be a *runner* . . . maybe she'll have *speed*."

Whether the new horse is a son of Danzig, looking past the Kentucky Derby to the mile and a half of Belmont, or a daughter of Special Effort, aiming for the 440-yard All-American Futurity, the word that will make or break its career is speed.

Thoroughbred Sprints

In comparison to the real tests of endurance of the past and those run in other countries today, virtually all North American races are sprints. A horse must have the potential for speed to run with top competition, whether a particular race develops with a slow pace or not. Quarter horse straightaway races are sprints of the highest order, but, with few exceptions, Thoroughbreds begin their lives as sprinters as well.

Races early in the two-year-old year begin at four furlongs and move progressively to five, five and a half, and six. This is the testing ground for Thoroughbreds, and those who can carry their speed further move on. Those that show no speed or no will to win—or who damage delicate two-year-old bones and joints—move back, to be hunters and jumpers in English riding schools or, if their bloodlines warrant, to be bred, for better or worse.

In the earliest days of semiorganized Thoroughbred racing in this country, up through the turn of the century, races were usually run in four-mile "heats"—at least two, on the same or succeeding days. Endurance and a propensity for soundness of bone and wind were both the requirement for the races and the result of selective breeding.

Today, for a variety of specific purposes and for general discussion, the *Daily Racing Form* and others make a division in Thoroughbred races between "long" and "short." Long races are considered to be a mile and over; short, anything less. Since these divisions are now used in the *Form*'s speed ratings, they are beginning to replace the older and less precise classes of "sprints" and "routes." But for our purposes the older names work as well, if they are defined in terms of the nature of the horses and the races.

The old terms have often been used differently by different authors and racing publications. One common definition of a sprint is that it is run around one turn of an oval track. But routes are defined as being one and one-sixteenth of a mile and over, so a one-mile race around two turns falls back into a sprint, fitting neither set of conditions.

The terms are better defined if they are based on the natural ability of horses to run. Turns are very important in horse racing and we will consider them in handicapping later. But for the moment, suppose the racetrack is a two-mile straightaway.

When horses break out of the gates, they are loaded with anaerobic energy, stored in their muscles and blood. Anaerobic exercise is the process of converting glycogen and glycerin in the cells into energy without the need for oxygen. The process, which provides the initial burst of speed for sprinting horses, is highly evolved in grazing animals because it allows for instant flight from predators. It can only be sustained for a short time, however. The chemical waste products of anaerobic exercise, which include ammonia and lactic acid, must be transported away from the muscles through the bloodstream. While the waste products are accumulating, the cells are shifting over to aerobic exercise, which requires oxygen but can be sustained for considerable periods. Anaerobic and aerobic exercise are two of the many factors that affect the times and speeds achieved by running horses at various distances and that underlie this approach to speed handicapping. The relationship of some of these factors to handicapping will be shown graphically in later chapters.

With the bells and bangs of the gate, and the jockeys' shouts and whistles, most horses blow out with little need for serious urging for about a quarter mile (two furlongs). For about this distance, the chemical energy stored in their muscles and blood has been converting to lactic acid and other waste products and the shift to aerobic exercise is well underway. This is where the jockey comes in.

In this imaginary race, the horse is looking down a two-mile straightaway and may or may not see the distance poles along the side, but certainly doesn't know which one is the finish line. The jockey does, and if it is the four-furlong pole (a furlong is one-eighth of a mile), just another quarter mile ahead, he will continue to urge the horse forward. With a true runner this can amount to as little as *thinking* speed and maintaining a speed position in the saddle. (If this sounds a little mystical, get on a good horse and try it.) As the four-furlong finish line approaches, the jockey starts urging more speed, because, unlike the horse, he or she knows where the arbitrary end line is. A true runner wants to win; the jockey knows *where* to win.

If the race had been to the five-furlong (5/8-mile) pole, the strategy of the rider would be a little different. The chemical conversion of energy, which starts with the first excitement before the race, has had more time to progress (and is not a linear progression, as will be seen later). Most true runners and most riders want "position" from the outset of the race, so there will still be a dash out of the gates. But once the horses gain stride and positions begin to be established, the riders—who know both the finish line and the capabilities of their horses—try, at least, to take control. They limit the level of urging. If they are third and satisfied, they may not push their horse ahead. If their horse is one that hates to be behind but tends to burn himself out if he makes his own pace, they will pull him in and make him "rate" the rest of the field.

The riders may not know or care a thing about anaerobic and aerobic exercise, but they know that their horses get tired going full tilt for five furlongs, and this is where pace enters the picture. They are reserving their horses' energy and attempting to limit the buildup of lactic acid for when they must urge their horses as they approach the finish pole.

At six furlongs, the central part of the race becomes increasingly important. The moment-to-moment decisions of the jockey, about whether to let a speed horse push ahead or "rate," whether to urge a late runner at two furlongs or just 200 yards before the finish, can become the deciding factor of the race. The skill of the jockey also moves away from centering almost solely on the ability and condition of his own horse to the moment-by-moment assessment of the condition and placement of the other horses. Is the lead horse, who has weakened before, showing surprising strength today? Is the footing, two lanes over, worth the burst of energy to push ahead and take it? If he does attempt to move for the lane, is the horse or jockey next to him likely to fight for it? At six furlongs, on this hypothetical, two-mile straightaway, the race moves toward a balance between the horse's ability and condition and the jockey's skill in metering it out.

At seven furlongs, these factors fall into equilibrium. At a mile, the balance has tipped away from speed toward strategy. At each intermediate distance after a mile, the other important balance, between the horse's inherent speed and endurance, tips along with the importance of the jockey's strategy, until, if the full two miles are run, endurance, speed, and strategy come into three-way balance.

These changes and shifts in the horse's physical ability to run with speed and endurance and the balance between natural ability and jockey strategy are of critical importance in handicapping.

Speed is the most powerful handicapping tool available to race fans whose lives do not revolve around the track—but its effectiveness is in direct proportion to this balance. The natural balance between speed and strategy, on an imaginary straightaway, would probably be between six and seven furlongs. As we will see later, there is some evidence that this distance is the physiological outer limits of a true sprint.

Real Thoroughbred races are run on ovals, not straightaways, so the balance is artificially tipped earlier. Most tracks are one-mile ovals. On these tracks, six- and seven-furlong races are run around one sweeping turn. At tracks like Hollywood Park and Belmont (Belmont's one-and-a-half-mile oval is the largest in the United States), one-mile races are also run around one turn. Many smaller tracks may be seven-furlong ovals or even smaller, so races at those distances are run around two *tight* turns. The nature of the track can therefore affect the definition of a sprint. Six- and seven-furlong races run around two turns result in disproportionately slow times (with a disproportionate shift toward strategy), which make them difficult to classify as sprints. But since the same horses appear in one-turn races at the same and other tracks, they can be a handicapping tool, which can separate you from the crowd. We will discuss these and other "track constants" when we move into handicapping.

For speed handicapping, a sprint is a race of up to seven furlongs in length run around no more than one turn. This carries handicapping from the virtually pure speed factor of the quarter horse dashes to the balance point of speed and other handicapping analyses before strategy and endurance come to the forefront. Speed continues to be a consideration in handicapping races around two turns, and at a mile and over, but its importance in making handicapping decisions must stay in proportion to the importance of speed in the race.

Even the *Daily Racing Form*, with its extraordinary data banks, does not tabulate how many races are run at different distances each year. But it is safe to say that across the country over half of the Thoroughbred races run are at distances of seven furlongs and less, so at most tracks the *majority* of your Thoroughbred handicapping and betting opportunities will be in sprint racing.

Quarter Horse Dashes

Quarter horse racing, quite simply, is the most exciting horse racing on earth. If you have only seen it on television or from a soundproof grandstand, you have not experienced it. You must stand at the rail near the finish line and hear the roar of oncoming hooves, feel the ground shake under your feet, and then squint and cover your head in your arms as the clods fly and the horses disappear with incredible *speed*. Or see it from the rarer vantage point, at the gates, where the assistant starters shout, *"No, no, Boss! No, no!"* until each horse is standing straight, and then there is the blast of the bell, instantly drowned out by the thunder of hooves and the jockeys' screams and whistles. Your breath goes with them down the track into silence and then you hear the sudden roar of human voices as the horses approach the first seats of the grandstands.

Quarter horse racing is not only the most exciting form of horse racing to be near, it is also the most easily handicapped—which is just the opposite of what most handicappers think. Lots of things can lose a quarter horse race, but only one thing can win it.

Speed is the single overriding factor in handicapping quarter horse races, and everyone in the grandstands at Los Alamitos and Ruidoso knows it. The crowds at other mixed meets of Thoroughbreds and quarter horses and at offtrack-betting locations might not be quite so sure, but they certainly have an inkling. Why, then, at Ruidoso Downs, New Mexico—playground of the Texas and Oklahoma oil-rich who come to the mountains to vacation with their quarter horses—is the percentage of winning quarter horse favorites a bare seven points above the Thoroughbreds? Both winning favorites and favorites in the money in quarter horse races at Ruidoso *dropped* from 41 percent and 74 percent in 1989 to 37 percent and 71 percent in 1990. These percentages are higher than corresponding percentages for Thoroughbreds at Belmont and Hollywood Park, but they are far from what could be expected—and they would be *death* to your bankroll, only a little slower and more agonizing, if you practiced blind favorite betting.

Even with these higher percentages of favorites in the money, there are still great opportunities for finding good odds bets in quarter horse racing. The crowd is using the improved speed figures provided by the *Daily Racing Form*, and an increasing knowledge of handicapping, but very few are taking the steps to break beyond them. When the break is made, whether it is in microtrip handicapping in the short dashes or in making unique speed figures—or ideally a combination of both—the success ratio and the sound selection of higher-odds horses shoots up dramatically.

Quarter horses are run at distances of from 220 to 1,000 yards. The official running distances are 220, 250, 300, 330, 350, 400, 440, and 550 on a straightaway; 660, 770, 870, and 1,000 yards around one turn. By far, the most common races are those between 350 and 440 yards, which is the true speed domain of the quarter horse. Races at 220 and 330 are usually run early in the year at smaller tracks as prep races for two-year-olds, although you may occasionally see older horses, sometimes as the track secretary accommodates personal challenges between owners. Races at 660 and 770 are rare and are often the result of track size and layout at small tracks and fairs. The 870-yard distance, however, has become firmly established at larger tracks. Especially at mixed meets of quarter horses and Thoroughbreds, you will often see at least one 870-yard race per day. This distance originated to provide racing opportunities for quarter horses that may have lacked the blinding speed necessary for the straightaways and as a showcase for direct competition between quarter horses and Thoroughbreds. Aside from steeplechasing, the 870-yard race may be the most grueling distance in horse racing.

In top competition there is no pace in an 870-yard race. There is strategy, since a turn must be negotiated and position can mean everything, but the horses break out of the gates like quarter horses and run as fast as they can as far as they can to the finish. These races are timed and listed in the *Daily Racing Form* as quarter horse races (in other words, in hundredths of a second, not fifths, and in the quarter horse past-performance format), but the field may often be half or more Thoroughbreds. As a result, they can be difficult for the crowd to handicap—which is exactly why some handicappers specialize in them.

The 1,000 yard distance was introduced in the 1980s, specifically as a sponsored quarter horse/Thoroughbred "challenge." A limited number of qualification races are run, leading to a championship in which the winner (or the winner's owner) receives one of the sponsor's fancy four-wheel-drive vehicles in addition to the purses. You should get one too, if you can handicap a race in which first-time Thoroughbred starters are listed in Thoroughbred times and distances against both Thoroughbreds and quarter horses listed in the quarter horse format.

The Horses

Speed in horses is developed and perfected through conditioning, but the innate desire to run is bred into both Thoroughbreds and quarter horses. Many handicappers place great weight on breeding, even to the exclusion of other factors, especially in the first races of two-year-olds before performances are established. Breeding can mean everything or it can mean nothing.

Race horse genetics are as tantalizing and frustrating to breeders as past performances are to handicappers. It is long-term, high-stakes gambling, with the teasing possibility that a scientific solution lies ahead, just out of reach. There have been almost as many theories, schemes, and systems devised by breeders and bloodstock consultants as by handicappers. As in handicapping, it is often easier to say that a system works than to explain *why* it works—and it is often just as deceiving.

Modern Thoroughbreds and running quarter horses are so closely related, it is hardly useful to consider them separately. The origins of the American Quarter Horse (a trademark of the American Quarter Horse

Association) and the American Thoroughbred are hazier than either breed organization would have you believe.

A mixture of horses were raced on the Colonial Eastern seaboard and new blood was imported continuously from England and Europe, initially to make up for the ones they had to eat over the winter and later for racing. Since the Eastern seaboard was dominated by English colonies, which later dominated the central continent, English bloodlines in draft, carriage, and racing also dominated the horse gene pool.

Both Thoroughbreds and "short horses" were selected for their ability to run at the distances that paid. Since Thoroughbreds can trace ancestry to European and particularly English Thoroughbreds, which were already established as "blood horses," Thoroughbred advocates enjoy feeling superior on the issue of breeding. But the fact remains that from the introduction of European horses to the Eastern seaboard until the limitations struck by the breed registry in 1873—about fifty horse generations—all types and descriptions of mares were bred to imported stallions, and back to their mixed offspring, to populate the expanding country. As a result, the Thoroughbreds of America, Australia, and other former colonies are not identical in type or bloodlines to each other or to those of England, Ireland, or France. American Thoroughbred racing has focused on shorter, "flat" racing, at distances generally under a mile and a half on controlled, flat dirt or grass courses, and the intensive breeding focus has followed.

Race horses are a combination of genotype and phenotype. The genes of two parents provide a range of possibilities that becomes fixed in the gene combination of the offspring. The phenotype is the combination of genetic potential with environment and experience, which together make up the individual. The same two horse parents can produce a vast variety of gene combinations in their offspring, and an even broader range of phenotypes.

When a stallion tends to pass on certain desirable characteristics to a high percentage of his offspring, he is considered "prepotent." The "high percentage" is often deceiving; many stallions that are considered prepotent will produce dozens, if not hundreds, of offspring that do not possess the outstanding characteristics that make the stallion famous. No business has a greater propensity for forgetting failures and remembering successes than horse breeding.

When a stallion produces a high percentage of outstanding foals with a particular mare or line of mares, he is said to have "hit a nick" (which may be derived from the term "genetic niche," which is a totally different but vaguely analogous notion). "Nicks" tend to be more readily observed than general prepotency when viewing a particular stallion with a particular mare or small line of mares, where the numbers of successes and failures are small and easy to recognize. When the idea expands to lines of stallions and lines of mares, then the notion of a "nick" becomes almost as difficult to pin down as the population genetics at large.

Although everyone knows that genes are a combination of those of the male and female parents, horse heredity is overwhelmingly biased toward tracking male lines. There are two primary reasons for this. One is the pure chauvinism of the traditionally male domain of horse breeding; the other is the fact that even a marginally fertile stallion can produce vastly more offspring than the most nubile mare. This disproportionate representation of males complicates analysis of bloodlines beyond the Mendelian, classroom-pea examples, which are complicated enough already. To complicate matters further, when female lines are traced, it usually is in terms of the mare's sire, or more distant male ancestor. Thus, you will often read or hear that Grey Dawn mares are a good cross on such-and-such a line of stallions.

You will occasionally hear a trainer or breeder say that the mare contributes *more*—"sixty or sixty-five percent"—to the foal. This is usually more a statement of liberalism than genetics, unless they are referring to phenotype, where the mare's ability to produce milk, her mothering instincts, spirit, and disposition are passed to her baby in the months they are together. These can be profound contributions to the development of the individual race-horse, but they hedge the question of genetics.

Even the best stallions are bred to a wide variety of mares. Owners of top stallions are often selective in the class of mares they will allow to be bred, but more often the stud fee itself creates a form of natural selection. Horses tend to be bred within their value classes. The owner of a $2,500 claiming mare is not likely to pay a $25,000 stud fee (although it does happen). This might be expected to create de facto levels of potential in the foals born each year, and to a certain extent it does. Cheaply bred horses very, *very* rarely rise into the highest ranks of competition; but, on the other hand, a great many of the highest bred horses fall dismally into the cheapest claiming barns and become available for breeding at low stud fees. Genetic failure may be a greater force than success in keeping the blood circulating.

One breeding analysis system that has moved into handicapping and is widely acknowledged as working—but no one can explain (beyond intuition) *why*—is "dosage analysis." This system produces a mathematical index, which is useful not so much in predicting which horse will win a race, but which horses will not. It was devised in France at the turn of the twentieth century but has become notable in recent years as a result of its very high success in picking *nonwinners* of the Kentucky Derby.

The analysis of pedigrees identified *chefs de race*—stallions that have shown profound influences on the breed and that tend to produce certain qualities in their offspring. These stallions are divided into ascending categories of early to late maturity, and concomitantly, of speed toward endurance: brilliant, intermediate, classic, solid, and professional.

Chefs de race are classified according to the performance of their off-spring, so that sires such as Bull Dog, whose offspring are viewed as general-ly early maturing and possessing great speed over short distances, are considered Brilliant only, while others, such as Bold Ruler, straddle the categories of Brilliant and Intermediate. When a *chef de race* such as Bull Lea, a son of Bull Dog, is classed differently than his sire, it is considered to be the result of the influence of some other *chefs de race* in either his sire or dam's ancestry.

In order to calculate the mathematical dosage index, you need at least a four-generation pedigree. Only *chefs de race* are counted, and if they appear in the first generation, they are given 16 points in whichever category they fit. Horses like Bold Ruler, which span categories, would be split 8 and 8. Each more distant generation is given half the value (8, 4, 2), so the more distant the *chef de race*, the less influence on the horse at hand. To arrive at the dosage index, you add up the score in each of the separate categories for the horse you are analyzing, then divide the speed half (scores for Brilliant, Intermediate, and *half* of the Classic) by the endurance half (the other half of Classic, Solid, and Professional). There are other calculations that can be made with the figures, but this is the basic one.

Dosage analysis reveals that no winner of the Kentucky Derby has ever had a dosage index greater than 4. In other words, at the classic distance of a mile and a quarter for three-year-olds, the "speed dose" from its ancestors must not be more than four times greater than the "endurance dose"—or your favorite is going to lose. On an ordinal scale, a 4 looks pretty innocent. Why it is the breaking point in a process of mathematical division of subjec-tively assigned classes is anybody's guess.

Although the dosage system is on a roll with nonwinners of the Kentucky Derby, you don't have to look far to start scratching your head.

The 1983 champion sprinter was Chinook Pass. Listed beside him in *The American Racing Manual* (the annual summary of Thoroughbred racing published by the *Daily Racing Form*) is the great champion "steeplechase or hurdle horse" Flatterer, who remained champion through four successive years. Chinook Pass has an impressive eight *chefs de race* in his background and is heavily weighted in the Brilliant and Intermediate classes with one fourth-generation Professional in Admiral Drake. He won most of his races at six and six and a half furlongs, and yet his dosage index is 3.3—hot stuff for a Kentucky Derby winner.

Flatterer has four *chefs de race* in his background, all of which are Brilliant through Classic, with no Solid or Professional. Flatterer's 1983 races were all won at distances of two to two and three-quarter miles. He shares two ancestors with Chinook Pass, in Royal Charger and Bull Lea, and would share another, if you went back a generation from Nasrullah (Brilliant) to

Chinook Pass, 1983 Champion Sprinter, was one of the few champions who specialized in sprint distances. *Photo by Four Footed Fotos.*

Nearco (Brilliant/Classic). His dosage index is *11!* According to dosage, the racing distances of their two careers should have been exactly reversed.

It is often unclear what marks a horse as a sprinter. Secretariat would probably be classified as a Classic performer. One of his good sons, Pancho Villa, was a sprinter and stands as a new sprinting sire.

What made Pancho Villa, Chinook Pass, Forego, or any of the others sprinters? Some may have been intentionally bred for it, but probably most were not. Most elite Thoroughbreds are raised with one objective in mind, and it is the Triple Crown—at distances of one and an eighth, one and three-sixteenths, and one and a half miles. Becoming tagged as a "sprinter" can be a natural reflection of a horse's ability to run or a fluke in the development of his career.

Chinook Pass, during his championship sprinting year, ran seven races, six at distances of seven furlongs or less, and one at a mile. He won all but one at six and one at seven furlongs. Since he was a four-year-old and qualified to run at longer distances, it is clear that his connections believed they had a sprinter on their hands and shaped his career accordingly.

Forego was sprinting champion in 1974 and made thirteen starts, winning

One of the great horses of all times, Forego could run at any distance. Champion sprinter of 1974, he was also Horse of the Year at route distances three years in a row. *Photo courtesy of* The Blood-Horse.

eight and showing in the money in all but one. He ran three races at seven furlongs, winning two and coming in second in one. He placed second in the Metropolitan Handicap at a mile. The other nine races of his championship sprinting year were at distances of at least one and an eighth mile—up to the Jockey Club Handicap at Aqueduct, at two miles, which he won by two and a half lengths! (Forego was also champion "older colt, horse, or gelding" for that year, and Horse of the Year for 1974, 1975, and 1976.) Each of the last four years of his remarkable five-year career, Forego began by winning a tune-up race or two at seven furlongs or a mile, then moved on to true "routes." Forego was not a sprinter in the planned sense of Chinook Pass; he was simply an exceptional racehorse that could run with speed at any distance. Like several other superior horses with long and distinguished careers, such as Kelso and John Henry, Forego was a gelding, so we will never know if he would have been a *chef de race*.

While the genetic background of a horse can often suggest whether it is likely to be a sprinter, the phenotype is what decides. The phenotype covers everything from disposition to scars, but in racehorses centers on conformation of muscle and bone. No two horses, even from the same parents, are built quite the same. Subtle differences in conformation are difficult to observe and describe, and even more difficult to place values on, because there is no single ideal.

Secretariat's running style, huge build, and intangible presence might be considered an ideal. On the other hand, Northern Dancer was a short-bodied, almost ponylike horse in comparison with Secretariat, who became one of the great sires of the century after knocking two-fifths of a second off the Kentucky Derby record of his era and going on to win the Preakness. There are two ways of running fast: one is to take long fast strides, the other is to take short strides even faster.

The only law of horse conformation is that it is a lot easier to see faults than it is to identify and define advantages. The library is full of books that will show you graphic photos of cow hocks, ewe necks, upright pasterns, toed-in and toed-out front hooves, etc. It is also true that for every conformation defect there is an example of a horse that possessed it to some degree and yet performed well as a runner.

The real masters of conformation evaluation, who successfully buy runners out of auctions such as Keeneland, cannot tell you, beyond the well-known structural composition, why they see a horse as a runner. This is because there is no "mental template" of an ideal horse, but rather a mental simulation of how the composition of body and mind will operate.

There are some broad conformation traits that identify sprinters and long-distance runners. The most obvious is pure mass. As in the definition of "Brilliant" runners, sprinters do tend to mature earlier, with greater muscle mass at a younger age than long-distance endurance runners. This is brought to an extreme in the quarter horse futurity sprinters, who may weigh half a ton before they reach their second birthday.

Early quarter horses and some that resemble the type today were called bulldogs because of the huge muscle mass of both their shoulders and

Top: Every trainer's dream of conformation, Secretariat was perfection of mind and body. Notice his size in relation to on-lookers and the depth of his chest at the girth. *Photo by Bob Coglianese.* **Bottom:** A dream in a different body, Northern Dancer ran with short legs and small torso in perfect combination. His ability to pass on his running traits made him one of the great sires of the century. *Photo courtesy of* The Blood-Horse.

Count Fleet shows the lean, lanky look of a router, although his conformation was considered far from perfect. Perfection is what works, and Count Fleet was Triple Crown winner and Horse of the Year of 1943, and in the dosage system he is now considered a Classic *chef de race*. *Photo courtesy of* The Blood Horse.

A modern sprinter of great ability, Smile could also run a route. Shown here winning the Breeders' Cup Sprint, making him Champion Sprinter of 1986. *Photo by Bob Coglianese.*

Clabber was the first World Champion running quarter horse, crowned in 1940. His stocky build is classic quarter horse, but many other early runners showed strong thoroughbred characteristics. *Photo courtesy of* The American Quarter Horse Association.

Some modern running quarter horses are difficult to distinguish from thoroughbreds but 1987 World Champion, First Down Dash, is not one of them—even though thoroughbreds are predominant among his ancestors. Note the similarities with Clabber, fifty years his senior. *Photo courtesy of Vessels' Stallion Farm.*

hindquarters, which made their relatively short legs appear even shorter, and because of the massive round muscles of their jaws in contrast to the desired short, foxlike ears. They were also higher in the croup (top point of the rump) than at the withers (top base of the neck)—which is considered a conformation fault in most other breeds, but which apparently worked in the all-purpose days. Now the croup height is not selected against, but is becoming less pronounced, especially in racehorses.

There is more to sprinting than mere muscle size. There afe different types of muscle fibers in the same muscle mass and they are present in different proportions in different horses. Studies have shown that quarter horses on the whole have a higher proportion of "fast twitch" muscles than Thoroughbreds. But the proportion can also change over time, depending upon the work the muscles are called upon to do in training and racing. Which is one reason why very fast Thoroughbreds can compete successfully in the mixed-breed 870-yard races, but seldom in their first attempt in stepping down from six and seven furlongs.

Much of quarter horse racing is based on anaerobic energy supplied by prestored glucose and supported by removal of exertion products, such as lactic acid, which is what makes muscles "burn" when overexerted. Blood cell volume, therefore, is important, both in the early stages of running and when the need for oxygen takes over. Both Thoroughbreds and quarter horses have been shown to have a higher "packed cell volume" (measured by spinning blood samples in a centrifuge, or simply letting them settle) than either standardbreds or endurance horses (of the separate sport of endurance riding, mostly dominated by Arabian horses). These data are averages, and individuals may excel in these and other yet-to-be-identified physiological traits. Characteristics such as these may be what quarter horse breeders have been selecting for all along, and they may be only partially reflected in the more obvious quarter horse conformation.

Historically, the "short 'horse" might have almost died out, if it were not for its lingering popularity in the deep South, notably in Louisiana—and for the fact that when the West was opened, cowmen needed sturdy, dependable horses capable of quick bursts of speed to turn, rope, and work cattle. While racing continued, most of the breeders were cowboys of the finest tradition. Speed, dependability, reasonable disposition, and cow sense became virtually equal breeding objectives. These efforts culminated in about the 1930s, when quarter horses bred true to type and had developed such an enthusiastic following that the breed registry was founded in 1940.

Thoroughbreds were used continually for breeding short horses, from Colonial times through the cow horse era, when the King Ranch's almost bizarre but scientifically devised and successful inbreeding program was based on *El Alazán Viejo*, the Old Sorrel. (The King Ranch breeding theories also produced world-class Thoroughbreds and the Santa Gertrudis breed of beef cattle.) The first quarter horse to be registered, by prior agreement, was the winner of the 1941 Fort Worth stock show, which turned out to be Wimpy, a closely inbred double grandson of Old Sorrel.

Both of Wimpy's parents were by Old Sorrel, out of different *Thoroughbred* mares. Old Sorrel himself was out of a Thoroughbred mare, by Hickory Bill, a son of Peter McCue. Peter McCue's breeding is debated, since he was listed in the *American Stud Book* as the son of a Thoroughbred, while quarter horse people prefer to think he was by the quarter horse Dan Tucker. In either case, Peter McCue's dam was Norma M.—a Thoroughbred.

So the first registered quarter horse was—*at a minimum*—15/16 Thoroughbred.

In spite of the obvious, there was considerable debate and dissension in the newly formed AQHA about closing the registry to Thoroughbreds. The result was a compromise, and Thoroughbreds and their "half"-Thoroughbred offspring have been held in an appendix ever since, until their performance meets the criteria for full registry. This was a lucky thing for the quarter horse breed.

Innumerable top-running quarter horses have been first-generation outcrosses to Thoroughbreds. Great runners like Strawberry Silk have resulted from crossing the best quarter horse mares to dominant Thoroughbred speed, found in sires like Beduino. Strawberry Silk's pedigree is typical of the modern running quarter horse, but it is not only modern—it is the history of the breed.

The unlucky thing for the quarter horse was that the old cowboy breeders had developed such a fine horse, with so many desirable traits, that as the following grew, it began to segment into groups that focused both their activities and their breeding on single talents of the horse.

It is no longer an obscure worry of quarter horse conservatives, but a simple fact, that the quarter horse breed has diverged into varieties that cannot crossover in areas of performance. The reason has much less to do with Thoroughbred outcrossing, which produced Wimpy and virtually all of the "foundation" sires, than with the original versatility of the quarter horse itself.

Since quarter horses are such a pleasure to ride, they are natural standouts in the "pleasure" show classes. The "cow sense" bred into them by their cowboy breeders created the amazing phenomenon and athletic sport of "cutting" cattle. Quarter horses are also beautiful and their strength and beauty led to halter classes, where horses must do nothing but stand straight and refrain from biting their owners. Meanwhile, although the median purses for quarter horse racing remain far below those for Thoroughbreds, the single-minded quest of quarter horse racing—the All-American Futurity—has grown to $2.5 million in total purse money (the race itself is $2 million, the consolations $500,000).

"Performance" horses (cutting, roping, and reining) probably remain

Strawberry Silk ran with a rare combination of breeding, condition, and charisma that transcended betting. Thousands who lost money cheered when she ran way from the colts in the 1989 All-American Futurity. Her breeding is typical of modern quarter horses, but also reflects the history of the breed. *Photo by Bill Pitt, Jr. Courtesy of Ruidoso Downs.*

Bred in Kentucky, but running only in Mexico, Beduino was a thoroughbred sprinter of blazing speed. The quarter horse world lost face when Beduino won a match race against the world champion quarter horse, but gained a great sire, when he moved to California. *Photo courtesy of Vessels' Stallion Farm.*

Beduino (TB)	Romany Royal	Grey Sovereign
		Romany Belle
	Jo-Ann-Cat	Rejected
		Quick Eye
Painted Bug	Shawne Bug	Lady Bug's Moon
		Shawne Win
	Miss Painted Clown (TB)	Dead Ahead
		Talk About Run

FIGURE 3.1: STRAWBERRY SILK'S PEDIGREE. SHADED AREAS DENOTE 4TH GENERATION THOROUGHBREDS

Shawne Bug, Strawberry Silk's maternal grandsire, is a masterpiece of quarter horse conformation. The smashing success of Strawberry Silk cemented his reputation as a broodmare sire, but his immediate sons and daughters are also top-rank performers. *Photo by Orren Mixer courtesy of Bowlan Farms, Tecumseh, Oklahoma.*

truest to the quarter horse breeding at the time of the founding of the registry, but racehorses follow the pre-cow horse tradition of outcrossing to Thoroughbred speed.

There is no quarter horse winning races in top competition today (and maybe none at all) that is not, at the least, half Thoroughbred. This does not mean that the sire or dam was pure Thoroughbred, which has always been common. It does mean that if you go back through the generations and tally a percentage, not accepting ancestors as "quarter horse" simply because they have a permanent registration number, you will arrive at the conclusion that the American Quarter Horse is actually a strain of Thoroughbreds that could be added to the dosage system as "Blindingly Brilliant."

PART TWO

The Noise of Time

4

CLASS IN RACES AND HORSES

> When Protagonist rallied to beat Stonewalk by two lengths, I could not explain the outcome of the race in any way that was consistent with my own philosophy.
>
> —ANDREW BEYER
> on reconciling speed and class, in
> *Picking Winners: A Horseplayer's Guide*

Horses live and race in a fairly rigid class structure. The classes of the races are easy to describe, but *class in a horse* is the most elusive of all handicapping factors. It exists only in the minds of horses.

Most trainers will insist that a \$15,000 horse will lose a \$20,000 race, even if it has run consistently faster than any other horse in the field—are you ready for this?—because it *knows* it is not as good.

Quite often, they are right.

This holds not only for lower ranked, but also for highly bred horses, which have fallen into the lower ranks to be claimed and then are placed back up out of their class by overly optimistic new owners. What the horse knows is another story.

Fleeting Ben *
LOPEZ A D **116**
Own.—Molinaro K R

Dk. b. or br. g. 5, by Plotting—Fleet Maid, by Sandy Fleet
Br.—Salamoni B (Cal) **1990 5 3 1 0 \$17,600**
Tr.—Molinaro Kent \$12,500 **1989 10 3 0 4 \$14,295**
Lifetime 25 8 3 7 \$48,250

14Apr90-7GG	6f	:21^4	:44^4	1:10^{1}ft	*4-5	119	8^7	$8^{7\frac{1}{4}}$	$4^{3\frac{1}{2}}$	$1^{\frac{3}{4}}$	Hansen R D^7	c10000	87-15	FleetingBen,ThisIsForevr,SocilMn	11
9Mar90-6GG	6f	:22	:44^2	1:09^{3}ft	4	117	$5^{5\frac{1}{2}}$	3^4	$3^{1\frac{1}{2}}$	2^{hd}	Warren R J Jr^1	12500	90-15	KingSkipper,FletingBn,SuchMrcnry	6
19Feb90-9GG	6f	:21^4	:44^3	1:10^{2}gd	*3-2	119	$5^{7\frac{1}{2}}$	$4^{3\frac{1}{4}}$	3^2	$1^{1\frac{1}{2}}$	Long B^5	10000	86-17	FletingBn,RoyllyGood,B.J.'sPockts	7
10Feb90-9GG	6f	:21^3	:44^3	1:09^{3}ft	5¾	117	$7^{4\frac{3}{4}}$	$4^{5\frac{1}{2}}$	$4^{4\frac{1}{2}}$	$5^{1\frac{1}{2}}$	Warren R J Jr^8	12500	88-12	RatherOdd,KingSkipper,Clehuche	11
14Jan90-3BM	6f	:23	:47	1:12 sy	*8-5	116	3^3	2^{hd}	1^1	$1^{2\frac{1}{2}}$	Warren R J Jr^3	10000	80-24	FleetingBn,HstyTobin,B.J.'sPockts	4
24Dec89-3BM	6f	:21^4	:44^1	1:09^{2}ft	2e	117	6^5	7^8	6^6	$5^{6\frac{1}{4}}$	Maple S^2	12500	89-07	Lot'sCurosty,NvdSwngr,SchMrcnry	8
24Dec89—Wide on turn															
3Dec89-7BM	6f	:22^1	:44^4	1:10 ft	10	117	$4^{3\frac{1}{2}}$	$4^{3\frac{1}{2}}$	$4^{4\frac{1}{2}}$	$3^{1\frac{1}{2}}$	Privitera R^2	10000	90-12	Fast Foods,Generator,FleetingBen	12
3Dec89—Lost whip 3/8															
12Nov89-5BM	6f	:22^3	:45^2	1:10 ft	3½	119	2^{hd}	1^{hd}	1^{hd}	1^2	Hansen R D^5	[S] 6250	92-08	FleetingBen,DevilishPirte,Guggen	12
13Oct89-9BM	1	:45	1:09^4	1:35^{1}ft	14	117	$6^{2\frac{1}{2}}$	2^1	$7^{6\frac{3}{4}}$	$6^{5\frac{1}{2}}$	Chapman T M^4	8000	86-14	OnzsChmpion,DrouillyFuss,Mr.Fudd	9
29Sep89-3BM	6f	:22^3	:46	1:11 ft	2¾	117	$4^{2\frac{1}{4}}$	$3^{\frac{1}{2}}$	3^1	3^4	Privitera R^3	8000	80-15	Mc Gruff, Tashes Only,FleetingBen	6

Speed Index: Last Race: +2.0 3–Race Avg.: +3.3 9–Race Avg.: +0.7 Overall Avg.: +0.7

May 13 GG 5f ft 1:04 H Apr 10 GG 6f ft 1:16^3 H Apr 4 GG 6f ft 1:17^3 H Mar 27 GG 4f ft :49^2 H

Class in Races

Racing classes are the foundation of most modern approaches to handicapping, since they offer a means of categorizing levels of performance and times that horses can be expected to attain. Virtually all current theories take off, at least, from the work of William Quirin, Tom Ainslie, Steven Davidowitz, and Andrew Beyer, all of whom developed ingenious uses for racing class par times.

Class in both its meanings (racing categories and in the individual horse) will be used in this approach, but not as the foundation. The resulting difference in the baselines used for comparison of performances will be shown later.

A horse's racing class is based on the marketplace. A horse's value, both in its breeding and performance potential, determines where it will start its career.

A horse is a maiden until it wins its first race, when it is said to have "broken its maiden." This is such an old term in racing that horsemen seem to be confused about its origin; newcomers aren't. Maidens can be of either sex, or gelded (castrated), which does sometimes confuse newcomers, who assume they are watching a field of fillies. A female horse is a *filly* until she is five years old, when she is called a *mare*; a male horse is a *colt* until he is five, when he becomes a *horse*. A *gelding* is a gelding whenever the misfortune befalls him.

When a foal is born, and perhaps before it is conceived, in spite of all the hopes and dreams, there is probably some fairly realistic expectation of where it will race. While a few of the owners and trainers of national stature, such as D. Wayne Lukas and Shug McGaughey, may jet their horses around the country on the Grade I circuit, most know from the outset that they will be racing in their home region or at a specific track. The hope may be for a good runner to take the state-bred futurity or an important regional handicap. Of course, if the colt is launched from there into the Kentucky Derby, that would be all right, too. Since every unraced two-year-old is a potential Kentucky Derby winner, it has to find its own class.

One of the primary jobs of the racetrack, in addition to providing stables and getting the public to attend, is to organize balanced races. This is a lot more complicated than just seeing that horses of approximately equal potential run against each other, and it is the job of the racing secretary.

About twelve races will be run every race day, and over a hundred horses will compete. Meanwhile, several *thousand* are waiting on the backside, at a $15- to $50-a-day training fee, for the right time and race to run.

The balancing process begins with the issuance of stables. At most tracks they are provided free to trainers, or at some nominal fee for utilities. At most tracks, too, the preseason requests for stalls greatly exceed the number available. The distribution of stables is *not* first come, first served. Leading trainers, of course, are given not only the number of stalls they want, but usually the finest accommodations; maybe tulips along the side in their stable colors.

All trainers must provide information on the breeding and past performance of their horses with their applications, so that the track can select what they feel will provide the best racing for the public. This makes perfectly good sense, but you can picture the rest.

Racing continues year-round across the country, but racing seasons vary considerably. Individual tracks close as others in the same state open, according to the dates assigned by the racing commissions. The time of year assigned to the meet is the first determinant of the races to be organized.

Spring/summer meets usually begin on or before Memorial Day and end on Labor Day in September. Two-year-olds usually appear on the track for the first time in the early weeks of these meets, although some may be moved in after one or two training races toward the end of a winter season. Since every one of them, in the mind of someone, is a potential winner of the Triple Crown, the racing secretary must ensure enough races to accommodate all of them without the danger of claiming. All he or she has to do is count noses and divide by twelve to book races with the simplest conditions of all: Maiden. 2-year-olds.

A "condition book" covering the first weeks of racing is put out before the meet begins, and it is usually based on last year's meet, with modifications to fit any changes in the horse population that the racing secretary knows will be arriving. After the races take shape and the secretary learns more about the horses (or is shaken by the lapels a few times at meetings with the horsemen), succeeding condition books are issued to keep all segments of the population racing.

Meanwhile, the racing secretary has two other constituents to accommodate: the public and the racetrack owners. The public hates two-year-old maiden races, cheap claiming races, and too much duplication in a day's program. The track owners hate low attendance and weak betting. It is not a job for the sensitive. But with the onset of the "exotics," the secretaries have found their revenge. Races have to be placed in the program with a view of both the flow of the day's entertainment and the types of betting offered on individual and sequential races. So these are the fellows you can thank for those second halves of twin trifectas, in which the most recent past performance was a 2.7-kilometer hurdle race in a suburb of Caracas, or when the field is otherwise pitiful (see next page).

There are two broad conditions of races: those in which the horses are vulnerable to be sold and those in which they are protected from loss. To say that claiming horses are "for sale" is a little too euphemistic; most owners would probably prefer that their horses not be claimed, although every imaginable permutation occurs.

Claiming races create a natural classification of horses, since every horse entered in a race is subject to being lost at the stated price. This keeps horses

Pittiful Prince — Ro. g. 4, by T V Minstrel—Fantazac, by Order Up
BAZE R A — 120 — Br.—Pitti C C (Cal) — 1990 4 M 0 0 $575
Tr.—Smith Kenneth D Jr — $28,000 — 1989 6 M 0 0 $2,280
Own.—Pitti C C — Lifetime 10 0 0 0 $2,855

20Apr90-2SA	6f :22 :453 1:111ft	65	1135	85½ 97¼ 97½ 810¾	Davenport C L 9	M45000	70-20	LnLghtFoot,OrgnlTrp,CstmSttchs	12
25Feb90-1SA	1 1/16 :473 1:124 1:452ft	113	119	64½ 3½ 710 922	Cedeno E A 11	M50000	54-24	St. Elmo, Coronado Bay, Event	12
25Feb90—Wide									
2Feb90-6SA	1 1/16 :472 1:123 1:453ft	92	119	1211 1213 813 615¾	Meza R Q 5	M50000	59-26	CrckInThIc,TrEnogh,Gbson'sChoc	12
15Jan90-6SA	6f :221 :453 1:094gd	54	119	118¼ 119¾ 811 516¼	Meza R Q 4	M50000	71-13	Shadowy Smile, Geyser, Jane'sRaj	12
16Dec89-2Hol	6f :22 :451 1:102ft	64	118	85½ 54¾ 68 66¾	Meza R Q 8	M32000	82-09	King Saros, Geyser, Pappy Yokum	12
16Dec89—Lugged in 3/8									
17Nov89-2Hol	6f :223 :46 1:111ft	49	118	73¼ 63½ 66½ 79	Patton D B 9	M32000	76-12	PerfectPtient,Gllon,Gibson'sChoic	11
8Nov89-2SA	6½f :214 :444 1:17 ft	88	118	34 32 53 1013¼	Patton D B 1	M32000	76-12	MoreGolden,Jane'sRaj,NobleVlint	12
26Sep89-8Fpx	6f :22 :453 1:11 ft	17	116	57 49 57½ 416½	Sibille R 9	Mdn	75-13	TryANtive,IslyPrince,OnForAdrno	10
26Sep89—Very wide early									
8Sep89-4Dmr	6f :221 :45 1:102ft	4¾	1125	4nk 63¾ 129¼ 1216¼	JureguiL H 11	[S]M32000	70-12	OhDatFox,BolderStrategy,Interpol	12
8Sep89—Wide into stretch									
29Jly89-4AC	6f :223 :451 1:103ft	*2¾	115	1½ 11 1hd 42½	Lopez A D 7	AlwM	83-11	MoneyAura,ClassicAmerican,Shunl	7

Speed Index: Last Race: −10.0 3–Race Avg.: −11.6 8–Race Avg.: −11.8 Overall Avg.: −13.2
May 20 Fpx 3f ft :352 H ●May 13 Fpx 1 ft 1:422 H May 4 Fpx 7f ft 1:284 H Apr 12 Fpx 4f ft :482 Hg

Fiscal Fiasco — Ro. g. 3(May), by Spanish Drums—Miss Ali Dal, by Affiliate
Br.—Baumohl & Fernung (Fla) — 1990 5 M 0 0
Own.—Hanafin M — 1065 — Tr.—Bailie Sally A — $45,000 — 1989 5 M 0 2 $3,120
Lifetime 10 0 0 2 $3,120 — Turf 1 0 0 0

18May90-9Bel	1 1/16 :473 1:134 1:46 ft	9¼	113	106 106½ 915 925¼	Bruin J E 7	M32500	47-28	Duck Calling,Cucho,Life'sSurprise	12
28Apr90-7Aqu	1⅛ (T):483 1:124 1:512fm	49	115	78 87¼ 1019 1115¼	Smith M E 7	Mdn	79-05	Rubigo, Apple Current, Theurgist	12
17Apr90-3Aqu	6f :222 :46 1:112ft	43	113	1010 1010 810 711¼	Bruin J E 14	M32500	72-17	IftsfrItsform,HomrmDncr,Skyfrng	14
26Jan90-4Aqu	6f [•]:222 :462 1:124sy	23	118	911 99¼ 1017 1022¼	MrtinezJRJr 11	M30000	60-13	Border Captain, Three Lyrics,Heat	12
15Jan90-4Aqu	6f [•]:222 :464 1:124ft	113	118	813 810 812 69¼	McCarthy M J 5	M45000	73-16	Ack'sRddl,OlympcImg,ComdyRotn	12
4Oct89-2Bel	7f :231 :474 1:262ft	74	114	1118 1116 1020 1026½	Cruguet J 7	M70000	43-27	Flthorn,MysteryLovr,FltCommndr	11
13Sep89-2Bel	6f :23 :463 1:131ft	5¼	118	79½ 512 410 310¼	Cruguet J 6	M35000	63-20	Dr.LouieD.,Overndovrgin,FisclFisco	8
22Jly89-4Bel	6f :23 :471 1:123ft	6½e	114	84¾ 99 814 816	Santos J A 5	M70000	60-23	NorthrnBb,FnlDstnton,SpnshLgnd	11

Speed Index: Last Race: −11.0 3–Race Avg.: −16.3 6–Race Avg.: −18.8 Overall Avg.: −19.2
May 13 Bel 5f ft 1:013 H May 7 Bel 4f ft :49 B Apr 23 Bel tr.t 4f ft :493 B Apr 14 Bel tr.t 5f ft 1:013 H

of approximately the same abilities together, since the owner of a solid $10,000 horse is very unlikely to try to slip into a $2,500 claiming race to steal a $1,700 purse. That is the basic theory—to which there are infinite possibilities.

Tracks set the claiming prices according to tradition and the horses on the grounds. Every track has a base price, which usually continues from year to year. It can be as low as $1,000, but at most moderately sized tracks the minimum is $2,500. Large tracks may have top claiming prices of well over $100,000.

Claiming prices step up incrementally and, in the lower classes, are a fair indicator of the abilities of the horses in them. There is a major paradox here, though, which we will get to in a while.

Horses are grouped not only according to value, but also according to age. The conditions for a claiming race will almost invariably include both.

Claiming. ($3,250) 3-year-olds and upwards.
Claiming. ($30,000) 2-year-olds.

Many other conditions can be set on claiming races, such as weight for age and weight for price.

> Claiming. ($5,000) 3- and 4-year-olds. Weights, 3-year-olds, 117 lbs. 4-year-olds, 122 lbs.
>
> Claiming. ($32,000) 3-year-olds and upward. $28,000 allowed 2 lbs.

There is also weight-for-performance.

> Claiming. ($150,000) 4-year-olds and upward. Weight 122 lbs. Nonwinners of two races at a mile and over since March 1 allowed 3 lbs. Such a race since then, 5 lbs. (Races when entered for $100,000 or less not considered.)

3rd Hollywood

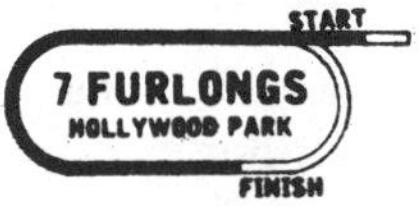

7 FURLONGS. (1.20%) MAIDEN. Purse $34,000. Fillies and mares. 3-year-olds and upward which have not won $3,000 three times other than maiden, claiming or starter. Weights, 3-year-olds, 114 lbs.; older, 121 lbs. Non-winners of two such races since March 15 allowed 2 lbs.; two such races since February 15, 4 lbs.: such a race since March 1, 6 lbs.

Hidden Garden — B. f. 4, by Mr Prospector—The Garden Club, by Herbager
DELAHOUSSAYE E 115 — Br.—Farish W S (Ky) — 1990 2 0 0 1 $14,550
Tr.—Drysdale Neil — 1989 5 3 0 1 $50,750
Own.—Farish W S — Lifetime 7 3 0 2 $65,300

12Feb90-3SA 1 :46^3 1:11^3 1:37^{3}ft 3-2 117 2½ 2½ 3^3 3^{6½} DlhoussyE^3 ⒻAw47000 72-25 FantasticLook,Felidia,HiddenGrden 6
20Jan90-8SA 7f :22^3 :45 1:22^{2}ft 2½ 115 5^{5½} 4^{4½} 4^{5½} 4^{3¾} McCrrCJ^1 ⒻSt Mca H 87-17 Stormy But Valid,Survive,HotNovel 5
20Jan90—Grade I; Broke slowly
29Dec89-7SA 6f :21^3 :44^2 1:08^{4}ft 2¾ 117 7^{6½} 5^{3¾} 3^3 1^{2¾} DlhoussyE^2 ⒻAw30000 94-13 HiddenGrden,Unpinted,RunwyBlues 8
25Nov89-7Hol 6½f :22^2 :45 1:15^{4}ft *8-5 119 2^1 2^{hd} 1^{1½} 1^4 DlhoussyE^2 ⒻAw27000 96-08 Hidden Garden, Onyx, Sharmoon 5
6Aug89-6AP 1 :46^1 1:12^2 1:39 ft *2½ 116 3^{2½} 1^1 2^{1½} 4^{5¼} Gryder AT^8 ⒻAw20000 61-27 Toiny,FlagsWaving,WckyPrincess 10
15Jly89-2AP 7f :22^1 :46^3 1:26 ft *9-5 115 7^6 7^{4¾} 4^{2½} 1^2 Day P^{10} ⒻMdn 72-23 HiddenGrden,Gesundheit,Agneshk 12
20May89-3Hol 6f :22 :44^3 1:08^{3}ft 2¾ 116 5^{2¾} 4^5 3^7 3^8 DelahoussyeE^1 ⒻMdn 90-07 WhtHsBeen,JustBLucky,HiddnGrdn 7
20May89—Broke slowly

Speed Index: Last Race: +4.0 3–Race Avg.: +5.0 5–Race Avg.: +1.4 Overall Avg.: –1.1
May 12 Hol 4f ft :51^2 B May 6 Hol 6f ft 1:18^1 B Apr 24 Hol 4f ft :47^3 B Apr 19 Hol 4f ft :52^3 H

Sing Sweet Syl — Dk. b. or br. m. 5, by Singular—Sweet Syl, by Sette Belle
SOLIS A 115 — Br.—Siegel Jan (Fla) — 1990 4 0 1 1 $16,325
Tr.—Stute Melvin F — 1989 15 3 4 1 $88,225
Own.—Siegel Jan — Lifetime 22 3 6 2 $111,100 — Turf 10 1 3 1 $57,250

28Apr90-9Hol 1$\frac{1}{16}$ Ⓣ:47 1:11^{1}1:42 fm *3¾ 116 3^1 3^1 1½ 5^{5¼} Solis A^8 Ⓕ 80000 80-15 Nimes, Belle Poitrine, Seaside 12
5Apr90-8SA 1 Ⓣ:45^{3}1:10 1:35^{3}fm*8-5 115 4^4 5^{4½} 7^{6¼} 6^{7¾} McCrrnCJ^5 ⒻAw47000 77-15 Kiwi, Hickory Crest, Remedios 7
5Apr90—Wide into stretch
22Mar90-8SA a6½f Ⓣ:21 :43^{1}1:13^{3}fm 3¼ 115 2½ 2^{hd} 1½ 2½ Solis A^4 ⒻAw42000 92-07 IvoryTower,SingSwtSyl,ExclIntLdy 7
5Jan90-8SA 1 Ⓣ:45^{4}1:09^{1}1:33^{4}fm 7 117 4^2 3^3 3^{3½} 3^{4½} Solis A^5 ⒻAw47000 89-07 Agirlfromrs,CollctivJoy,SingSwtSyl 8
5Jan90—Rank 3/4
24Nov89-9Hol 1$\frac{1}{16}$ Ⓣ:45^{3}1:09^{2}1:41 fm 3½ 117 3^{5½} 3^6 6^4 6^{4¾} Solis A^7 ⒻAw32000 84-11 MammaRosit,Remedios,SilverLne 11
8Nov89-7SA 1 Ⓣ:46^{2}1:09^{3}1:34^{1}fm 3½ 117 2^{1½} 2^{1½} 2^2 1^{nk} Solis A^8 ⒻAw37000 100 — SingSwtSyl,SingngPrt,HthrAndRos 9
4Oct89-3SA 1⅛ Ⓣ:45^{3}1:09 1:45^{2}fm 8 116 2^{1½} 2^{1½} 3½ 2^{1½} Solis A^1 ⒻAw37000 98 — Agirlfromrs,SingSwetSyl,MjoliquII 8
4Oct89—Veered out start
7Sep89-3Dmr 1$\frac{1}{16}$ Ⓣ:47^{3}1:12 1:44^{2}fm 8¾ 119 7^{17} 4^{11} 4^{3½} 2^{nk} Solis A^3 ⒻAw40000 78-19 DnsusDLun,SngSwtSyl,RoylApprovl 7
7Sep89—Off very slowly
26Aug89-7Dmr 1 Ⓣ:48 1:12^{3}1:36^{4}fm 21 119 4^{1¾} 3^1 4^{2½} 4^{1½} Solis A^6 ⒻAw38000 85-16 PrincssRy,DuckingPrk,DnsusDLun 10
4Aug89-11LA 6½f :21^1 :45^1 1:15^{4}ft 3¾ 122 1^{hd} 1^{hd} 3^{2½} 3^{8¾} CstnAL^1 ⒻⓇChapman 87-11 DfndYourMn,ISrHopSo,SngSwtSyl 6

Speed Index: Last Race: –2.0 1–Race Avg.: –2.0 1–Race Avg.: –2.0 Overall Avg.: –3.3
May 15 Hol 3f ft :37 H ●May 8 Hol 4f ft :48 H ●Apr 19 SA 5f ft :59^2 H ●Apr 12 SA 4f ft :46^4 H

These conditions can be combined in various ways to either remain open to all horses of several overlapping classes or narrowed to a handful of specific horses that the racing secretary has in mind.

In a sense, maiden races are "allowance races," since the owner is allowed to keep the horse. The term actually works the other way, limiting what a horse is allowed to have accomplished before it is overqualified for the race. Theoretically, the allowance for maidens is zero; they must never have won a race. However, a number of allowances can be made so that winners remain eligible. If I ever own a 5-year-old "maiden," may it be one like Sing Sweet Syl (previous page).

Allowance races are a way of ensuring some balance of competition without holding the horses up for sale. Allowances are run in all age groups, the simplest being

Allowance. Purse $31,000. 3-year-olds which have not won two races.

Allowances are sometimes so complicated, you will hear trainers reading them out loud, over and over, trying to figure out if any of their horses fit. The intricacies are not particularly important to handicappers once the field is set.

The higher levels of races are just the opposite; a horse must earn its way in. Some handicaps are open, but most of the higher handicap and stake races are filled either by invitation or subscription—sometimes a few weeks in advance, sometimes before the horses are born. These races usually have money added to the purse, either by the track or an outside sponsor, and subscription races require periodic payments by the owners, often beginning long before they are run. Most, however, allow penalty payments up to a certain date, when an unsubscribed horse can be bought in ("supplemented") if it shows late promise.

Both Thoroughbred and quarter horse stakes are divided into categories of Grade I, II, and III, according to the purse money and corresponding quality of horses drawn into competition. Until just a few years ago, the quarter horse All-American Futurity, at $1 million, was the richest horse race in America. Now numerous Thoroughbred stakes are run at $1 million, and the All-American is in multiple Thoroughbred company at $2 million. The Breeders' Cup Classic currently tops them all, with a $3 million purse.

Handicap races can occur at almost any purse level and, in theory, are designed to provide the most balanced competition between higher grades of horses. The conditions may be very elaborate for classes of possible entries or tailored to the specific horses after they apply. The horses are "handicapped" in the same sense that we use, and then weighted—*literally*, with lead. This is to "handicap" the stronger horses and give advantage to the weaker horses, so that in the best judgment of the racing secretary all horses should put their noses to the wire at the same instant. The idea is to give every horse an equal chance of winning (which is the idea of all classes, taken to the extreme) and to allow truly superior horses to show their abilities. Great horses, like Dr. Fager and John Henry, have competed at outlandish weights and still defeated the best of their eras. They are usually geldings, since if they are that great, and a stallion or mare, they would usually be retired before they reach the age that would allow the weight.

Class in Horses

There are two ways in which a horse can perform well on the racetrack. One is to have the correct physiology for speed and endurance and be driven to win by the jockey; the other is to have the same ability, or even less, but with the innate *desire* to beat other horses. That is the undefinable side of "class."

Horses have obtained their speed through evolution as plains-grazing animals. You can see horse evolution in action by watching films that follow prides of lions on the plains of Africa. Adult zebras that fall prey are usually not the fastest stallions or mares in the herd. The fast ones get to breed. Young zebras often do fall prey, not only to lions later, but to smaller predators moments after birth, so there is a real advantage in being able to stand and run within minutes of being born. But there is more to the evolution of speed than the black-and-white question of whether or not an individual gets to breeding age without being eaten.

The social structure of horses developed as a reproductive mechanism under strong predatory pressure. The indefinable "class" in racehorses may have its distant background in the requirement of speed to escape predators, but its *active* process is in the evolution of the reproductive social order within the herd. There are many orders of dominance within a wild horse herd. One is that of the herd stallion over the mares; another is the herd stallion over competing outside stallions; and another is the pecking order among mares and foals within a stallion's band. Exactly the same mechanisms can be seen in domestic horses when a stallion is turned out with a band of mares for "pasture breeding."

As in other herd species with single male breeding individuals, stallions have evolved to be stronger and more aggressive than mares. Pure aggression can make up for size both in herding and holding the mares and in warding off competing bachelor stallions. When wild herds move with speed, which they might do once or twice a day when colts are maturing, stallions use both speed and aggression to keep the band from scattering. When challenged by an outside stallion, aggression may explode in a fight that can lead to death, but much of the time challenges are met with lesser aggression, the main component of which is speed. All but the most determined bachelors can be driven off by circling and dodging—*getting a head or a nose in front*—so that the challenger knows he is outclassed.

Dominance between mares is more subtle. Every band will have a "boss mare," second only to the herd stallion and perhaps outranking him in matters such as when to move to water and other daily movements of the band. The adaptive advantage is that she is likely to hold the best grazing when resources are patchy and her offspring will be first to drink, first to run when danger appears. More important, regardless of available resources, their foals learn the dominant role. They learn they don't have to be third to drink. If they are males, they may be more likely to become breeding herd stallions, and if females, more likely to assume their mother's rank.

There are no geldings in the wild and, although they have existed almost as long as horses have been domesticated, there are clearly no genetic traits to be passed along. They are the safest horses to be around and they are far and away the preferred working horses. Geldings are generally even tempered and can be pastured with mares with few problems. When they are, however, there is a serious problem for racehorses. When a new horse is introduced into a pasture or corral, a rearrangement of the pecking order begins instantly. *Rarely* will a gelding come out on top. An almost certain way to drop a gelding in racing rank is to rest him in a pasture where he drops in social rank.

Social dominance is the closest analogy to "class" in a racehorse. Among the volumes of studies of genetics and breeding, no one has ever recorded how many "class" horses have been the foals of dominant mares in mare bands. For centuries, though, buyers with the resources and an understanding of the process have preferred to purchase runners in person at the stud farms of Ireland, England, and Kentucky, so that they can watch the interaction of the mares and foals in pasture rather than the view foals in isolation, which is how they are displayed at the big auction sales.

In Thoroughbred racing, the basic difference of gender is often an important handicapping factor. Stallions are often physically larger, stronger, and possess greater endurance than mares. And depending upon the development of both the stallion and the gelding, a stallion may possess a greater imperative to win than a gelding. These attributes may play a considerable role in the shaping of an individual's career, but once shaped by past performances, they are manageable handicapping factors.

Many handicappers will discount a mare simply because she is a mare. But mares and fillies that have shown the ability to run in mixed competition can be handicapped right along with the other horses, based on their actual performance. There is a danger, however, since more and more races are being conditioned for fillies and mares alone. When a mare moves from a background of only these races into mixed competition, her past performances must be carefully examined. In order to be competitive, her past performances must be either a little better than those of the colts and geldings in the race or she must show some inkling of condition and handling to indicate that she can move in the dominance battle of the race.

In quarter horse racing, mares compete on a much more equal basis. Two-year-old and three-year-old fillies often mature as quickly as colts, and they have proven that speed is equal between the genders. Fillies like Strawberry Silk and Dash For Speed can run and win in any company. The same caveats apply to handicapping quarter horse fillies and mares in lower classifications and older age groups, but to a much lesser degree than to handicapping Thoroughbreds.

The phenomenon of class and dominance is what makes a true runner: a horse that would rather die or drop in exhaustion than let another horse put its nose ahead. In this life there are few true runners, while there are many horses that can be driven to use the speed and endurance bred into their bodies. The ability to run is genetic, the desire to win is ephemeral.

Even more elusive is the class structure within a race. It is easy to understand dominance in theory, but as noted at the beginning of this chapter, many of those closest to the horses believe that "class"—translated into the claiming prices and allowance levels of a race—is somehow *understood* by the horses.

Every day, and thousands of times in the course of a year, horses that have performed very well as $5,000 claimers move up into an $8,000 race and lose—at slower times than those in any of their previous races. Horses that have been winning $4,000 purses in claiming races move into a $4,000-purse allowance race and lose at slower times—they can't be *driven* past the allowance horses. After performing dismally three or four times, they drop back down into their original rank and murder the competition. What in the world is going on here?

Nobody knows. But my guess is that the dominance interaction begins at the crossroads in the stable area, where horses that may never have seen each other before meet as they are led from their scattered stables into line on the way to the paddock. They act and see each other's actions as they are saddled and led in the post parade. An experienced racehorse knows what the gates mean, and their actions there and what they see in the others may be significant. The real dominance play begins in the first strides as the gates open and continues throughout the race.

In a Thoroughbred race, even in the shorter sprints, there is considerably more time and there are many more incidents of body language and placement than in quarter horse racing, and the phenomenon of intrarace class distinction is much stronger. Both Thoroughbreds and quarter horses moving up in class must be scrutinized very closely. Their past performances must be strong and usually not just comparable to but a little better than their new competition—and yet they remain a riskier bet than if their past performances had been within their new class.

With quarter horses, however, especially if they are two-year-olds or lightly raced three-year-olds, time will tell—meaning their past performance times. These horses can frequently move up and post the same times in higher-grade races. For quarter horses in general, "class" is much more directly equated with the ability and condition to run with speed. Aside from any bullying that may occur in the paddock and post parade, there is very little opportunity in the blur from the gates to the finish line for dominance posturing. There is also a different class structure in quarter horse racing, particularly in the higher ranks at Ruidoso Downs and Los Alamitos, because of the intensity of competition for berths in the big futurities and derbies. A two-year-old quarter horse may remain a maiden after three races in which its losing time would set new track records at two-thirds of the tracks in the nation. The purses in futurity qualifying races are notoriously small, and this horse, having lost at maiden purses of $1,700, may step into top allowance competition and blow more experienced horses away—if it hasn't learned how to lose.

Dominance interaction before and during competition may influence the outcome when it is fresh, but sooner or later, a horse often learns its place in a race. The true runners are those who *believe* with all their heart and soul that their place is in front. It may not take very long to shatter that belief. Every handicapper has a story of a horse he or she has followed and how it learned to be polite.

Polite horses can learn their skills in the pasture with the mares and other foals or on the racetrack in competition that is beyond their reach. They drive handicappers to distraction. A horse may lose by one and a half lengths in a very fast maiden race, lose by a length in another, drop to a lower group of maidens and perhaps win one, posting an identical time to its two losing efforts. Then it moves into the allowance ranks for winners of one race, with times better than any of its competition, and begins its career as the speed favorite, who always loses—no matter how far it drops through the claimers. These horses can sometimes be identified in the past performances by simply looking down the corresponding racing class and finish placement columns. (If you look back to the Introduction and the finishes of Sir Hon, you may find cause for suspicion.)

Class, like most attributes, is a combination of genetic potential and learned behavior. The trainer's most important job in awakening class in young horses is to place them not where they have a wild card, but a *good* chance to win, and where they will be beaten by as little—and as seldom—as possible.

Class Pars and Variants

One of the foundations of speed handicapping is a set of "par times," based on racing classes, which performances can be judged against. The best par times are from an established season, currently underway; but as a season begins, it is necessary to have something to go on. To develop par times for a new season, Andrew Beyer recommended a day in a closed room with a complete set of last year's *Forms* for your home track—and a bottle of Jack Daniels. A lot of people took his advice; apparently on both counts. It is hard to explain, otherwise, why so many fight reality the way that they do.

If you intend to be a serious handicapper, you will need to either utilize established par times and track variants, create your own, *or* understand fully why you don't. To build your own par times, the first step is to set out the classes of horses, however they occur at your track:

Maiden Claiming, $2,500 . . . (in increments to however high they go)
Maiden, 2-year-olds
Maiden, 3-year-olds (etc.)
Claiming, $2,500 . . . (to however high they go)
Allowance (broken down in purse levels and by age)
Handicap (broken down)
Stakes, Grade I, II, III

Then, start with a distance, say 6 furlongs, and record every time posted on a "fast track" in the previous year under the appropriate class. When you are done with all distances run at the meet, you take the mathematical average in each class and you have the "par time" for class and distance. Thus, at the ideal track, you would end up with something like this, for every distance run:

Distance: 6 Furlongs

Class	Time
Maiden claiming <$5,000	1:14:3
Maiden claiming >$5,000	1:14:1
Claiming, $2,500	1:14:2
Claiming, $3,250	1:14:1
•	
•	
Claiming, $10,000	1:12:1
Allowance, $4300 purse	1:11:3
•	
Allowance, $10,000 purse	1:11:0

And so on, up through the stakes.

Notice that every track will be different in both the classes of horses and the times that they average. Notice, too, the nice progression. With a little logical lumping of similar classes, and just a couple of adjustments—the times stair-step and become faster as the races go up in class. That is because I made them up.

On real tracks, in real seasons, there might be only three, 7 furlong races for $8,000 claimers and they may vary wildly. But suppose you analyze the figures more deeply, and find that the time range at 7 furlongs for $6,000 through $10,000 claimers overlap sufficiently for you to logically lump them and have 24 times and a better mathematical average? This looks pretty good, until you run the 16 finish times for $5,000 claimers through the calculator and find that they averaged 2/5s of a second *faster*. The $3,250 claimers' average time looks about right; the higher levels above $10,000 look about right; so, it must be the lumped $8,000 range that is off. This is where the Jack Daniels comes in. *You adjust the averages to fit.* Not just one, but maybe three or four, to arrive at the stair-step progression. Every handicapper who makes par times has done this.

Par times by themselves don't do much. But they do provide a starting point for a variety of comparisons. They let you see that a $5,000 claiming horse ran 1/5 second faster or slower than the "average" $5,000 claimer. Most people set the par time at some arbitrary number, such as 100. They then attach another arbitrary value to time fractions, such as 2 points per fifth of a second. So, if a horse was 1/5 second slower than the average, its handicapping value for that past race is 98. A 5th of a second faster: 102.

With an average—*par*—time in hand, you can evaluate each day's racing and create a "track variant." This is the average that all times for races on a particular day vary from the par. You get this by checking the time for each race against the average for that class of horses. You get something like this:

1st Race, 6f, $5,000 Claimers	+2 (1/5 fast)
2nd Race, 1m, Alw, $4,500 purse	−4 (2/5 slow)
3rd Race, 5.5f, Mdn	−6 (3/5 slow)
4th Race, 7f, Alw, $20,000	+4 (2/5 fast)

And so on.

You then add up the plus and minus figures, divide by the number of races, and you have the track variant for the day. In the four races above, it would be −1. (Your eyebrows should be rising.) If there was a drastic change in track condition during the day, like a downpour after the sixth race, most handicappers will separate the races for separate averages to apply in their figures.

Then, if a horse's past performance was on a −6 track—three-fifths of a second slower than the average—the 6 points are *added* to his score. So, a horse that ran a 98 is given credit for the slow track and becomes a 104. If the track was a +8—four-fifths fast for the day—the horse's time is considered to be inflated, and 8 points are subtracted, giving the 98-horse an actual score of 90.

This works—some of the time.

The process of creating your own par times for your home track, or several tracks you are most interested in, can be tedious, but worth the effort—even if you never use them to adjust a speed or pace figure. If you are very careful and very conservative in using them at first, you may develop an approach that is more accurate and much more meaningful to you than commercial variants, such as those published in the *Daily Racing Form*, or built into the published Beyer Speed Figures. The real value of your labor, however, will be in developing a personal understanding of the factors that win races at your tracks. The work can be done with a Big Chief tablet and a pencil, but it is much more valuable to run the numbers through a computer spreadsheet such as Quattro Pro or Lotus 1-2-3, where you can also sort, rearrange, and save them (see Chapter 9).

On many tracks, especially at lower levels of competition, you will probably find that the range of time-overlap between classes makes an average for a class highly suspect. For most tracks there will be a mild, over-all statistical correlation between time and class. You may well find, however, that there is no way to predict whether a $20,000 claiming race will be run faster or slower than a particular $15,000 race—or for that matter, the *average* $15,000 race.

Quarter horse racing categories follow almost exactly the same pattern. The only noticeable difference is that the times for the large class of "futurity trials" are often off opposite ends of the scale—which skews class-par-times and the resulting track variants even further.

You will need to be very careful in applying daily track variants. You will no doubt find days when all twelve races range between +1 and +3, giving a clear and probably true picture that the track was a little fast that day. You will find classic cases where the first six races are all perfect +7s and the last six perfect -8s, and you can probably split the ratings for the day with confidence.

Then you will find—and quite often—days that look like this: +2, −1, +3, −22, +4, +16, −11, par, +6, −2, −9, +10. The track variant for the day is −0.33? Egads.

I have never heard anyone argue that class-par-times and track variants are science. Andrew Beyer states flatly that the variants used in creating the Beyer Speed Figures are subject to artful judgments by his team.

One of my best handicapping friends, Tim Menicutch, makes his own artful daily variants for both Thoroughbreds and quarter horses. There are many ways to approach handicapping and Tim is living proof that hard work, rigorous betting discipline, and total emersion in *a single racing meet* can pay. You cannot practice Tim's brand of absolute emersion from a Las Vegas book or an off-track betting location. Tim has detailed personal knowledge of every horse on the grounds and probably knows the local trainers and jockeys better than most of their respective spouses. He is an advanced speed handicapper and his daily track variants are fundamental to his approach—yet probably don't consume more than about five minutes of his working day once the season is underway. He jots them down, doing the math by sight, from his par times and, therefore, they are an integral part of his decision-making, but not at anything like the level of daily work you might imagine from the preceding pages. This is classic home-track handicapping and I admire it greatly.

On the other hand, I also admit I love the atmosphere of the Las Vegas casino race books; the machine-gun betting opportunities, the quality of racing competition, and the ability to be extremely selective as races are run around the country in rapid succession. (Not to mention the opposite perspective on customer service: casinos *give* you comps—tracks take them.) Even in the intense atmosphere of race books, however, it is possible to conduct the research required to build class par times and resulting daily variants. The only question is, do you really *want* to?

Few people have focused more on par times than Gordon Pine, a colleague of Dick Mitchell and the Cynthia Publishing group. Pine has published a widely respected set of pars for tracks around the country which are free of the basic pitfalls that many home-made pars incorporate. These may be worth the investment and the time required to construct daily variants from his baseline if your interest includes numerous tracks from around the country.

If you calculate your own daily variants from pars, it is important to remember that pars and variants both make the *a priori* assumption that each race is run to the ability of the horses in the field. Any variation from the par is traditionally viewed as the result of some outside factor—primarily the speed of the racing surface. Actually, a very fast race may result from a maximum effort with some assistance from a hard track or a tail wind (discussed later)—but, other than bonuses gained from wind, altitude, and such, there is nothing the jockey can do to exceed a horse's natural ability. (That is legal.) Conversely, some portions—*or all*—of a race may be run at significantly *less* than the natural ability of the horses. This occurs in every race in which a jockey rates his horse, but particularly in higher levels of competition on the dirt when jockeys know they have tactical reserves—and the *majority* of races on the grass. Unless you are able to view the race, there is no way to judge by simple variations from the par times, whether the horses are expending real effort against a genuine, slow bias, or if they are cruising at an easy gallop, waiting for tactical moves that never happen. Such races do not represent a slow track bias and should not be included in your daily variant.

In my experience, errors result much more often from over-representing variants, rather than under-representing them.

An even riskier solution to the variant problem is to utilize readily available variants such as those published in the *Daily Racing Form*. There have been several approaches to improve upon the published daily variants by using derivations of them rather than using them uncritically, or the alternative of building pars and variants entirely from scratch. William Scott, Dr. Howard Sartin, Tom Brohamer, and others have all investigated the problem with similar results as summarized by Brohamer (1991, pp. 247–259). As Brohamer notes, this is not the most advanced approach to variants, but it is by far the easiest.

The computer program in the appendix includes an option that utilizes a reduced variant based upon the Scott/Sartin/Brohamer approach to the *Daily Racing Form* variant. The math is more consistent with my own approach to speed, however, since it employs the actual race time-per-length, rather than the 1/5 second rule-of-thumb. Still, if you use that option of the program, be cautious at first—and test your results until you are sure that using the variant is a *current* advantage at a *particular* track. Variants tend to be artsy. That should be why we call them "variants," but unfortunately it is not.

5

THE MECHANICS OF TIME

A longshot wins a race. A disappointed bettor consults his *Form* and
discovers that the longshot had been timed at 36 seconds in a
breezing three-furlong workout a couple of days ago. No other horse
in the race had worked so rapidly so recently. Powie! A new system
is born!

—TOM AINSLIE,
Ainslie's Complete Guide to Thoroughbred Racing

*I*f you stand at the finish line and look back toward the grandstand, and
then almost straight up, you will see two dark vertical slits in the face of
the highest girderwork—one very narrow and barely visible (perhaps
three feet high by six inches wide) and another, offset a few feet, maybe a
more normal-looking window.

If you watch closely, while the crowd is occupied looking across the track
at the horses being loaded into the gates, you will see the wider one open.
Look again when the horses round the curve and break onto the straightaway and you may see him—a face back in the shadows. When the leaders
approach about 30 yards from the line, his head may pop out and then
immediately jerk in as he slams the opaque window behind him. The moment the race is over, he locks himself in darkness.

As the roar of the crowd subsides and strangers debate the winner, he
conducts a brief ritual with foul-smelling chemicals and bursts of light. While
he works, mortals squirm. He opens a tiny trapdoor and lets the image shine
down on the judges. The crowd roars again at the first news of his work, and
runners move quickly through the grandstands posting copies of what he
saw. He goes back to reading his novel until it is time to do it again. Very
rarely, he may slip down into the crowd for food and then run, two stairs at a
time, back up into the darkness. To identify him at the hot dog stand, watch
for overconstricted pupils and strange odors from his clothes. It might be
him . . . then again, it might not.

The photo-finish operator does not usually work for the racetrack; he is
generally employed by one of several companies that contract with tracks to
provide photo and video coverage with their own specialists and equipment.
The narrow, vertical slit is the opening for his camera lenses, always a bank
of at least two, stacked vertically in perfect alignment with the finish line.

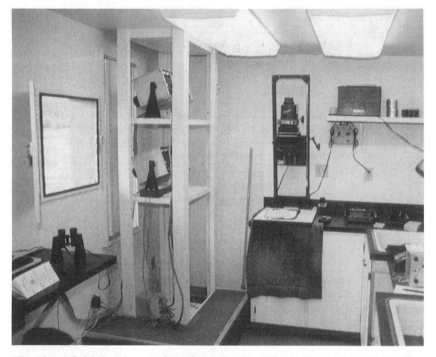

The photo finish booth at Ruidoso Downs, New Mexico. Notice the bank of two cameras, aligned through a slit-window on the finish line. By closing the slit and observation window, the room becomes a darkroom. Few are this neat. *Photo by author.*

The darkroom is like most others except the equipment is more specialized. There is a heat-controlled bath of developer and fixer, sized and shaped to fit the film; a vertical enlarger for making enlargement prints; and an instant print machine. The only thing unusual is the trapdoor, where the film negative is projected straight down onto a white table in the stewards' room, where the official judgments are made.

Thoroughbred and quarter horse times are recorded using entirely different methods, and these are very important to understand in handicapping.

Thoroughbreds are timed from a flying start, with the gates set back from the starting post. The run from the gates to the post is not counted in the time or racing distance.

Quarter horse times and distances begin at the gates, from a flat-footed, standing start.

This has created immeasurable confusion and debate, not only among casual fans, but within the inner circles of both breeds. Thoroughbred enthusiasts relish the idea that Thoroughbred first-quarter times, even in extended route races, are sometimes as fast or faster than quarter horse 440-yard dashes. Quarter horse breeders themselves, in presenting Thoroughbred sires for outcrossing, have advertised things like: "Theoretically 8 1/2 lengths faster than Dash For Cash in the quarter mile."

Wrong theory.

The AQHA (American Quarter Horse Association) has dabbled strangely with the problem. Without knowing this for a fact, I will give you 8-to-5 that the 870-yard distance for quarter horses was sanctioned as 10 yards short of four furlongs to retain the standing start, yet in hopes of making quarter horse times appear more respectable. We'll see later why this doesn't work. As I write this, the AQHA Racing Council has made its first major concession to the problem for both status and handicapping by passing a rule that from now on all quarter horse races over 870 yards will be timed from a flying start, to become directly comparable with Thoroughbreds. Times will still be recorded to hundredths of a second, which will be easy to convert to fifths, and presumably the times of nonwinners will still be given, so this is an important landmark for handicapping. The only problem is that at present the only sanctioned distance over 870 yards is 1,000 yards, which is 30 feet longer than four and a half furlongs, and 300 feet shorter than five. In the future, it is likely that the AQHA will adopt the Thoroughbred measures of distance for at least the longer races. And if we all live long enough, we may see the Thoroughbred world adopt the vastly superior quarter horse method of measuring time.

Thoroughbred Time and Track Constants

The distance of the Thoroughbred flying start varies from track to track and, notably, from different starting arrangements at different distances on the same track. This was determined consciously—sometimes apparently semiconsciously—when the track was designed and built. It is well worth noting, if you are going to dissect racing times, how the starting gate is positioned in relation to the starting post at various distances at the tracks that you follow.

The Jockey Club rule (Part XIV, No. 149) is a little obscure on the issue: "The horses shall be started *as far as possible in a line*, but may be started at such reasonable distance behind the starting post as the starter thinks necessary" (emphasis added). Stewards and starters I have asked agree that the distance should be about 35 feet. But the actual distance may vary from about 8 feet to 35 yards and is determined by the layout and construction of the track.

When races are started from midway in a chute (an offset or extended "ear" of the track), there is generally room to position the gates at about the optimal distance. When racing distances are started at the end of the chutes, or at certain locations on the oval, the start is often constricted. If you check different starting positions on ovals, you may come to suspect they are where they are because the construction contract called for hinged rails for the passage of the gate truck off the track after the start—without specifying *where they should be placed.*

The running distance of the Thoroughbred flying start has considerable effect upon first-quarter times and final times at different distances on the same track. If the distance is short, such as the "one jump" start shown in the photograph, first-quarter times will be slow. And since a greater portion of the acceleration period is included in the race, final times should average somewhat slower than times at the same distance at different tracks, which are started at speeds closer to a full run. These are one form of "track constants."

A more obvious track constant, affecting both splits and final times, is the layout of the race—for example, one-turn miles at physically large tracks like

A "one-jump" thoroughbred start. Notice the starting post, just ahead of the horses' noses. This location is constrained by a tunnel between the infield and the grandstands, right behind the gate truck. Starting distances will vary at other tracks for a variety of reasons. First-quarter times at this distance will always be slower on the average than times begun after a longer initial run. *Photo by author.*

Hollywood Park and two-turn miles on ovals like Golden Gate Fields. Mile-and-a-sixteenth races at Belmont are run around one turn; the same distance at Charlestown is run around three turns.

Less apparent constants can be seen when comparing times between similar, large-oval tracks and at different distances on the same track, when for example, five-furlong races are started on the curve, while six-, six-and-a-half, and seven-furlong races are started at progressively longer distances back on the straightaway.

At the other extreme, on the bull rings (five-, six-, and seven-furlong ovals), six-furlong races may be started from a chute, with an exceptionally long straightaway before the turn. Horses have considerably more time to come up to racing speed before they negotiate the corner, while on other small tracks they may be started on the oval, with two tight turns and a very short initial run that does not even require a lead change. (Horses run with one foreleg extending further and exerting more power than the other. On a curve, this lead leg must be on the inside or the horse can go seriously out of balance—to the point of falling down. Most horses have a strong preference for a left lead, and so are naturally prepared for starts on the curve in this country, where races are run counterclockwise. If a horse prefers a right lead, or inadvertently starts on the right leg, the jockey must cue the lead change before banking into the turn. The lead leg also tires more quickly, so jockeys try to balance the fatigue by cueing changes to the left going into turns and right coming out of them. Brief mishaps observed going into turns, and recorded as "checked" by trip handicappers, are often fumbled lead changes, with the jockey trying to save his life before either going down or shooting off to the far rail. This happens fairly frequently. If you watch at

"Horses are all in line. . . the flag is *UP!* " This is the traditional alert to the crowd from the track announcer in thoroughbred racing, even if the flag has been replaced by an electric eye. Time begins when the horses reach the post and the flagman snaps his flag down. When electric eyes are present in the starting posts, they are connected directly to the internal camera timers. *Photo by author.*

about the 3/8 pole on the backside turn, you will occasionally see a horse drop its head and be lifted back up by the reins, with a significant loss of momentum, until everything is working again in left gear.)

All new tracks and many older ones have installed electric-eye timers in the starting post, call posts, and finish line. The first horse breaks the light beam and sets the time. This has not put the clockers, who back up each race in case of a malfunction, out of work.

A first-rate, experienced clocker is almost as accurate as the electric eye. The clocker usually sits with or next door to the stewards, where he or she can have the finish line in direct sight, but since the angle to various starting positions around the track varies in his view, there will often be a flagman stationed at the starting post. The job of the flagman is to stand in direct line with the starting posts and raise the flag overhead when the horses are all in the gates. This is when you hear the track announcer say, "Horses are in the gates . . . flag is up."

Neither the clocker nor the flagman watch the horses. The flagman stares directly at the opposite starting pole, and the clocker watches him. The instant that the first horse's nose passes his, the flagman drops the flag and the clocker starts his watch.

With a hand-timed race, the "splits" are made with the same technique used in timing the morning workouts. Marker posts for the split times at the 1/4, 1/2, 3/4, etc. are set back off the rail for the safety of the riders in case of a fall, and each has a different angle of projection from the clocker's view. The result is like looking across the rear sight of a rifle instead of directly down the barrel at the point where the horse will pass. Because the angle varies, there are usually marks on the rail that the clocker uses to catch the time of the first horse as it passes. The angle of projection works to a lesser extent, affecting the accuracy of the timing, depending upon the distance of the horse from the rail. In all cases, whether electrically or hand timed, it is the first horse through that sets the time for the call.

As the horses reach about 30 yards from the finish line, the photo-finish operator turns on his cameras. Both are turned on simultaneously so that if one malfunctions, the other will capture the finish. In Thoroughbred racing the photo may be used both for time and lengths-back placement—or strictly for the stewards to declare the official placement of the horses. As we will see, this is a *big* difference.

Quarter Horse Time

Quarter horse distances are measured entirely in yards, as listed earlier, but it is interesting to note that 220 yards (the shortest sanctioned distance) is 1/8 of a mile, or a furlong; 330 yards is one and a half furlongs; the classic quarter horse distance, 440 yards, is two furlongs or a quarter of a mile (hence the name of the breed). The 550-yard distance is two and a half furlongs; 660 yards is three furlongs; 770 yards is three and a half furlongs. The other distances, 250, 300, 350, 400, 870, and 1,000 yards—don't line up with anything. Both the distance and the time are measured from the instant the gates are opened.

The photo-finish cameras perform a far more complex job in recording quarter horse races, but each quarter horse race is also hand timed in case of a complete electrical failure. The electric eyes of the Thoroughbred course play no part in quarter horse timing.

As the horses enter the gates, the photo-finish operator turns on an internal clock in the camera. No film moves, no time begins, and no human hand introduces error in the process. The starter's button opens the gates, but has no direct connection to the cameras in either Thoroughbred or quarter horse racing. The clocks in each camera only stand ready until the gates fly open, tripping the "whisker" switches that start them running. This is when you may get to see the photo-finish operator's head pop out of his window. Still, no film has moved. The operator watches until the first horse approaches within about 30 yards of the finish line, then manually turns on the cameras.

The "whisker" switches are also set in pairs in case of a malfunction—one

Gate clock "whisker" switch (center). In quarter horse racing, time is started when the gates fly open, tripping these electric switches tied directly to the internal timers of the cameras in the photo finish booth. *Photo by author.*

on the door of the first gate and one on the 12 hole. This is why you will always see the last gate closed in a quarter horse race, whether there is a horse in it or not. You will notice in the photograph two vertical springs in addition to the angled spring of the whisker (there are numerous types of whiskers). The vertical springs are part of a sandwich break, which grabs a plate on the gate door to prevent it from bouncing back at the horse.

If you have ever looked around the finish line and at the finish-line photos posted around the track, you may suspect that there is an electric eye somewhere that trips the camera and snaps the photo. The actual technology is a lot more interesting.

The photo-finish cameras have no shutter that trips, and there is no snap of a picture. The aperture of the lens, instead of round, is a tiny, vertical slit, fixed precisely on the finish line. As the horses approach, from the cameras' left to right, and the operator turns them on, the film begins moving in the opposite direction, from right to left, at first taking no image but the ground and rail within its narrow range of vision. If a stationary object, like a basketball, were placed on the finish line, its image would "flow" onto the moving film and look like a hot dog. For moving objects, the film speed is calibrated for both the speed of the passing object and the distance from the film plane, so that the objects appear almost as they would in life.

As the first hair of the first horse's nose reaches the finish line, it enters the vertical aperture and is exposed on the film as it moves away in the opposite direction. As each succeeding hair enters—then the nose, the neck, and the body—they are smeared across the moving film.

At the same time, the clock, which was started independently and which has been recording time all along, begins printing the time and time dots along the top or bottom of the moving film. All is calibrated precisely so that the times appear in the right places and the horses don't look like dachshunds or giraffes. If the film speed were too fast, they would stretch out; too slow, they would be tall and skinny. The speed of the race does affect the image, and a very fast horse will be compressed and a slow one will be

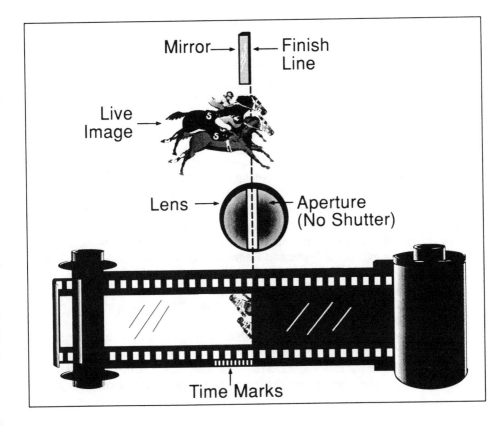

extended. Some cameras can compensate for this with adjustable film speeds, which are set according to the distance of the race.

The vertical mirror that you will sometimes see on the opposite rail of the finish line has nothing to do with time. Its tall, thin shape is aligned with the camera aperture, so that as the horses streak past its surface, their reverse sides are streaked on the film. This gives the stewards the opposite view, which they can't see during the race, so that when horses' noses are hidden behind bodies, they can usually accurately call their placement. Still, a nose can sometimes get lost between bodies.

When the film is exposed and the race is finished, the photo-finish operator immediately locks himself in and works in total darkness. The film is unloaded, agitated in developer, then fixer, washed in the sink, given a quick wipe, and loaded on the projector, still wet. The image is projected, about fifteen times its actual size, onto the table of the judge, who makes the calls of the race. The order of finish of each horse, not just those in the money, is called by the placement judge. Usually, in both Thoroughbred or quarter horse racing, the lengths-back placement is not determined by the stewards.

Paradise Lost: Quarter Horse Lengths Back

Quarter horse times are extremely accurate. The speed-strip films require only minor visual extrapolation to arrive at three-decimal-place (thousandths of a second) accuracy. The error introduced by the visual reading is probably in the $\pm$ 0.002 range, which is far below the range of significance for speed handicapping.

Immediately after the placing judge has made the position calls from the projected image, the film is taken from the projector and placed on a narrow light box under a perpendicular thread, which is used as a visual finish line. With the first horse's nose exactly tangent to the thread, its time is read from the time strip along the edge of the negative, and recorded on a finish call slip. Some error in the recorded time can occur if the thread is not perfectly aligned with the alignment ticks on the top and bottom of the negative; but the AQHA Racing Division rechecks races on contact prints for their records toward Registers of Merit and Championships and say they rarely find an error.

Where things can go haywire is in the next step. Some handicappers place great importance upon "beaten lengths" when evaluating a horse's past performances.

Since the *Daily Racing Form* now publishes finish times for each horse in quarter horse races—not just the winner—the lengths-back call is no longer essential to speed handicapping. Many handicappers still use it, however, and if you do, you need to first determine how accurately it is calculated at the tracks that you follow. The methods may be entirely different and can vary from pretty accurate to atrocious.

At some tracks, the lengths back are taken directly off the film by the photo-finish operator. This method is probably fairly accurate, although the operator must mentally superimpose horse lengths, which can vary and become distorted, depending upon racing speed, film speed, etc. At other tracks, the lengths back are extrapolated from the finish times.

After the winner's time is recorded, the film is slipped forward to be tangent with the second horse's nose and its time is recorded, and so on. Then, either before or after making the enlargement prints that are posted around the track, the photo-finish operator begins the calculation of the lengths-back calls. This is done, not visually on the photograph, but mathematically, on the finish call slip. Following is the conversion table used on some quarter horse tracks:

	Less Than 870-Yard Races	870-Yard Races
Nose	0–2	0–2
Head	3–4	3–4
Neck	5–6	5–6
1/2 Length	7–8	7–8
3/4 Length	8–11	9–12
Length	12–14	13–16

(Time Ranges in Hundredths of a Second)

Photo-finish operators do not seem to own calculators and do both the subtraction and the conversion in their heads. Even if they had the finest scientific model made, suppose a winning time is 17.76 seconds and the fifth or sixth horse came in at 18.31. The difference is 0.55 seconds. The table does not extend beyond one length, so the operator does this in his head. But if it did continue, it would look like this:

For Distances Less Than 870 Yards

Lengths	Range	Width of Range
1	12–14	2
2	24–28	4
3	36–42	6
4	48–56	8
5	60–70	10

(Time in Hundredths of a Second)

Is the lengths back for 0.55 four lengths because it falls in the four-lengths range or is it $48 + 7 = 4\ 1/2$? Or does 4 1/2 lie somewhere in the gap between 56 and 60?

This should be a moot point, now that quarter horse nonwinners' times are published; but if you already handicap them and take lengths back into account in your method, it is handy to know whether they are accurate or atrocious at your tracks. To check, simply subtract the winner's time from the nonwinner's time and divide by the lengths-back call.

	Race 1	Race 2	Race 3
Loser's Time:	18.40	18.31	17.86
Winner's Time:	−18.00	−18.05	−17.59
Difference:	.40	.26	.27
Lengths Back:	3	1.5	1
Time Per Length $=$	.40/3	.26/1.5	.27/1
Time Per Length:	.13	.17	.27

These examples are not hypothetical. They are taken from the most recent past performances of a horse entered in a 350-yard race (all past times were also at 350 yards). We will be looking closely at time per length in chapter 7, but for the moment, just consider the track's own conversion table given above. A time of .13 is within the range; .17 has already left the range of quarter horse sprints and moved into that of Thoroughbreds finishing a route; .27 is about the equivalent of crossing the finish line at a high trot.

Under the calculation method, errors are most common when the time difference is great, but they do occur at smaller margins, as in this case. If you would like to see how accurate the overall lengths-back placement is at your track—and possibly deduce which method is being used—try a calculator on past performances picked randomly from the *Form.* What you are likely to find with a sample of forty or more is that *over half* will fall outside the ranges, generally on the high side, and there will be some wild "fliers." We will pay no attention to quarter horse lengths back in handicapping.

Thoroughbred electric-eye timers are also extremely accurate, although by tradition they are still recorded only to fifths (0.2) of a second. At tracks where they have not yet been installed, the hand-timed Thoroughbred races are probably only slightly less accurate. Hand timing is an acquired skill, and good clockers are extremely consistent. Some tracks use only one clocker and watch; others use several and take an average. In most cases, the range of accuracy is within the 1/5-of-a-second measure for Thoroughbred races.

Other methods, such as those used by Steinley's Photochart Systems, employ a combination of film and hand timing. With this method, the split times and final time are recorded on the film by the official clocker, who presses a remote cable button simultaneously with his stopwatch. At each split, the time is flashed on the film through an internal prism system long before the horses approach the finish line where their images will be recorded. The clock is started remotely by the clocker as the horses pass the starting post and, as they enter camera range at the finish, the photo-finish operator turns on the film motors and the time is printed along the top of the film, just as in quarter horse races. And, as with quarter horse races, the measurement of time itself is rarely a problem.

Thoroughbred Lengths Back

Unlike quarter horse racing, the lengths-back placement of Thoroughbreds is *absolutely critical* to virtually every handicapping method. Trip handicapping requires some concept of each horse's actual time, and speed

Quarter horse "speed strip" print. The streak of horses along the top is the mirror image of the horses in the foreground. The white finish line is superimposed during print making—in this case inaccurately. Note that the line is on the winner's nose in the foreground, while almost at the same horse's eye in the mirror image. This time, which would be read as about 17.392, should actually be about 17.38. The same type of misalignment can occur when the official times are read from the negative in both quarter horse and thoroughbred racing. (This print was made long after the race.) *Photo by Steinley's Photochart Systems courtesy of Sweetwater Downs.*

Thoroughbred speed strip print, indicating the time of the third horse back, showing that thoroughbred non-winners' times need not remain a mystery. The time is in the thoroughbred format of fifths-of-a-second (58:4 rounded), but all the points are present for a decimal reading of 58.815 seconds. *Photo by Steinley's Photochart Systems courtesy of Les Bois Park.*

handicapping centers on it. Pace handicapping employs not only the final lengths-back placement, but, depending on the method, calculates each horse's "actual" time from lengths back at some or all of the splits.

So far, all of the data recorded on the running and outcome of the race is gathered either by an independent contractor, who provides the photo-finish equipment and the personnel to operate it, or by the official clockers, who are employees of the track. This information is compiled by the track and transmitted to the *Daily Racing Form* either by hand to the *Form* representative ontrack, over a fax machine, or through a direct computer link.

In some cases, such as the Steinley method, the *final* lengths-back placement for Thoroughbred races is taken directly from the film by the photo-finish operator. In others, it is called and compiled by the *Daily Racing Form* itself. Every track, no matter how small, has at least one employee of the *Form,* who writes the lead articles you read, handicaps the races for the

"Experts' Selections" and "Graded Handicaps," follows the horses, trainers, and jockeys, and calls the placement at the splits and (sometimes) the finish line.

In the past, and at some tracks today, the split and finish calls are made at racing speed. The fact that lengths-back calls are of any use at all in computations of speed is testament to the skill and experience of the "trackmen." The placements have always been referred to as "calls," and that is often exactly what they are. The trackman locks on the racing field with binoculars and calls the placements to an assistant, who quickly jots them down. The trackman not only calls positions and lengths back, he or she also makes calls of horses in trouble, "Three, five wide; Six, no running room . . . ."

If you have any hopes of handicapping, pray for either photo interpretation of lengths back or experienced trackmen at the tracks that you follow. It doesn't matter if their trip notes require the CIA to decipher—or if their top picks in the "Experts' Selections" are wrong all the time (all the better)—as long as their lengths-back placement is accurate, they are heroic figures.

More and more, trackmen are using video replays to be certain of the calls, but the need for skill remains. Even with a frozen frame, it takes considerable experience to decide accurately if a horse is five and a quarter or five and a half lengths behind the winner. The proof of their skill can be seen when you find very consistent horses who win and lose at almost exactly the same time in different races, at different tracks, with different trackmen placing them.

Naturally, they can also be wrong—occasionally, grossly so. At one track recently, the show of the day was one trainer gloating to all who would listen about the odds he would get because his horse, which had come in fifth by four and a half lengths, had been placed *ninth by five and a half* by the trackman.

In the excitement and euphoria of watching history being made as Secretariat blasted into ever faster quarter times, leaving great horses far behind him, the experienced track announcer at Belmont screamed, "It's Secretariat by *twenty-two!* Secretariat still drawing *away!* Secretariat by *twenty-four LENGTHS!*" It brings tears to my eyes to recall it, and I suspect the announcer had tears in his own, because a stupendous race like this is always reanalyzed a thousand times, and the first thing that was noticed was it was actually *thirty-one.*

Misjudgments of Thoroughbred lengths-back placement occasionally occur, and there is no way you can guard against them. They may sometimes explain mysterious results, when a horse that you discounted wins, by posting the same time that you would have calculated, if you had had the correct information. With the many improvements the *Form* has made, the single one which would help speed handicappers most is one they haven't yet implemented, which would be to take the lengths-back at the finish directly off the photo, with a template or interactive measuring device calibrated with the film speed.

As can be seen in the earlier photo-finish "speed strips," the technology presently exists to provide actual finish times for Thoroughbred nonwinners in the same manner as quarter horses. If you are already an experienced speed handicapper, there is no need to start the car with the garage door closed. Nonwinner times have been available for several years to quarter horse crowds, and their success in putting favorites in the winner's circle has improved only a few percentage points over their picks of Thoroughbreds in the same day's racing. Since quarter horses also have the characteristic of running a little more consistently up to their potential than Thoroughbreds, the actual improvement is minuscule. The crowd doesn't know what to do with the information, so life only gets better for the few who use it well.

The Dirt Mystique: Track Variants

The whole notion of "track variant" is based on the theory that the racing surface changes mysteriously from day to day and hour to hour. Many handicappers view the track surface as a malicious chameleon, forever frustrating their best efforts to analyze and understand racing times.

The racing surface—the dirt—is a primary factor in racing speed and times. But it combines with a number of other factors, which can be equal or overriding, to result in times that vary from expected times in ways that are difficult to model and test. The vast majority of handicappers either ascribe some mysterious and mystical powers to the dirt or, like good scientists, argue that the untestable does not exist.

We will see later that wind is a significant factor in quarter horse races that can be quantified and utilized. It is not recorded for Thoroughbred races for the obvious reason that its direction changes in relation to the horses as they round the track. However, the average difference between a headwind and a tailwind in a two-furlong (440-yard) quarter horse race is *two lengths*, while the horses are running in a maximum, all-out effort.

Suppose Thoroughbreds run the first five furlongs of a seven-furlong race into a headwind, then into an angling headwind on the curve before picking up a tailwind on the stretch. They are not running with the same intensity as quarter horses, so the wind could be expected to have a greater effect, but even at the quarter horse average, they would be five lengths behind their potential in still air. This creates a minus-5 track variant for the race with no need for intrusion of the track surface whatsoever.

This can't be tested and proven for Thoroughbred races, except by analogy to quarter horses, so you will have to draw your own conclusions when you see the quarter horse information.

If you could be sure that this is what happened—and if you utilized the more accurate time per length that will be presented later—you would have a valid "race variant" to apply to future handicapping of the horses in this race. But *do not* add them up for the day and divide by the number of races, or the validity will be lost again, this time in a false "average" of wind speed and direction.

This is not to say that wind is the single or overriding cause of variation in race times. It is one of several that have been veiled in the mystery of dirt. In the March, 1995 issue of *The Quarter Racing Journal*, George Pratt quantified the combination of wind and altitude. He found that even without wind, the same quarter horse would run 440 yards at a rate 0.218 seconds faster at 7,000 feet altitude (approximately the elevation of Ruidoso Downs, New Mexico) than at sea level (the elevation of Los Alamitos). That's about 1.7 lengths (at 440 speeds) for every 2 furlongs, due to the relative density of the air alone.

The official condition of the track is called by the stewards from their glass booth high above your head. Some of the conditions are easy and natural; if the weather has been clear and dry for days and the track has experienced only normal grooming by the harrows and water trucks, calling it anything else but "fast" would take some explaining. If there has been a quick downpour and there are standing puddles that send rooster-tail splashes over the jockeys' heads as they ride, it is pretty definitely "sloppy." Somewhere in between are "muddy," "slow," "heavy," and "good."

Tracks are not just rototilled out of the native earth, but are constructed by, first, excavating up to a couple of feet below the existing ground surface. A bottom layer, usually of crushed stone, is applied for drainage; then a middle layer, or "cushion," which is sometimes composed of "decomposed" granite or limestone; then the final racing surface, which is usually a mixture of sand with clay and silt or more exotic components.

If you have ever had gravel delivered for your driveway, or a yard of sand for mansonry work, you can imagine the expense and volume required for filling an eighty-foot-wide mile oval to a depth of several feet with carefully blended soils. This is why racetrack construction and maintenance is big business, with its own experts who travel the world.

There have been endless experiments with each component of the track, ranging from porous-pipe systems in the drainage layer to polymer and oil coating of each individual grain in the top racing surface. The cushion and top layer have considerable influence on both the speeds that horses can attain and the safety with which they do it.

Water hits the track regularly between races, when the water truck and tractors zoom around, erasing the evidence of the last race. The amount of water applied can adjust the speed of the track and, if different from a normal run, the adjustment is directed by the track superintendent. The rate of flow is controlled by the spreader bar and speed of the truck. It can range from a light sprinkling to keep down the dust to a thorough soaking, which builds up over the course of the day.

The optimum (safe) track conditions for speed are a soil mixture and moisture content that springs back slightly as the force of the horse's hoof is released, helping the foot lift into its next stride (described by Dr. George Pratt of MIT in the wonderful PBS NOVA documentary on Thoroughbreds, "A Magical Way of Going"). No matter what the soil mixture, each type has two moisture thresholds, where the spring turns first to a dead blow and then to a "slurp." These can be achieved with a water truck, without the need for Mother Nature. At the second threshold (the "slurp"), instead of a minuscule assist with every step, the horse gets a jerk. These thresholds are occasionally achieved in the course of a normal race day—but if any steward ever downgraded a track from "fast" to "good" as a result of track maintenance, he is probably working in a different maintenance field today.

When Mother Nature does intervene, the fast to good (and reverse) breakover is usually determined with intuitive par times. The stewards do not take the elevator or jog down their long stairs from the crow's nest to shoulder through the crowd and squeeze a handful of dirt. They look at the times. If top allowance horses on a drying track post six furlongs in 1:13:4 and cheap claimers in the next race do it in 1:12:3, then the track is obviously speeding up dramatically . . . or the wind changed.

The climate in different parts of the country often affects the way that natural moisture is applied to the tracks. On the East Coast and in the Northwest, there is more of a tendency for long, soaking rains. You will

Whiskey Jack			B. g. 3(Apr), by Pac Mania—Trinidad Doll, by Ack Ack			
STEVENS G L		**115**	Br.—Stolich Mr-Mrs R (Cal)		1990 7 M 4 1	$17,650
Own.—King & Taber			Tr.—Barrera Lazaro S $32,000		1989 2 M 0 0	$475
			Lifetime 9 0 4 1 $18,125			
26Apr90-2Hol	6f :22² :45⁴ 1:12 ft	*2 115	3½ 21½ 2½ 22¾	Stevens GL ³ Ⓢ M32000	77-10 CharRog,WhiskeyJck,ExclusiveKl 12
20Apr90-1SA	6f :21⁴ :45³ 1:13 ft	5 118	1hd 1hd 2½ 95¾	ValenzuelaPA ⁸ M32000	65-20 Fast Roller, Dr.Hyde,DebetteGlory 12
28Mar90-4SA	6f :21⁴ :45³ 1:11³ft	4 118	53½ 22 2² 21¾	Stevens GL ⁴ Ⓢ M32000	76-23 Hghty'sNotn,WhskyJck,Crcmstllr 12
28Mar90—Lugged out 3/8					
23Feb90-2SA	6f :21² :45¹ 1:12³ft	*8-5 116	3½ 21½ 24 89½	McCarronCJ ¹¹ M28000	63-26 Hostettle, Sumbanaire, Free Bail 11
23Feb90—Wide 3/8 turn					
9Feb90-1SA	6f :22¹ :45⁴ 1:13²ft	*9-5 116	1¹ 1½ 1hd 2hd	VlenzuelPA ⁴ Ⓢ M28000	69-23 EsyBrzy,WhskyJck,RunRunRdolph 12
17Jan90-1SA	6f :22² :45³ 1:12²m	3½ 117	21½ 2½ 21½ 22½	Pincay L Jr ⁷ M28000	71-25 Fitchburg,WhiskeyJck,DrumHouse 10
12Jan90-1SA	6f :21⁴ :45³ 1:12²ft	4½ 116	2hd 2hd 2hd 36½	VlenzuelPA ² Ⓢ M28000	68-23 TellAThief,CaletteKit,WhiskeyJck 12
12Jan90—Veered in start					
24Aug89-4Dmr	6f :22² :45⁴ 1:11 ft	9 115	1hd 31 45½ 613½	Meza R Q ¹ M28000	70-13 Pleasurekite,CrigsReb,VerblLeder 12
24Aug89—Lugged out badly					
30Jun89-4Hol	6f :22¹ :46² 1:12¹ft	*2½ 117	1½ 1hd 23 59½	ValenzuelaPA ⁷ M40000	70-16 Stratified,RisingForm,LucindaLce 11

Speed Index: Last Race: -13.0   3-Race Avg.: -9.6   9-Race Avg.: -10.2   Overall Avg.: -10.2
May 18 Hol 5f ft 1:01⁴ H   May 10 Hol 5f ft 1:01² H   Apr 18 SA 4f ft :47³ H   Apr 12 SA 5f ft 1:01⁴ H

more often see track conditions of muddy and heavy, and when they use those terms, they usually aren't kidding. Because of clouds and overcast, these conditions may last for some time. In the Southwest, rains often come as short, intense cloudbursts, with immediate clearing and just as intense drying, so that official conditions can go from fast to sloppy and back to fast again with hardly a pause for good.

The conditions are a gradient, and since to some extent they are based on times, the times naturally co-vary.

Most speed handicappers base their comparisons of horses strictly on fast tracks. If you are a complete slave to numbers, this is the only way to do it. However, it often pays to look at past performances under other track conditions. In Whiskey Jack's January 17 race, his 1:12:2 less two and a half lengths in the mud showed strength over his previous races, sending him off as the favorite in his next race, which he lost by only a head.

In the handicapping examples in later chapters, you will notice several offtrack times that serve well when carefully selected.

Track conditions in order of wetness are

Fast: moisture content in the neighborhood of optimal for spring from the soil

Good: spring disappears

Slow: spring turns to pull

Heavy: thick mud, clings to the horses' hooves so they carry the weight with them (in real time, this may come either before or after muddy); the slowest track

Muddy: closes in around the horses' feet and lets go with rude noises

Sloppy: surface puddles and very soft mud that splashes away in a crater, leaving the horses' feet free

In order of *speed*, the track conditions would be better listed fast, sloppy, good, slow, muddy, heavy—with sloppy and good interchangeable. For that matter, the first three might be interchangeable, because it is in the category of fast where handicappers have their fits. Times on fast tracks can easily encompass sloppy and good, and only stretch a little to catch the top end of slow.

Some horses get an absolute kick out of running on a sloppy track. Some of the fastest workouts I have ever seen have been on sloppy tracks, where the rider was actually trying hard to hold the horse to prevent slipping and injury, but the horse wouldn't listen to reason. Under just the right conditions, sloppy tracks can be lightning fast. I don't think I'd care to get close enough to confirm it, but I believe what is happening is that the top few inches of silt and sand grains are partially suspended in water and splash clear of the hoof, giving the horse a good bite of the harder undercushion and a bit of a hydraulic lift as the force is released. At any rate, it appears to feel good, and some horses seem to love it.

When the current day's condition turns to an "off" track, many handicappers will simply fold their *Forms* and go home. This is especially true of speed handicappers, who invariably seek their key past performances from fast tracks. In my experience neither is entirely necessary.

Speed figures and their supporting evidence hold until one of two things happen: the footing becomes so heavy that endurance shifts the balance, or things start flying in the air. When one or both become apparent, it is time to decide whether to drastically change your strategy or if your money should stay in your wallet. Unless you are already a mud guru and have a strategy to change to, the best fallback you can assume is to lower your betting to experimental. Water opens the door wide for chaos to slide through.

Endurance strategy is the tougher switch, when conditions change through a race day. Horses that may not have your top speed figure, but have shown strength late in their races or are shortening their distance today, might be possibilities. But *might* is a mighty word.

When water and mud start flying, the old axiom holds true: Look for a horse that can get to the front and stay there—to be the "mudder" rather than the "muddee." The same horse that prances like an antelope, all alone on a sloppy workout track, and runs for the pure joy of being is going to take a different view of matters when mud starts flying up his nose. Horses that consistently break to the front at the first call might get to stay there, while the mud that they fling discourages better horses behind them. Again, *might* is the word.

It doesn't take mud to observe this. Every trip handicapper will strongly question a horse that wins only by going to the front and staying there, as was the case with Soltau's two lonely wins.

Aside from his two stay-in-front wins, take a look at Soltau's history of odds. He has been the crowds' favorite in four of his ten races (noted by the asterisk). He went off as the 8-to-5 favorite in his very first race and did abysmally, then went off at 3.5-to-1 in his next race and was eased—to come back as the 6-to-5 favorite in his next? Was he running against camels?

When a horse does not push through the barrage of clods and slime in a mud race, it probably will not be affected when it races again on dry land. A bad race in mud is a valid excuse and can usually be discounted.

The symbols used in the *Form* to designate mud runners are, not surprisingly, a little nebulous. Many horses will get an asterisk (*), the sign of a "fair mud runner," beside their name for life if they simply win one mud race. An ✕ for a "good mud runner" comes with good showings in two or more races, and a "superior" (⊕) when a horse shows a pattern on offtracks. Many people simply bet these symbols when the rain begins to fall. But they are no substitute for handicapping, especially if you know ahead of time that the

Soltau

CHAPMAN T M

Own.—Qvale K H

B. g. 3(Mar), by Silveyville—Bright Daisy, by Trondheim
Br.—Qvale K H (Cal)
Tr.—Hollendorfer Jerry $10,000

						1990	6	2	0	0		$9,425
						1989	4	M	0	1		$1,250
Lifetime	10	2	0	1	$10,675							

2May90-9GG	6f :214 :45 1:11 ft	4 115	42 33 34½ 44	Gonzalez R M 11	10500 79-20 DncngCrzr,StrttnJyP.,MnOvrMscw 12
19Apr90-7GG	6f :22 :45¹ 1:10²ft	*2½ 117	13 13 1² 11	Chapman T M 2	8000 86-15 Soltau, Coloneoric, Ocotillo 10
30Mar90-3GG	6f :22 :45 1:10²ft	13 117	3¹ 53½ 55 55½	Chapman TM 5 Ⓢ	12500 80-15 Zumbi, BuckStealer,ColonelRumbo 8
28Feb90-3GG	6f :21³ :44⁴ 1:10⁴ft	7½ 117	5³ 55½ 58 57½	Long B 1	18000 76-13 OnMorFrtn,MnOvrMscw,ShrThDrm 6
7Feb90-3GG	6f :22¹ :46 1:11⁴ft	5 118	1hd 1½ 13 13	Lambert J 8 ⓈM12500 79-17 Soltau,Commissio,HveYouSeenMe 12
10Jan90-5BM	1 :46 1:13² 1:40³ft	*9-5 118	2⁴ 1hd 4³ 8¹⁴	Hansen R D 9 ⓈM12500 54-32 Baron O' Fire, U. O. Me, Pilfering 10
13Dec89-2BM	6f :22² :45² 1:11³ft	5½ 118	4² 79½ 8¹¹ 9¹¹	Hansen R D 8 M12500 73-13 CurrghView,NoLoitering,Grimmst 12
13Dec89—Steadied 3 1/2					
15Nov89-1BM	6f :22³ :46 1:12¹ft	*6-5 118	3½ 3² 2³ 34½	Judice J C 6 ⓈM12500 76-15 Scarlet Groom,CoulDorado,Soltau 11
23Sep89-1BM	1 :45² 1:10⁴ 1:37²ft	3½ 118	36 6¹³ — —	Chapman T M 1 Mdn — — SfeToSy,PortRinbow,MissionSttion 7
23Sep89—Eased					
9Sep89-5BM	6f :22 :44³ 1:10¹ft	*8-5 118	65½ 78¾ 7¹⁰ 6¹⁰¾	Chapman T M 5 Mdn 77-10 VlntnLd,MssnSttn,McClymndsHgh 9

Speed Index: Last Race: –1.0   3–Race Avg.: –1.6   8–Race Avg.: –7.0   Overall Avg.: –7.7

May 15 BM 4f ft :49 H   May 9 BM 4f ft :48³ H   Apr 25 BM tr.t 4f ft :50¹ H   ●Apr 12 BM 4f ft :47 H

---

track is going to be muddy. Often the majority of the field will have no past racing experience in the mud, and a "fair mud runner" may find himself beside a horse that is about to prove himself a "superior" one.

Under the best conditions, handicapping is a complexity of variables that you try to hold constant and balance. When you add the flier of offtracks, the gyroscope starts to wobble. This isn't necessarily a time to stay home, but it is definitely a time to back off on the intensity of your bets and enjoy other aspects of the game.

Dirt Biases Between Lanes

When lane biases occur because of mechanical conditions, such as starts on curves and extended-width starting gates, they are "track constants." When they occur as a result of track maintenance—or are due to totally baffling conditions—they join the class of "track variants." One thing you can be assured of, even though the track management may bitterly debate you, is that lane biases do occur.

The Downs at Albuquerque is a fine small-city racetrack that, along with many others, is beginning to find its way in the new world of modern marketing and simulcasting. Attendance is up, handles are up, purses are up, horsemen are about as happy as horsemen get, and the public is more comfortable, as profits are put back into the facilities. Last year, after a motorcycle race over the winter ripped the track down to the drainage base, a new surface was installed. It is black, which seems a little odd in New Mexico, where the whole fad of earth tones originated. I asked Casey Darnell, one of the deans of New Mexico trainers, if it seemed to run any differently. "Nope," he said. "Fast horses run fast—sorry horses run sorry."

This wasn't the case the previous year, when I stopped by the track for just one day to renew acquaintances before the races and ended up staying on after I wandered down by the empty track.

Lane biases are usually invisible, but in this case, even from the grandstands you could see that there was a six-foot-wide ditch along the rail. The Thoroughbred stretch runs had dug a trench six or eight inches deep, and about three horses wide from the stretch curve to the finish line. Across three-quarters of the track the surface was flat and hard, then it dropped— not gradually, but like a New Mexico mesa, into the hole, where the sand was deep to the rail. It would probably only occasionally affect the Thoroughbreds, who would not normally be running that wide in the stretch, but, Albuquerque is a mixed meet, and I was dying to see the quarter horses.

In the first quarter horse race, it became apparent that the mesa edge lay between the 3 and 4 holes, and as the jockeys approached it from the flat chute, the 3 horse was eased down to squeeze side-by-side with the 1 and 2 horses in the softer footing of the valley, while the 4 horse was eased slightly to its right, to stay on the mesa top. The 5 horse won.

In the next quarter horse race, several races later, the 3 horse was more than "eased"—he was *charged* up onto the hard surface, forcing the whole field to the right. He won. The next race would have been funny, if I hadn't been worried for the horse and rider. The jockey never quite "got hold" of his horse, and it went up and down the talus all the way to the finish line, which it crossed last.

This would be a tough bias to handicap, because although quarter horses can and do move around between lanes, a straight line in a straightaway race is the quickest way to the finish line. A 45-degree angle across 50 feet of track adds 20.5 feet to the distance run—in a race that is often won by inches. When drastic lane changes are made, it is usually not the jockey's idea. On this track, the outside post positions clearly had a harder and faster footing; and on this day, at least, no horse could win from the first two post positions. So if the situation persisted, with a little study you could determine how much to subtract from a horse's time if it ran on the inside lanes last time and appears on the outside today—and how much to add if it did the opposite. But—what do you do with the 3 and 4 holes? No jockey in his right mind would drop the 4 horse into the valley, but in the instant-to-instant trips of quarter horse racing, what the jockey has in mind doesn't always prevail. For the 3 horse, you would have to be able to read the jockey's mind and the tea leaves to see if he had the intention—and the opportunity—to climb out.

The Works

Many handicappers place great emphasis on workouts, even to the exclusion of other factors. Before you do, you had better know a little about them.

A runner on ice. This allowance-quality thoroughbred stands in ice to soothe joints, tendons, and muscles after workouts and races. For some claimers, this is the extent of their training; their time between races is for recovery, not conditioning. *Photo by author.*

The first and most important thing to know about the actual times is that they are absolutely meaningless.

Unless there is some dubious practice afoot, a horse will *never* be run in an all-out, racing-level effort while conditioning for its next race. Many horses, especially in the lower claiming ranks, race on a one-week cycle. They may race every Saturday or every Wednesday, often against each other in almost identical fields, and they may show no workouts for months. This may mean that they "train" in an ice bucket—that they are on a routine of resting, walking, and light galloping between races—or that their trainers are very adept at avoiding timed workouts.

All major tracks have rules about workouts. If a horse has never appeared on the track before, or if it has been laid off for sixty days, it must usually record two, or at least one, "work" from the gates before it is allowed to enter a race. This is for the safety of the jockeys and gate crews, who need to know if a horse is likely to rip the gates, and maybe them, apart.

There is almost no way an unscrupulous trainer can avoid recording these times, but there are innumerable ways he can alter them. The recorded times mean almost nothing until they approach what would be respectable racing speeds. Then they become suspect. They may be a trainer's trick to pacify a waffling owner or an overdone "blowout," two days before a race, that will hurt rather than help the horse. On the other hand, they may be a real show of top condition and a horse that feels terrific. There is no way for you to know, unless you have coffee with the jockey.

Workout figures are a secondary handicapping factor both for condition and for speed. In no case should they be any part of a mathematical formula, since they are subject to adjustment by the trainers, exercise riders, jockeys, and, very rarely, the clockers.

If a horse shows one or more workouts at regular intervals since its last race, it is probably a fair indication that it is not crippled. If a horse shows *consistently* fast workouts—not just one aberrantly fast time—this may be good *supporting* evidence for decent racing speed figures. Period.

"Bullet horses" are probably a sly joke from the stats room of the *Daily Racing Form.* Horses are given a "bullet" (●) next to their workout time if it was the best posted for that day. There is a little section in the *Form* each day listing the horses entered that received bullets in one of their last four works. Occasionally, this may mean that a horse is sharp; it *can* mean that there was

Comedy Routine — B. c. 3(Apr), by Tsunami Slew—Giggling Girl, by Laugh Aloud — Lifetime 3 0 0 2 $3,360 — 1990 1 M 0 1 $1,800
$70,000 Br.—Harbor View Farm (Ky) — **118** — 1989 2 M 0 1 $1,560
Own.—Sommer Viola — Tr.—Martin Frank

15Jan90- 4Aqu	fst	6f	⊡:22 2/5	:46 4/5	1:12 4/5	Md 47500	10	2	2^{1}	$4^{1\frac{1}{4}}$	$4^{2\frac{1}{2}}$	$3^{3\frac{1}{4}}$	Madrid A Jr	120	5.70	79-16	Ackie'sRiddle118^nk OlympicImge118^3 ComdyRoutin120^2 No match 12
24Dec89- 4Aqu	fst	6f	⊡:23 4/5	:49	1:15 3/5	Md 35000	11	8	$8^{6\frac{3}{4}}$	$7^{5\frac{3}{4}}$	5^{4}	3^{3}	Smith M E	118	4.80	65-22	Chronoscope114^2 Dn'sProspect114^1 ComdyRoutin118^2¼ Rough trip 12
5Nov89- 7Aqu	fst	6f	:22	:45 1/5	1:10 4/5	Md Sp Wt	11	2	3^{2}	8^{8}	13^{18}	$13^{23\frac{1}{2}}$	Rojas R I	118	136.60	62-19	PolishNumbers118^4 BambooShoot118^nk FirstndOnly118½ Gave way 13

Speed Index: Last Race: –5.0 3–Race Avg.: –12.3 3–Race Avg.: –12.3 Overall Avg.: –12.3

LATEST WORKOUTS Jan 24 Bel tr.t 4f gd :48 H ●Jan 9 Bel tr.t 3f my :36 2/5 H Jan 3 Bel tr.t 4f fst :49 2/5 B Dec 20 Bel tr.t 4f fst :48 Hg

↑

a particularly poor crop of horses working that morning or that everyone else was just out for the morning air.

There is only one reason why a trainer wants an extremely fast workout to be actually recorded by the clocker and published in the *Form:* the owner is losing heart. Fast published workouts can keep a loser on the payroll for a few more weeks or months. When a trainer wants a fast workout strictly for conditioning—or his own betting plans—he often will try to mask it.

Trainers have three basic sources of income: the training fees paid by the owners, which cover horse feed, grooms' salaries, and equipment (vet, farrier, and jockey fees are extra); race earnings, of which the trainer receives 10 percent (unless he personally owns the horse); and betting. Betting is legal for trainers, not because it is a desirable part of racing, but because there is no way on earth to stop it. It is, therefore, a fundamental fact of handicapping.

Whenever a horse makes a change in its racing habits, such as stepping up from a $25,000 claimer to a $32,000 race, from routes to sprints, or from turf to dirt, there is an excellent chance that the trainer is testing the horse to see if it will find its "nick" on the track. There is an equally excellent possibility that the trainer fully expects the horse to do poorly and is using the race or a series of races to establish a history of poor performances for the handicapping crowd, so that when he drops it into the race he has planned he will make much more on the bet than from his percentage of the purse. Andrew Beyer called this "larceny." In its purest form, it may not be. Many horses—perhaps most—do not round into full racing condition until they begin a regimen of racing on a regular basis. No workout compares to an all-out race for both training and conditioning.

Many trainers have theories about conditioning through racing distances and may, for example, place a sprinter in a mile-and-an-eighth route to build up its wind, then at five-and-a-half-furlongs with a hot field to make it stretch for speed, then come back on the fourth or fifth week of the cycle to the race they actually had in mind—to blow them away at six furlongs. If their horse comes in ninth by twenty-four lengths in the route, and fifth by five and a half in the first sprint, all the better for the odds. It doesn't always work in the last race, or the first—sometimes the horse will surprise everyone and win in the misplaced route. Many times handicappers will do better than the trainers in spotting horses that will perform out of their element.

The larceny comes in when a trainer tells a jockey where to place the horse. This happens every day, at every track in the country, from Belmont to the bull rings. The trainer may not specifically call for a fifth, but while he's standing there in the paddock with his hands in his pockets and the jockey is boosted aboard, he may just murmur, "Don't push him," and the horse that would have made your exacta with one easy crack of the whip comes in fourth at a canter. The jockey, who would have made an extra $100 or $200 for third- or second-place money knows that he will have the ride and a bet in his name (which is legal) when the money race is run.

A good clocker keeps a "book" for the workouts, with notes on every horse on the grounds. Large tracks may have four or five clockers, while even fairly good-sized tracks might have only one, plus a backup. In each case the clocker is responsible for the long-distance identification of up to several thousand horses. The registration papers of all horses are kept in the racing office, both as a means of identification and as collateral for unpaid bills owed to feed suppliers, farriers, and vets. The clocker will go through all of the papers immediately before the meet and as horses come and go, making notes on each horse's markings.

When a horse that is to be run for an official time enters the track in the morning, the rule is that its name and the trainer's name must be reported to the clockers.

Along with the hundred or so horses that may come onto the track for an official time are five hundred or a thousand who are just out for a gallop. Aside from owner manipulation, the only other time that many trainers want an officially clocked time is when they have to meet track regulations of one or more works or gate trainings. And so the game begins.

Horses hit the track before dawn, when visibility is 50 yards. Like every good horse movie, there are speed works in pitch darkness, when only the rider knows what happened. Horses "just out for a gallop" break for speed between poles, with no reference points for the clockers. The clockers fight back, catching unscheduled runs at distances the trainer never planned. Allowance horses with a white blaze and left hind foot, from the same or an ally's barn, just out for a romp, are called in to the clocker under the name of a cheap claimer with similar markings to post a time to amaze the owner. Or, simplest of all, as the riders approach the beginning time pole at a gallop, they simply don't "break" until they are a few strides beyond it. The horse gets the recorded time it needs for entry and/or the blowout the trainer wanted, but you see a time in the *Form* considerably slower than its actual work, which will be slower than race time to begin with.

There is room for conniving between trainers and clockers, but they generally don't get along that well. Usually, it remains in gamesmanship.

Workouts are also given a rating by the clocker, which is transmitted to the *Daily Racing Form* and published for the public (opposite page).

Many handicappers pay close attention to these, since *breezing* means that the horse was worked under a tight hold by the rider, without urging. "Handily" means that the horse was urged, if not whipped. Obviously, if two horses record identical recent workout times—say three furlongs in 36 and 4/5, and one did it under restraint (breezing), while the other had to be urged (handily), then the first can be assumed to have more "run" in him than the second.

WORKOUTS

Each horse's most recent workouts appear under the past performances. For example, Jly 20 Hol 3f ft :38b indicates the horse worked on July 20 at Hollywood Park. The distance of the work was 3 furlongs over a fast track and the horse was timed in 38 seconds, breezing. A "bullet" ● appearing before the date of workout indicates that the workout was the best of the day for that distance at that track.

ABBREVIATIONS USED IN WORKOUTS:

b—breezing   d—driving   (d)—worked around "dogs"   g—worked from gate
h—handily   bo—bore out   ⑪—turf course   Tr—trial race
tr.t following track abbreviation indicates horse worked on training track

At some tracks, you will *never* see identical breezing and handily times. They are mutually exclusive categories. Rather than evaluate the level of restraint or urging, the clockers simply observe the time. If it was fast, it gets an *H*. If it is slower than some threshold for the distance, a *B*—whether the rider was whipping like a demon or standing erect in the stirrups. At other tracks, you will rarely see a *B*, which may result from the fact that most horses are urged to some degree or it might just be a convention of the clocker.

What means more, when it appears, is the little *g* beside the *H*. This means that the time was clocked from the starting gate. The time will be slower than race times for Thoroughbreds and usually much slower than nongate works for quarter horses, because both of the others represent only a shift in gears at the distance pole, from a gallop to a run. But gate works are the most accurate and there is less room for manipulation, although many horses are purposely broken slowly to avoid both times and injuries, and then pour on the coals down the track.

Gate works and faster, well-spaced nongate works, are more significant in handicapping quarter horses, since they not only give you an idea of what the horse may be capable of—with some of the caveats of slower work times that apply to Thoroughbreds—but they tell you that for this work, at least, the horse didn't tumble head over heels when it broke from the gates. Quarter horse experts (owners, trainers, and track officials) go back and forth on this, saying in one breath that the race is won or lost in the gates, and in the next—when they realize what this means for the promotion of quarter horse handicapping—that a good horse can overcome a bad start. Both are true, but there is a big difference between *can* and *will*.

When you bet on a quarter horse race, part of your bet is on the *luck* that your horse will get out cleanly. The same kind of luck permeates Thoroughbred racing and every other sport, although it is usually less dramatic.

Workout times are, perhaps, one notch above totally meaningless in handicapping, even after all this is taken into account. They are a secondary factor, but *never* a data point for computation. If a horse is returning to the track after a six-month layoff, and shows a well-spaced series of works, at least someone is trying to bring it back into form. For shorter layoffs of a few weeks, decent workouts may show that the horse at least isn't crippled, and you can handicap its past races with only moderate paranoia. The workouts are usually worth a glance, to run through the possibilities, but to analyze them in much greater detail is an exercise in futility.

6

CHAOS
WHY THERE ARE HORSE RACES

Any horse can be beaten on any given day.
—ANGEL CORDERO, JR.

The Butterfly Effect. *Photo by author.*

Horse race handicapping turned from an art to a science in the 1960s and '70s along with such unrelated, former academic arts as sociology and anthropology. It was the spirit of the times. Engineers had raised the rallying banner with the hardware of space travel, and every child knew that one day he or she *personally* would understand the universe. All we had to do was reduce it to its fundamental parts, understand those, explain how to put it back together again, and Nirvana was at hand.

In the glory years of science, physicists *reduced*, from atoms to quarks; biologists *reduced*, from cells to electrochemistry; handicappers *reduced*, from hot tips to track variants and par times. Handicappers borrowed from science, and scientists became handicappers. All of it was based on the clear vision that the universe was orderly and that the laws of Newton and thermodynamics hold, whether you are looking at wrinkles in a distant galaxy or Thoroughbreds running out of gas. It was simply our job to measure, define, and explain. Physicists, biologists, and handicappers worked in parallel, looking for clear-cut, linear relationships.

The mood coincided with the introduction of the computer, so the next step was natural: run a bazillion or two race factors through a mainframe for statistical analyses never dreamed of by the old school handicappers and find out which factors predict—and to what degree—the outcome of a race. The task of converting this into a mathematical formula would be child's play after the job of punching ten thousand computer cards.

Some of the factors were made to order: weights come in numbers; changes in weights are the same way. They are mathematically sexy: you can use the Greek alphabet, with terms like ΔW, to represent weight changes. Track variants are numerical. Jockeys are a little trickier, but you could assign some numerical value based on dollar winnings, percentage of rides in the money, standings at the meet, or whatever tickled your fancy.

To find the universal truths of horse racing, all you would have to do is, first determine what the elements are, and then put the correct algebraic symbols between them.

You might come out with a probability equation that looked something like this:

$$P_1 = (S/d - T_v) \, {}^*(x)\Delta w \, {}^*(y)j - P_2..P_n$$

where the probability of a particular horse winning is equal to some measure of time in relation to distance, minus the track variant, times some function of weight, times a jockey factor—minus the probability of winning of each of the other horses in the race. Today you can buy very expensive computer programs that not only do something similar to this, but supposedly learn from their mistakes.

While this was going on, physicists were learning from their mistakes. Not mistakes, really, because quarks do exist (one supposes), but as they and the biologists and meteorologists found more and more subparts, they found less and less reason why the parts—taken as a whole—should work. The "smaller" you looked, the more elusive the answer, like looking through an electron microscope at your genes and realizing periodically that it is your genes that are looking at you.

In many cases order didn't just slip away, it plummeted into an abyss. The more you learned, the less likely it became that you could predict what would happen the next instant in whatever dynamical system you were studying, even if you had a good idea of what the general trend should be a year from now. Chaos was found not only in the depths of microanalysis; once the monster was recognized, it started turning up everywhere. Classic toys of physics, such as pendulums and pulley machines, used for teaching high school students—after two thousand years of order—began running erratically and unpredictably. But nothing had changed—it was only when you looked at them differently.

The answer from academic science was the same as that from the wise mother you tell, "My leg hurts when I do this." "Well," she says, "stop doing that." Graduate students were taught how to look, and if what they saw looked odd, they were taught a name for it. It was "noise."

Every science, from the hardest to the softest, developed mathematical modeling to explain its problems. Just ten years ago, some of the most complex problems in some fields were ground out on programmable hand calculators. If you had a hot-rod "HP" or "TI" (Hewlett-Packard or Texas Instruments), you were not only the envy of your graduate school classmates, you could actually do front-line work on the theoretical frontiers of biology and anthropology. If you knew how to talk the card language of a mainframe, you were the darling (and the lackey) of your professor. Whatever topic you studied, you blasted over the "noise" like an airboat over the weeds.

When you create a vastly simplified mathematical model of a dynamical system, like the "blooms and crashes" of algae in a pond, it will *always* work, because, unlike the system, the math is self-contained. Once you get rid of any blatant mistakes, you check against what you know about the general idea of "blooms" and adjust the math until the model is up and humming. Then comes the scary part: you try it with real data. To get this, you applied for your grant from the National Science Foundation for a year "in the field" to count algae strands, or calories expended in swidden agriculture, or whatever you were studying. And usually, by the time the leech bites faded, you had your graduate committee's approval of your Ph.D. thesis, based on the neat, linear relationships of the data run through your model.

Sometimes, though, when the real data were applied, strange things happened. The predictable became unpredictable; laws seemed to be broken. It was easy to explain. *Real* data are subject to human errors in counting; models can't account for everything, like algae-eating pollywogs, which might or might not bloom along with it; the statistics of gathering large enough samples constantly introduced errors—*noise*. "Noise" became such a readily recognized answer for complex problems that it entered the language to dismiss anything that seemed to distract from the real meat of the matter.

But independently, in different fields, at different times, from the 1950s into the '80s, a few mathematicians, physicists, and, notably, one meteorologist stopped to wonder if maybe the noise might be important. Edward N. Lorenz, a meteorologist at MIT, was running a mathematical weather model on an archaic computer of 1961, when one day he introduced some noise. He simply rounded the starting data, a seven-digit number, to three digits—which the computer did anyway in its printouts—and went for a cup of coffee.

The model, which was mathematically simple but elegant, should have continued making the same numerical weather changes over and over through eternity, or at least until it ran out of paper. When Lorenz returned an hour later, it was fluctuating wildly and randomly away from its normally fixed weather pattern. Instead of dismissing the chaos that had resulted from the tiny amount of noise he had entered, Lorenz thought about it.

From that hour of fluctuations away from expected weather patterns came ideas that are yet to be fully realized outside a small segment of the scientific community. The most practical is that weather can probably never be predicted beyond a general pattern. The deeper ideas were that chaos is as much a part of reality as order and that the "butterfly effect" exists.

Lorenz wrote and published a paper on the effect, in a meteorological journal that wasn't "discovered" by scientists facing similar problems in other fields for another decade. Then they gave the theory a more academic-sounding name and started holding conferences on the topic. "Sensitive dependence on initial conditions" became one of the hallmarks of a revolution in science.

Lorenz's point was simple. Slight variations in points of departure can result in not only radically different destinations, but totally unpredictable paths. The "butterfly" was a little tongue in cheek—but not much. Weather patterns were affected and changed by factors as remote and seemingly trivial as the beat of a butterfly's wings.

In his excellent overview of the topics of chaos for laymen (*Chaos: Making a New Science*, New York: Viking, 1987), James Gleick suggests the bus you miss that runs every ten minutes, which causes you to miss the train that runs every hour, as an example of small changes producing large effects. Taken further, of course, you miss the plane that flies once a day.

What initially stunned scientists who came to recognize the process was that you didn't have to look to the vast complexity of interaction between the earth and the atmosphere's heating and cooling to see transitions in chaos and order. You could look at the steam rising from a cup of tea. Or you could watch a horse race.

In dynamical systems, random aberrations are not noise in the system—*order* is the system in the noise. Scientists in many fields have accepted two new fundamentals: You can't know all the parameters; and the ones you do know probably aren't connected in any linear fashion.

Linear equations can be solved if you have a few key pieces of information. Once solved, they can tell you many things about the relationship of the variables. Most nonlinear equations *cannot* be solved. The devastation

FIGURE 6.1

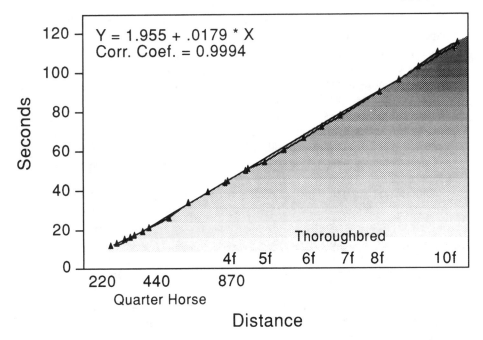

comes with the realization that most of the relationships in the universe are nonlinear.

The second law of thermodynamics says that all systems run out of gas. Energy dissipates; the universe is expanding; running horses get tired. You can see a linear relationship as fine as any by looking at the time it takes a horse to run greater and greater distances.

Figure 6.1 displays a near-perfect linear relationship of racing distance and time. For every distance on the X axis there is a time on the Y axis that corresponds with almost perfect regularity. In this case, they are the fastest times officially recorded for quarter horses and Thoroughbreds taken together—as if one superhorse took off out of the gates and was clocked at each intermediate distance from 220 yards to ten furlongs. If the second law holds, then each time should increase in direct proportion to the increase in distance. Some of the distance gaps are only 20 yards (for example, 330 to 350 yards in the quarter horse portion of the scale), some are an eighth of a mile. The linear regression shows how close the relationship of time is to distance.

A perfect correlation of time and distance would give a correlation coefficient of 1.0. In this case, it is .9994, which is totally acceptable as "perfect" in almost any academic science. The tiny variation is *noise*, because we used real data. It can be explained in a variety of ways. Since these are absolute records, some of the times were achieved by megahorses, like Dr. Fager at a mile. Others, such as the 1,000-yard quarter horse distance, haven't been run enough for records to reach the predictable limit for 1,000-yard races. The noise is acceptable; the correlation is *very* strong; the second law of thermodynamics works; all is well with the world.

To see the second law even better, look at times in a different way. Convert all of the times to seconds and all of the distances to feet. Divide the feet by the seconds and you have feet per second (fps), which is no longer time but *speed*. Since the second law holds, the feet per second should taper off over distance, which, of course, it does, as a mirror of the first equation (Figure 6.2).

One of the characteristics of such a strong linear relationship is that you can predict with measurably precise accuracy what the X is for a given Y, and vice versa. Pick any distance on the X axis on the first graph, or something in between, and you can solve the equation to see what the ultimate time should be. If you would like to know with 99.94 percent certainty how far away this ultimate horse would be in thirty seconds, insert thirty seconds into the equation as Y.

But suppose we look at a smaller piece of the line—the quarter horse portion alone. The times are components of the same "perfect" linear system (Figure 6.3).

The 20-yard and 50-yard distance times are not official; they are times that I clocked for handicapping purposes. The rest are the fastest official

FIGURE 6.2

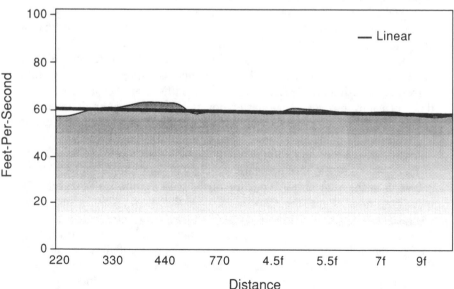

FIGURE 6.3

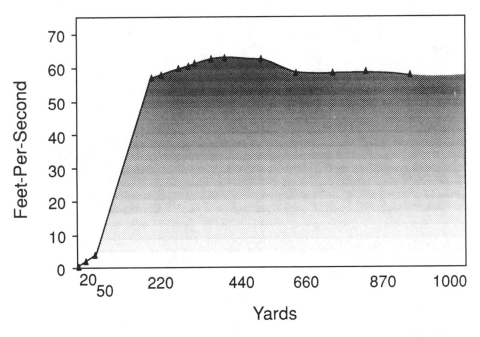

times recorded by quarter horses at those distances. It doesn't look very straight and it's not.

There are parameters you could not have known by looking at the first large-scale graph, even though the main components were all included. This graph starts at zero, with the quarter horse standing in the gates, while the jockey "ties down" with a handful of mane, and several assistant starters scream, "No, Boss, no!" The gates open, the whiskers trip, and the clock begins running.

Twelve hundred pounds of horseflesh, 110 pounds of jockey, and maybe 6 or 12 pounds of lead are standing still, tied down by inertia. As you can see in the top photograph, the gates are open, but only three horses have peeked out; the rest are inside, contemplating the law of gravity.

Any quarter horse aficionado will tell you that a quarter horse reaches peak speed two jumps out of the gate. It is in every piece of literature ever written about them. Jockeys will tell you this and they, more than anyone, should know. But it seems they may be confusing G's with speed. The 20- and 50-yard times were hand timed and they are not a gigantic sample, but two things are patently clear: the first is that quarter horses may come out of the gates faster than any other horse alive, but they are not exempt from the laws of inertia and gravity. The other, which you can't see in the graph but is

Gravity. Five horses are still inside, pondering Newton's law. *Photo by author.*

Inertia. With the enormous exertion of getting 1200 pounds into motion, the rider's position is critical. The jockey in the foreground is a little high, but in the right position, far forward. The rider in the center is sitting back almost to the lumbar, and will lose almost a length by the time his horse's blurred feet come down for a second stride. *Photo by author.*

"linear" in the data, is—to paraphrase Casey Darnell—that good horses start fast, "sorry" horses start "sorry."

This was a devastating blow to what I thought was going to be the greatest quarter horse handicapping tool of all times. I thought that—perhaps—quarter horse class and speed would show itself further down the track. And of course it does there, too. But since all horses are charged to go in the gates and it is an explosive time of bangs, buzzers, and yells, I wondered if *maybe* the $2,500 claimers would get out just as fast—for at least the first jump—as allowance and even Grade I horses. If that were true, then maybe you could hold the first part of the curve constant and do wonderful things with the rest. Instead, it is just another unknown in the nonlinear equation. A horse's ability to run with speed starts with the first push against inertia, and not all horses are equal.

Twenty yards is 60 feet, or about three jumps, with running horse strides of about 20 feet. Twenty-five-hundred-dollar claimers cover the distance in about 2.2 seconds. Grade I horses do it in about 1.85 seconds. At full running speed, a length is about 0.10 to 0.12 seconds, so the Grade I horse would be *three lengths* ahead of the claimer, *less than three jumps out of the gate.* Of, course, the whole point is, they are not running at full speed. (Since this work was done, Dr. George W. Pratt has filmed quarter horse races at Los Alamitos using high-speed timing cameras, with somewhat different results. Most of the differences are easily explained. For example, my consistently faster times stem from the fact that with hand-timing, one must react to the opening of the gates; this always places the start a hair after the timing switch on the gates. Horses passing the 20 yard mark are much more accurately anticipated and observed, thus shortening elapsed time. Also, in Dr. Pratt's published explanation, the horses may be running faster at Ruidoso due to the reduced air resistance at high altitude. His top speed and mine, which will be discussed later, are virtually identical but were found at different distances down the track. The discrepancy is more complicated, but can be explained through the data. What I cannot explain is that with much more sophisticated methods, he found very little difference in start-up times and speed between his two categories of "superior" and "average" horses at Los Alamitos. While my data would err toward faster times, it was consistent and the start-up difference between low-priced claimers and Grade I horses at Ruidoso was clear. Dr. Pratt's results can be found in the April, 1991 *Quarter Racing Journal.*)

At 20 yards, the fastest time per length recorded in this sample was 0.25 (in the 1990 All-American Futurity, First Consolation). About one-half full speed. But, again, this speed is an *average* that includes both the instant of dead standstill shown in the first picture and the acceleration portion of the curve. The curve shoots up drastically, as can be seen in the graph, after the horses pass 50 yards. Since the start-up time is included in it, the horses are gaining speed at 50 yards, but are still far from full bore.

Although start-up times are not constant, which introduces some noise, they are always part of the total times recorded in quarter horse races. In the mechanics of starting, the first "jump" is more of a *hop* to overcome inertia, as can be seen in the lower photograph. Close analysis would probably show that fast horses are better hoppers than slow ones.

The two start-up photographs are in immediate succession on a roll, taken with a motorized winder that touches off shots at half-second intervals. The top photo was obviously taken the instant after the starter pressed his button while the horses are in the first microseconds of reaction. In the bottom photo, 0.5 seconds later, they have made their first hop and have planted their hind feet for the first stride, which will be a longer hop against inertia. If you look at the distance from the gates (not the front of the open doors, but back where their noses had been), it appears that a horse can hop, flat-footed, about its own body length, or approximately eight feet.

If this is a moderately fast race, with the first 20 yards run in about 2.0 seconds, the overall (average) time per length would be about 0.27. Since 0.5 seconds, or 25 percent of the time, was spent getting 8 feet from the gates, it leaves 1.5 seconds to get the other 52 feet—which gives an average time per length of 0.23 seconds for the rest of the distance. If the assumption were true that quarter horses reach full speed two, three, or even four jumps from the gate, then eliminating this relatively huge segment of time spent moving 8 feet should drastically lower the time per length of the remaining run—toward the 0.12 – 0.14 range. Since it barely touches it, it is clear that horses are still overcoming inertia at 20 and 50 yards.

But there is another side to inertia, if you recall: "Bodies at rest tend to stay at rest; bodies in motion tend to stay in motion." Just as there is an anaerobic/aerobic threshold, there is also an inertia drag/propulsion threshold, where momentum catches up with the horse and, instead of pulling it back, drives it forward. This is when quarter horses start to fly.

The anaerobic/aerobic threshold and inertia drag/propulsion threshold are related. The tremendous exertion of overcoming inertia is probably where most of the glycogen and glucose of anaerobic exercise is expended. The gradient of a horse converting from anaerobic to aerobic energy is no doubt a function of the gradient of inertia. And the relationship is probably nonlinear.

If you look at Figure 6.3 again, you will see that there is not only a drastic start-up curve, but a hump, out around 440 to 550 yards. Quarter horse speed, in feet per second, begins to taper off as they approach 660, 770, and then 870 yards. There is a good reason for the initial downturn because, as they go around the corner from 550 to 660 yards, the "curve" is literal. Five-hundred-fifty-yard races are run on a straightaway; 660 and up are run around one turn. Somewhere, at about the curve in the track, between 550 and 770 yards, but probably closer to 550, the gradient of quarter horse anaerobic and aerobic exercise comes into balance. If you extend the curve out to Thoroughbred distances, it is pretty much downhill from here (with an expected ripple from the introduction of the flying start and a few very interesting wiggles).

Quarter horse speeds, when viewed broadly as components of how fast horses can run over distance, are linear and predictable, fitting perfectly the laws of thermodynamics. When viewed in isolation, as a picture of how horses do run, they create a bump in the expected entropy and, although other good laws—such as Newton's—apply, the relationship becomes non-linear and far less easy to solve. With a little advanced math, you can *approximate* where a horse would be 15 or 24.176, seconds after the time starts, given the fixed parameters of the graph. But in real life, with real horses on real dirt, you cannot know the rest of the parameters. Determining "instantaneous speed," in systems that can slow down as well as speed up unpredictably, is an insolvable problem.

Conventional entropy seems to be the steadying factor for dynamical curves after bursts of life—or a good start in a quarter horse race. The trouble is, the path can't be predicted—even though in two dimensions the curve resembles graphs that *can* be. A rifle bullet's trajectory looks a lot like quarter horse speed, but it is a *solvable* equation because there is only one burst of energy.

Rocket trajectories can also be calculated, even though there is a pro-longed force applied, as long as you know that the force is constant, or when and how it changes—which was a lucky thing for John Glenn when it came time to find him. What no one, including NASA, can predict are systems in which an unknown force is applied at imprecise intervals—systems as simple as a child's swing or the strides of a running horse.

Sensitive dependence on initial conditions is difficult to describe, and the path that results is impossible to predict in systems that are given minor perturbations at start-up, like Lorenz's weather machine. In the world that we know, *there is no start-up*. All systems are already running. There is no butterfly—there are billions of them, flapping on, and between, every instant.

Everything we have looked at and talked about so far in horse racing is noise—breeding theories, jockeys' and trainers' tricks, par times, and track variants. But the system is the noise. One of the things that comes with recognizing disorder and chaos is that order comes and goes within it—but order of a different kind. Each component of horse racing that we have reviewed is its own system, with its own frequency of chaos and order.

The breeding of racehorses does not ensure the occurrence of "runners." Runners can occur with seeming regularity in a stallion's or mare's offspring,

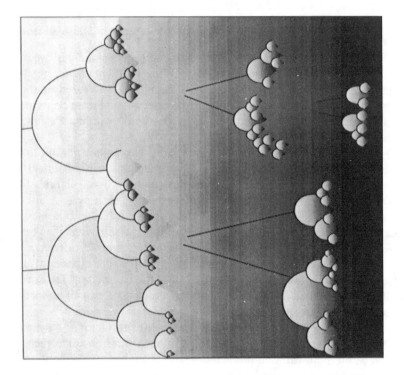

FIGURE 6.4: BIFURCATION

and then disappear to pop up randomly with no predictable pattern. Runners, and the genetic material that creates them, can occur with every third foal, even with the same stallion and mare combination.

Since "runner genes" can occur in third-combination cycles, another realm of chaos may apply. In a 1975 paper, James Yorke and Tien-Yien Li proved that if a system can fluctuate on a period of three, then it can also fluctuate on any period—including periods of total randomness (recounted in Gleick, 1987, pp. 73 – 80). When graphed, the purely mathematical model of bifurcation (two-way splitting) dramatically resembles a horse's pedigree.

The bifurcations produce ancestorlike splits—2, 4, 6, 8, 16, 32—until the splits become almost infinitely small and begin to fill space randomly. Order falls apart. But in spots the randomness reorganizes and begins again, with a new cycle and new multiples. If you recall the organization and values of each generation in the *chefs de race* system, the analogy is a little uncanny.

In the flow from left to right in a pedigree diagram, the generations cannot become random. But genes flow in the opposite direction—from right to left—and split in a vastly more complicated pattern. It may be that "runners" and *chefs de race* occur at the points of reorganization.

There are other realms of chaos and other forms of "galloping." For several years, I chaired the research and development committee of an electrical utility, where one of our projects involved putting a damper on galloping power lines. When the wind blows directly parallel to a wire strung in the air, the line can begin to "gallop." In a sustained wind ripples in the wire become waves, which reach the next pole and roll back, like breakers on the seashore. At higher wind velocities, the orderliness of the waves can break over into turbulence. Forceful waves from one end meet declining waves from the other and chaos sets in. The disorderly thrashing may settle back to orderly waves of the same or different period—*or* may build to wild, random thrashing, to snap the cable or the poles at both ends.

It has been suggested recently that catastrophic failures in horses' leg bones while at training and racing speeds, such as the heartbreaking fall of Go For Wand in the 1990 Breeders' Cup, may result from undetected hairline fractures developed before the massive failure. This is no doubt true in some cases. There is also the possibility that the rhythmical running of a horse sets up harmonic stress in the bone structure, which is the perfect environment for chaos. If this is true, there would be the tendency to look for factors that disrupt the rhythmic stresses—a missed step, a thin spot in the track cushion—but chaos doesn't need this kind of outside intervention. Randomness and disruption are already part of the system. If hairline fractures precede the final failure, their origin may be the same. Somewhere among the causes for unsoundness, between mechanical slips on the track and plain, overzealous training, may be a realm of biomechanical chaos, possibly with elegant mathematical and graphical possibilities—which shows up on the racetrack as rotten, egg-sucking luck.

Chaos has been found and described in various forms in every imaginable system, from living structures to pure mathematics. But far and away its most understandable variety is "sensitive dependence on initial conditions," which could be used as an alternate definition for "horse racing." The delicate network of tiny differences with large effects begins when a breeder first starts *thinking* about breeding two horses. When a mare carries a foal, she has butterflies in her stomach. If twelve precisely matched horses step up to the gates, a glance from one can make it impossible for another to pass him.

Every handicapper has seen more cases than he cares to remember, when horses have won races and there is no rational explanation on this earth. When a good horse like Strawberry Silk loses, there can be ready explanations: subclinical illness, pulmonary bleeding, a stumble at the gates, a bad lane on the track. But when a dismal horse runs faster than it ever has in its life, or ever will again—and the drug test is negative—you can spend the rest of your life in a monastery and never find the answer.

It will not get you your money back, but it may give you some peace of mind, to think of the race as an energetic system subject to the rules of both order and chaos. This is easiest to visualize in a quarter horse race. All of the surrounding subsystems of breeding, training, and betting wind up centered on five or six tons of horse energy about to be released from the gates. The center of energy moves up and down the line as horses "blow up" or fight their heads loose from the assistant starters to look over the divider and see if that big sorrel is really glaring. When the gates open, the whole system moves forward and the center of energy shifts. Body language and relative position, to and from horses in sight, pushes and pulls both energy and conviction. One or more centers of energy can form in clusters across the track: slow horses run faster with fast ones; faster horses drop back from dominant ones; the jockeys introduce major butterflies with their whips, which act more like yellow jackets. This environment is to chaos as the Everglades is to mosquitos.

At the same time that the hard sciences like physics discovered that their bugs were nonlinear and shifted paradigms to face up to it, horse players lost heart with their search for linear equations and moved on to trip handicapping. Since order and chaos repeat in horse racing with some pattern, if not exact predictability, trip handicapping works because it is an observational approach to chaos. Speed handicapping works because speed is the order to which chaos returns.

Chaos and order pervade not only the race, but the pari-mutuel system of betting, so chaos is not a reason to give up hope, but a new way of looking for fun.

PART THREE

The Elements of Speed

7

TOP SPEED

It may be that the race is not always to the swift, or the battle to the strong—but that's the way to bet.
—DAMON RUNYON

*T*o recognize order within chaos, we need some indication of what order is. Handicappers have always searched for a valid baseline against which to compare the variation of individual horses' performance. This would be a much simpler proposition if all races were run on two-turn miles, 6 furlong hooks, or, simpler yet, 440 yard straightaways. Since they are not, you need some way of dealing with the range of variation in racing distances and track constants (which affect times at seemingly equal distances), before you can consider the variation in running ability of individual horses.

"Parallel speed" is an essential concept for handicapping, since you will almost always have to compare horses which have recorded past performances at different distances. How can you know if a time at 5 1/2 furlongs would be relatively faster or slower than one at 6? Is a quarter horse time of 17.88 seconds for 350 yards "faster" or "slower" than 20.21 at 400?

There were several basic flaws in many of the early approaches to speed and pace handicapping. Most of them revolved around the baseline problem and the mathematical factors used to compare performances to the standard. The flaws didn't matter much when speed and pace were in their early years; each provided a fresh new edge that often allowed you to find classic overlays on horses that the crowd simply couldn't see without figures.

Tom Ainslie, Andrew Beyer, Steven Davidowitz, and notably, William Quirin, among others, produced state-of-the-art parallel speed charts that were drawn from analyses of par times and adjusted by experience. My first revelations of the power of figure handicapping came from visually running down tables of numbers created by Ainslie and Beyer, making simple comparisons, and *winning bets*. Unfortunately, those days are long gone.

The problems with many of the baselines, particularly homemade ones that attempt to follow the lead of the various writers, are mainly caused by class-par-time charts that incorporate false averages and flyers, and the concomitant overuse of daily track variants derived from the same pars. They are compounded by the wide-spread acceptance of the old axioms that one losing length is equal to 10 feet and 1/5 of a second.

Modern speed and pace handicapping have advanced beyond many of the pitfalls of pars discussed earlier, but the mathematical constants for time and distance of one length are still widely used.

Some handicappers, who loathe numbers entirely, have told me that the differences are trivial: two feet, and a *few hundredths of a second* per length. They may wish to skip the next two paragraphs.

A six furlong race covers 3,960 feet. Ten-foot Clydesdales run 396 lengths from start to finish. Eight-foot Thoroughbreds run 495. Generally it is best when your errors are not magnified by things like *"99"*—the number of lengths difference between Clydesdales and Thoroughbreds running 6 furlongs. At the Kentucky Derby distance of 1 1/4 mile, the difference is *165*.

Many current approaches to speed and pace handicapping use beaten lengths only for the purpose of calculating "feet-behind" at the finish or splits, which are immediately converted to something else, like feet-per-second, so they're quickly out of mind. The difference then, of course, is much smaller. A Clydesdale, beaten by four lengths, is 40 feet behind the winner at the finish. A Thoroughbred is 32. The difference is 8 feet—one length for every four. (Quarter horses and Thoroughbreds are the same length . . . so don't divide by four.)

So hey, *what's a length or two at the finish?*

The Beyer Speed Figures now published in the *Daily Racing Form* do not use 10-foot lengths, and they are far-and-away the best figures ever given universal distribution. The differences you will find between the Beyer figures and those that you create yourself will often be significant enough to produce respectable differences in odds. They will result from differences in the baseline, the difference of using a closer approximation of actual time-per-length instead of the 1/5 second axiom, and in the differential application of track constants and variants.

3-YEAR BEST TIMES FOR SPEED RATINGS

Below are the best times for various distances during the past three years at selected tracks on which the Speed Ratings are based and incorporated into the Speed Index.

Track	5 Fur.	5½ Fur.	6 Fur.	6½ Fur.	7 Fur.	1 Mile	1 Mile,70 Yds.	1¹/₁₆ Miles	1¹/₈ Miles	1¼ Miles
AGUA CALIENTE	:55⁷/₅	1:02⁴/₅	1:07⁴/₅	1:16²/₅	1:23¹/₅	1:34	1:38²/₅	1:41¹/₅	1:47¹/₅	2:02¹/₅
AK-SAR-BEN	:58⁴/₅	1:03¹/₅	1:07¹/₅	—	—	1:38²/₅	1:40¹/₅	1:42⁴/₅	1:48²/₅	—
ALBUQUERQUE	:57¹/₅	1:03¹/₅	1:09¹/₅	1:15¹/₅	1:22⁴/₅	1:36⁴/₅	—	1:44²/₅	1:50	2:04¹/₅
ARLINGTON PARK	:57¹/₅	1:04³/₅	1:09¹/₅	1:16¹/₅	1:22	1:34¹/₅	—	—	1:48²/₅	2:02²/₅
AQUEDUCT	—	—	1:08	1:15¹/₅	1:20²/₅	1:32²/₅	—	—	1:47¹/₅	2:00¹/₅
AQUEDUCT (Inner)	—	—	1:09¹/₅	—	—	—	1:41	1:41¹/₅	1:48²/₅	2:03³/₅
†ASSINIBOIA DOWNS	:57¹/₅	1:03¹/₅	1:09	—	*1:24¹/₅	1:36¹/₅	—	1:41¹/₅	1:49¹/₅	2:05¹/₅
ATLANTIC CITY	:56⁷/₄	1:03¹/₅	1:08¹/₅	1:16	1:21¹/₅	—	—	1:41¹/₄	1:49¹/₄	2:03³/₅
†FERNDALE	:58²/₅	—	1:15	1:19²/₅	1:25²/₅	—	—	1:47	1:53¹/₅	—
FAIR GROUNDS	—	1:04³/₅	1:09¹/₅	—	—	—	—	1:43¹/₅	1:50	2:05⁴/₅
FINGER LAKES	:57¹/₅	1:02⁴/₅	1:09¹/₅	—	—	1:36⁴/₅	1:41²/₅	1:43³/₅	1:50²/₅	2:05¹/₅
FAIR MEADOWS TULSA	—	1:05¹/₅	1:13¹/₅	1:18¹/₅	—	1:39¹/₅	—	1:47²/₅	—	—
FRESNO	:56¹/₅	1:02³/₅	1:08¹/₅	—	—	1:35¹/₅	—	1:41⁴/₅	1:47³/₅	2:03¹/₅
†FONNER PARK	—	—	1:10	1:17	—	1:37	1:40	1:45	1:51⁴/₅	—
FAIRMOUNT PARK	:56⁴/₅	1:03³/₅	1:08⁴/₅	—	—	—	1:39⁴/₅	1:40⁴/₅	1:47³/₅	2:03
FAIRPLEX	—	—	1:09¹/₅	1:15²/₅	1:23²/₅	—	—	1:42²/₅	*1:49¹/₅	—
†GREAT FALLS	1:00	—	—	—	1:25¹/₅	—	1:45³/₅	1:48³/₅	1:57³/₅	—
GOLDEN GATE FIELDS	:57	1:02³/₅	1:07³/₅	—	—	1:33	—	1:39³/₅	1:45	2:01
GULFSTREAM PARK	:59²/₅	—	1:09	—	1:21¹/₅	—	—	1:42¹/₅	1:47²/₅	2:00¹/₅
†GREENWOOD	—	—	—	1:17¹/₅	1:21³/₅	1:34	—	—	—	2:03³/₅
†GRANTS PASS	1:02²/₅	1:06	—	1:16²/₅	—	—	—	1:46³/₅	—	—
GARDEN STATE PARK	:57³/₅	1:03⁴/₅	1:08³/₅	—	—	1:35⁴/₅	1:40²/₅	1:41⁴/₅	1:49²/₅	2:00⁴/₅
†HARBOR PARK	—	1:09²/₅	1:15	1:23⁴/₅	1:28	1:42²/₅	—	—	—	—
HAWTHORNE	:58¹/₅	1:04¹/₅	1:08²/₅	1:14²/5	—	—	1:39¹/₅	1:41³/₅	1:49⁴/₅	2:00¹/₅
HIALEAH PARK	:58¹/₅	1:02³/₅	1:08²/₅	—	1:20³/₅	—	—	1:41⁴/₅	1:47²/₅	1:59²/₅

*(Discussed in Chapter 11.)

Before introducing the baseline for this approach, there are other types of speed "indexes" published by the *Form* for Thoroughbred and quarter horse past performances that are worth knowing about—so that you won't use them. Both are based upon yet another form of baseline.

Thoroughbred Published Speed Ratings

The *Daily Racing Form*'s baseline for Thoroughbred speed indexes is the fastest time at each distance, at each track, over the past three years, which is given the value of 100. To compare a winning horse's time to the baseline, one point for each 1/5 of a second faster or slower than the base is added to or subtracted from 100.

In the major editions of the *Form*, you will find the baseline times featured occasionally in a large table, tucked in around the past performances and the news columns. The table includes all tracks in the United States, Canada, and Mexico, and the times should change occasionally at most tracks, so there is little purpose in reproducing the entire chart (page 124).

The base point time for six furlongs at the first track listed, Agua Caliente (Tijuana, Mexico), is 1:07:4. If a horse wins with a time of 1:09:0 today, he was 1 1/5 second, or 6/5, slower than the base, so 6 is subtracted from 100 for a 94 speed rating. A horse in the same race that finished one length behind the winner will not have a published time but is assumed to be 1/5 of a second slower, or 7/5 off the baseline, so it receives a 93. If the final finisher in the same race was 24 lengths behind the leader, it is 30/5 off the base and receives a rating of 70. The ratings are then combined for various averages and used as described by the *Form* (page 126).

Quarter Horse Speed Indexes

Quarter horse speed indexes are computed and published by the *Daily Racing Form* according to the American Quarter Horse Association's method for determining awards and "Registers of Merit" (ROM's) within the association. Their baseline for comparison is either the *average* of the fastest three races at that track over three years (nine races), or the AQHA "Minimum Standard Times" (if the track has not been in operation three years— or if any *one* of the nine times falls above the minimum). In either case, the baseline is given a value of 100. A horse receives an ROM when it achieves a speed rating of 80 or greater. The ROM means absolutely nothing to bettors but a good deal to members of the AQHA, when it comes time to set breeding fees.

Under this method, if a horse runs 350 yards in 17.885 seconds on a track where the Minimum Standard Time (MST) is used for the 350 yard base

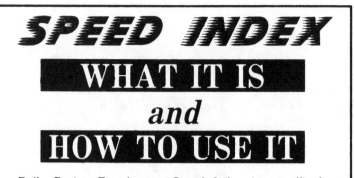

SPEED INDEX

WHAT IT IS
and
HOW TO USE IT

Daily Racing Form's new Speed Index is actually four information-packed tools in one. The Speed Index figures, evaluating every horse's speed record, provide a rapid calculation of speed ability.

The Speed Index par is 0.0. A rating of 0.0 is better than all minus (−) ratings and inferior to all plus (+) ratings. The higher the plus rating the better; the lower the minus rating the worse.

A Speed Index figure of +6 is better than an Index of +2.

On the minus side, a − 2.8 Speed Index is better than a − 5.6 (since − 2.8 is closer to the 0.0 par). A dash within parentheses (−) indicates the horse has no Speed Index for the distance and track surface.

There are four Speed Index categories for each horse:

● The first one (farthest to the left) is computed for the most recent start at today's conditions. Conditions refer to distance (shorter than one mile or one mile or longer) and surface (dirt or grass).

● The second Speed Index number is computed for the three (or fewer) most recent starts at today's conditions. The horse's three most recent Speed Index numbers for the applicable races are totaled and divided by the number of starts (up to three) to reach an average.

● The third Speed Index number is computed from all starts, but only for races with conditions similar to those of today's (to a maximum of 12).

● The fourth Speed Index number is computed from ALL starts, (up to the 12 most recent races), without regard to distance or track surface.

Each of the four Speed Index categories must be regarded separately. The reader should first rank the top three or four horses in the first category, then do the same for the three other categories. Then, by reading the rankings for each horse in each category, a quick determination can be made as to the horse's overall speed capability.

point, it is 0.035 seconds slower, which is one point on the scale, so it receives a 99. If it had run 17.815, it would be 0.035 seconds, or one point, faster than the minimum, and would receive a speed rating of 101.

Actual Time:	17.885	MST Baseline	17.85
MST Baseline:	17.85	Actual Time	17.815
Difference:	+.035	Difference:	–.035
Speed Index:	99	Speed Index:	101

The factor for calculating the quarter horse speed rating is adjusted for both the distance and the weight carried. The standard weight for the computations at all distances is 116 pounds. If a horse carries less than that amount, 1/10 of a second is added to its time for each 4 pounds or fraction of 4 pounds. (There is no adjustment for carrying over the minimum.) So if a horse ran a distance in 17.7 seconds, carrying 111 pounds—5 pounds less than the standard—0.2 seconds would be added to its time before computation of its speed rating, which would then be based on a time of 17.9.

Quarter horse times and speed indexes are calculated in very fine increments and you have to look closely to see the distinctions. It is worth the trouble, however, even if you don't handicap them, since their running parallels the early stages of a Thoroughbred sprint without the unknowns of the flying start.

When you look at the raw times for each distance (Figure 7.1) the AQHA MST's are very close to the average track records for all tracks at the corresponding distances, and both are close to the fastest times ever recorded for quarter horses at the distance, regardless of the track.

EXPLANATION OF QUARTER HORSE SPEED RATINGS

Speed index ratings are based on an average of the three (3) fastest winning times run each year for the immediate past three (3) years for each distance at each track The average of the nine (9) times (to the nearest 01 [1/100] of a second) will represent a speed index rating of 100

In the event that the average time or any of the fastest times included therein are slower than the Minimum Standard (Time[s], the Minimum Standard will be used to compile the average(s) from which the speed index ratings will be computed the following year No horse will be used more than one time in any one year at a particular distance at any one track in calculating the nine fastest times

Horses starting at tracks eligible for recognition by the American Quarter Horse Association for the first time or when a new distance is being run will receive a speed index rating based on the Minimum Standard Times

A speed index point varies according to the distance of the race as follows

04   (four one-hundredths of a second) equals speed index point at 400 and 440 yards

035 – (three and one-half hundreds of a second) equals one speed index point at 350 yards

03 – (three one-hundreds of a second) equals one speed index point at 300 and 330 yards

02 -- (two one-hundredths of a second) equals one speed index point at 220 and 250 yards

The times listed below shall be used to compile speed index ratings at tracks where the average times are slower than the Minimum Standard Time

Distance	220	250	300	330	350	400	440
Minimum Standard Time	11 95	13 35	15 55	16.94	17 85	20 15	22 05

FIGURE 7.1

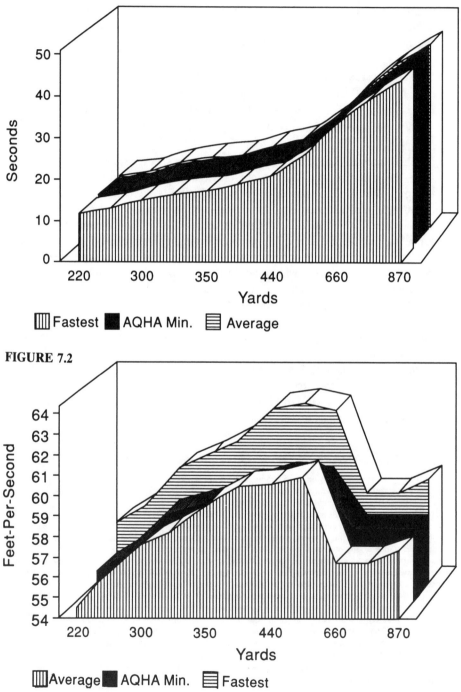

FIGURE 7.2

However, if you look at the same data a little differently (Figure 7.2), in terms of one measure of *speed* (feet per second), the curves start to separate. The fastest recorded times stand apart, above the rest, and there are several things you can observe about the average of records at all tracks and the AQHA minimum standard time. The average is a little slower than the MST at 220 yards and they stay close until the average starts to become a little faster than MST, from 350 to 550, before they both plummet off the edge—around the turn—between 550 and 660 yards.

Since the MST curve is dead level from 660 to 870 yards, it is pretty clear that someone in the AQHA calculated these times from some factor of speed, so that the times for the distances (34.6, 40.36, and 45.6 seconds, respectively) are in exact proportion. The real speeds for 660 and 770 (both for fastest and average) dip below the speed for 870 rather than continuing the downturn of the curve smoothly, as might be expected. This may be explained by the fact that these distances are rarely run, and even more rarely by top-quality horses. Therefore, the AQHA flat-line approach may be a reasonable average, about halfway between the expected and the actual.

Another measure of speed is time per length. In order to calculate it, you first need to decide how long a length is. Visually—as it is called in the races—it is from the tip of the nose to the rear curve of the buttock, not including the tail. There has been some debate over the years about whether 8 or 9 feet should be used. Horses, of course, vary. And so does the same horse, depending upon which phase of a running stride it is in.

After several attempts at measuring and scaling running horses over the years, both in person and in photos, it finally dawned on me to simply *try* 7 and 9 feet in the computations. When you do, you get impossibly fast and slow speeds, respectively, which make it clear that 8 feet is the best average. You are welcome to try this, and—at any time in the handicapping computations in this and following chapters—insert a measure for length that you like better. Maybe there is a quintessential average, like 7.839 or 8.021—but it is not 7.5 or 8.5; they've been tried.

With 8 feet as the average, you can divide any racing distance into lengths. For quarter horse distances in yards, multiply the yards times three for feet, then divide by eight. There are 82.5 lengths in a 220-yard race; 326.25 in an 870.

For Thoroughbred distances, in furlongs, a mile is 5,280 feet, so a furlong (1/8) is 660 feet, divided by 8 = 82.5—the same as a 220-yard race. For weird distances like 1 mile, 70 yards, the answer is: 5,280 + (70 X 3) = 5,490 feet ÷ 8 = 686.25 lengths.

To calculate time per length, divide the time by the number of lengths. For example, the AQHA MST for 220 yards is 11.95. So convert the 220 yards to 82.5 lengths; then divide 11.95 by 82.5 = 0.14484848 . . . *ad infinitum.*

Time per length gives you a different measure of speed, with a graph that is the mirror image of feet per second. The new graph, Figure 7.3, is the same

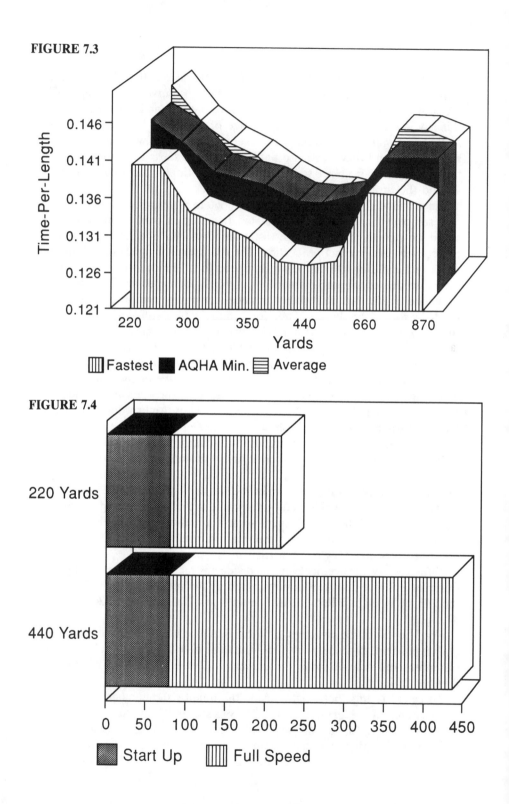

FIGURE 7.3

Time-Per-Length

0.146
0.141
0.136
0.131
0.126
0.121

220   300   350   440   660   870

Yards

▥ Fastest   ■ AQHA Min.   ▤ Average

FIGURE 7.4

220 Yards

440 Yards

0   50   100   150   200   250   300   350   400   450

▨ Start Up   ▥ Full Speed

as Figure 7.2 turned upside down, except you can see the value of how long it takes to run a length along the left axis. You can also see something else, which is apparent in Figure 7.2, but perhaps a little more vivid in terms of time per length.

It takes a quarter horse significantly *longer* to run an average length in a *short* race than it does in a long one. The reason was suggested in chapter 6. In spite of the myth of quarter horses reaching full speed two jumps out of the gate, they do not cross the threshold from inertia drag to propulsion until they are much further down the track. The time it takes varies with class, but the law is universal.

We will see later that the inertia drag/propulsion threshold is probably never reached in a 220-yard race; but if the start-up distance were as little as 80 yards, it would comprise 36 percent of a 220-yard race. The same start-up segment in a 440-yard race would comprise only 18 percent of the distance.

Since, as can be seen in Figures 7.2 and 7.3, a quarter horse can run full blast out to 550 yards (the average track records are actually faster at 550 than 440 yards). There is no downturn of speed due to fatigue in a straight-away race, only longer periods of high speed (Figure 7.4).

Like the Thoroughbred speed ratings, the published quarter horse speed indexes cannot be used for comparison between tracks. And although they don't suffer from the assumption of one length being equal to 1/5 of a second, you may have noticed a problem in the last three graphs that would affect comparison of speeds between distances.

From a handicapping standpoint, the published speed index figures for both Thoroughbreds and quarter horses are a little worse than useless—they can lead to totally false conclusions. At times, they will parallel the speed figures that you create yourself; when they do, you can count on low odds. The strength of speed handicapping arises when the published figures stumble over their baggage, leaving you alone with your numbers.

A Foundation in the Rafters

The baselines for the published Thoroughbred and quarter horse speed ratings are quite different from each other, but are fairly straightforward in comparison with other methods that have tried to take more variables into account.

There are numerous factors that make tracks intrinsically fast or slow, so that the same horse, expending the same effort, will run faster on one than the other. Track speed can also change from day to day and hour to hour, as the wind dries the surface and impedes or speeds the horses. The problem of developing a baseline to account for these differences is compounded by the fact that different tracks draw different qualities of horses as a result of purse money and the prestige of the meeting.

Individual horses can also skew the averages and the records, for example, when a quarter horse like Junior Meyers shows up at a place like La Mesa Park in 1969 through '71. Junior Meyers created several world records at La Mesa; his 11.62 at 220 and 13.0 at 250 still hold. But he was not alone; numerous world records have come from La Mesa Park in Raton, New Mexico. La Mesa is a *fast* track. Figure 7.5 gives an idea how fast in comparison with the average track records of all quarter horse tracks.

FIGURE 7.5

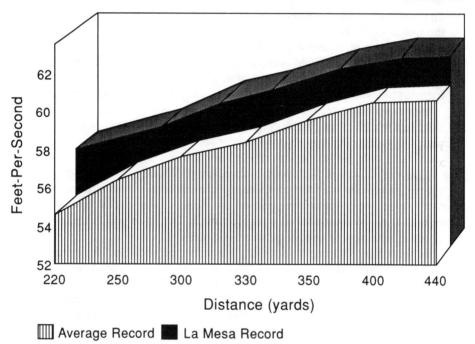

Since there are so many sources of variation, there are a number of approaches that can be used to establish a baseline for comparison of times between tracks and at various distances. The most widely used are parallel class par times. Probably the next most widely used are methods similar to those used by the *Form*, which the handicapper compiles himself using some average of the past year's times (broken down by something other than class) rather than the fastest time of the past three years, and for *each distance* rather than lumped into "long" and "short."

The purpose of a baseline is to establish a standard for comparison. In my view the ideal baseline is the ultimate speed that could be achieved by the ultimate horse, given the physical and mechanical properties of a track. You can figure down from there, while with a midpoint or average you have to figure in both directions.

This is partially a matter of taste, but also one of theory. Since horses are limited by their own physiology and the laws of physics, there is a speed ceiling for every racing distance—and every point in between. Just like human runners, modern horses have been "pushing the envelope," but the advances have become smaller and smaller as they approach the limits.

It is likely that new racing surfaces will have more profound effects on horse longevity than on speed, since there is a limit to how fast a horse can move its legs before disaster sets in. Under the present conditions, which balance between speed and safety, the ultimate physiological potential for speed is almost entirely written.

Rather than have half a dozen baselines, one for each track that you follow, it is far less prone to introduced error, and a lot easier, to have a single baseline—for *horse racing* in general—and then apply variables to account for "track constants" and "race variants."

Even if you don't have something as obvious as a two-turn, "short" race, you may find clues in the times that you analyze that suggest that constants and variants are needed. For example, on a one-mile oval, if you find that first-quarter times from the six-and-a-half- and seven-furlong chute are consistently, proportionately slower than times for races started on the oval, you may want to customize the data you apply to your baseline to account for a slow chute. We will see how to make such refinements later.

If you handicap quarter horses, you will need two baselines, because quarter horse and Thoroughbred distances and times don't mix. The breeds do mix in 870- and 1,000-yard races, but once Thoroughbreds have run at these distances, their past performances are recorded in the quarter horse format.

The Quarter Horse Baseline

The quarter horse speed curve is nonlinear and insolvable, but, luckily, the existing times for the most hotly contested distances sit very close to the edge of the envelope. The baseline, therefore, is ready-made.

Time per length will be the primary measure of speed used in this approach to speed handicapping, since it has some very useful characteristics. The baseline for quarter horses will be the fastest times ever run, viewed in terms of time per length (Figure 7.6).

The world records can be expected to change over time, but since the curve is nonlinear, it is best to revise them periodically and let the horses solve the equation. The changes are usually minute, except where the optimum hasn't been achieved. In 1987, Go Lika Rocket tied Junior Meyers' 1971 record for 250 yards by running the distance in 13 seconds flat at Helena Downs.

Since 250 yards is a hotly contested distance for futurity hopefuls, and the 13.0 time has held for twenty years, the flatness in speed between 220 and 250 yards (Figure 7.6) is probably "real," suggesting that the full shift from

FIGURE 7.6

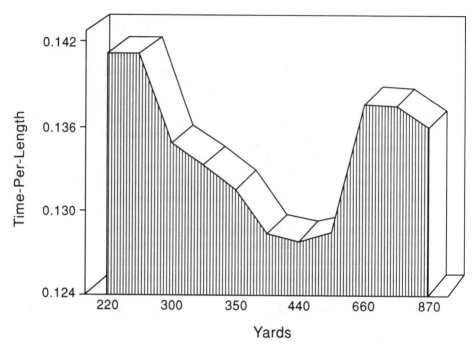

inertia drag to propulsion occurs between 250 and 300 yards—much farther down the track than intuition would suggest.

Real Speed

A better picture of the potential for speed at racing distances can be achieved by looking at smaller segments of distance. For example, there are 11.25 lengths between the distances of 220 and 250 yards, so the time per length of the hypothetical superhorse running at world record time between those two points would be 0.1226. If the same horse continued between 350 and 400 yards, there would be 18.75 lengths covered in 1.97 seconds, which is a time per length of 0.105.

This time per length is approximately *one-half* the 1/5-second axiom (0.2) for Thoroughbreds—the horses are running *twice* as fast.

If chaos ensues from the minuscule changes of the butterfly effect, what do you suppose happens when you *begin* with a 50 percent error? For one thing, you lose bets.

To view this different picture of speed, Figure 7.7 traces the speed, in feet per second, of a hypothetical horse traveling at world record speed *between* the quarter horse distances.

This curve suggests that the anaerobic/aerobic threshold lies between 330

FIGURE 7.7

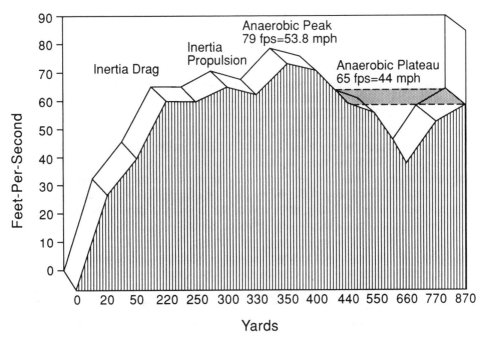

and 350 yards, where an almost incredible anaerobic peak speed of 79 feet per second—or *53.8 miles per hour*—can be achieved. This speed may be maintained for just a few strides, but it is consistent with the earlier observation that the inertia drag/propulsion threshold lies between 250 and 300 yards, since it would be shortly after the threshold is passed and before anaerobic energy degrades when the peak speed could be reached. The horse first breaks loose from drag, then raises propulsion to its full potential using anaerobic energy, then shifts to aerobic running.

The world record speeds for 440 and 870 yards are almost precisely the same. Part of the reason for the extreme dip in speed between 660 and 770 yards, aside from the fact that the 770 distance is run infrequently, is an artifact of the math, which also accentuates the dips and peaks between 220 and 350 yards and drags down the speed for 550—which would be at least equal to 440 and 870 if 660 were not so slow. Mathematicians will see the problem, but it is not crucial to the point that if the artificial dip is ignored, there appears to be a plateau after the anaerobic peak. This may be a period during the gradient shift from anaerobic to aerobic exercise, when horses can run at an optimum level—which happens to be about 65 feet per second, or about 44 miles per hour—before the shift to aerobic exercise and the chemical and physiological effects of fatigue begin the steady reduction of speed.

Figure 7.8 is free of the mathematical skewing and displays speed in feet per second for quarter horse and Thoroughbred distances in accurate proportions.

This graph demonstrates the drastic acceleration against inertia in the start-up distance; the continuing acceleration from 220 yards past the anaerobic peak at 330 to 350 yards, to a plateau of anaerobic performance between 400 and 550 yards for quarter horses; then a plateau of optimal anaerobic/aerobic performance between 660 and 1,000 yards/4 furlongs, which is shared by very close speeds for both quarter horses and Thoroughbreds. At 5 furlongs there is another minor peak, analogous to the middle quarter horse distances, where the start-up curve is dampened by prolonged optimal aerobic speed, followed by another, sloping plateau of entropy from 5.5 furlongs to 7 furlongs, after which, the downward slope (slowing) of the line increases in another linear segment. So the original linear relationship of the speed of a running horse over distance (Figure 6.1) is actually composed of one major and at least four minor nonlinear components, and four internally linear segments, directly tied to laws of physics and the physiological changes within the running horse.

The records that form the baseline for the handicapping examples used in this book will change over time, and you may want to revise them—with caution, as we will see—in the future. Thoroughbred world records are

FIGURE 7.8

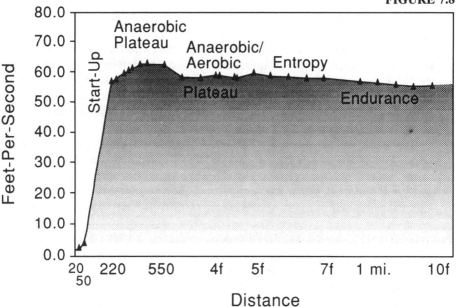

published annually by the *Daily Racing Form*, in *The American Racing Manual*. Quarter horse world records are published in the March, annual review issue of *The Quarter Racing Journal* of the American Quarter Horse Association.

The current quarter horse world record speeds for each distance and the corresponding basepoints are:

Quarter Horse World Record Times and Speeds

	Time	Lengths	Time-Per-Length
220 yards:	11.62	82.5	.1408
250 yards:	12.92	93.75	.1378
300 yards:	15.06	112.5	.1339
330 yards:	16.43	123.75	.1328
350 yards:	17.19	131.25	.1310
400 yards:	19.18	150	.1279
440 yards:	21.02	165	.1274
550 yards:	26.33	206.25	.1277
660 yards:	32.67	247.5	.1320
770 yards:	39.53	288.75	.1369
870 yards:	43.99	326.25	.1348
1000 yards:	51.81	375	.1382

The Thoroughbred Baseline

Thoroughbred record times have an important taming characteristic, but it must be used with care. While quarter horse times over distance create a nonlinear measure of *acceleration*, Thoroughbred times present an almost-perfect linear measure of *entropy*. The Thoroughbred "curve" is very close to flat, and although each race will include a start-up period similar to the bottom of the quarter horse curve, part of it is absorbed by the flying start, and the times for distances beyond about 4 1/2 furlongs become almost a pure gradient of aerobic exercise and entropy—when viewed from afar.

Since Thoroughbred times over distance are "linear," the ultimate-horse baseline provides not only a nearly perfect transition of relationships of time and distance at the top of the scale, *it is solvable*. It has a short, simple equation into which you can plug values and get an answer with a high degree of testable certainty that you are right.

As an example of how the graph equation works, there is no world record for 7 1/2 furlongs on the dirt, although there is an American record of 1:26:4.

FIGURE 7.9: Y = –5.5846 + 12.292X; CORRELATION COEFFICIENT = .9994

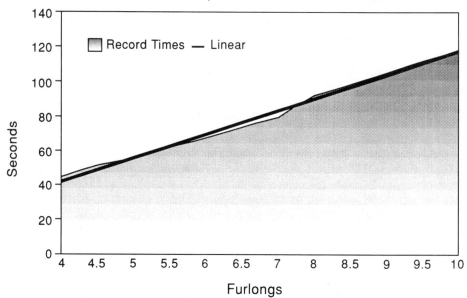

With a correlation coefficient of .9994, you can plug 7.5 into the equation for the line in Figure 7.9 and be 99.94 percent certain that the world record for the distance should be 86.6 seconds, or 1:26:3.

Ninety-nine point nine percent is pretty certain when viewing the whole curve, but it can be deceiving when you look closely at the segments. The Thoroughbred curve can be treated as linear for most purposes, but it is actually only linear between nonlinear bumps, which occur at each progressive threshold.

The 7.5-furlong distance lies within the nonlinear ripple created by the internal sprint/endurance threshold. When you view speed between distances, time per length drops significantly between 7 and 8 furlongs. This supports the idea that the physiological outer limits of a sprint, and the threshold for the shift from aerobic speed to endurance capacity, is right around 6 1/2 to 7 furlongs.

There is another interesting property of the linear relationship, which rides over the humps. While instantaneous speed (the speed that a horse is traveling at a particular instant) is insolvable on the quarter horse curve, it cannot only be solved in a linear equation, it is constant—and it is equal to the slope of the line. The slope of this line is 12.2924 (seconds per furlong), which translates to a hair under 0.15 seconds per length, or 36.6 miles per hour, which is virtually identical to the optimum aerobic level identified at the longer quarter horse distances (not the anaerobic/aerobic plateau found between distances, but that shown earlier in Figure 6.3).

The shortest Thoroughbred distances are the tail end of a *nonlinear* equation, resembling the quarter horse curve, which doesn't stabilize until five furlongs are run.

Optimum aerobic performance can be carried out to 10 furlongs (the "classic" distance of 1 1/4 miles), where it begins to taper off and then slopes continually toward 2 miles and beyond. This suggests a fourth threshold in Thoroughbred races (inertia, anaerobic, aerobic, endurance), where the offspring of Solid and Professional *chefs de race* take over.

Thoroughbred world records, for at least the most commonly run distances, are fairly well established. When a distance such as 4 1/2 furlongs shows eight co-record holders, it suggests that the time (50:2) is close to the wall for the distance. Since 1987 three co-record holders have been added at this distance (two at the brand-new and apparently fast San Juan Downs, New Mexico), but none have been able to beat the time, which has stood for nearly twenty-five years.

Like La Mesa in the quarter horse world, several tracks have been disproportionately represented in the American and world records for Thoroughbreds, suggesting that they are inherently fast. At the shortest distances, of 2 to 4 furlongs, the records are held in Mexico and Canada, where these distances are more commonly run than in the United States. At the more common American sprint distances, 4 1/2 to 7 furlongs, there are eight distances, with eighteen co-record holders. *Six* were set at Turf Paradise in Phoenix, Arizona; four at Longacres (three have been recently surpassed, leaving only the 55:1 for Chinook Pass at 5 furlongs); and two (co-records at 7 furlongs) at Hollywood Park, California.

At the more commonly run route distances, the scene of the dirt records changes to tracks like Saratoga, Belmont, and Santa Anita, and the horses' names become more prominent, with the likes of Dr. Fager, Riva Ridge, Spectacular Bid, Man o' War, and Secretariat.

The speed of a sprint race is much more dependent upon the speed of the track than the longer distance races, which the great, "classic" horses run. To get an idea of just how fast tracks can be, Chinook Pass's fastest 6-furlong time in his 1983 championship sprinting year was 1:08:3, at Del Mar. That same year, the 6-furlong world record was jointly held, one at Turf Paradise and one at Longacres—in the then incredible time of 1:07:1—by two six-year-olds named Grey Papa and Petro D. Jay.

The time of 1:07:1 stood as "incredible" until 1987, when Zany Tactics redefined the word by running 6 furlongs in 1:06:4. Two guesses where, and it wasn't Longacres.

Zany Tactics was a *very* fast horse, who died too young of a heart attack after a gallop. He was so fast that his speed, in combination with the surface at Turf Paradise, creates a flier, which would distort all 6-furlong speeds (toward slow) when compared to speeds at neighboring distances.

Unfortunately, the linear equation is no help at all in establishing a more reasonable base time. The 6-furlong distance lies in a nonlinear segment of the line where physiological factors are working, and numerous horses have shown that they can run faster than the time that would be predicted, of only 1:08:1. Since the base point can't be solved, it has to be tested against real data, and I have found that the old record of 1:07:1 holds.

If you are handicapping at Turf Paradise, Longacres, or other tracks with disproportionately fast surfaces (or at tracks where horses move in from faster ones), you might seriously consider devising track constants, as will be demonstrated in chapters 9 and 11.

The baseline that we will use is comprised of the following speeds:

Thoroughbred Base Points

Distance	Time	Lengths	Time-Per-Length
4 furlongs	44.2	330	.134
4.5 furlongs	50.4	371.25	.1357
5 furlongs	55.2	412.5	.1338
5.5 furlongs	61.4	453.75	.1353
†6 furlongs	67.2	495	.1358
6.5 furlongs	73.6	536.25	.1372
7 furlongs	79.4	577.5	.1375
8 furlongs	92.2	660	.1397
††8.182 furlongs	95.0	675	.1407
††8.318 furlongs	96.7	686.25	.1409
*8.5 furlongs	98.4	701.25	.1403
*9 furlongs	105.0	742.5	.1414
*9.5 furlongs	112.4	783.75	.1434
*10 furlongs	117.8	825	.1428

†See text
††1m 40yds and 1m 70yds extrapolated times
*American Dirt Course Record

With this baseline, you can get away with murder. Even though handicapping can be considerably improved with the addition of track constants and (in some cases) race variants, a weekend handicapper can get by at most tracks with conservative betting and this ultimate-horse baseline alone.

8

PARALLEL SPEED

Happy Idiot

DAVIS R G   **117**

Own.—Sunflower Farms

Ch. g. 5, by Genuine Guy—Lucky Jackie, by Piaster
Br.—Sunflower Farms (Cal)
Tr.—Jenda Charles J $40,000
Lifetime 21 6 · $82,825

											1990	5 2 1 1		$31,650
											1989	11 2 2 1		$32,775
											Turf	2 0 0 0		$1,725

15Apr90-2SA 6f :21⁴ :45 1:10⁴ft 4½ 118 4½ ⁵½ 3² 4³½   40000 79-18 FrontlineFbl,OhDtFox,‡RightRuddr 8
    15Apr90—Placed third through disqualification; Broke in, bum...
11Mar90-3GG 6f :22 :44³ 1:09³gd *2½ 119 1½ 1² 1¹ 1hd Hummel C R² 40000 90-17 HppyIdiot,IslndDyBrek,DytimBrgin 6
25Feb90-7GG 6f :21³ :44 1:09 ft 5½ 117 3¹½ 3¹½ 1½ 1³ Kaenel J L⁵ 32000 93-13 Happy Idiot, Craig Ronald, Stogie 9
    25Feb90—Bumped start
31Jan90-7GG 6f :22 :45 1:10 gd 4½ 117 43½ 42½ 53½ 43 Kaenel J L⁶ 32000 85-14 GoToThWndw,DytmBrgn,SndncSqr 8
13Jan90-1BM 6f :22 :45¹ 1:11²sy *2½ 117 2¹ 2½ 1hd 2² Kaenel J L⁴ 25000 81-17 GoToThWindow,HppyIdiot,ZrMoro ⅚
16Dec89-9BM 6f :22 :44³ 1:09²ft 2½ 117 2³ 2² 2² 2¾ Kaenel J L⁴ 25000 94-08 SundncSqur,HppyIdiot,DytimBrgin 8
19Nov89-8BM 6f :22² :45 1:09²ft *2½ 119 2½ 2hd 1hd 2hd Kaenel J L⁹ 25000 95-09 Vancelot,HppyIdiot,SundnceSqure 10
25Oct89-8BM 6f :22³ :45¹ 1:09¹ft *2-3 119 1½ 1hd 2½ 44½ Kaenel J L¹ 40000 91-11 BayIndian,DaytimeBargain,ZrMoro 5
    25Oct89—Bumped start
28Sep89-8BM 6f :22 :44³ 1:09 ft *6-5 117 3³ 3¹½ 1½ 1¹½ Kaenel J L⁵ Aw18000 94-14 HppyIdot,DlghtflDoctor,DytmBrgn 5
30Aug89-8BM 6f :21⁴ :44 1:08²ft 6½ 117 1² 1¹½ 1² 1⁴ Hummel C R¹ Aw17000 97-15 Happy Idiot, Damaskim,EagleLeash 5
   Speed Index: Last Race: -3.0   3–Race Avg.: +3.3   10–Race Avg.: +3.5   **Overall Avg.: +3.5**
May 11 Hol 4f ft :49¹ H   ●May 1 SA 4f ft :46 H   ●Apr 25 SA 4f ft :47 H   Apr 11 GG 4f ft :48⁴ H

Selecting Past Performances

Happy Idiot is a pretty good journeyman racehorse. At the age of five, he has run in twenty-one races, won six, placed in the money twelve times for a 57 percent average, and winnings of $82,825. Seventeen of his twenty-one races were run in 1989 and '90 as a four- and five-year-old, so he was apparently judiciously raced at two and three. We don't know what classes of races he ran in before the ten past performances listed, but the two earliest are $17,000 and $18,000 allowance races at Bay Meadows, and he won both in very good times: 1:08:2 and 1:09 flat at 6 furlongs. He was then moved into a $40,000 claiming race. Rather than a step down in racing class, from allowance to claiming, this was a step up in purse money. He finished out of the money, but ran credibly.

The only question in his management comes in the next three races, where he was dropped to a $25,000 claimer. You might question the other trainers at Bay Meadows too, because at $25,000, they may have missed a bargain. He placed in the money in all of his $25,000 races, then moved to Golden Gate Fields, where he stepped up to $32,000 and ran his worst race so far, which was still not bad, at a new track on less than a fast surface. Then he nailed a $32,000 claiming race at what seems to be his fast track, 6-furlong time, of 1:09 flat. He stepped up to $40,000 again and won it wire to wire. He moved to Santa Anita and ran his first race there in a very similar fashion to his first race at Golden Gate (although this time he received third money due to the disqualification of Right Rudder). These past performances are listed in preparation for his entry in a 6-furlong, $40,000 claiming race at Hollywood Park, with a purse of $23,000.

Happy Idiot is a pretty likable horse. You would almost have to give him a chance in this race without even looking at the other horses, unless all of the rest regularly run in the 1:08s, which would be highly unlikely. He always puts in a good effort, and he is running at his distance and in his class—even though his owners apparently didn't think so for a while. Since he occasionally wins races, you can see the times that he is capable of running directly in the *Form*.

But his best time of 1:08:2 was a full season and three tracks ago. After his coming race, it will drop off the bottom of his ten listed past performances, so you won't even know it existed unless you keep long-term records on all of the horses in the meet. While some people keep such records for personal interest, there is no handicapping reason to do so.

The theory of speed handicapping is that the fastest horses most often win races and that final times are the best component measure of speed. The *method* of speed handicapping is to determine the *current* speed potential of each horse in the race, to predict where they should be in relation to each other at the finish line—*if* each runs up to its potential.

In earlier chapters we covered some of the factors that affect a horse's potential for speed, and you may already know or have guessed some of the laws speed handicappers impose upon themselves in selecting past performances as representative of a particular horse's potential. Obviously, the best times for comparison are those recorded at the same distance, under the same track condition, on the same track, and—you could quickly add—with the same jockey, under the same weight, with the same rate of flow from the spigots on the water truck, and the same ambient air density. The first and most time-honored law is to simply limit all comparisons to fast tacks.

We will cover some of the methods of amending the laws by addressing some of the factors that create them, such as track constants and track variants. However, we won't replace them with other laws, but rather with approaches that you can use, if you choose, to refine your methods, specifically for the tracks that you follow.

With the Happy Idiot past performances above, it doesn't take any calculation at all to see that this horse's potential lies right around the 1:09+ range. If you look closely at his most recent past performance at Santa Anita, you will see that he was running in a tight pack in a quick 21:4 quarter-mile. He was fourth, and yet only three-fourths of a length behind the leader. The pack then slowed down to make the half mile in 45 flat, where he remained third, by only half a length.

With a second lost off some of his earlier half-mile paces of 44 flat, the leader's race must have progressed at a pretty steady pace from the half to finish at 1:10:4—about a second slower, overall, than Happy Idiot's usual capabilities. It is pretty easy to see that three or four good speed horses burned each other up in the fight from the gates to the half-mile pole.

Happy Idiot put in a good race, in spite of the poor losing time, and has had two workouts since, one at Santa Anita and one after moving to Hollywood Park, which suggest he didn't cripple himself in the process. I would forgive him the embarrassment of coming in 3 1/4 lengths behind a 1:10:4 at a new track and look to previous races for a better estimate of his capabilities. In his case, it presents a bit of a dilemma because his second previous race was on a "good" track, where he won in 1:09:3—which is a very decent time, for him, on a less-than-fast track. I would break the first law and take it.

This is a rule that I break occasionally, when I feel there is good reason. Happy Idiot is a journeyman, but his two worst races each came after a move to a new track. He has moved again and is starting at Hollywood Park for the first time today. If Happy Idiot stays sound, his potential for speed is right around 1:09 flat, and he will probably run that time again—but not today. On the other hand, he is unlikely to run 1:10:4+ like he did in his last race, which was his slowest time to date. Happy Idiot's capability—which is what we want to compare with the other horses entered in the race—is in the neighborhood of 1:09:2 or :3. There are plenty of clues available in his winning past performances, which can be readily seen without calculation. Most horses aren't so convenient.

When the race was run, he finished second, in about 1:09:3 behind the winner's 1:09:1, and paid $6.00 to place and $44 in the exacta.

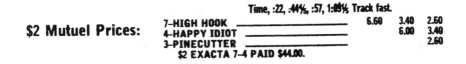

Time, :22, :44⅘, :57, 1:09½ Track fast.

$2 Mutuel Prices:				
7-HIGH HOOK		6.60	3.40	2.60
4-HAPPY IDIOT			6.00	3.40
3-PINECUTTER				2.60
$2 EXACTA 7-4 PAID $44.00.				

In practice, you will rarely have or be willing to spend the time to run down a horse's past performance in the detail above, but rather will do it in a few seconds and glances, first in selecting the past performance times for speed calculations and *again* when you have the results for analysis.

Rather than start with rigid laws and a roaring example of the success of some "system" of picking a winner at huge odds, it is more realistic to show an example of a horse that would appear with several others in the analysis of a race and that would be overrated or underrated, if strict rules were followed.

In general, it is best to compare recent performances on fast tracks. And never, never break the fundamental laws—like accepting offtrack conditions or subjectively changing a horse's time—*unless you have very good reason.* If you believe in it, do it—and bet at whatever level your belief dictates. Horse racing is a great testing ground for ideas. Answers are quick and resounding.

It would be great if there were rules for breaking the laws, but there aren't. For example, one might be: Never go back several months in a horse's past performances to pick up a fast one if the horse has been racing every week in the meantime with poorer showings. It is a lot safer to go back a couple of months with a higher-class horse that runs only on a monthly schedule, if you see a strong reason why that time should be representative. Hopefully, even if your experience with horse racing is limited to reading the earlier chapters of this book, you should be able to think of a dozen reasons why either side of this law wouldn't hold. When you apply that reasoning to the analysis of each horse in a race, it is called handicapping.

Calculating Thoroughbred Time

Duck Butter is a pretty good horse, too. He is a four-year-old and has won $109,460 on the claiming and allowance circuit by placing in the money in fifteen of his twenty-six races. He is a son of Duck Dance (who also stands to quarter horse mares and produced Merganser, a winner of the All-American Futurity). Duck Butter is entered today in a 7-furlong claiming race at a $25,000 price. His past performances show only one previous 7-furlong race, which he lost by 8 3/4 lengths to So Private, who ran a 1:22:4. What was Duck Butter's time?

If one length were equal to 1/5 of a second, his time would be the winner's (1:22:4) plus 9/5 (rounded), or 0:01:4, which equals 1:24:3.

Duck Butter						B. c. 4, by Duck Dance—Cinderella's Sister, by In Reality					
						Br.—Hobeau Farm Inc (Fla)		1990 8 2 2 1			$44,620
Own.—Evans R M			**1107**			Tr.—Prainito M	$25,000	1989 11 2 3 2			$39,460
						Lifetime 26 6 6 3 $109,460					
30Mar90-3Aqu	6f :221 :453 1:102sy	4½ 119	33½ 33½ 58 613¾	Smith M E 2 Aw31000 74-19 Paul's Way, Scuba, CourageousTry 7
19Mar90-7Aqu	7f :223 :452 1:224ft	*3½ 1145	2½ 2hd 73 78¾	Toscano P R 6 Aw31000 79-16 So Private, Termez, Slick Jack 8
8Mar90-6Aqu	6f ⊡:223 :454 1:112ft	8 1175	2¹ 1hd 1½ 2no	Toscano P R 3 Aw31000 89-15 AccipterStep,DuckButtr,DrrlWltrip 8
21Feb90-7Aqu	6f ⊡:222 :452 1:104ft	7½ 1107	1¹ 11½ 1³ 1nk	Toscano P R 5 Aw30000 92-09 Duck Butter, SoPrivate,EvenFaster 9
10Feb90-4Aqu	6f ⊡:223 :47 1:12 m *6-5 1107		1hd 1hd 2½ 36	Toscano P R 3 Aw30000 80-15 Fancy Raja, Sam Sam, Duck Butter 7
10Feb90— Brushed				
31Jan90-7Aqu	6f ⊡:221 :45 1:10 ft	14 1107	3¹ 3nk 2½ 23½	Toscano P R 6 Aw30000 92-07 SovereignSmoke,DuckButtr.Tlwtch 9
22Jan90-5Aqu	6f ⊡:222 :46 1:122gd	5½ 1107	1¹ 11½ 12½ 12	Toscano P R 6 17500 84-16 Duck Butter,FastTrick,WillCojack 10
8Jan90-5Aqu	6f ⊡:223 :461 1:12 ft	8¼ 119	41½ 53¾ 56 89½	Smith M E 2 25000 76-15 CountOnRomo,DsrtDvl,KngdomKy 12
Speed Index: Last Race: -7.0		3–Race Avg.: -2.6	8–Race Avg.: -2.7	Overall Avg.: -2.7
●May 12 Aqu 6f ft 1:133 H		May 3 Aqu 4f ft :492 B	●Apr 10 Aqu 4f ft :463 H	●Mar 26 Aqu 4f ft :464 H

There is another way to look at this. The winner, So Private, ran the 577.5 lengths of the 7-furlong race with an average time per length of 0.143. You arrive at that figure by converting 1:22:4 to 82.8 seconds and dividing by 577.5 lengths. Duck Butter finished 8 3/4 lengths back, so his finish time is approximately the winner's time, plus 8.75 x 0.143. His time is 82.8 + 1.25 = 84.05 seconds, or, converting back to the traditional format: 1:24 flat.

This result is 3 lengths different from the result of the rule of thumb—using the rule—or *4 lengths,* by using the closer estimate of a length being worth 0.143 in *this race.* By any measure, Duck Butter ran faster than the traditional method would suggest.

There is a pitfall in this method of calculation that you need to be aware of from the start. If a horse is far off the pace of the race, the winner's average time per length—which is the only one you have to work with from the *Form*—is not going to be an approximation of this horse's. Even though Duck Butter was dropping back at the finish, he was not far off the pace, and his average time per length will be *very* close to So Private's. The problem occasionally becomes important when you are comparing past performances from an entire racing field, but only under unusual circumstances. If a horse ran very far behind a blazing speed winner—say 24 lengths behind a 6-furlong time of 1:08:1—its time will be inflated in comparison with the times of winners that have won with slower times. This is usually not a serious problem, since 15- to 30-length losses would be highly suspect for speed analysis anyway.

In my own handicapping I occasionally penalize a horse a fifth of a second or more in the calculations if I am using a loss by a significant distance in comparison with times of much closer finishers or winners. Which is a euphemistic way of saying I sometimes break the cardinal law and *change* a horse's time to suit what I believe—and what I know about the mathematical method. It's my money.

Since yours is what this is about, I would suggest that you don't compare losing efforts beyond about 10 lengths to closer finishers or winners until you are very familiar with the process. If this means passing a bet on a race, pass it. Or work with the figures—see where the horse stands with his "actual" figure and what happens if you penalize it a fifth, or a fraction. If it gives you what you believe is a clear picture, test it on paper, or with a cautious bet.

On the other hand, you will often run across races where all of the past performances are in the dismal range, and in these you can generally get away with using the speed calculation without adjustment. All of the times will just look slightly better than they really are. These types of races show up quite often in twin trifecta and other exotic slots with, for example, a field of older maiden claimers who have never come within 25 lengths of a winner in their lives. The whole reason, of course, is that they are very tough to handicap. Even though they may be the bottom of the social order of racehorses at the track, the outcome may be more a matter of "class" than in the higher ranks. Sometimes speed plays a primary role; sometimes it doesn't. I often pass on these races simply because they take far too much time to handicap when there are five or six better races to study—and because only about one in five or six races of this type will produce an opinion strong enough to put money on. When they do, they usually produce good odds and excellent quinella and exacta payoffs. I have met a few people who semispecialize in them, but they can be frustrating and *costly* if you are just starting out. If they interest you, and you have a real compulsion for accuracy, you may want to figure out a sliding scale for adjusting the time per length for increasing losing distances, but it really isn't necessary. The time is better spent handicapping.

Thoroughbred Parallel Speed

Very often you will be faced with a horse like Duck Butter, who is entered at a distance that he has run only once or never before in his life. In Duck Butter's case, I would not be satisfied with a figure from one losing 7-furlong effort and would want a second opinion. Unfortunately, all of his other listed races are at 6 furlongs. I would forgive him the poor 13 3/4 length-back finish in his last sloppy race, but the time is useless. (Note that, as discussed earlier, a leader's time on certain sloppy tracks may be as fast or faster than his time on a dry one; this time is not dismissed solely because of the sloppy conditions, but because once a horse gets caught behind a rooster tail of mud, there is a little guy on his back who probably agrees there will be better days in the future.) In spite of his somewhat quicker, earlier times, I would not give him much better than his 1:11:2 performance in his third-last race, which he lost by a nose. That selects a past performance, but it is at 6 furlongs, and I want to know what it would translate to at 7.

The *Daily Racing Form*'s speed index method views all sprints together and all routes together and does not allow comparison of times at different distances within the broad categories. Any small advantage over the information available to the crowd magnifies itself in handicapping—and the advantage of being able to compare speeds at specific distances is a huge one. This is why class-based, parallel-speed charts have been an advantage to those who have used them, even though most of them are fundamentally shaky in origin. They have just enough basis in fact that the butterfly effect is dampened.

The central flaw of speed handicapping has been that it analyzes time, not speed, which is a function of *distance over time*. We have set time per length as the baseline for comparison of speed at sprint distances. You can set a value for the baseline at any level you like, but I prefer to use 1,000, since it provides the necessary level of distinction, which would require a decimal point if you use 100.

You can do the following calculations with a pencil and paper or with a $3 calculator; but they are vastly less tedious with a programmable calculator or computer, which will do the same thing over and over again. All you have to do then is enter the numbers. The process will be automated in the next chapter, and a functional, albeit inelegant, computer program in BASIC language is listed in the appendix.

For Thoroughbreds, after you have selected the past performances you want to compare, the first step is to convert the "minutes-seconds-fifths" time format of the *Form* to decimal seconds. This is one step that is easier to do at a glance than to program for a computer, but once programmed, it's a breeze. Without a computer, you just have to remember to mentally convert the fifths of seconds to multiples of 0.2.

If a time for 5 furlongs is published in the *Form* as 59:2, the decimal equivalent is 59.4. Times over a minute, such as 1:23:2 are: 60 + 23 + .4, or 83.4. If the horse was a winner in this past performance, you are through with this part. If not a winner, use the method shown earlier to approximate the time of the losing effort: first, calculate the winner's time per length by dividing the decimal time, 83.4, by the lengths in the 7-furlong race, which is 577.5, from the earlier table. The result is 0.1444. In this case, if the horse was 4 1/2 lengths behind the winner's time, the 4 1/2 length losing effort was 4.5 * 0.1444 = 0.65 seconds slower. (The asterisk indicates multiplication.) Add 0.65 to 83.4 and you have a pretty close approximation of this horse's losing time of 84.05 seconds.

It is still "time," so convert to speed by dividing it by the lengths of the race (84.05 ÷ 577.5) and this horse's speed was approximately 0.1455 (seconds per length).

The baseline speed for 7 furlongs is 0.1375, which has an arbitrary value of 1,000. To get a comparative value for 0.1455, you simply divide the baseline speed, 0.1375, by the actual speed, 0.1455, multiply by a thousand, and, if necessary, round to a whole digit:

$$0.1375 \div 0.1455 = 0.945$$
$$0.945 \times 1,000 = 945$$

As you can see, what you are doing is asking the question "What percentage of the speed ceiling for this distance did this horse run?" In this case, it was 94.5 percent. In speed-handicapper parlance, this horse "ran a 945."

Viewed this way, it will be interesting to note when you begin calculating real times that the racing speed range, even for maiden claimers, seldom drops below 90 percent of the superhorse. A figure in the 800's is extremely poor. A horse can be 90 percent as fast as Secretariat or Dr. Fager and never win a race.

The decimal equivalents for lengths back are shown in Figure 8.1. The fine distinctions of 0.15 for a head and 0.06 for a nose are approximations, since you will never know unless you have the photo whether the nose or

Decimal Lengths

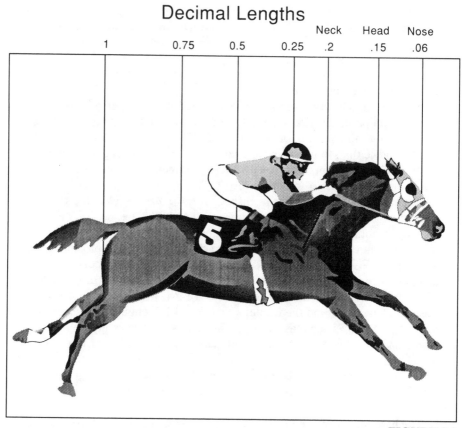

| 1 | 0.75 | 0.5 | 0.25 | Neck .2 | Head .15 | Nose .06 |

FIGURE 8.1

head was "long" or "short." This is true of every lengths-back call and injects some noise into every Thoroughbred calculation. All you are doing with the nose or head fractions is docking a horse for losing, so there is room for art in choosing the decimal.

Obviously, the strongest use of speed figures occurs when you are lucky enough to have past performances for comparison from the same distance that is to be run. The next is when you are comparing distances that are closely allied on the physiological scales that we have discussed. Sprinters will frequently move up and down in distance, from 5 1/2 furlongs to 6, to 7, and back. Because of individual abilities to maintain aerobic levels, the closest comparisons are always best.

When selecting past performances for analysis, remember that the objective is not to find out what a horse *could* run, if it duplicated the best performance of its life. The objective is to determine what a horse *should* run, given its demonstrated ability—and to consider the secondary factors that we have covered, which include track constants and variants (which can be applied mathematically), and class, condition, race placement, post position, and all of the other "noise" factors that you will probably apply subjectively. As a result, I often use two, and sometimes three, past performances for comparison.

When you find a horse that, for example, ran a 963 and a 967 at 5.5 furlongs and a 965 at 6; and is entered again today at 6 furlongs, with no clues that suggest a drop; *and* it is running against horses that have never run better than a 959, you have a bet. Period. No further analysis, no soul-searching. The horse may fall down, may run wide on the turn or be pinched back. That is horse racing; chaos happens. But the chances of this horse placing in the money are as good as you will ever get. Such clear-cut choices in a field of horses don't happen every day, but they are not impossibly rare, either. A horse that shows such consistency is a journeyman, whether it is the greatest journeyman of all time, John Henry, or a seven-year-old $2,500 claimer.

More often, an individual horse's times will be erratic, and your objective and subjective handicapping are called into play.

In either case, making the figures is just the first step in a three-step process, and each step is important. Making figures is simply mathematics. You make some handicapping decisions when you go through the *Daily Racing Form* to select the past performances to analyze, but this is usually quick and superficial. Once you have the figures in hand, you go back to the *Form* and *handicap*, applying your best deductive and inductive logic.

When you are finished and have a clear opinion of what the outcome of the race should be—which will not be the case in every race—you then move to the step that is more important than the other two put together: you decide how to bet your opinion. It's all academic until you lay your money down, and we will get to that in the last chapter.

It may seem odd that I have included distances out to 10 furlongs (a mile and a quarter) in the baseline for a book that is explicitly centered on sprint horses. In the balance between speed, endurance, and strategy, speed becomes much less powerful as the distances extend beyond 7 furlongs. It does not disappear, however, and you may want to use it in a strategy that takes the balance into account. *In no case* do you want to use the neat, linear relationship for comparison of speed between distances on the opposite sides of a major threshold, such as 5 furlongs and 1 1/4 miles. If your only times for comparison are at, say, 7 furlongs and a mile, use them—but then *handicap* carefully in the second step, after you have the numbers.

Occasionally, you will find a horse in a sprint race that has only run extended routes in its most recent 10-race history—or the reverse, in a route race. In all but the highest ranks, the chances of a horse adjusting to such drastic changes in one race are so slim that unless it is truly an exceptional

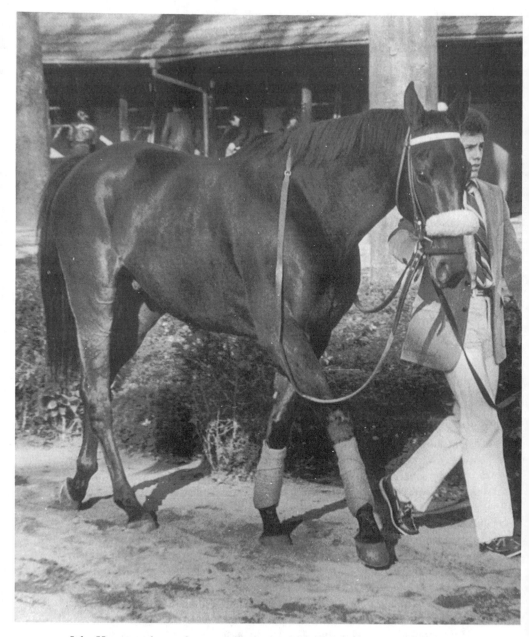

John Henry was by an obscure stallion named Ole Bob Bowers, yet became arguably the greatest journeyman race horse of all times. Along with several other superb geldings, including Forego, he is in retirement at the Kentucky Horse Park, where he can be visited by his fans. *Photo courtesy of* The Blood-Horse.

animal with splits that pace handicappers love or is gifted with a perfect trip, you can very nearly ignore it.

The same is true of quarter horses moving for the first time between short distances on the straightaway and 870 races around the curve. Except in the highest ranks of both Thoroughbred and quarter horse racing, these moves are usually because the horse is doing so poorly that the trainer and owner are looking for a distance where it is better suited. Sometimes they find it. Sometimes they find that distance has nothing to do with it.

Quarter Horse Parallel Speed

Calculating quarter horse parallel speed is considerably easier than calculating it for Thoroughbreds and usually much more accurate. The *Daily Racing Form* gives you each horse's *actual* time, whether it won or lost the race. And it is *already* in decimal seconds. All you have to do is divide it by the lengths of the race to get time per length and then divide the baseline time per length by your result and multiply by 1,000. For example:

> Horse's actual time (winner or loser): 20.35
> Lengths (400 yards, in this example): 150
> 20.35 ÷ 150 = .1357
> 400-yard baseline speed: .132
> .132 ÷ .1357 = .973
> .973 * 1000 = 973

One of the characteristics of quarter horse racing that you will find as you use this method is that at top tracks like Ruidoso Downs and Los Alamitos, the higher classes of quarter horses run more consistently close to the ceiling than their Thoroughbred counterparts. This is because in quarter horse racing there is only one strategy: go from the gates to the finish line as fast as you can. No quarter horse straightaway race was *ever* won by setting a slow pace to throw off the competition. Speed figures in the 990's are not uncommon, even though world records are not often broken. This suggests that top quarter horses run in a very thin margin, within sight of the absolute limit.

9

COMPUTING SPEED

Anybody can win unless there happens to be a second entry.
—GEORGE ADE

*I*t is easy to compare one horse to the baseline with a pencil and paper, and it is not difficult to compare several horses to each other with a calculator. Comparing all of the horses in a race, in six or eight races a day, is no harder—just more tedious.

Selecting the past performances involves some handicapping, but making the figures involves none and is time borrowed from handicapping and making betting decisions, where time is much better spent. In the next chapters we will look at the most important phases of handicapping, which are selecting races where speed is likely to play the greatest role, managing time, and making betting decisions. Here we will look at methods to speed up the calculations, so that making figures doesn't overshadow the rest, and ways that horse racing data can be viewed to develop track constants and variants, to take your own ideas and theories beyond the crowds' and mine.

Calculators

This approach originated on a hand-held calculator, a few years before the price of computers came down out of the clouds, and the basic calculations can still be made with nothing more. Even if you have the finest, hotrod test computer on hand, you may still want to mark your figures on the *Form* for reference while handicapping, just as you would with a dime-store calculator, so the result is the same once you settle down to handicap.

Most inexpensive calculators have a memory feature with which you can store the result of one computation for use in another, and this can be used to slightly speed up the pencil-and-paper approach for arriving at parallel speed.

The steps shown in the last chapter for both Thoroughbreds and quarter horses are almost a straight progression on a calculator, so that most results flow directly into the next computation. But without the calculator memory function, you will have to enter the winner's time and lengths of the race twice and write down the loser's time per length (TPL) in the second-last step, so that you can enter the baseline TPL from the table, then reenter the figure you saved on paper to divide for the answer.

To save a few steps with a memory calculator, store the winner's time and lengths of the race in memory locations (usually something like "<time>-2nd-STORE 1", "<lengths>-2nd-STORE 2"). If it uses algebraic steps (like Texas Instruments and others), then hit "RECLAIM 2" "÷" "RECLAIM 1" "=" and you have the average TPL. Then, each time one of the stored numbers is called for, hit the correct mathematical symbol and "reclaim" it. When you get to the loser's TPL, instead of writing it down, store it in memory location 3, enter the baseline TPL "÷" and "RECLAIM 3." The result will be in the format 0.9999, and you won't want to waste the button pushes to multiply by 1,000, so simply move the decimal point over three digits (rounding) and record the answer in or around the horse's past performances on the *Form*.

If your calculator has lots of memory locations, and will hold figures in them when you turn the power off, you can make it into a semidedicated speed calculator, even if it is not otherwise programmable. In this case, leave the first two or three memory locations open for active calculations and enter the baseline times per length into the others. Then, instead of five or six button-pushes to enter them, you can just hit "RECLAIM 4" for 4 furlongs, or however you arrange them. You could even enter and save the lengths for each distance for use in the calculations, but unless you have a good mnemonic system for remembering which one is where, chances are your own memory will run out before the calculator's.

There are some pretty remarkable calculators and even tiny, palm-sized computers available that cannot only be programmed to store the numbers, but also the sequence of calculations, so all you have to do is enter the variables for each past performance, which are distance, time, and lengths back. The "languages" used by these little things vary considerably, and are necessarily short and compressed. If you already have one on hand, you may want to program the steps to speed up the calculations. I would not run out and buy one until you have tried the method for a while on the dime-store variety—and then consider a full-grown computer.

Computers

The only real advantage of a computer over a programmable calculator for these basic calculations is that instead of dealing with one past performance at a time and writing the single result onto your *Form*, you can efficiently store and sort the results of an entire field of horses and print hard copies of the sorted results on paper.

If you decide to go beyond the basic calculation of parallel speed and do things such as add track constants and variants, develop your own customized baselines, or do your own research on the tracks that you follow, then a computer has it all over anything you can hold in your hand.

If you already own a computer, or use one in your work, you are well aware of its advantages, but if you don't own one, this doesn't mean that you will have to mortgage the house, or hire a computer consultant. Computers can be complicated and expensive—or cheap and simple.

Luckily for most of us, the deeper levels of computer programming are like layers of an onion; you can make soup while barely disturbing the surface. With a disk drive, you can not only save work (or "data"), you can also save the step-by-step instructions of a program, so you don't have to rewrite it every time you want to do some work.

"Software" is simply your own or someone else's saved program that you copy into the workspace so that you can use those steps again without rewriting them. In the onion layers of deep programming already contained in the computer, there are different "languages" that address different layers and instruct the steps to be taken. The further you go into the onion, the more tears you will shed, especially if you are already fluent in normal human language (the best programmers seem to be thirteen-year-olds who can transfer concepts of Lego building blocks into logical programming steps). Unless you already are a programmer (or thirteen), there is hope in BASIC programming language.

BASIC uses fairly straightforward commands and symbols, and its mathematical steps follow intuitive algebraic logic. BASIC comes with most computer operating systems, so you won't need to buy it—you probably already have it. The program segments used here and the complete program in the appendix are written in QBasic, which comes with Microsoft DOS 5.x and higher. If you try it in other forms of BASIC, the lines that won't work will kick you out with an error message, telling you at least where the problem is. Compare the commands and syntax of the line with your BASIC manual, correct it, and try again, until you stop getting errors.

Since the information provided in the *Daily Racing Form* is slightly different for Thoroughbreds and quarter horses, there are two slightly different sub-programs needed. All of the rest of the much longer program just consists of ways of getting in the race number, track name, and date for reference, storing the results of calculations, sorting them, and printing them out on the screen or printer.

In BASIC the mathematical operators are normal-looking, with an asterisk "*" representing multiplication and a slash "/" representing division. The "Input" command in any line tells the computer to stop and wait for you to enter something from the keyboard.

The quarter horse routine is best to show first, since there is no need to approximate the horse's actual time, and the times are already in decimal seconds. In all of the program lines, things in brackets are comments and not part of the program.

The BASIC routine to conduct the same calculation of quarter horse parallel speed shown in the previous chapter is as follows:

```
Input "Time: ", T [Actual time, this horse]
Input "Distance: ", D [Distance in yards]
S = D [D is about to change, so S will work later]
D = D*3 [Convert yards to feet]
LR = D/8 [Lengths = feet ÷ 8]
TL = T/LR [Time-per-length = time ÷ lengths]
```

The next steps insert the baseline times-per-length for each distance:

```
IF S=220 THEN S=.1408
IF S=250 THEN S=.1387
IF S=300 THEN S=.1344
```

And so on, up through 1000 yards (completed steps are shown in the appendix). You then want to find out what percentage of the baseline time-per-length this horse ran in its past performance, so you divide the baseline (now "S") by the approximated time-per-length ("TL"):

```
P = S/TL [P = "Parallel Speed"]
```

This will give you a long, and sometimes endless decimal number, so you need to round it down to three digits and in the process make it a whole number so it's easier to look at:

```
P = (P+.0005)*1000
P = INT(P)
```

The first "P" rounds the number at the third digit; the last command ("Integer") knocks off the decimal fraction. The computer now knows the answer, but you don't, so you need one more line to display the answer on the screen:

```
Print P
```

This little routine (with a few completing lines) can give you one parallel speed for one past performance. You can type it in, *save it*, and use it over and over again by giving the command "RUN," each time. It will ask you three questions about this particular past performance, which you type and "enter."

It is also short enough (and can be made much more compact) so that it will easily fit in a programmable calculator or pocket computer.

Thoroughbred parallel speed requires a few more steps because you must first approximate a non-winner's time. It is not difficult to convert the minutes-seconds-fifths format of Thoroughbred times to decimal seconds in your head, but it is easier (and a little less prone to error) to simply enter them as you would say them without punctuation (for example, "1113" for "one-eleven-and-three"). This conversion requires a string function which you will have to look up in your BASIC manual, if you are dying to know how the program in the appendix works. For now, assume you will be converting to decimal seconds in your head:

INPUT "Distance: ", D [Distance in furlongs]
S=D [store furlongs as "S"]
INPUT "Winner's Time: ",T [Decimal seconds]
INPUT "Length's Back (Winner=0): ",L
D = (D/8)*5280 [Convert furlongs to feet]
LR = D/8 [Lengths Run = feet ÷ 8]
TL = T/LR [Time-per-length = time ÷ lengths run]
IF L=0 THEN GOTO Basepoints [Tells the computer: if this horse was a winner, skip the next two lines]
T = T+(L*TL) [Non-winner's time = winner's time + loser's lengths back, times the TL]
TL = T/LR [Loser's time-per-length]

This brings you to the same point as in the quarter horse routine, with an approximated time-per-length for both winners and non-winners. You now need to retrieve the basepoints for Thoroughbred distances:

Basepoints:
                        IF S = 4 THEN S = .134
                        IF S = 4.5 THEN S = .1357
And so on, for as many baseline times for distances as you want to put in. The remaining steps are the same:

P = S/TL [Parallel speed]
P = (P+.0005)*1000:P=INT(P):Print P [Round and Print]

This routine is also compact enough to use with either a calculator or pocket computer, which may also be able to handle the string function to allow you to program the conversion to decimal seconds.

These two little routines give you all that you need for weekend handi-capping. The significantly longer program in the appendix adds some ma-jor refinements, but most of its length is involved in storing results from multiple past performances, for sorting and printing hard copies. We will see how to use the results in the following chapter, and some ways to im-prove them next; but even with the raw figures, you will be far better off than the crowd.

Refinements and Research

Computers are a lot more valuable in handicapping than simply acting as calculators, doing the same routines over and over again. There are two important realms in which they can help you: one is to search for—and, equally important, to *test*—objective measures that affect the outcome of races; the other is to lead into deeper research, where you might not find a mathematical law, but rather build your subjective handicapping skills.

The larger issues of the *Daily Racing Form* contain dozens of computer programs that offer to do your handicapping for you, according to someone else's theories. Like handicapping at large, they all probably work some of the time. But handicapping is a lot more interesting when you win and know why. Since winning is a combination of objective and subjective theories, deductive and inductive logic—and pure, rabbit-ass luck—the approach is to develop the first four and to narrow the field on the latter.

The most useful commercial software for background handicapping are "spreadsheets." These work like a bank of hotel mailboxes, where you can put notes for future reference. The power of a spreadsheet is that you can specify relationships between boxes, so that it creates a new note in an empty hole. State-of-the-art spreadsheets, like Lotus 1-2-3 and others, can set up extraordinarily complex relationships between thousands of boxes and do tedious, repetitive calculations with just a few keystrokes, almost instantly. Even the best, however, are presently limited in the level of statistics that they can apply to your data, and if your interest is in deep handicapping, you will have to add a separate statistical software program.

These can cost as much or more than the spreadsheet—and they take you into the maddening realm of "compatibility" of moving data back and forth between commercial programs. Before you throw up your hands, let me quickly add that all of the original work for this book was done years ago, first on a hand calculator and then on a Commodore-64 with a functional little spreadsheet that cost less than $20.

With an advanced spreadsheet, it is possible to do front-line handicapping by programming the steps of the BASIC program above right into the spreadsheet. To calculate parallel speed with this method, you could enter the horse's number (or name, if you really enjoy typing), winner's time, and loser's lengths back into boxes, and have the parallel speed appear in an empty box that you assign. I find this a cumbersome approach, and there are some drawbacks with certain spreadsheets, which, for example, can't hold information side by side, if you want to sort from fastest speeds to slowest and hold the horse's number next to the speed. (The program in the Appendix does do this.) A far better use of a spreadsheet is in your background handicapping and personal research.

A spreadsheet is the perfect work space in which to identify "track constants" for the tracks that you follow, and it is also useful if you simply want to learn more about speed and time factors between distances or tracks and develop ideas. The problem of acquiring data to put into them (which used to be only by painful transcription from the *Form*) has disappeared. Both past performances and results charts are available in various file formats from a number of computer services. Computer addresses for several data sources such as *Bloodstock Research Information Services*, *Dark Horse*, *Equibase*, *International Thoroughbred Superhighway*, and *Thoroughbred Sports Network* are listed in the Appendix. Other sources will no doubt be available by the time you read this.

You can use spreadsheets in a number of different ways, as they have been in the background of earlier chapters of this book, or you can break beyond these to develop and test your own theories—which is the whole idea.

To start with a simple example of spreadsheet use, a table of quarter horse track records is published monthly by *The Quarter Racing Journal* of the American Quarter Horse Association. To enter these into a spreadsheet, about the only thing you have to do is create a wide first column so that the track names will fit and label the first row along the top with the distances (only the first four distances are shown; empty cells are distances where no track records are recorded).

Track Dist:	220	250	300	330
ALB Albuquerque			15.7	17.3
ASD Assiniboia Downs				
BCF Brown Co. Fair			15.82	
BEU Beulah Park	11.94	13.3	15.5	16.77
BKF Eastern Idaho Fair		13.44	15.63	16.94
BM Bay Meadows	12.21	13.57	15.43	16.81

The track record times are entered as pure data, with no operators assigned to their boxes. Once they are in, you can do anything your imagination or spreadsheet operations allow. For example, if you are doing this a few years from now, it is likely that some of the records will have improved. You will probably want to see what the new average record times are for each distance and whether the world record times have changed, for use in your baseline. Each spreadsheet has its own secondary language for conducting operations between the boxes, and the following commands are based on Lotus 1-2-3.

In a blank row above or below your data, and in the 220-yard distance column, insert the formula: $@AVG(B2..B_n)$, where B2 is the box address of your first 220-yard time, and B_n is the address of the last. As soon as you hit Enter, the average record time will appear in the box. Copy the formula across the row using the Copy command, hit Enter, and all of the averages appear. (Averages shown are for the six tracks only.)

Track Dist:	220	250	300	330
ALB Albuquerque			15.7	17.3
ASD Assiniboia Downs				
BCF Brown Co. Fair			15.82	
BEU Beulah Park	11.94	13.3	15.5	16.77
BKF Eastern Idaho Fair		13.44	15.63	16.94
BM Bay Meadows	12.21	13.57	15.43	16.81
Average:	12.075	13.437	15.616	16.955

To see what the current world records are, take another blank row, and insert the formula: $@MIN(B2..B_n)$, hit Enter, and the *smallest* number in the 220-yard column will appear in the box. Copy the formula across the distances, and you'll have a row of the fastest officially recorded times for quarter horses.

This is the kind of stuff that used to take a full day and a fifth of Jack Daniels. Look through the manual of commands for your spreadsheet and you will find other interesting manipulations you can perform with the data.

Later versions of Lotus (and other current spreadsheets) can hold adjoining data side by side when you sort one column, so you may want to use the "Sort" function to see if your tracks (or their best horses) are relatively faster or slower at different distances. If one track is significantly faster across the board, it may be more than just exceptional horses, and you may be on the trail of a track constant—but you won't know until you dig deeper and move from the records into the charts. This is just playing with the data for ideas; you can also create new information.

The racing distances are in yards across the first row. You can insert a new blank row under it and the mathematical formula: (B1*3)/8, which gives you lengths of the race. (Copy it across the row.) Insert another blank row and the formula: $B_x/B3$, where B_x is the address of any time, such as fastest or average (and B3 is now the lengths of the race), and you have the time per length for that time. For feet per second, use the formula: $B1*3/B_x$, and you have another measure of speed for whichever time you have selected.

If you want to visually compare your home track to the average or fastest track records, you will find that most spreadsheets have a fairly simple graphing function, where you can set the distances in yards from row 1 along the X axis, and whatever row of times you select as your Y-axis function, and get an instant (almost) picture for comparison (see Figure 7.5).

Unfortunately, the statistical capabilities of most spreadsheets—beyond simple mean, median, and variance—are wretched. To look for the "true meaning of life," you need a separate, specialized statistical "package." Unfortunately, too, the data entry and manipulation features of most statistical packages are weak. So what you will usually find yourself doing is entering the data into a spreadsheet like Lotus 1-2-3, where entry is fairly easy and where you have much easier methods to extract certain sets of data, then translating the extracted data into .DIF or ASCI-II files that can be imported into the statistical program. Some statistical programs are better than others in letting you rearrange data within them, but since you will probably want to use features of both types of programs, you may want to stick with your spreadsheet for holding the main body of data.

The second example takes a step beyond simply rattling data around in the boxes and into some actual analysis. Class-par-times can be fairly stable, but they do change over time or sometimes abruptly, for example, when a new racing surface is installed. Track variants derived from the pars are a moving target, so having records to keep track of them and keep yourself informed can be valuable. The process for testing class pars is one of the most useful you can know.

Statistics don't work on words, so racing classes must be converted to numbers, first for entry into the spreadsheet, then for translation into a file that can be exported into a statistical package. Assuming your spreadsheet is one that can hold information side by side when it sorts one column, you can enter the race results from an entire year of racing, or as many as you choose, simply in chronological order, without separating distances. You can then sort by the distance column, which will group all of the same distance races together, and extract each distance as a block into a separate file for further sorting, and/or applying statistics. The following shows how you might arrange the columns for data entry before sorting:

Class	Distance (Furlongs)	Time (Decimal Seconds)
3	6	70.6
12	6.5	77.8
6	5.5	65.8
9	6	70.2

The spreadsheet formula for converting minutes-seconds-fifths to decimal seconds is simple and allows you to enter the times in the format "1 <enter> 10 <enter> 3 <enter>" with limited brain strain and mistakes, once the formula is in place. To arrange it, set up four narrow columns—say, C through F. Enter minutes in C, seconds in D, and raw fifths in E. In F place the formula: $+C*60+D+E*0.2$. You don't need any parentheses to schedule the calculations, since the computer will do each multiplication before adding.

This method can be used to test the importance of any factor in horse racing for which you can find reliable data in the *Form* or other source and which can be logically represented by a number. Age is simple to add and was used in the original analysis. You just have to settle on a convention to handle the "and ups," so that two-year-old and three-year-old races are pure 2's and 3's; three-and-up races are 4's; four-and-ups are 5's.

The class-value system of races is not in numbers, but can be easily represented as a numerical progression, as shown earlier (chapter 4). The greatest danger to your ultimate analysis of the results of assigning numerical values to nonnumerical data lies in ensuring that the number progression is sound and logical. With racing classes, the progression from best to worst is fairly straightforward. Grade I stakes, for example, can logically be assigned a "1," as the best. Claiming races are simple (once you have stepped down through the higher ranks): $25,000 races might turn out to be "6"; $20,000, "7"; $15,000, "8"; and so forth.

Where you will run into trouble, at first, is in the highest and lowest ranks, but if you have a great many races for data and considerable patience, you should be able to come up with reasonable rankings to start. You will see the problem as soon as you get a little way into the data: is a $100,000 claiming race better or worse than a $30,000-purse allowance race; and is either better than a minor stakes or handicap?

Assigning numerical values to nonnumerical data is done with a pencil and paper, before you go near the computer, by paging through *Form*s or charts and writing down every different class of race you come across. At this stage, the best advice is: don't anticipate saving work on the computer by "prelumping" information. This will be a temptation, as you get familiar with the times for different classes by simply glancing over them, and you start to see similarities. This may be absolutely correct, or it can be deceiving. At this stage, be a "splitter," not a "lumper." You can lump later, when the computer gives you reasons.

Other nonnumerical data, such as jockeys and trainers, are much less straightforward than race classes, but this doesn't mean they can't be studied. The first thing you have to decide with jockeys or any other nonnumerical factor is what there is about them from the information available that allows them to be ranked. Money won, races won, percentage of wins, percentage in the money are not corresponding categories for any given jockey or trainer. You will have to start with a "theory" of what you think is important, with the explicit purpose of changing and improving it as you test it against the actual data of wins, times, or whatever fixed (independent) data you select. Theory building is where many handicappers lose their bets— making the variables fit the theory rather than rethinking the theory to explain the variation—and then testing it all again.

If you survived the chapter on chaos, you should have a major reservation about where this is leading. Not every theory, even if it is based in some kernel of truth, is going to have explanatory power, and you can't know all the parameters.

Jockeys and trainers are powerful factors in horse racing, *but* can you find a *valid, quantifiable factor* from all this work to plug into a handicapping equation—which would be better than simply knowing that this guy is pretty good, or does well with new horses, or is scared to death about mixing it up in traffic because he fell and fractured his spine last year? I doubt it. What you can do, though, is greatly refine your own understanding (theory) about which published information is relevant—and thereby improve your subjective handicapping skills.

By following your own interests into these analyses, you may also turn up *objective* secondary factors, which affect the most objective factor of all—speed. When you find one, you have really got something.

To follow the process beyond data entry into simple statistical analysis, here is an example of a concrete speed factor that can be quantified. It uses exactly the same process that can be used to study race-class structure, trainers, jockeys, or other nonnumerical factors. You will find the results built into the quarter horse speed equation in the program in the Appendix.

All quarter horse aficionados know that wind affects final times in races. At tracks like Ruidoso, where wind occurs and is listed in the *Form*, it is usually not in the nature of little dancing zephyrs, but at a magnitude to issue small-craft warnings. The *Form* lists head wind (hw), tail wind (tw), crosswind (cw), or a blank space next to the winner's time meaning "no wind."

When applying numbers to words, it is critical that the number progression reflect the physical or theoretical progression that they represent. Wind is fairly easy:

$$1 = \text{tail wind}$$
$$2 = \text{no wind}$$
$$3 = \text{crosswind}$$
$$4 = \text{head wind}$$

This is based on the extent to which wind would be expected to help or impede a horse running down the track. A tail wind will obviously help, "no wind" is neutral; a head wind will impede, a crosswind is a lot less certain. A perfect 90-degree crosswind is going to impede somewhat; an angling crosswind from the front is going to impede more; an angling crosswind from behind is going to *help*. This effect (and the fact that wind is recorded by direction, not velocity) affects the "tightness" of the correlation in the statistics and the relative position of the crosswind category.

This 1–4 progression works at Ruidoso Downs, where the layout of the track and prevailing winds make crosswinds more often an impediment (clearly, in some races, it swings around to the east and helps the horses along). At other quarter horse tracks, such as Sunland Park, the layout of the track and prevailing winds may make assisting crosswinds more common, and you may want to test this by reversing the values of "no wind" and crosswind. If this sounds a little wishy-washy, it is only for crosswinds.

The difference between tail wind and head wind is the single most powerful speed factor that can be quantified for quarter horse handicapping. *Wind works.* It works so well that it is worth your time to determine where "crosswind" belongs at your tracks.

The process of finding out is a simplified example of the methods you can use if you want to venture into the real mysteries of horse racing. To do it, you need a set of the previous year's charts, or at least a good portion of the current season's. One warning is to plan the data categories carefully, before you begin.

Suppose, for example, you decide to set up a spreadsheet for three categories of information: distance, wind direction, and winning time, and select the data only from races on fast tracks. Later you may decide you want to see what happens with class or weight. It is easy to add a parallel column for class and go through the charts again to add the new factor for each race. However, if you are jumping over offtrack conditions, the chances for error in this tedious operation are great, and, for example, if you miss one fast-track race after a series of sloppy ones that you are skipping, every single piece of data after that will be wrong—and so will your conclusions. You will lessen your chances for error and add the opportunity for analysis of offtrack conditions if you include a column for track conditions, assign them numbers (in the order suggested earlier), and enter every single race from your collection. You only have to do it once; you can sort later for only "fast" or any category of surface you want. With computer disks, it's yours forever.

To test the effect of wind, you need only three columns of data from the charts—distance, time, and wind. If you use more categories in your initial pass through the charts (such as class, age, etc.), it is easy to move the columns around so that the three relevant ones are side by side to be extracted and exported for statistics.

Distance	Wind	Time
350	1	17.66
400	4	19.92
350	2	17.81
440	1	21.47

With the three columns either rearranged to be side by side in the data, or copied (duplicated) in a blank area of the spreadsheet, you can then "extract" only the columns you want by blocking them and saving them separately as a new file on disk.

If you tend to vent frustration on expensive, inanimate objects, now is the time to open the bottle. Some commercial software is known as "user friendly." (Lotus is, for the most part, although it is user ambivalent in spots.) The more powerful statistical packages are user hostile. The majority will accept .DIF or ASCI-II files, translated from Lotus data sheets, which Lotus will do for you very easily as it bids you a friendly farewell.

Now, batten down the hatches and move all sharp objects out of reach while you crank up the statistical package. Depending upon which one of these sadistic little monsters you own, you will find out all kinds of things about their inner workings that you never wanted to know before you successfully end up with your translated Lotus file in a form that will work.

If both you and your computer live through the translation of your data from your spreadsheet into something the statistical package can read, the rest is interesting, and usually pretty easy.

There are a number of ways you can look at your data to get ideas about what is going on, and a number of tests that can be performed to see if you are right.

Time will usually be your "dependent variable," because you want to see how it changes, depending upon other factors, such as wind or class. With the data already sorted by racing distance, you can start with a simple breakdown of times by wind category. The following is for all 440-yard races run (under fast track conditions) at Ruidoso Downs during the 1988 and 1989 seasons:

Wind	Average Time
1 (tw)	21.60
2 (nw)	21.64
3 (cw)	21.77
4 (hw)	21.81

For the seventy-six races that are summarized, a tail wind—on the average—provides a 0.04 second assist over no wind at all. If you hold "no wind" as the baseline, then the average crosswind is a 0.13 detriment, a head wind slows the horses down by 0.17 seconds, and the overall difference between tail wind and head wind is 0.21 seconds.

Since these figures are composed of all classes of races, intense winds and mild winds, crosswinds from 45 degrees behind and others from ahead, the correlation of wind and time and, especially crosswinds, is not perfect, but the general trend is clear. When this is carried out for all races at all distances over a three-year period, some of the smaller samples will vary, but the tail wind average is *always faster* than the other three categories and the head wind average is *always slower*.

A tail wind provides less of an assist to speed than a head wind impedes it, because of the horse's speed relative to the air. If a horse is running with a ground speed of 40 miles per hour into a 20-mile-per-hour head wind, its relative air speed is 60 miles per hour. With the same velocity tail wind, it quickly passes the wind velocity and is running with a relative air speed of 20 miles per hour. So tail wind velocities of less than about 40 miles per hour are not "assists" at all, but a reduction from the basic impediment of still air.

The larger sample does not smooth the variation significantly, and the time differences between wind directions remain essentially as they are in the 440-yard sample.

This presents a problem for converting these observations to a speed handicapping factor. The effect of wind can be much more drastic than the average that these numbers reflect, but even the averages are too big to use at face value—especially the crosswind factor, which can reverse itself, depending upon which way the wind blows. Then, too, suppose a horse runs an extremely fast time *into a head wind*. If you subtract the full 0.17 seconds (about 1 1/2 lengths in a quarter horse race), you may push the time into the impossible zone.

This is not fighting reality, because the reality is that the components of the averages contain a lot more unidentifiable parameters than some of the other factors we have looked at. What we want is a *relative* factor to apply uniformly to all past performances. Since at Ruidoso the average crosswind is a substantial detriment to times (0.13—or about a length), subtracting a factor from the recorded time is going to be correct most of the time. But sometimes it is going to be dead wrong. At other tracks you may find that crosswinds more frequently assist with times, and you may want to add a factor to account for them.

With the possible exception of crosswinds, the following factors, developed from the averages by trial and error, will probably hold for most tracks:

tail wind = +0.04
no wind = 0 (par)
crosswind = –0.06
head wind = –0.13

When wind is recorded in quarter horse past performances, these factors can be added and subtracted from the horse's actual time to account for its effect. A horse is slightly penalized for a time run with a tail wind and given substantial credit for having run into the wind. At Ruidoso, it is also given credit for a crosswind, with the knowledge that this will be wrong some of the time. Until the unlikely event that the *Form* adds categories of "rcw" (rear crosswind) and "fcw," this is the best you can do—unless you are there personally to record the azimuth of the flag for every race. (Checking the

National Weather Service isn't going to do you much good unless their instruments are at the track.)

It takes about twenty steps to include the wind factor in the basic quarter horse parallel speed routine, and you will find them within the full program in the Appendix should you wish to insert them into the short program shown earlier.

Most statistical programs will allow you to do considerably more than simple breakdowns of data, and you may try various forms of regression analysis, factor analysis, cluster analysis, and other approaches to both generate ideas and test them against independent data. The results of such analyses have been presented in earlier chapters. Your imagination is limited only by the data available.

If you are able to define track constants and variants from your work, their insertion into the calculation of parallel speed is usually simple. Say, for example, your handicapping centers on three tracks, where horses may move from one to the other as seasons close or between them if they are open simultaneously. If you find that the average times for the tracks vary predictably across the board, you can set one track's times as par, as we did with "no wind" above. This can be the major track among the three, or any one you prefer. Set that track as par, so that its times will be used at face value when you enter them. If one track is consistently faster than par, use as a model the wind factor (as shown in the program in the Appendix) to add a line so that you can identify which track the time comes from and subtract the track constant from the faster times before time per length is calculated. If the third track is three-fifths slow, add the lines to add 0.6 to the times when you tell the computer it is Track 3.

As with the wind example, you may find that, while the general trend is correct, the apparent factors derived from averages may be too large or too small to function reliably. When you add a factor like this, be sure to save the program both in its original form and under a new file name so you can test your ideas against the old one on real race results.

Track constants, of course, are seldom so convenient as occurring across the board for all distances. You may find that times between tracks are pretty similar (or vary mildly) except for one radical departure at one distance, at one track. If it is the result of a track constant, such as a one-jump flying start or two-turn "sprint," it can be quantified and tested just like the broader constants above, and added to the program with a few more programming steps. If you find several, and can identify concrete reasons why variation is occurring, the programming gets a little thicker, but it will probably be worth your time. If you find *lots*, it may be time to step back and decide if they are really track constants or artifacts of the data. In every case, remember that it costs nothing to test your ideas with real data from the *Form* before your start betting that you are right.

..

10

HANDICAPPING SPEED

> If certainty about the past is so limited, must not certainty about the
> future be terribly slight? How can anyone wrench a profit from such
> confusion?
>
> —TOM AINSLIE
> *Ainslie's Complete Guide to Thoroughbred Racing*

Time Management

Until fairly recently, handicapping was centered around one track. If you
were based in New York, your summer hours were spent at Belmont, your
winters at Aqueduct—unless you wanted to get really Runyonesque and
"winter" at Caulder in Florida. On the West Coast, you only had to worry
about shifting your handicapping knowledge up and down the seacoast from
Hollywood Park, to Del Mar, to Caliente. Even if seasons overlapped, you
might only have twenty-four races to worry about and two sets of track
variants to juggle, so your biggest concern might have been how to be certain
that your partner laid the right bet down at Hollywood while you were at
Golden Gate.

Now offtrack betting and ontrack simulcasting present serious time management problems. Even if you center your work at your home track, you
still may be offered two or more races a day simulcast in from across the
country. If your home track is Playfair in Spokane or Prairie Meadows in
Altoona, you might find yourself also handicapping races from Pimlico,
Belmont, or Del Mar.

Like the tracks themselves, offtrack betting facilities are beginning to
realize that if you give the average bettor a comfortable chair to sit in—and
restrooms that don't gag the rats—people will actually come and enjoy the
sport. As a result, Thoroughbred racing attendance, including offtrack,
actually surpassed baseball in 1990 as the leading spectator sport in the
United States. Offtrack betting is a major, expanding industry yet to find its
full market. It presents added complexity for handicapping, but also great
opportunities.

Four tracks, each with twelve races a day, offer forty-eight races for
handicapping. It takes at least a minute or two to decide *not* to handicap a
race, and it takes at least fifteen minutes to handicap and make betting

decisions on the easiest and most clear-cut races. On the average, it takes about thirty minutes to form an opinion on a race and decide on betting, depending upon how strong the opinion is. At that rate, it would take twenty-four hours to handicap one edition of the *Form,* which is often less than you have in total from the time the *Form* hits the streets.

Your first decision has to be whether you are willing to spend a couple of hours, a long evening, or every waking moment to participate in the sport. Even if it is the latter, offtrack-betting opportunities make it impossible to handicap every available race. But it offers two major, new alternatives: you can now center on one or two tracks, even across the continent, and learn the idiosyncracies of their constants and variants and the horses that run there. Or you can specialize. With forty-eight races a day, you can probably find *something* to handicap, even if your specialty is races run solely by horses named after famous comedians. If your specialty is something broader—like sprint handicapping—you have the advantage of being able to pick and choose only those that best suit your handicapping and betting methods.

I have visited several tracks where the *Form* and track employees have kept a season record on their picks of winners. These are the inner circle of handicappers described in the first chapter who devote 100 percent of their working hours to horse racing and have access to all the backside informa- tion they care to gather. Their season percentages are *dismal* . No one whom I have ever seen has broken out of the 30 percent range; most are in the 20's, and a few are actually in the *teens* . Since the crowd at large is also in the 30- percent range of picking winners over a season, it is clear that even the very best handicappers would lose horrendously *if they chose only winners and bet every race.* But this is *not* what they do, so even those in the teens are often strong winners.

Whether you have forty-eight races to choose from at an offtrack facility or twelve at your home track, you will have to decide which races are best suited to your methods and worth your time to handicap and then which results of your handicapping show the strongest betting possibilities.

If your methods center on speed handicapping, the first decision is clear: speed is most powerful at sprint distances. Within the sprint distances are a wide variety of races. Every class and every level of competition is represented.

Really bad races in which none of the horses have ever come within thirty lengths of a winner are easy to dismiss and you can feel a little superior for it. Really good races can be just as impossible to handicap, and it may be just as wise to pass them, but it always feels like a defeat when you do. Both categories, however, can sometimes be handicapped using a higher degree of subjective and secondary factors, and the rewards are sometimes substantial for the one out of five that may result in a strong conviction. But the time involved is usually two to three times that of a middle-of-the-road race—or about *fifteen* times, if you consider all of the ones that never result in a bet.

Even if you are just starting out, it will take no time at all to figure out which kinds of races are your strong suit. These are the ones that you win and know why.

One approach to efficiently using limited handicapping time is to page through the races first, noting which are likely to be prime races for your methods. See how many there are—if any—and limit your first attack to these. If it takes an hour or two to go through them and you can still see straight, take the next most likely, or the other race to fill in the daily double, or triple—if you have a strong opinion for part of it and the additional one looks possible. Forget about races where half or all of the field are unraced two-year-olds, unless you are loaded with time and the fever to gamble.

Once you select a race to handicap, glance over the past performances of the field to get a first impression of the balance of talent. Then number the horses in post position order. This is extremely important if you are not able to purchase the track program at the same time as the *Form,* because the post positions and betting numbers may become completely scrambled if there are couplings or scratches. It will also help you avoid errors as you look back and forth from the *Form* to your calculator or computer. It is bad to lose a bet because your logic or method failed; it is worse to lose one you would have won if you had not miscounted the horse's number or inserted the time from one race and the lengths back from another.

Start with the first horse and select the past performance(s) that you think will best represent its capabilities in the upcoming race. Mark them with a "tic" in this first pass, so you don't have to refind them later. If you come to a horse that you believe (glancing around and about the other times and positions) stands no chance in this race, cross the imposter out and forget it—at least for a while. As you select past performances, you will also get a clearer picture of what the horses are doing in the race and begin to build subjective opinions. When you have selected what you think are the significant past performances, move to the calculator or computer and enter them all. You will learn more about the horses as you reread and enter the information.

If you are working with a calculator or the short, one-run computer program, you will want to record the speed figure with the horse's past performances on the *Form.* I don't like to cover information by writing directly on the past performances, so I squeeze the figures above, using the convention that if two or more figures are calculated, they are placed in the same order as the "tics" below, so I know immediately which is the most recent.

With the longer program in the Appendix, the speed figures and other information can be sorted and printed from fastest to slowest to give a far better visual impression of the results for comparison. In either case, when the figures appear, handicapping does not stop, it begins.

Assessing the Field

This wouldn't be a handicapping book without an example of a race with the win, place, and show horses picked in exact order of finish, at big odds, with minimal need for a thought process, as if this were some reflection of reality. The reality is that this might happen once a month per track. Real day-to-day races are more like the eleventh at Longacres on August 25, 1990.

11th Longacres

6 FURLONGS. (1.07⅕) CLAIMING. Purse $4,200. 4-year-olds and upward which have not won a race since April 3. Weight, 122 lbs. Non-winners in 1990 allowed 3 lbs. Claiming price $4,000.

LASIX—Nijinsky's Promise, Kalahari Kid, Memory Lapse, Big Time Louie, Western Nifty, My Picture Time, Smoother Sailing, Green Echo, Lord Emmaus.
BUTAZOLIDIN—Nijinsky's Promise, Kalahari Kid, Memory Lapse, Sir Edward, Big Time Louie, Western Nifty, My Picture Time, Smoother Sailing, Green Echo, Seatonic, Lord Emmaus.

Nijinsky's Promise — **B. g. 4, by Nijinsky's Secret—Bold Essie, by Bold Forbes**
Br.—W. Paul Little (Ky) — **1990 5 0 0 2 $1,292**
CORRAL J R **119** **Tr.—Chambers Mike** **$4,000** — **1989 12 1 1 1 $7,260**
Own.—MacadmsR&SeHorseSixStble — **Lifetime 18 1 1 4 $9,487**

Entered 23Aug90–10 LGA

→8Aug90-3Lga	6½f	:22^1	:45^1	1:18 ft	16	LB	116	12^{12} 11^{10} 9$^{4\frac{3}{4}}$ 3$^{3\frac{1}{4}}$	Corral J R 7	4000	78-17	PrncZm,FryChmp,Njnsky'sPrms	12
27Jly90-5Lga	6f	:22^1	:45^3	1:10^2 ft	19	B	114	11$^{9\frac{3}{4}}$ 11^{20} 11^{13} 10$^{16\frac{1}{2}}$	Kaenel J L 9	5000	71-19	CoulTrip,CocolallaKid,BeringStr	11
1Jly90-5EP	6½f	:21^4	:45^1	1:18^1 ft	4e		117	8^{11} 8^{12} 8^{10} 6$^{12\frac{1}{4}}$	Noguez A 5	10000	73-19	SunrisTquil,FritttdiRoni,Kyl'sDvil	8
16Jun90-5EP	6½f	:22^1	:45^2	1:18^3 ft	15		117	6$^{9\frac{1}{2}}$ 6^9 4$^{4\frac{1}{2}}$ 3$^{3\frac{1}{4}}$	Noguez A 6	10000	80-19	Lrn'sSrprs,BldGlxy,Njnsky'sPrms	7
3Jun90-8EP	6½f	:22^2	:46^1	1:20^1 m	31		117	5$^{7\frac{1}{2}}$ 7^{10} 8^{10} 8$^{10\frac{1}{4}}$	Noguez A 2	16000	65-29	Barbex, Proud Winds, Vihuri	8
28Oct89-8San	6f	:22^4	:46^4	1:13^3 gd	9¾		117	6^6 4$^{2\frac{1}{2}}$ 4$^{3\frac{1}{2}}$ 4^3	Curcio C M 6	15000^c	— —	BrndyShooter,TrueBrt,Kyle'sDvil	6
14Oct89-9EP	6½f	:22^2	:46^1	1:20 sl	4e		117	10^9 10^{14} 7$^{7\frac{1}{4}}$ 6$^{4\frac{1}{4}}$	Krasner S 8	16000	72-29	TrueBrt,Kyl'sDvil,OnMyGoodSid	10
22Sep89-6EP	1$\frac{1}{16}$	:47^4	1:12^4	1:45^4 ft	6½		116	2^1 3$^{1\frac{1}{2}}$ 5^6 6$^{8\frac{3}{4}}$	Loseth C 4	16000	73-21	ErriglRod,MotvPowr,VctorClppr	10
26Aug89-7EP	6½f	:22^1	:45^4	1:18^3 ft	4¼		117	3$^{3\frac{1}{2}}$ 3^2 6^4 8$^{4\frac{3}{4}}$	Loseth C 6	20000	78-21	Pacific Briar, Big Bad Lu, Funlad	9
16Aug89-7EP	6½f	:22^1	:45^4	1:18^2 gd	3¼		117	7^9 7$^{6\frac{1}{4}}$ 5^7 3$^{5\frac{1}{2}}$	Loseth C 2	20000	78-17	Ginnd,Kyl'sDvil,Nijinsky'sPromis	7

Speed Index: Last Race: –5.0 3–Race Avg.: –7.6 8–Race Avg.: –4.3 Overall Avg.: –4.5

Jun 25 EP 5f ft 1:03^1 H

Kalahari Kid — **Ch. g. 4, by Pirateer—Aswan, by Nantequos**
Br.—Kem Diane C (Wash) — **1990 9 1 0 1 $2,464**
BELVOIR V **117^5** **Tr.—Fisher Steve** **$4,000** — **1989 10 2 1 0 $5,481**
Own.—Jones O M or Jean C — **Lifetime 21 3 1 1 $8,143**

→15Jun90-2Lga	6f	:21^4	:45^1	1:11 ft	7¾	122	8^8 10$^{8\frac{1}{4}}$ 8$^{5\frac{3}{4}}$ 7$^{7\frac{3}{4}}$	Comber J 3	4000	77-15	FirwyChmp,KntuckyTrip,Wvlgnd	11
26May90-6Lga	6½f	:22	:45^3	1:18 ft	3½	122	6^3 8$^{4\frac{3}{4}}$ 11^{12} 11$^{12\frac{3}{4}}$	Delgadillo C 4	6250	68-16	JericoJke,KnifeRiver,MmoryLps	12
13May90-2Lga	6f	:21^3	:44^3	1:10^2 ft	7¾	122	7$^{7\frac{1}{4}}$ 5$^{4\frac{1}{2}}$ 4$^{2\frac{1}{4}}$ 4^1	Corral J R 6	6250	87-12	Empror'sCort,StrctCnfdnc,SHslr	11
29Apr90-11Lga	6f	:23^1	:47	1:12^3 gd	6¼	120	5$^{1\frac{3}{4}}$ 4^3 5$^{2\frac{3}{4}}$ 4$^{1\frac{3}{4}}$	Corral J R 10	6250	75-18	ApplSlwdl,GottHvSol,TwDysAwy	10
6Apr90-1Lga	6f	:22^1	:45^2	1:12 ft	15	122	7$^{5\frac{1}{4}}$ 7$^{6\frac{3}{4}}$ 6$^{4\frac{1}{2}}$ 6$^{3\frac{1}{2}}$	Aragon V A 9	6250	76-15	BordE.Z.,GodTmBddy,LllnsPrnc	12
18Mar90-12PM	6f	:22^1	:45^4	1:12 ft	12	119	6$^{9\frac{1}{4}}$ 7$^{7\frac{3}{4}}$ 7$^{3\frac{1}{4}}$ 5$^{3\frac{1}{4}}$	Bergsrud S A 3	4000	90-18	DcortdHro,MountinMnMl,Bobndr	9
25Feb90-12PM	6f	:23^1	:48^1	1:14^4 ft	3¼	120	7$^{3\frac{1}{4}}$ 3^2 3^{nk} 1$^{1\frac{1}{2}}$	Bergsrud S A 2	5000	79-20	KlhriKid,TintdEvidnc,FrnchActon	8
20Jan90-6PM	6f	:22^3	:47	1:13^3 ft	2½	120	3^2 2^1 4$^{2\frac{3}{4}}$ 5$^{6\frac{1}{4}}$	Bergsrud S A 5	5000	79-17	BigSilnc,DdictdLd,KnowsNoLimit	8
11Jan90-7PM	6f	:22^2	:46^1	1:13 gd	3¾	120	6$^{4\frac{1}{2}}$ 5$^{3\frac{3}{4}}$ 3$^{3\frac{1}{2}}$ 3$^{2\frac{1}{2}}$	SouthwickWE 9	5000	85-12	MoonPlace,CraftyCrafty,KlhriKid	9
17Dec89-4PM	6f	:23	:47^3	1:14^3 ft	*7-5	120	5$^{1\frac{1}{4}}$ 1^{hd} 2^{hd} 4$^{1\frac{3}{4}}$	Bergsrud S A 9	5000	78-13	B.B'sChrmer,BossGen,ShrkAttck	12

Speed Index: Last Race: –8.0 3–Race Avg.: –8.3 10–Race Avg.: –5.8 Overall Avg.: –5.8

● Aug 21 Lga 5f sy 1:00 B   Aug 15 Lga 5f ft 1:00^4 D   Aug 9 Lga 4f ft :50^3 B

Memory Lapse

Ch. g. 4, by Tantoul—Reasonable Force, by Forceten
DREXLER H — 122 — Br.—Harris Farm Inc (Cal) — 1990 15 2 1 4 $6,362
Tr.—Samuels Bruce — $4,000 — 1989 10 M 0 1 $1,538
Own.—Dbts Stable — Lifetime 25 2 1 5 $7,900

9Aug90-5Lga 1¼ :471 1:383 2:063ft 18 LB117 49 712 713 910¼ Bayer J D2 4000 68-23 NohlmWnd,DckStrt,SlfDtrmntn 10
1Aug90-5Lga 1 1/16 :474 1:132 1:462ft 26 LB1125 65¾ 63¼ 69 66¾ Keckler R1 4000 65-27 Dli'sBrtt,GrtstOfAll,FlyingOfficr 10
8Jly90-11Lga 1 1/16 :471 1:12 1:452ft 13 LB1155 97¾ 87¼ 57½ 66¾ Belvoir V4 5000 70-20 BillyDay,IvoryMerchant,Nmeske 12
24Jun90-2Lga 6f :214 :451 1:111ft 13 122 77¾ 68 47½ 66¼ Jauregui L H11 5000 77-14 Kentucky Trip,FireAlley,SoTesty 12
6Jun90-10Lga 1 1/16 :491 1:132 1:461gd 3¾ 117 45 45½ 59¼ 510 Bayer J D7 c4000 63-27 Cpitlist,LillinsPrince,ImATrooper 8
26May90-6Lga 6½f :22 :453 1:18 ft 8 122 128¾116½ 88¾ 32 Bayer J D6 6250 79-16 JericoJke,KnifeRiver,MmoryLps 12
16May90-1Lga 6½f :221 :454 1:18 ft 7¾ 119 75½ 63¾ 42½ 41¼ Bayer J D3 4000 80-15 BestMark,MariniRed,LordEmmus 8
6May90-6Lga 1 :464 1:112 1:384ft 6¼ 120 79½ 811 77½ 77¼ Best F5 6250 68-24 GdTmBddy,RdwdStr,Pppg'sPrnc 10
22Apr90-3Lga 1 :463 1:123 1:382m 6½ 1155 812 57 44½ 35 Belvoir V8 6250 72-26 TemprsFlr,RdwoodStr,MmoryLps 9
15Apr90-6Lga 1 :484 1:144 1:411gd 4½ 1155 1½ 11½ 1hd 43¾ Belvoir V1 6250 59-37 DoMAFvorit,RyDlRobl,LillinsPrnc 9

Speed Index: Last Race: –9.0 3–Race Avg.: –6.3 3–Race Avg.: –6.3 Overall Avg.: –7.0

Aug 16 Lga 3f ft :373 Bg Jly 22 Lga 4f ft :50 B

Sir Edward

Ch. g. 4, by Sir Paulus—Ocean Dew, by Oceanus II
SOUTHWICK W E — 119 — Br.—Hagan E J Jr (Wash) — 1990 2 0 0 0
Tr.—Jones Michael David — $4,000 — 1989 14 1 3 5 $12,772
Own.—Jones & Hagan Jr — Lifetime 24 2 6 6 $16,487

11Aug90-11Lga 6½f :221 :451 1:181ft 19 B 116 97½ 86½ 910 87¼ Jauregui L H2 6250 73-22 RnnngProspct,BrngStr,ContyJrk 11
2Aug90-5Lga 6f :221 :453 1:102ft 65 B 116 76¾ 88¼ 915 912¼ Jauregui L H8 12500 76-18 O.K.Yt,PrintsChrming,Bmn'sBndt 9
24Jun89-6Lga 1 1/16 :47 1:112 1:433ft 7¼ 114 65½ 54½ 54 76¼ Aragon V A 2 16000 75-15 Arktikos, ClassyBoss,Pappa'sBrat 8
11Jun89-3Lga 1 1/16 :473 1:124 1:441ft *2 115 86¾ 78 89¼ 711 SouthwckWE 7 12500 67-16 Arktikos,FrnchFoxtrot,CountyJrk 9
11Jun89—Bumped 7/8 turn
24May89-6Lga 6½f :22 :452 1:163ft *3½ 117 85¾ 83 69¼ 33 SouthwckWE 6 16000 83-15 Bldr'sBoy,HoYnMmors,SrEdwrd 10
24May89—Wide 1/4 turn
14May89-8Lga 1 1/16 :473 1:12 1:44 ft 9 114 66 65¼ 66¼ 53¼ SouthwckWE 7 40000 76-16 TroysFriend,DrkFleet,Lord'sLnes 8
30Apr89-5Lga 6½f :223 :461 1:171ft 2½ 117 43 41½ 32 2nk SouthwckWE 4 16000 83-17 PlyMony,SrEdwrd,RnnngProspct 8
15Apr89-8Lga 6f :221 :452 1:101ft 7½ 114 55 53½ 54 33 SouthwckWE 6 20000 82-19 Zoot'sLdy'sMn,Arktikos,SrEdwrd 6
2Apr89-9PM 1⅛ :47 1:114 1:542sy 16 117 612 59 34 33 SthwckWE 5 Ore Dby 69-23 PrimEdton,GoodPhyscn,SrEdwrd 9
19Mar89-9PM 1 1/16 :472 1:13 1:47 ft *8-5 118 57½ 58½ 56½ 57 SouthwickWE 6 InvH 74-20 GoodPhyscn,HbbBbbBr,PrmEdtn 7

Speed Index: Last Race: –5.0 3–Race Avg.: –4.3 5–Race Avg.: –2.4 Overall Avg.: –6.1

Jly 28 Lga 3f ft :371 Bg Jly 22 Lga 5f ft 1:02 B Jly 14 Lga 5f ft 1:002 H Jly 7 Lga 4f ft :483 H

Big Time Louie

Dk. b. or br. g. 4, by Just the Time—Tidy Bubbles, by Windy Tide
MAELFEYT B J — 119 — Br.—Hudson–Gray–Harwood (Wash) — 1990 6 0 0 1 $1,050
Tr.—Drebin Keith — $4,000 — 1989 12 1 2 0 $3,503
Own.—Gray–Harwood–Hudson — Lifetime 18 1 2 1 $4,553

→8Aug90-10Lga 6½f :22 :444 1:174ft 22 LB117 96 118¾ 911 32 Maelfeyt B J3 4000 80-17 ApplMrkt,Jm'sGodOl'By,BgTmL 12
28Jly90-11Lga 6f :214 :451 1:114ft 29 LB119 1013 911 811 74 Cedeno E A6 5000 77-19 Jayndr,MyPictureTime,FireAlley 11
1Jly90-6Lga 1⅛ :484 1:132 1:514ft 22 LB120 2hd 2½ 914 1017 Cedeno E A7 4000 60-27 MostGllnt,CosnAbby,WndsngLd 11
16Jun90-4Lga 6½f :22 :443 1:171ft 24 116 1110 1112 912 88¾ Fox W I Jr 10 5000 76-13 ClssicQuick,KrftyGuy,HloExprss 12
25May90-6Lga 6f :221 :46 1:113ft 7½ 117 1013 1011 99½ 78 Aragon V A 10 6250 74-19 Emperor'sCourt,BstMrk,Csy'sDl 10
17May90-1Lga 6f :213 :452 1:114ft 10 117 811 812 79½ 43¾ Aragon V A 1 6250 77-19 GrysRdr,MyPcturTm,IvoryMrchnt 8
8Dec89-7PM 6f :223 :461 1:123gd *2½ 120 64 66 68 54¼ SouthwickWE 5 8000 86-14 Pul'sSong,MndysResen,ReblsFir 12
19Nov89-12PM 6f :224 :464 1:123ft 7¼ 120 84¼ 53 34½ 26 SouthwickWE 3 8000 84-14 SJudgmnt,BgTmLou,Unqstonbly 11
19Nov89—Wide 1/4 turn
4Nov89-6PM 1 :482 1:142 1:413ft *2 120 63½ 33½ 33½ 68 SouthwickWE 7 8000 75-14 WldToby,Unqustonbly,JustABm 10
27Oct89-6PM 6f :23 :471 1:134sy 2½ 120 62¾ 55 32½ 2nk SouthwickWE 2 8000 84-15 MndysRsn,BgTmLo,WtchAdmCls 9

Speed Index: Last Race: –3.0 3–Race Avg.: –6.0 8–Race Avg.: –4.0 Overall Avg.: –5.6

Jly 24 Lga 4f ft :491 B

Western Nifty

Dk. b. or br. c. 4, by Capt Don—Yu R Nifty, by Yu Wipi
BOULANGER G — 119 — Br.—Henderickson J C (Wash) — 1990 4 0 0 0
Tr.—Smith Larry — $4,000 — 1989 10 1 0 0 $3,305
Own.—Western S Stables — Lifetime 16 1 0 0 $3,305

3Aug90-1Lga 1 3/16 :48 1:14 1:592ft 20 LB114 23 2½ 712 79¼ Delgadillo C 2 5000 66-29 MobsStrp,Ab'sDbbdbbdo,C'EstRn 7
22Jly90-2Lga 6½f :221 :451 1:174ft 25 LB116 62½ 107 1214 1012¼ Delgadillo C 11 5000 70-17 RedwoodStr,RiderBustin',Stonic 12
13Jly90-10Lga 6f :213 :443 1:10 ft 39 LB116 43½ 42½ 33 74¼ Delgadillo C 7 6250 86-14 ScrtForFiv,BrngStr,ClockrsChoc 10

1Jly90-7Lga 6f :213 :444 1:101ft 62 LB116 65¾ 76½109¾ 910½ Bayer J D 7 8000 78-12 SltyShoes,Thorp,CourgeousGorg 12
23Sep89-2Lga 1 1/16 :464 1:121 1:434ft 65 120 33 12161226 — Mercado V V 8 8000 — — Salt Hay,LilliansPrince,TallTales 12
23Sep89—Distanced
15Sep89-5Lga 6f :214 :45 1:103ft 37 120 75 99¼ 911 910 Mercado V V 9 10000 73-23 RushOrder,Tllrun,RunningProspct 9
20Aug89-4Lga 6½f :214 :443 1:154ft 8½ 120 2hd 53½1118 — Lamance C 11 8000 — — ChmpgnB,JyBrCptn,BlckZootZt 11
20Aug89—Eased
11Aug89-2Lga 6½f :22 :453 1:184ft 32 115 11½ 12 11 1nk Lamance C 7 M12500 75-22 WstrnNfty,MontryMgc,Hot'NRn 10
26Jly89-2Lga 6½f :22 :443 1:174ft 43 120 42½ 46 37½ 410½ VlenzuelFZ 3 M12500 69-21 MckyMgmbo,PwrLftr,OnBBrwn 12
14Jly89-1Lga 1 1/16 :472 1:131 1:462ft 23 120 2hd 41¼ 920 926¾ Aragon V A 5 M12500 40-23 IronLord,ChstnutChrl,Andy'sGft 12

Speed Index: Last Race: -13.0 3-Race Avg.: -7.6 6-Race Avg.: -6.6 Overall Avg.: -10.2

Aug 17 Lga 4f ft :494 H Jly 10 Lga 4f ft :483 H

My Picture Time

Ch. g. 4, by Peterhof—Fancy Tish, by Grey Dawn II
BARNESE V J 119 **Br.—Trilogy Farm (Ky)** 1990 12 0 3 0 $2,893
Own.—Jensen Luella M **Tr.—Kenney Dan** $4,000 1989 11 2 0 2 $8,340
Lifetime 24 2 3 2 $11,233

15Aug90-11Lga 1 1/16 :47 1:123 1:454ft 12 LB117 1½ 1hd 68 814 Corral J R3 4000 61-29 CosnAbby,C'EstRn,InstntChckt 12
5Aug90-11Lga 6f :214 :451 1:113ft 5 LB116 2½ 22½ 23 65¾ Best F8 4000 76-19 Can'tCtchRoni,Setonic,BigBdLu 11
→ 28Jly90-11Lga 6f :214 :451 1:114ft 11 LB119 32 43¼ 44 21½ Best F8 5000 79-19 Jayndr,MyPictureTime,FireAlley 11
18Jly90-5Lga 1 1/16 :464 1:123 1:452ft 7½ LB1095 2½ 52 9141017 Belvoir V9 4000 60-22 FlyingOfficer,Cpitlist,HloExprss 12
31May90-10Lga 1 1/16 :473 1:132 1:474m 4½ 117 1½ 11 56½ 28 Barnese V J8 4000 57-34 SlfDtrmntn,MyPctrTm,NhlmWnd 9
17May90-1Lga 6f :213 :452 1:114ft 13 117 1hd 1½ 1hd 23 Best F3 6250 78-19 GrysRdr,MyPcturTm,IvoryMrchnt 8
5May90-6Lga 6f :214 :444 1:11 ft 4 117 1hd 1hd 32 53½ Boulanger G8 6250 81-12 HllowedEnigm,Csy'sDl,NightDrift 9
25Apr90-10Lga 6f :22 :451 1:11 gd 8½ 117 1½ 32½ 614 716½ Olguin G L3 8000 68-16 BigGossip,GarysRaider,KraftyGuy 7
12Apr90-10Lga 6½f :214 :45 1:173ft 7 119 1hd 11½ 11½ 64¼ Best F12 6250 79-11 RysonFether,KrftyGuy,JericoJke 12
25Jan90-11TuP 1 :471 1:123 1:383ft 7¼ 117 51½ 51¼ 41¾ 52½ Guerrero A7 5500 78-18 SightSekr,MnOfArn,SyonrTootsi 10
25Jan90—Stumbled break

Speed Index: Last Race: -5.0 3-Race Avg.: -3.3 6-Race Avg.: -7.1 Overall Avg.: -8.4

Jly 15 Lga 3f ft :37 B Jly 4 Lga 5f ft 1:02 B

Smoother Sailing

Ch. g. 4, by Eagletar—Sand Sailing, by Windy Sands
JAUREGUI L H 119 **Br.—Pacesetter Farm (Wash)** 1990 5 0 0 0 $385
Own.—Collicott G L & MercerBetty **Tr.—Collicott Gary L** $4,000 1989 11 2 1 1 $6,575
Lifetime 20 2 2 2 $8,575

4Aug90-3Lga 1 1/16 :473 1:132 1:46 ft 52 LB114 31½ 33 47½ 79¼ Comber J10 Ⓢ 6250 64-28 DDDddy,HubbBubbBr,Imprimtur 11
4Aug90—Broke in air
28Jly90-5Lga 6f :214 :451 1:11 ft 31 LB119 121411161015 79½ Comber J10 5000 75-19 BgJohnP.,Jm'sGdOl'By,MnyTrns 12
28Jly90—Steadied start
14Jly90-5Lga 6½f :221 :452 1:17 ft 34 LB116 42 52¾ 33 44¾ Comber J11 5000 81-14 NonStop,LittlD'Arcy,V.C.Svings 11
30Jun90-11Lga 6½f :214 :45 1:174ft 52 116 43 87¼1111107¼ Comber J9 6250 75-14 ‡ClsscQuck,Imprmtur,OhHowJst 11
22Jun90-7Lga 6f :213 :442 1:104ft 44 116 85 111212141212¼ Comber J7 8000 74-16 CorgosGorg,BstYrBttns,BgJhnP. 12
1Dec89-9YM 6f :23 :46 1:121ft 6 120 3½ 52¾ 66¼ 612¼ Walker M4 10000 69-19 ‡DcdlyBst,Shrt'NDrty,Emprr'sCrt 6
10Nov89-8YM 6f :223 :453 1:111ft 3½ 120 1hd 1hd 1hd 1hd Walker M7 Ⓢ 12500 86-12 SmothrSlng,DcdlyBst,PrfctAddtn 7
17Sep89-2Lga 6½f :222 :454 1:171ft 15 1155 21 1hd 2½ 65¾ Kimes C9 8000 77-17 Pel'sBucky,LotTim,PrinciplWilli 10
8Sep89-3Lga 6½f :221 :46 1:19 ft 13 120 31½ 32½ 42½ 53½ Steiner J J10 8000 70-25 MnyTurns,Pppgo'sPrince,AGmbl 12
12Aug89-2Lga 1 1/16 :47 1:123 1:461ft 6 120 48 12161226 — Baze G3 10000 — — Digger Will, Writer, Iron Lord 12
12Aug89—Eased

Speed Index: Last Race: -6.0 3-Race Avg.: -7.3 8-Race Avg.: -7.1 Overall Avg.: -7.2

Jly 26 Lga 3f ft :373 B Jly 11 Lga 3f ft :362 B

Green Echo

B. g. 4, by Greenough—Forest Echo, by Tompion
DELGADILLO C 119 **Br.—Roffe S (Wash)** 1990 9 0 0 0 $1,685
Own.—Gentry J **Tr.—Mullens H R** $4,000 1989 2 1 1 0 $1,776
Lifetime 11 1 1 0 $3,461

→ 17Aug90-10Lga 6½f :22 :444 1:17 ft 6½ LB114 31½ 63¼ 88¼ 75¼ Boulanger G 12 5000 81-15 P.J.'SNtv,CorgosFool,LllnsPrnc 12
28Jly90-11Lga 6f :214 :451 1:114ft 4 LB119 56 66¼ 79 43¾ Gonsalves F A 9 5000 77-19 Jayndr,MyPictureTime,FireAlley 11
→ 13Jly90-10Lga 6f :213 :443 1:10 ft 8½ LB116 22 32½ 67 84¾ Gonsalves F A 2 6250 85-14 ScrtForFiv,BrngStr,ClockrsChoc 10
1Jly90-7Lga 6f :213 :444 1:101ft 15 LB116 32 2½ 1hd 54 Best F 4 8000 85-12 SltyShoes,Thorp,CourgeousGorg 12
23Jun90-9Lga 6½f :221 :452 1:164ft 24 116 2hd 2hd 31½ 86¾ Best F 6 10000 80-16 JmesWillrd,CordovRed,NilBendr 12

2Jun90-9Lga	1	:474	1:133	1:401sl	4¾		115	2½	33½	56¾	811¾	Best F 7	12500	56-38	SpnshTsunm,Rgl'sFool,SJudgmnt	9
16May90-7Lga	6f	:221	:454	1:103ft	8		116	2hd	1hd	32¼	44¼	Best F3	16000	83-15	AgntNo.Svn,MontryMgc,HrnOfIss	7
5May90-9Lga	6f	:214	:443	1:093ft	8½e		117	94½	107¾	1014	912¾	Best F7	Aw10600	79-12	Aerodrmtics,RegIBilly,GretForm	10
21Apr90-10Lga	6½f	:214	:45	1:173gd	7½		117	23½	24	52¾	56½	Best F3	Aw10300	76-20	JustaCityBoy,EternlFire,RegIBilly	7
2Dec89-3YM	6f	:23	:453	1:113ft	8-5		122	32	3nk	1½	17	Best F7	Mdn	84-14	GrnEcho,SirLuckyStrk,StormyBy	8

Speed Index: Last Race: -4.0 3-Race Avg.: -3.0 9-Race Avg.: -3.6 Overall Avg.: -3.9

Aug 10 Bon tr.t 5f gd 1:053 B

Seatonic
CEDENO E A **119**
Own.—Holland L & P-Lang T

Ch. g. 8, by Native Born—Bou An Run, by Long Position
Br.—Qvale K M (Wash) **1990 6 0 1 2 $2,525**
Tr.—Holland Peter **$4,000** **1989 14 1 2 3 $15,195**
Lifetime 84 9 15 13 $66,913

→ 18Aug90-11Lga	6½f	:22	:452	1:173ft	8¼	B	116	76¾	76¼	55½	32¼	Cedeno E A5	5000	81-16	RiderBustin',FirwyChmp,Setonic	12
18Aug90—Wide 1/4 turn																
5Aug90-11Lga	6f	:214	:451	1:113ft	11	B	116	1010	68	55¾	2¾	Cedeno E A11	4000	81-19	Can'tCtchRoni,Setonic,BigBdLu	11
5Aug90—Wide 1/4 turn																
28Jly90-5Lga	6f	:214	:451	1:11 ft	6¾	B	119	97¾	1013	813	89¾	Aragon V A8	5000	75-19	BgJohnP.,Jm'sGdOl'By,MnyTrns	12
22Jly90-2Lga	6½f	:221	:451	1:174ft	4½	B	116	3nk	21	52¾	33½	Aragon V A7	5000	78-17	RedwoodStr,RiderBustin',Stonic	12
8Jly90-3Lga	6f	:22	:444	1:094ft	8½	B	116	52¼	66¾	59½	410½	Maelfeyt B J4	6250	80-14	GrysRider,HllowedEnigm,Ptpelli	10
13Jun90-10Lga	6½f	:214	:444	1:163ft	19		119	53¾	77½	97¾	96¼	Valenzuela FZ9	8000	82-16	‡FlshyA.J.,ScrtForFiv,CountyJrk	12
30Aug89-8Lga	6½f	:22	:443	1:161ft	7½		119	2hd	21½	22	33¼	Aragon V A1	10000	85-20	StormyRyStompr,WllPlnnd,Stonc	6
20Aug89-5Lga	6f	:212	:441	1:093ft	4¾		120	63¼	107¼	88¼	94¾	Hanna M A9	8000	83-11	Pt'sInvnton,AndovrWst,BrngStr	11
5Aug89-7Lga	6½f	:221	:451	1:16 ft	11		122	41½	41½	44½	55¾	Hanna M A7	12500	83-18	SassMeSam,ToothAdeenie,Prion	10
23Jly89-9Lga	6½f	:22	:444	1:154ft	6¾		122	3nk	11	42½	77	Hanna M A9	16000	83-13	Sylvia's Baby, Sass MeSam,Prion	9

Speed Index: Last Race: -3.0 3-Race Avg.: -3.0 10-Race Avg.: -2.6 Overall Avg.: -2.6

Jun 30 Lga 5f ft 1:002 H

Lord Emmaus *
D'AMICO D L **122**
Own.—Smith Jenny L

Dk. b. or br. g. 8, by The Irish Lord—Shirley Spragetti, by Umbrella Fella
Br.—Smith W A (Wash) **1990 11 1 0 4 $3,826**
Tr.—Smith Derry B **$4,000** **1989 17 2 5 1 $7,198**
Lifetime 86 12 15 13 $50,272

Entered 24Aug90-11 LGA

28Jly90-10HaP	6f	:223	:391	1:20 ft	*1		124	2½	2½	12	3½	JohnsonTim5	Aw1200	74-20	InstntChckt,RmndTTrl,LrdEmms	8
3Jly90-10Lga	6½f	:22	:452	1:173ft	13	LB	122	1½	21	56½	810	Cooper B3	4000	73-18	NorthernMrit,RossLk,RlNumbrs	12
15Jun90-2Lga	6f	:214	:451	1:11 ft	10		122	1hd	2hd	3½	45½	Cooper B10	4000	79-15	FirwyChmp,KntuckyTrip,Wvlgnd	11
25May90-5Lga	1	:462	1:123	1:402ft	13		1095	1hd	42½	89¼	88¼	Belvoir V5	5000	59-34	WhtstonBlu,Jnk'sFlyr,C'EstRon	10
16May90-1Lga	6½f	:221	:454	1:18 ft	19		119	1½	1hd	2hd	31¼	Cooper B1	4000	80-15	BestMark,MariniRed,LordEmmus	8
27Apr90-5Lga	6f	:214	:452	1:122sy	9		1115	2hd	22	53½	58	Belvoir V3	5000	70-23	BonePhysicin,MistrPppG.,Alstrnd	8
1Apr90-5YM	6f	:224	:452	1:104ft	2		122	1hd	1½	3½	32¾ ♦	Best F3	4000	85-13	DrivingVioltion,Knpl,LordEmmus	7
♦ 1Apr90—Dead heat																
16Mar90-7YM	6f	:223	:452	1:101ft	6¾		1175	1½	3nk	1hd	1hd	Belvoir V9	4000	91-08	LordEmmaus,Bill'NBob,GumFleet	9
3Mar90-5YM	6f	:223	:453	1:103ft	4½		121	11	1hd	31½	33½	Best F4	4000	85-11	Bob'sFlying,NowGon,LordEmmus	6
3Feb90-8YM	5½f	:222	:451	1:043ft	4		122	1hd	52¼	55	511¾	Bayer J2	4000	81-15	TrnTwRck,BrntGsOn,GrtsAndSplt	7

Speed Index: Last Race: -6.0 3-Race Avg.: -7.0 9-Race Avg.: -4.8 Overall Avg.: -5.1

Jly 18 Lga 5f ft 1:023 B

This is a $4,000 claiming race for four-year-olds and upward that have not won a race since April 3. There are no other limits, so you can find four-year-olds like Green Echo that have run only eleven races and eight-year-olds like Seatonic and Lord Emmaus that have both run over eighty and have won respectable amounts of money. This type of race, with a low frequency of winners, significant losing distances, and a low percentage of hot horses that regularly run close to contention, is the type of race you will find filling most of each day's opportunities at most tracks across the country. The claiming prices may be higher at Aqueduct, or they may be allowance horses at Hollywood, but the performance of the field is typical.

The tic marks show which of the past performances I chose to use for speed figures. This is both a subjective and objective process, but not objective in the sense of applying hard-and-fast rules. For example, by the time you get to Sir Edward, you can see that his time of 7.25 lengths behind a 1:18:1 winner is not going to come close to Nijinsky's Promise's most recent race, and Sir Edward has nothing else to recommend him, so there is no sense in bothering with his figures.

To run through the field briefly:

1. **Nijinsky's Promise.** Last race shows a vast, come-from-behind improvement over previous races, and you don't know yet if the time is competitive in this field, so use it.

2. **Kalahari Kid.** Performances are pathetic except third-to-last race (May 13, 1990), which is not only too old, but completely out of character with his previous times. Take his most recent, which is going to come in around 1:12-something and is more typical of him.

3. **Memory Lapse.** Doesn't stand a prayer.

4. **Sir Edward.** Discussed above.

5. **Big Time Louie.** Most recent race is his best, so try it.

6. **Western Nifty.** Showed early speed in his last route race, which is not a bad sign, and even made up a little ground toward the finish. I like this horse better than his second-last race, so I'll take his third last, which is aging but not quite moldy.

7. **My Picture Time.** Exactly the same as Western Nifty.

8. **Smoother Sailing.** You could use the same logic here, especially since he has a written excuse for his last two races, but the third last looks like it would overrepresent his potential in this race. You have to look back to November 1989 to find the last sign of life in this horse, unlike My Picture Time, who has run steadily, placing occasionally, and Western Nifty, who showed something in his last race. Smoother Sailing is unlikely to be a factor today.

9. **Green Echo.** Last race at 6.5 furlongs is not bad, now that the picture of the field is developing; use it. But this is a 6-furlong race, and looking back, this horse has run within about 4 lengths of the winners in four, higher-priced 6-furlong races this summer. Unlike Smoother Sailing, his third-last race is representative of a class of repeated efforts, so I'll take it, too.

10. **Seatonic.** This horse placed and showed in both of his two most recent races, gaining ground both times. The second last race is at

the current distance, but you can tell by looking at it, it is not going to compare with times of other horses already selected. Take the 6.5 furlong, most recent race.

11. **Lord Emmaus.** Not a bad finish in his last race—third by half a length—but look at the time! Six furlongs in 1:20 *flat?* You have to be on the lookout for typos in the *Form,* and if this were one where they left out a "1," making it 1:12:0, you could be in trouble. But without knowing a thing about Harbor Park, Washington, my bet is that it is a small oval and the time is real. His second-last race was poor; the third last is too old. Subjectively, I am going to pass him—knowing that he may be the ringer in the race.

With the speed figures calculated and sorted, the results look like this:

No.	Horse	Dist	Speed	Time
6	Western Nifty	6	952	70.6
9	Green Echo	6	951	70.67
9	Green Echo	6.5	946	77.75
10	Seatonic	6.5	944	77.93
5	Big Time Louie	6.5	942	78.09
1	Nijinsky's Promise	6.5	938	78.47
7	My Picture Time	6	933	72.02
2	Kalahari Kid	6	932	72.11

Many speed handicappers would bet Western Nifty on the basis of the numbers; others—and I am one—would prefer Green Echo, because he is the only horse in the field who can post two fairly recent times in the same range and he supports it with a series of earlier 6-furlong races at a fairly consistent distance behind 1:10+ winners. As a result, I like him better than Western Nifty, who has the top speed figure but has been inconsistent in his races.

The trouble is, I am not crazy about any horse in this race. With $4,000 claimers, or any other level of racing, you will occasionally find a field of horses that have been solidly consistent in their past performances and speed will lead you to a standout winner. More often, at all levels, the past performances are inconsistent and betting a winner is high risk.

The three most likely horses in the money are Green Echo, Western Nifty, and Seatonic, whom I like both for his figure and for being a steady old campaigner. Big Time Louie stands a chance, but I would make the arbitrary speed break at 944.

Turning the results of handicapping into bets is the most critical phase of the game. In a field like this, the chances of a fourth horse—perhaps one that was dismissed out of hand, like Memory Lapse—making a surprise showing is very high. I like Green Echo the most, but not enough for a large single win bet or enough to wheel him as the leader, so I would box him with the other two, in exacta and trifecta bets.

Seattle may be a good place to vacation, if you are a speed handicapper. In this race, at least, the Longacres crowd did what every speed handicapper dreams of—ignored speed and bet Seatonic down to the $2.30-to-$1 favorite on the basis of two respectable and consistent showings in his most recent

ELEVENTH RACE
Longacres
AUGUST 25, 1990

6 FURLONGS. (1.07⅕) CLAIMING. Purse $4,200. 4–year–olds and upward which have not won a race since April 3. Weight, 122 lbs. Non–winners in 1990 allowed 3 lbs. Claiming price $4,000.

Value of race $4,200; value to winner $2,310; second $800; third $610; fourth $375; fifth $105. Mutuel pool $50,377. Exacta pool $37,698. Trifecta pool $83,715.

Last Raced	Horse	M/Eqt.	A.	Wt	PP	St	¼	½	Str	Fin	Jockey	Cl'g Pr	Odds $1
17Aug90 10Lga7	Green Echo	LBb	4	119	9	3	3½	1hd	13	1½	Delgadillo C	4000	7.30
3Aug90 1Lga7	Western Nifty	LBb	4	119	6	5	5hd	31	3½	21½	Boulanger G	4000	10.80
18Aug90 11Lga3	Seatonic	B	8	119	10	6	62½	41	52½	31½	Cedeno E A	4000	2.30
15Aug90 11Lga8	My Picture Time	LB	4	119	7	1	12	21½	21	4½	Barnese V J	4000	5.50
8Aug90 3Lga3	Nijinsky's Promise	LBb	4	119	1	11	11	91½	63	51½	Corral J R	4000	9.60
8Aug90 10Lga3	Big Time Louie	LB	4	119	5	8	83	6hd	73	6½	Maelfeyt B J	4000	13.00
15Jun90 2Lga7	Kalahari Kid	LBb	4	117	2	7	41	73	42½	72½	Belvoir V5	4000	9.70
9Aug90 5Lga9	Memory Lapse	LBb	4	122	3	9	91	8½	93	82	Drexler H	4000	25.10
28Jly90 10HaP3	Lord Emmaus	LB	8	122	11	2	21	5½	8hd	9¾	D'Amico D L	4000	8.00
11Aug90 11Lga8	Sir Edward	B	4	119	4	10	10½	102	103	105	SouthwickWE	4000	12.90
4Aug90 3Lga7	Smoother Sailing	LB	4	119	8	4	7hd	11	11	11	Jauregui L H	4000	17.20

OFF AT 5:59. Start good. Won driving. Time, :21⅘, :45⅕, :57⅖, 1:10⅗ Track fast.

$2 Mutuel Prices:			
9–GREEN ECHO	16.60	12.00	5.40
6–WESTERN NIFTY		10.40	7.40
10–SEATONIC			2.80

$2 EXACTA 9–6 PAID $229.40. $1 TRIFECTA 9–6–10 PAID $407.60.

B. g, by Greenough—Forest Echo, by Tompion. Trainer Mullens H R. Bred by Roffe S (Wash).

GREEN ECHO, within striking distance early, drove through along the inside on the turn to take command, gradually drew clear and just lasted in the final sixteenth. WESTERN NIFTY, never far back, rallied slightly wide into the stretch and closed strongly. SEATONIC lacked early foot, came wide for the drive and finished willingly. MY PICTURE TIME sprinted clear early, could not match strides with GREEN ECHO nearing the stretch, gave way gradually. BIG TIME LOUIE raced wide. LORD EMMAUS stopped after showing brief speed.

Owners— 1, Gentry J; 2, Western S Stables; 3, Holland L & P-Lang T; 4, Jensen Luella M; 5, Macadams R & Sea Horse Six Stable; 6, Gray-Harwood-Hudson; 7, Jones O M or Jean C; 8, Dbts Stable; 9, Smith Jenny L; 10, Jones & Hagan Jr; 11, Collicott G L & Mercer Betty.

Trainers— 1, Mullens H R; 2, Smith Larry; 3, Holland Peter; 4, Kenney Dan; 5, Chambers Mike; 6, Drebin Keith; 7, Fisher Steve; 8, Samuels Bruce; 9, Smith Derry B; 10, Jones Michael David; 11, Collicott Gary L.

races and his $66,913 lifetime campaign. This is a traditional handicapping approach that sometimes works. I liked Seatonic, too—as a factor, not a winner. But what about My Picture Time, the crowd's second, albeit lukewarm, choice at $5.50-to-$1? Were they looking at his earlier 1:12:plus 6-furlong performances? Maybe. But my bet is there was some superficial pace handicapping afoot in his most recent 1 1/16-mile route where he led at the half and 3/4 with a 1:12:3.

Another place worth being is any track where quarter horses run in an extended meet, such as Remington, Ruidoso, and Los Alamitos. The period early in the meet and at short three-day fairs may be most exciting, as horses move in from various tracks and back roads, because the odds and performances vary wildly and speed frequently works. But once the horses settle in and establish themselves on the track, handicapping gets down to business.

The published speed indexes for quarter horses are somewhat more precise than for Thoroughbreds, and many handicappers simply use them. Their flaws do not become apparent until they are used for comparison of speeds between distances and between tracks—which, unfortunately, is necessary in virtually every race.

Dashing Lee Ann's 93 and 91 speed indexes in her second- and third-last performances fooled a good percentage of the crowd at Ruidos Downs, who, along with the fans at Los Alamitos, may be the most savvy quarter horse handicappers in the country. Even though she went off at 29-to-1 and 32-to-1 in her previous performances at Canterbury Downs, the Ruidoso crowd bet her down to 6.5-to-1 on the basis of her 93 speed index, which was recorded at the 440-yard distance of the upcoming August 2, 1990, race. She ran a full length *faster* on August 2, finishing sixth with a time of 22.13—for a Ruidoso speed index of 80. For the same performance at Canterbury, she would have received a 96.

Although you will often find the published speed indexes tracing your own, especially after performances at meets become established and between tracks with similar quality of competition, calculating your own figures

NO RIDER						Life	19	1	6	2	$18,216
Dashing Lee Ann			Ser. f. 3, by Streakin Six—Miss Dazzlin Dash, by Dash For Cash								
			Br.—Phillips B F Jr (Tex)				1990	6	0	1	0	$3,519
Own.—Henry L F		**120**	Tr.—Sanders Randall R				1989	13	1	5	2	$13,507
2Aug90-11Rui 440 :21.73 ft tw 6½		120	6½ 6³ Martinez AJ 4 Alw4000 :22.13			80 FlurDCoup,NtivGypsysJt,SmshdToAT 8					
2Aug90—Bumped at start											
3Jun90-9Cby 440 :22.00 sy tw	29	122	52½ 41¾	Miller D 1 Cby Dby 2 :22.27	93	PtrckRmbo,WhrlngLord,Sssysonhgh 11					
26May90-10Cby 400 :20.26 sy	32	119	51½ 41	MillerD 3 @Ssysnrtsk :20.34	91	ContssRon,Sssysonhghg,BrghtIdMrry 9					
5May90-11Cby 350 :17.95 ft	27	114	11⁶ 11³¼	BllngsG7 Dshngldshp3 :18.59	78	FAncyLorene,NuVision,MissieWhels 12					
27Apr90-9Cby 350 :17.99 ft	10	117	1012 10⁶½	CervantesE 9 InugrlH :19.36	56	Iris Top Bug, Honi Wins, Nu Vision 11					
7Apr90-10DeD 350 :17.87 ft	5½	124 7	2¹ 2ʰᵈ	Ortiz G7 Alw1700 :17.89	98	PhoebsScrt,DshingLAnn,LightOnCsh 10					
12Nov89-5BRD 400 :20.42 ft cw	11	118 4	4¾ 41½	Gentry D 9 Aw2700 :20.65	77	BgSmsh,HrlqnsTorndo,Whinthmony 10					
28Oct89-7BRD 330 :17.31 ft cw	5½	120 7	3¾ 2¼	Gentry D 4 Aw1400 :17.39	82	DellasChamp,DshingLeeAnn,Estrpde 10					
Jly 24 Rui 330 ft :17.56 Hg											

will always provide an edge in both accuracy and a systematic thought process as you evaluate the field. At some tracks speed indexes are occasionally or frequently omitted for various reasons, and when this occurs, the advantage is complete.

Transferring speed figures from quarter horse straightaway races to 870 sprints around one turn holds the same dangers as comparisons between large distance gaps in Thoroughbred sprints. But because of the intensity of 870 races, speed often holds, even in the lowest, maiden claiming ranks.

2nd Los Alamitos

870 YARDS. (:44.41)MAIDEN CLAIMING. Purse $3,000. 3- and 4-year-olds. Weights, 3-year-olds, 120 lbs.; 4-year-olds, 122 lbs. Claiming price $2,500.

GARCIA EDDIE
Win Burno Tb — Life 2 0 1 0 $777
Ch. g. 4, by Charisma II—Chrsity Sandsy, by Happy Harry F
Br.—Asadurian M & S (Cal) 1990 2 M 1 0 $777
Own.—Asadurian Manny & Sam 122 Tr.—Monteleone Frank J $2,500 1989 0 M 0 0

10May90-2LA 870 :48.05 ft 2¼ 122 5¾ 3nk 2nk Garcia E 3 M3200 :48.12 — Hallie Star Tb, Win Burno Tb, TheBrick 8
→ 5May90-2LA 870 :46.46 ft 3 122 45 46 56¾ Didericksen K 2 M4000 :47.68 26 DandyRenaTb,NoDeals,SherwoodBrown 8
5May90—Bumped at start

LACKEY JAMES
Sherwood Brown — Life 7 0 0 1 $658
Ch. g. 3, by Woodstock Brown—Wee Goletta, by Wee Folk Tb
Br.—Wells Martha or Dwayne (Cal) 1990 3 M 0 1 $542
Own.—Wells Martha or Dwayne 120 Tr.—Wells Dwayne $2,500 1989 4 M 0 0 $116

→ 5May90-2LA 870 :46.46 ft 3½e 122 22 34 32¾ Garcia E 5 M4000 :46.93 45 DandyRenaTb,NoDeals,SherwoodBrown 8
11Apr90-4BM 870 :47.33 ft 14 120 31½ 43½ 42¾ Solis W 2 M2500 :47.95 28 WhisprHisNm,SnppySmugglr,MissHsitll 7
11Apr90—Bumped 1/16
2Mar90-2BM 870 :47.81 sy 5 122 610 613 620 Meier J 5 M2000 :51.49 — MyGdDctr,LllByDncr,I'mAnIrshStrmTb 6
12Oct89-10LA 440 :22.51 ft 17e 122 84¼ 95½ 98¼ White S 8 M2500 :23.81 41 ChaseMeBaby,OttoMticDigger,GrnFvor 9
29Sep89-1LA 440 :22.43 ft 57 122 72¼ 63 52¾ Aguilar C 2 M2500 :22.83 65 VndysEsterJt,CliforniGrn,WhisprHisNm 8
22Sep89-1LA 350 :18.12 ft 96 122 72¼ 64 55 Aguilar C 4 M2500 :18.88 58 Tangibility, Cajun Delta, Mighty Dasher 8
22Sep89—Broke out, bumped
31Aug89-1LA 350 :18.26 ft 16 122 52 75 76¾ Aguilar C 1 M2500 :19.34 44 ElmersBest,GoneDshing,WhisperHisNm 9
31Aug89—Bore out

PROCTOR LUTE
Seattle Cindi — Life 5 0 2 1 $1,204
Br. f. 3, by Slewacide Tb—Cindio, by Jonny Apollo
Br.—Nakamura Frank (Cal) 1990 3 M 2 1 $1,204
Own.—Bloomquist Charles E 115 Tr.—Bloomquist Charles E $2,500 1989 2 M 0 0

→ 25Apr90-2LA 870 :46.84 ft *2-3 118 43¼ 44¼ 34¾ Proctor Lute 3 M4000 :47.18 — BirthdyDelightTb,GrlndBrown,SttlCindi 6
30Mar90-4BM 870 :47.09 ft *8-5 118 31 11 2hd Proctor L 5 M2500 :47.11 49 SpringAggrvtinTb,SttlCindi,DsrtMrrdoc 8
9Mar90-5BM 870 :47.31 ft 3 119 42½ 32½ 21¼ Proctor L 4 M2000 :47.57 38 Mepps, Seattle Cindi, Jojoba Okie 7
20Jly89-2LA 350 :18.37 ft 33 122 81¾ 92 62¾ Proctor L 9 ⒻM5000 :18.79 63 Oh Baby Me, Roys Doc, Rubinera 10
24May89-3LA 300 :15.90 ft 33 122 101½ 103 105¼ Proctor L 8 ⒻM20000 :16.63 57 Memesis, Smashed On Top,KimiBrown 10
24May89—Broke out, bumped

PAULINE RALPH
Tollson — Life 8 0 0 0
B. g. 3, by Tolltac—Archie Ann, by Dual Exhaust
Br.—Bickel Robert E (Cal) 1990 1 M 0 0
Own.—Bickel Robert E 120 Tr.—Cooper John L $2,500 1989 7 M 0 0

→ 5May90-1LA 350 :17.99 ft 14 122 71¾ 72½ 73 Pauline R 3 M2500 :18.48 69 ResluesGold,RamblinHope,BornToFight 9
5May90—Broke out, bumped
19Sep89-10LA 300 :15.83 ft 41 122 81¾ 71 83 Garcia H 1 M6250 :16.24 70 MrJerimihJohnson,BnkItNow,DrWhoop 9
8Sep89-11LA 300 :15.72 ft 78 122 5¾ 61½ 92¾ Garcia H 8 M10000 :16.13 74 CasdysRockett,StrikinFncy,SpecilSplsh 9
29Aug89-7LA 350 :18.03 ft 37 122 81¾ 83 84¾ Pauline R 2 M10000 :18.73 62 TripolisDshr,DmondsRSpcl,CsdysRocktt 8

16Aug89-10LA 350 :17.93 ft 26 122 6^{1} $6^{2\frac{1}{4}}$ 6^{4} Pauline R 5 Mdn :18.56 67 PyThChifDus,SmokumMyrs,ATinyRqust 8
7Jun89-4LA 350 :17.70 ft 56 122 $7^{1\frac{3}{4}}$ $7^{4\frac{3}{4}}$ $7^{5\frac{3}{4}}$ Pauline R 5 Fut Trl :18.54 67 StrwflySpecil,ShirleysStrdust,LsVegsDi 8
2Jun89-10LA 300 :15.74 ft 41 122 $10^{3\frac{1}{4}}$ $10^{4\frac{1}{4}}$ $9^{4\frac{1}{2}}$ Pauline R 3 Mdn :16.57 59 Teller Cash,LuvUMe,TheAtomicRocket 10
13May89-8LA 300 :15.66 ft 34 122 $10^{6\frac{1}{4}}$ 10^{10} 10^{12} Pauline R 3 [S]Mdn :17.49 28 Tickey Tack, Components,PocoDotDot 10
13May89--Broke very slowly
●May 12 LA 870 ft :48.00 D Apr 24 LA 350 ft :19.10 Dg

SPARKS KRIS
Little Bit Crisp
Own.—McDaniel Tommie L 117
Life 9 0 1 0 $577
Sor. m. 4, by Crispen Tb—Bonnie Bid, by Snooper Bid
Br.—Loeb Shirley&RynesBarbara (Cal) 1990 4 M 0 0 $232
Tr.—Berry Rick $2,500 1989 5 M 1 0 $345

→ 10May90-2LA 870 :48.05 ft 27e 117 3^{nk} 4^{nk} $4^{2\frac{1}{4}}$ Sparks K 4 M3200 :48.54 — Hallie Star Tb, Win Burno Tb, TheBrick 8
13Apr90-3BM 870 :46.57 ft 28 122 5^{2} 6^{8} 6^{11} Garcia E 6 M2000 :48.75 — Desert Merridoc,JojobaOkie,TustinFlyer 6
5Apr90-4BM 870 :47.59 ft 20 119 3^{2} 5^{5} 7^{8} Garcia E 3 M2000 :49.29 — Demarche, Jojoba Okie, DesertMerridoc 7
5Apr90—Broke in, bumped
22Mar90-6BM 870 :47.29 ft 24 117 $5^{3\frac{1}{4}}$ $5^{5\frac{1}{2}}$ 7^{4} Hearn L 6 M2000 :48.22 — Seenos Champ,Demarche,LillBayDancer 7
20Sep89-3Fpx 350 :18.09 ft 60 116 $5^{1\frac{1}{4}}$ $9^{6\frac{1}{4}}$ Stewart J 1 M3500 :19.08 58 FraudulentFreddie,‡HugoFst,CvirDrems 9
25Aug89-1Sac 870 :45.88 ft 31 114 6^{8} $5^{5\frac{3}{4}}$ Sparks K A 4 M2500 :47.11 54 Raise InClass,BornTrashey,FoolForLove 8
16Aug89-2Fer 660 :34.60 ft 11 113 $3^{6\frac{1}{2}}$ $2^{7\frac{1}{2}}$ Sparks K A 5 M5000 — RiseNFst,LittleBitCrisp,JtsMightyLgnd 5
2Aug89-1SR 870 :48.03 ft 47 114 7^{11} $7^{3\frac{1}{2}}$ Banderas A L 2 M3500 :48.94 — ShesGsMoney,PreppieNtive,FoolForLov 7
20Jly89-5Sol 350 :18.58 ft 35 118 $8^{5\frac{3}{4}}$ 7^{5} Banderas A L 6 M3500 :19.57 51 Rusty Replica,BlazingRoyal,TimelyAsset 9

DIDERICKSEN KIP
The Brick
Own.—Stanley Edwin 120
Life 3 0 0 1 $388
B. g. 3, by Circling Jim Tb—Nagoya Express, by Tiny Charger
Br.—Herburger Bob & Marion (Cal) 1990 1 M 0 1 $388
Tr.—Monteleone Frank J $2,500 1989 2 M 0 0

→ 10May90-2LA 870 :48.05 ft 4½ 122 2^{hd} 1^{hd} $3^{1\frac{3}{4}}$ Didericksen K 5 M3200 :48.44 — Hallie Star Tb, Win Burno Tb, TheBrick 8
16Nov89-11LA 400 :20.65 ft 38 122 9^{3} $9^{4\frac{1}{4}}$ 9^{6} Figueroa R 3 M2500 :21.65 52 ElRyPoquito,NturlSummit,ClifroniGrn 10
4Nov89-2LA 400 :20.49 ft 20 122 6^{3} $6^{7\frac{3}{4}}$ $7^{8\frac{1}{2}}$ Figueroa R 6 M3200 :21.83 47 WinForWoodstock,ClifroniGrn,GrnFvor 7
Apr 27 LA 870 ft :48.50 D

SEVILLE RALPH
Chielli Tb
Own.—Craigmyle J & N &EknolanT 115
Life 1 0 0 0
Br. f. 3, by Ponchielli—Easily Jean, by Easily Best
Br.—Lewis P & Lou Jeanne (Ariz) 1990 1 M 0 0
Tr.—Craigmyle Scott $2,500 1989 0 M 0 0
5May90-2LA 870 :46.46 ft 24 122 $8^{5\frac{1}{2}}$ 8^{11} 7^{13} Pauline R 8 M4000 :48.80 — DandyRenaTb,NoDeals,SherwoodBrown 8

MEIER JOE
Saras Revenge Tb
Own.—Benitas-Cassady-Sanders 115
Life 1 0 0 0
B. f. 3, by Spring Deer—Sea Reb, by Reb's Policy
Br.—Whisant L (Cal) 1990 1 M 0 0
Tr.—Cassady John $2,500 1989 0 M 0 0
→ 5May90-2LA 870 :46.46 ft 14 117 $7^{5\frac{1}{4}}$ $6^{8\frac{1}{2}}$ 6^{9} Fogner J 7 M4000 :48.11 — DandyRenaTb,NoDeals,SherwoodBrown 8
5May90—Bore in

Also Eligible (Not in Post Position Order):

PAULINE RALPH
D'Oro Bearer Tb
Own.—Begue-Dutko-Kent 122
Life 0 0 0 0
B. g. 4, by Color Bearer—Fiorina d'Oro, by Prince Little
Br.—Ribbonwood Farms (Cal) 1990 0 M 0 0
Tr.—Craigmyle Scott $2,500 1989 0 M 0 0

There is not much explanation needed in the selection of past performances in the second at Los Alamitos on May 17, 1990. With lightly raced maidens that have shown game, if not spectacular, finishes—as have almost all of the horses in this field—it doesn't matter if the price tag is $2,500 or $25,000—you are handicapping essentially the same race. Only the final time is likely to be different. Since actual finish times are published, you can see that Win Bruno's second-last race is his better effort, even though the first speed index is omitted and the second is horrendous. Tollson's published speed indexes in comparison to the field, and recent 870 workout, suggest that both he and his connections are serious about the switch off the straightaway. He can't be dismissed, so I will use his most recent 350-yard effort. Chielli has no speed index for her one previous race, but it is easy to see that her performance in relation to the other horses in that race and her 48.80 time are going to drop her off the scale.

No.	Horse	Dist	TPL	Speed	Time
2	Sherwood Brown	870	.1438	943	46.93
3	Seattle Cindi	870	.1446	938	47.18
4	Tollson	350	.1408	931	18.48
1	Win Bruno	870	.1461	928	47.68
8	Saras Revenge	870	.1475	920	48.11
6	The Brick	870	.1485	913	48.44
5	Little Bit Crisp	870	.1488	911	48.54

In this table you can see both the calculated speed figure and the time per length of the past race that it is calculated from. Note that Tollson's time per length is considerably faster, but earned only a 931 on the 350-yard baseline.

Unlike many approaches to speed handicapping, the value of a speed point was not the starting point in this method, but a product of the theory, so a speed point is not equal to a predetermined fraction of a second. For the quarter horse scale, it turns out that 10 points are equal to about 0.17 seconds, or about a length and a half (at quarter horse speeds), depending upon the distance and the speed of the individual race.

On the Thoroughbred scale, one speed point is equal to about one-half length, which again is a product of the theory and not an arbitrary starting point. The difference in scale is a reflection of the proportion of speed at quarter horse and Thoroughbred distances.

As you work with quarter horse times and speeds, you will come to share the amazement of how frequently quarter horses run within a half- or

SECOND RACE 870 Yards. (:44.41) Quarter Horses. MAIDEN CLAIMING. Purse $3,000. 3- and 4-year-olds.

Los Alamitos
Weights, 3-year-olds, 120 lbs.; 4-year-olds, 122 lbs. Claiming price $2,500.

MAY 17, 1990

Value of race $3,000; value to winner $1,650; second $675; third $375; fourth $225; fifth $75. Mutuel pool $20,812. Exacta pool $27,787.

Last Raced	Horse	Eqt.A.Wt PP	1	2	Fin	Time	Jockey	Cl'g Pr	Odds $1
5May90 2LA3	Sherwood Brown	b 3 122 2	2½	2²	1½	0:46.84	Lackey J	2500	4.80
5May90 1LA7	Tollson	b 3 122 4	1½	1²	2³½	0:46.93	Pauline R	2500	3.10
25Apr90 2LA3	Seattle Cindi	b 3 116 3	3½	3¹	3nk	0:47.55	Proctor L	2500	1.90
10May90 2LA2	Win Burno Tb	b 4 122 1	6¹	4hd	4nk	0:47.60	Garcia E	2500	3.70
10May90 2LA4	Little Bit Crisp	4 117 5	4½	5⁴	5½	0:47.67	Sparks K	2500	24.80
5May90 2LA7	Chielli Tb	b 3 122 7	7²	6½	6²½	0:47.96	Seville R	2500	67.50
5May90 2LA6	Saras Revenge Tb	b 3 122 8	8	7¹½	7½	0:48.42	Meier J	2500	41.20
10May90 2LA3	The Brick	b 3 122 6	5½	8	8	0:48.69	Didericksen K	2500	5.50

OFF AT 7:51 Start good for all but SARAS REVENGE. Won driving. Time, :46.84 Track fast.

$2 Mutuel Prices:
2-SHERWOOD BROWN	11.60	6.00	3.60
4-TOLLSON		5.20	4.00
3-SEATTLE CINDI			2.40

$2 EXACTA 2-4 PAID $50.40.

quarter-length (which is in the 0.06- to 0.03-second range) of their individual speed potential, whether they win at their own level or place three lengths behind the field when outclassed.

Sherwood Brown is 5 points over his nearest rival, Seattle Cindi, and a 12-point jump over Tollson's 931, earned at 350 yards. He has done much worse in the past, but there is nothing to suggest he will not do as well today and run at least a half-length ahead of the field. The major speed point break occurs between Win Bruno and Saras Revenge. Win Bruno's modest show of speed and second-by-a-neck finish holds him among the possibilities, especially since this will be only his third race. He apparently has some will to run and may improve. Chaos can happen, but without it no horse from Saras Revenge down stands a prayer. Sherwood Brown is strong enough to warrant wheeling him ahead of the other three in an exacta (2-3, 2-4, 2-1) and backing it up in the mutuel pool with win, place, or show bets, depending upon your conviction.

Seattle Cindi was the crowds' favorite in her last two races, both at Los Alamitos and Bay Meadows, and went off as the $1.90-to-$1 favorite in this race. The only real surprise in the odds was The Brick, who was bet down to $5.50 while theoretically outrunning only Little Bit Crisp in the past, who was a little overenthusiastically backed at $24.80-to-$1. This was no doubt based on The Brick's ride by Kip Didericksen, who was the leading quarter horse jockey in 1990 with earnings well over double his closest competition in the country. Even Didericksen can't get off and push.

Note that three horses in this race—Win Bruno, Chielli, and Saras Revenge—are Thoroughbreds that have started, and will probably finish, their careers at quarter horse distances. Saras Revenge is out of a Reb's Policy mare, which is one of the leading Thoroughbred sires of quarter horse runners, so her competition at the 870-yard distance may have been settled when the idea to breed her dam was conceived.

Wind is seldom a recorded factor at Los Alamitos, but it is a major one at Ruidoso Downs and other quarter horse tracks across the West. In each of the 870-yard past performances in the previous race, the wind factor was entered as "zero," which will be the case for all races around a turn, even if the gale is overturning cars in the parking lot. When wind is a recorded factor, it provides a major advantage over the published speed indexes.

The seventh race on August 11, 1990, was typical of Ruidoso, with wind recorded in many of the past performances.

Another thing that is typical of Ruidoso Downs is the quality of quarter horse breeding that appears in every level of racing. This is a $3,200 claiming race in which almost every horse is a son or daughter of a leading sire of the breed. Torch Run is by Easy Jet, the all-time leading sire. All of the other "Easy" sires listed are some of his top-producing sons. Dash N Breeze is an "own son" of Dash For Cash, the sire of the decade. Jets Special Dude is out of Special Effort, close behind Dash For Cash in most categories of winners and earnings. This is like seeing a whole field of sons of Danzig and Fappiano compete for a $10,000 tag at Belmont.

7th Ruidoso

350 YARDS. (:17.24)CLAIMING. Purse $2,800. 3-year-olds. Weight, 120 lbs. Non-winners of a race since July 10 allowed 2 lbs.; a race since May 9, 4 lbs. Claiming price $3,200. (Claiming races for $2,500 or less not considered.)

LASIX—Simon Six, Shoot Em Up Linde, Dandy Danny Boy, Working Class Man, Miss Julie Lark, Leave Em Lonely, Jets Special Dude, Lotta Toro.

MYLES L

Simon Six

Own.—McGuire & Rheudasil Mmes **120**

Sor. g. 3, by Streakin Six—Rare View, by Tiny Charger
Br.—Phillips & Rheudasil (Tex)
Tr.—Gilbreath C Dwayne **$3,200**

Life	10	1	0	0	$1,826
1990	7	1	0	0	$1,690
1989	3	M	0	0	$136

26Jly90-2Rui	400	:20.08 gd	hw	3¾	L	120	62¼	52¾	Myles L 8	3200	:20.45	82	CoolLadybug,MissJulieLrk,BornCool	10
4Jly90-1Rui	350	:17.96 sy	hw	18	L	120	91¾	92¼	Myles L 2	10000	:18.33	75	CoverdPolicy,StrkNCsh,HighSugrCrk	9
4Jly90—Bumped start														
1Jun90-9Rui	400	:20.47 ft	hw	54		120	3½	61¼	Baber W G 5	25000	:20.66	76	EsyPnnys,CovrdPolicy,HghlyFstdous	10
17May90-7Rui	400	:19.78 ft	cw	21		120	61¾	65	Baber W G 8	Dby Trl	:20.43	82	RRLeMistrl,TwoNSweet,PhoebesScrt	9
11Apr90-8Sun	350	:17.88 ft		16		122	4nk	4½	Myles L 3	Alw3300	:18.03	85	StreakNCsh,SureNufEsy,MelsBunny	10
11Mar90-5Sun	350	:17.66 m	tw	5¼		122	61¾	82¼	Myles L 5	Alw3500	:18.13	82	AzulRaposa,SailOnChico,FirstStanza	10
10Feb90-1Sun	350	:17.79 ft	tw	3½		122	1½	1hd	Myles L 10	Mdn	:17.79	95	Simon Six, Rocky Smash, Nintendo	10
1Sep89-2Rui	400	:20.24 ft	tw	2½		120	51¼	6¾	Myles L 5	Mdn	:20.40	83	LnlyArThbrv,MgcBdn,WndsOnAHgh	10
1Sep89—Bumped start														
9Aug89-1Rui	440	:21.88 ft	tw	16		120	61¼	51	Myles L 3	Fut Trl	:22.07	82	Feature This Cash,Jotsa,SafariSmoke	9
15Jun89-9Rui	350	:17.83 ft		19		120	41½	53	Myles L 7	Fut Trl	:18.20	79	CovrdPolicy,EsyBginnng,FstsDrkAngl	9

BROOKS R

Shoot Em Up Linde

Life 10 1 0 1 $5,760
Sor. g. 3, by Easy Linde—Bitty Bang Bang, by go With The Wind
Br.—Clemmons J (NM) 1990 5 0 0 1 $2,212
Own.—Clemmons J **117** **Tr.—Clemmons Jim R** **$3,200** 1989 5 1 0 0 $3,548

22Jly90-2Rui	350	:17.65 sy tw	13 L	118	4nk	4 2½	Dolphus S A 1	S 3200	:17.92	87	LgrimsAzul,ThSlvrMoolh,StrwMBrght	8
→27Jun90-8SFe	400	:19.92 ft tw	60	122	5 1¼	9 3¾	DolphusSA 2	S DbyTrl	:20.42	89	‡AbotTmHghTm,BcklUpJt,ClsscHnd	10
28May90-8SFe	400	:20.45 ft hw	3¼	118	8 1½	10 3	Harmon BD 3	Alw3500	:20.89	77	JeweledMoon,TateExpress,HicrdItch	10
28May90—Unruly gate												
20May90-6Alb	400	:20.10 ft cw	16	121	3½	3 2	HarmonBD 2	HrdTwst	:20.38	89	OhAlf,DustyMoolah,ShootEmUpLinde	4
28Apr90-8Alb	350	:18.04 ft cw	39	118	3nk	6 1½	HrmonBD 4	S Alw5000	:18.27	85	Easy Gaelic, Magna Glide, Easy Bits	10
22Sep89-10Alb	400	:20.37 ft cw	53	120	9 1½	10 5½	ThdfordR 3	S FutCon	:21.14	70	ClssicHnd,ColorMyWgon,HulkAMnic	10
12Sep89-9Alb	400	:20.30 ft cw	24	120	4 1	4 1¼	ThdfordR 10	S FutTrl	:20.50	86	ImSteppinOut,HolyBug,HrrierQueen	10
12Jly89-2SFe	350	:18.15 ft hw	48	120	6 1¼	7 2¾	Thedford R 3	Fut Trl	:18.55	79	StrkinShdow,EsyRxTwo,MjstysBunny	9
16Jun89-1SFe	350	:18.54 ft cw	2¼	121	1hd	1 1	Thedford R 6	S Mdn	:18.54	79	ShootEmUpLind,Emritus,ChmpsRlJt	10
16Jun89—Drifted out												
2Jun89-5Alb	350	:18.20 ft	8¼	122	5 1½	5 3¼	Thedford R 10	S Mdn	:18.67	73	Go Bimbo,JinglebobJim,ClassicHand	10

Jun 22 SFe 330 ft :17.80 H

NO RIDER

Dandy Danny Boy

Life 20 1 3 2 $3,572
Sor. g. 3, by Easy Dinero—Bobbies Dandy Jet, by Easy Dandy Dan
Br.—Fincher H O (Tex) 1990 13 1 3 1 $3,192
Own.—Fincher H O & Shelton G E **116** **Tr.—May E Lenard** **$3,200** 1989 7 M 0 1 $380

22Jly90-7SFe	350	:18.10 ft hw	16 L	118	6½	9 4¼	Fincher T W 1	2500	:18.68	76	HoppnForDoc,RockttAiird,RdnckPln	10
6Jly90-7Rui	350	:17.76 ft cw	10	116	4nk	6 2	Martinez A J 5	3200	:18.04	83	Gopen,LegendOfLeinster,RndomRyon	9
1Jly90-2Rui	400	:20.06 ft tw	27	116	6 1	6 1½	McGonagill M 6	4000	:20.33	85	Dark Jay, An EasyWinner,EaglesPatti	9
25May90-5Rui	350	:17.93 ft hw	23	120	7 1	7 4	Summerow D 10	3200	:18.47	71	AJSNtiveSmok,SilksTxsKid,PrlsAngl	10
4May90-5Sun	400	:20.42 ft	8	119	2½	2 1	Blevins D 4	3200	:20.57	74	DinnerDinh,DndyDnnyBoy,Hercomsbv	8
20Apr90-3Sun	350	:17.83 ft	21	122	5¾	7 2	Blevins D 3	3500	:18.16	81	MissJulieLrk,RiseYourWgr,Hrcomsbv	9
1Apr90-5Sun	440	:22.17 ft hw	6¼	117	7¾	8 3½	Briggs T K 2	2500	:22.64	72	Whtsoesy,FolsMgicRockt,SpcilSourc	10
23Mar90-2Sun	440	:21.85 ft	13	119	5½	6 3	Martinez A J 3	5000	:22.36	79	IndpndntJt,JhnnsIntnt,BrnHmThCsh	10
9Mar90-5Sun	400	:20.10 ft tw	7¾	122	1hd	2hd	Briggs T K 8	3200	:20.13	85	Dmndsnhrshs,DndyDnnB,KsAprlPrnc	10
23Feb90-1Sun	400	:20.35 ft	5½	122	1½	1nk	Briggs T K 10	M3500	:20.35	82	DndyDnnyBoy,DollyDsher,MsterForc	10

NO RIDER

Dash N Breeze

Life 20 1 2 3 $4,266
Sor. g. 3, by Dash For Cash—Miss Breezie Dawn, by With Ease
Br.—Hedlund G A (Tex) 1990 10 0 2 1 $2,020
Own.—Lewter J T **116** **Tr.—Cross Timothy W** **$3,200** 1989 10 1 0 2 $2,246

→2Aug90-6Rui	350	:17.76 ft tw	13	117	5nk	7 1½	Summerow D 4	4000	:17.96	86	HesMstrBug,FolsUpdt,KissMyStormy	9
14Jly90-2Rui	350	:17.73 sy hw	13	120	7 1½	7 2½	Summerow D 2	6250	:18.08	82	Plum Pie, Fleet Sky, HesaMasterBug	7
14Jly90—Stumbled start												
7Jly90-8Rui	400	:20.07 ft hw	20	116	5 1¼	7 3¼	LidbergMW 6	Alw4000	:20.50	80	DosChivs,NtiveGypsysJet,BlstABuck	10
17Jun90-1Rui	350	:18.07 ft hw	*2	120	1 1	2 1	Baber W G 10	5000	:18.18	80	An Easy Winner,DashNBreeze,Sistex	10
10Jun90-5Rui	350	:17.50 ft tw	19	120	4nk	6 1½	Baber W G 4	12500	:17.72	92	Roman Roula, GameRebel,DosChivas	10
30Mar90-5Sun	400	:19.52 ft tw	20	122	4 2	10 5¼	Baber W G 2	Alw3500	:20.19	83	DoNoWrong,HighlyFstidious,Outlws	10
11Mar90-5Sun	350	:17.66 m tw	23	122	4 1	4 1	Barber W G 6	Alw3500	:22.90	89	AzulRaposa,SailOnChico,FirstStanza	10
7Feb90-3Sun	350	:17.71 ft	*2½	119	5½	8 3	Sauceda J 1	Alw3300	:18.14	85	MrActonBug,CuchlloRojo,JtForPlsr	10
20Jan90-7Sun	350	:17.95 ft	2	116	2hd	2½	Sauceda J 2	Alw3500	:18.03	88	HighlySpecil,DshNBreeze,RiseYouNin	6
10Jan90-5Sun	400	:20.00 ft	18	119	1hd	3¾	Sauceda J 5	Alw3300	:20.12	87	DashingRuler,FancysZevi,DshNBreeze	9

YOAKUM J

Working Class Man

Life 10 1 2 1 $2,828
Sor. g. 3, by Board Chairman—Rocket Miss Hempen, by Rocket Wrangler
Br.—Kennedy Ellen (Okla) 1990 9 1 1 1 $2,628
Own.—Kennedy M Ellen **120** **Tr.—Howell R C** **$3,200** 1989 1 M 1 0 $200

26Jly90-2Rui	400	:20.08 gd hw	*8-5 L	120	3 1½	4 2¾	Yoakum J 5	3200	:20.44	82	CoolLadybug,MissJulieLrk,BornCool	10
→15Jly90-7Rui	400	:19.71 ft tw	6¼ L	120	6¾	6 1½	Yoakum J 2	12500	:20.94	94	StreakNCash,DineroDrem,MoodyEye	10
7Jly90-8Rui	400	:20.07 ft hw	*2½ L	118	6 1¼	6 2¾	Dolphus SA 5	Alw4000	:20.44	82	DosChivs,NtiveGypsysJet,BlstABuck	10
7Jly90—Bumped 1/8 pole												
22Jun90-7Rui	400	:19.81 ft tw	3¼	120	2hd	3nk	Yoakum J 4	Alw4000	:19.88	96	RmblngMnyMn,Jtt276,WrkngClssMn	10
8Jun90-1SFe	350	:18.05 ft cw	9½	122	8 1½	2½	Wilson L 8	Alw3500	:18.12	92	EsyCrossing,WorkingClssMn,EsyBits	10
8Jun90—Bumped start												

2Jun90-2SFe 400 :20.71 ft cw 2¾ 120 1hd 11½ Wilson L 9 Mdn :20.71 81 WorkingClassMn,FortunesRod,Krtell 10
2Jun90—Stumbled start
22Apr90-1Alb 400 :20.37 ft hw 13 121 82½ 73 Wilson L 8 8000 :20.80 78 SomRwrd,AboutTmHghTm,NcklPltd 10
31Mar90-5Sun 400 :19.69 ft tw 3 122 52¼ 63¼ Williams J 5 Mdn :20.15 84 Sound Victory, Nintendo,DipsyMoon 10
31Mar90—Bumped start
9Mar90-3Sun 350 :17.94 ft tw 2½ 122 1½ 11½† Williams J 10 M5000 :17.94 88 †Pl10]‡WrkngClssMn,BbbJyBg,KtyFl 10
9Mar90—Veered in

NO RIDER
Torch Run
Sor. c. 3, by Easy Jet—Hempens Easy Tam, by Hempen Tb
Br.—Kissee & Merrick (Okla)
Own.—Allen M J (Lessee) **116**
Tr.—Allen Mark J $3,200

Life 11 1 1 1 $4,561
1990 8 0 1 0 $1,239
1989 3 1 0 1 $3,322

→ 23Jly90-8Rui 350 :17.79 ft tw 12 116 5nk 6½ Martinez A J 2 3200 :17.91 87 CosmicBndito,LgndOfLinstr,PcificSl 10
23Jly90—Bumped start
27Jun90-7RP 350 :18.38 ft hw 7¾ 118 52½ 53¼ 53 Carter G R 9 Alw5500 :18.86 68 EffortsAwrd,Boonyboyboon,TxsJtski 10
10Jun90-7RP 400 :20.56 ft hw 6 119 41½ 43¼ 43½ Carter G R 3 Alw4300 :21.10 71 HeavenlyCent,FeaturedEffort,ImaLrk 9
1Jun90-10RP 350 :18.36 ft hw 8 119 31 31½ 21¾ Carter G R 1 Aw3800 :18.63 75 RentAWreck,TorchRun,LucksKitagy 10
18May90-3RP 400 :20.41 ft 21 122 7½ 7¾ 72¼ Hodges W 6 Dby Trl :20.77 79 Hatefuls Only, Turn Point, Nitpikins 9
11Apr90-8Sun 350 :17.88 ft 63 122 91¾ 104 Baber W G 2 Alw3300 :18.52 71 StreakNCsh,SureNufEsy,MelsBunny 10
16Mar90-5Sun 400 :19.75 ft tw 34 122 92¼ 94 Nicodemus J 8 DbyTrl :20.27 81 VerySpecilTip,HighBoogi,AngisRqust 9
10Jan90-5Sun 400 :20.00 ft 5 119 5¾ 82¼ Baber W G 1 Alw3300 :20.35 81 DashingRuler,FancysZevi,DshNBreeze 9
28Jun89-9RP 400 :20.16 ft 2¼ 122 42 43 43 Suire L 1 Ⓢ Aw6200 :20.62 86 Pl3]ShwneSvge,GoforBigs,CrystlJelly 9
28Jun89—No excuse
11Jun89-1RP 350 :18.11 ft cw *6-5 122 1 1no 1½ Suire L 6 Ⓢ Mdn :18.11 92 TorchRun,SnekAPeekLdy,IchintoRign 8
11Jun89—Driving finish

NO RIDER
Miss Julie Lark
Sor. f. 3, by Moon Lark—Julie Jet, by Jet Deck
Br.—Bud Boschert's StablesInc (Okla)
Own.—Gist M C **120**
Tr.—Bustamante Johnny $3,200

Life 26 3 3 4 $8,891
1990 11 2 2 2 $4,694
1989 15 1 1 2 $4,197

26Jly90-2Rui 400 :20.08 gd hw 5½ L 122 21 22¾ BustamanteRT10 3200 :20.42 82 CoolLadybug,MissJulieLrk,BornCool 10
14Jly90-5Rui 350 :17.86 gd hw 6¼ L 122 5¾ 52 Bustamante RT5 3200 :18.15 80 LottaToro,AnEsyWinner,FrenchDelt 10
1Jly90-2Rui 400 :20.06 ft tw 16 122 5½ 41 Bustamante RT2 4000 :20.21 88 Dark Jay, An EasyWinner,EaglesPatti 9
17Jun90-1Rui 350 :18.07 ft hw 4¼ 122 61¼ 82½ Bustamante RT4 5000 :18.42 72 An Easy Winner,DashNBreeze,Sistex 10
9Jun90-5Rui 350 :18.03 ft cw 4¾ 122 7¾ 91½ Bustamante RT2 3200 :18.26 77 LgndOfLnstr,GngrsDozn,MgnfcntRlr 10
20Apr90-3Sun 350 :17.83 ft 5 LB 119 1hd 1hd Martinez A J9 3500 :17.83 91 MissJulieLrk,RiseYourWgr,Hrcomsbv 9
20Apr90 - #Stumbled at start
13Apr90-1Sun 400 :19.97 ft tw 3 114 3nk 41½ Martinez A1 2500 :20.23 82 MissMstern,RisYourPyroll,LtMTllYou 8
13Apr90—Bumped start
11Mar90-1Sun 350 :17.98 m tw *9-5 114 2½ 3nk Martinez A J6 2500 :18.06 84 KristisGlss,RisYourPyroll,MissJuliLrk 9
14Feb90-2Sun 350 :18.17 ft tw *2 114 31 2nk Martinez A J 7 3200 :18.24 82 WillingtoTry,MissJuliLrk,MissMstrn 10
31Jan90-2Sun 350 :17.70 ft cw *6-5 117 3nk 31¼ Martinez A J 3 2500 :17.86 93 DeerMry,Herecomesbev,MissJuliLrk 10

NO RIDER
Bar One Lil
Sor. f. 3, by Hear The Band—Liberty Doll, by Chichester tb
Br.—Barone L or Carol (Fla)
Own.—Barone L & Carol **120**
Tr.—Buchanan Iris M $3,200

Life 10 2 1 0 $2,837
1990 4 0 0 0 $195
1989 6 2 1 0 $2,642

30Jun90-9SFe 350 :17.82 ft hw 5¼ 122 105 97¼ Chavez L 6 4000 :18.72 75 DancingDeborh,GerrisChnce,EsyUrlt 10
30Jun90—Broke awkwardly
→ 20Jun90-3SFe 400 :20.40 ft hw 7½ 117 41¼ 41¾ Lidberg M W 6 5000 :20.63 83 MkingAHnd,GerrisChnce,NickelPlted 8
20Jun90—Stumbled start
6Jun90-10SFe 350 :18.07 ft cw 7½e 121 81¼ 94½ Pierce H 1 6250 :18.65 77 AbotTmHghTm,SttnOnOl,MkngAHnd 9
6Jun90—Unruly in gate
12May90-3Rui 350 :18.05 ft hw 10 120 7¾ 62 Pierce H 6 8000 :18.32 75 LdySyntrit,RebelToro,RyonsTopGun 10
10Dec89-6RWD 330 :17.13 ft 4 120 41½ 2hd Luce S 8 5500 :17.15 90 Jet City Gent,Baronelil,Letmetellyou 10
26Apr89-1Sun 350 :18.05 ft tw 6-5 118 1½ 11 Pierce H 4 10000 :18.05 87 BarOneLil,TrytDnce,SmokyInspirtion 7
31Mar89-3Sun 350 :18.33 ft hw 5¼ 120 41½ 1no Pierce H 4 ⒻMdn :18.33 79 Bar One Lil, SpecialLans,GoinAllOut 10
3Mar89-11Sun 330 :16.87 ft tw 37 120 4¾ 42¼ Pierce H 2 Fut Trl :17.17 88 DevilsDgger,CocoSwet,ToroToroToro 9
3Mar89—Bumped start
12Feb89-9TrM 300 :16.14 ft 122 4 4¾ 41½ Tidwell R3 Si49 :16.34 73 Power Train, Intimate Miss, JazBlues 4
29Jan89-8RWD 250 :13.85 sy tw 118 5 51 54 Lewis B5 ⒻAlw500 :14.50 42 MrsMgoo,JohnnysMthLod,TrxStopGl 5

NO RIDER

Leave Em Lonely

Own.—Pool Merlane **116**

B. g. 3, by Viking in the Sky—Lonely Oh Lady, by Jody Oh
Br.—Fry R & Brown K & B (Tex)
Tr.—Thompson William A **$3,200**

Life	22	5	4	1	$14,367
1990	11	3	2	0	$7,894
1989	11	2	2	1	$6,473

14Jly90-5Rui	350	:17.86	gd hw	$3\frac{1}{2}$	L	118		$6^{\frac{3}{4}}$	$9^{3\frac{1}{2}}$	Koyle K 9	c3200	:18.32	75	LottaToro,AnEsyWinner,FrenchDelt	10
→ 1Jly90-2Rui	400	:20.06	ft tw	*8-5	L	118		$4^{\frac{1}{2}}$	$5^{1\frac{1}{2}}$	Koyle K 1	4000	:20.28	86	Dark Jay, An EasyWinner,EaglesPatti	9
10Jun90-9Rui	550	:27.31	ft hw	*$2\frac{1}{2}$		116		1no	$5^{1\frac{1}{4}}$	Koyle K 9	10000	:27.50	88	StnsEsyJt,SmokyInsprton,HghlySpcl	10
13May90-1Rui	400	:20.04	ft hw	$2\frac{1}{2}$		120		2^{hd}	2no	Koyle K 5	6250	:20.05	92	GmeRebel,LeveEmLonely,EsyShower	8
22Apr90-1Alb	400	:20.37	ft hw	*9-5		122		$6^{1\frac{1}{4}}$	$5^{1\frac{1}{2}}$	Chavez L 7	8000	:20.60	63	SomRwrd,AboutTmHghTm,NcklPltd	10
28Mar90-6Alb	400	:20.31	ft hw	$3\frac{1}{4}$		122		$1^{\frac{1}{2}}$	2no	Chavez L 3	8000	:20.32	90	MjestysBunny,LevEmLonly,NttysBob	7
11Mar90-5Alb	350	:18.09	m hw	$4\frac{1}{2}$		122		2^{hd}	1no	Harmon B D 2	8000	:18.09	90	LeveEmLonely,GmeRebel,RblPssWst	9
4Mar90-3Alb	350	:17.91	ft hw	*6-5		122		2^{hd}	$1^{1\frac{1}{2}}$	Harmon B D 6	5000	:17.91	95	Leave Em Lonely,HumANote,AzGone	8
18Feb90-6Alb	350	:18.07	ft hw	$8\frac{1}{2}$		120		6^{1}	$5^{1\frac{1}{4}}$	Cogburn K L 5	10000	:18.25	85	NettysBob,ImpressiveNavn,GmeRebel	6
18Feb90—Stumbled start															
4Feb90-1Alb	350	:17.93	ft	18		120		3^{nk}	$5^{\frac{1}{2}}$	Harmon B D 1	10000	:18.05	91	AboutTmHghTm,GmRbl,HunMoonLrk	9

PAYNE L D

Jets Special Dude

Own.—Gustafson Deborah **116**

B. g. 3, by Special Effort—Miss Jet Eternal, by Panama Jet
Br.—Burbank J H (Cal)
Tr.—Werner R W **$3,200**

Life	12	1	0	3	$1,924
1990	5	0	0	2	$994
1989	7	1	0	1	$930

→ 11Jly90-5RP	350	:18.20	ft tw	16	L	119	2^{1}	$3^{2\frac{1}{2}}$	$3^{2\frac{1}{4}}$	Payne L 3	5000	:18.55	77	ImLittleHnk,EsyMnorJt,JtsSpcilDud	10
28Jun90-5RP	350	:18.74	ft	$9\frac{3}{4}$	L	120	9^{3}	9^{4}	$9^{3\frac{1}{2}}$	Suire L 4	7500	:19.28	56	LassieKirk,BadJoeMondy,JetsCshDel	9
10Jun90-5RP	400	:20.70	ft hw	17		119	1^{nk}	1^{hd}	3^{2}	Payne L 7	Aw 4300	:21.02	73	RunnnByron,BstEffortYt,JtsSpclDud	10
28May90-5RP	350	:17.98	ft cw	$9\frac{1}{4}$		119	$8^{1\frac{3}{4}}$	8^{2}	7^{5}	Payne L 8	20000	:18.76	71	ImLittleHank,DutyDuke,TakeEsyFive	8
18May90-7RP	400	:20.45	ft hw	18		119	2^{1}	2^{1}	$5^{1\frac{1}{2}}$	Payne L 5	Aw 3800	:20.71	80	MissRcyVike,ImLittleHnk,SixKinRzz	12
23Aug89-5Rui	440	:21.83	ft hw	34		120		$9^{2\frac{1}{2}}$	$9^{5\frac{3}{4}}$	Sumpter G 5	Fut Trl	:22.57	69	ContessaCsh,RecklessDsh,RebelDsher	9
23Aug89—Lugged in start															
9Aug89-11Rui	440	:21.88	ft cw	21		120		3^{2}	$3^{1\frac{1}{4}}$	Layton L 3	Fut Trl	:22.04	82	ImaLark,MoonLarky,JetsSpecialDude	9
13Jly89-10Rui	400	:20.19	gd hw	17		118		$6^{1\frac{1}{2}}$	4^{2}	Layton L 7	Aw3200	:20.45	81	FlyMoonlrkJr,StrkNCsh,DoNoWrong	10
15Jun89-2Rui	350	:17.67	ft	13		120		3^{nk}	5^{2}	Layton L 6	Fut Trl	:17.94	87	BlnkrsCommnt,DshForPrks,MonLrky	8
3Jun89-10Rui	350	:17.97	ft hw	11		120		$4^{\frac{3}{4}}$	4^{1}	Layton L 6	Alw3600	:18.12	82	CovrdPolicy,LottToro,SumLilNumbr	10

Also Eligible (Not in Post Position Order):

YOAKUM J

Lotta Toro

Own.—Searls R S Jr **120**

Ch. f. 3, by Easy Toro—Precious Charger, by Heza Charger
Br.—Copeland C (Tex)
Tr.—Yoakum Jesse E **$3,200**

Life	14	3	2	0	$5,366
1990	6	1	0	0	$1,794
1989	8	2	2	0	$3,572

3Aug90-8Rui	350	:17.88	ft cw	$5\frac{1}{2}$	L	120	1^{hd}	6^{1}	Yoakum J 10	3200	:18.06	83	AJSNtiveSmoke,Bobbon,DncersGem	10
→ 14Jly90-5Rui	350	:17.86	gd hw	17	L	120	$1^{\frac{1}{2}}$	1^{hd}	Yoakum J 6	3200	:17.86	88	LottaToro,AnEsyWinner,FrenchDelt	10
29Jun90-2Rui	350	:17.94	ft	14		120	$7^{1\frac{1}{2}}$	7^{2}	McDaniel C W 1	4000	:18.26	77	PontotcCnty,AJSNtvSmk,MyEsySht	10
17Jun90-1Rui	350	:18.07	ft hw	20		120	2^{1}	$6^{1\frac{1}{2}}$	Yoakum J 2	5000	:18.30	76	An Easy Winner,DashNBreeze,Sistex	10
17Jun90—Stumbled bore 1/8														
28May90-2Rui	350	:17.50	ft cw	$8\frac{3}{4}$		120	$8^{2\frac{3}{4}}$	$9^{9\frac{3}{4}}$	Baber W G 3	6250	:18.69	65	RyonsTopGun,DucksFlyHighr,Bobbon	9
19May90-3Rui	350	:17.98	ft hw	16		119	9^{1}	9^{5}	Yoakum J 3	16000	:18.56	68	ShootNo,EsyBginning,OvrhndEffort	11
19May90—Bumped 1/8 pole														
20Aug89-6Rui	350	:17.85	sy hw	*9-5		118	6^{1}	$6^{2\frac{1}{2}}$	Yoakum J 8	10000	:18.21	79	SmshItHi,RiseYourWger,JesseMorgn	8
5Aug89-6Rui	350	:17.95	ft	$7\frac{1}{2}$		118	$5^{\frac{1}{2}}$	1^{hd}	Yoakum J 3	10000	:17.95	86	LottaToro,EasyPearlieJet,Hoofbeats	10
13Jly89-10Rui	400	:20.19	gd hw	14		118	4^{nk}	5^{3}	Yoakum J 1	Aw3200	:20.58	78	FlyMoonlrkJr,StrkNCsh,DoNoWrong	10
30Jun89-6Rui	350	:17.82	ft hw	47		120	$2^{\frac{1}{2}}$	$7^{2\frac{1}{2}}$	Yoakum J 3	Fut Trl	:18.15	81	Obelisk, Do NoWrong,CoveredPolicy	10

DOLPHUS S A

An Easy Winner

Own.—Talley W R **118**

Br. g. 3, by Easy Dozen—Gingers Wrangler, by Rocket Wrangler
Br.—Talley W & Dee (Tex)
Tr.—Atkinson Glen D **$3,200**

Life	13	3	4	2	$9,077
1990	5	1	2	0	$3,144
1989	8	2	2	2	$5,933

→ 5Aug90-1Rui	350	:17.62	ft tw	3	120	4^{nk}	$5^{1\frac{3}{4}}$	Dolphus S A 6	5000	:17.83	89	RndomRyon,StrekToBRich,SpdYouBt	7
14Jly90-5Rui	350	:17.86	gd hw	*3-2	120	$2^{\frac{1}{2}}$	2^{hd}	Dolphus S A 1	3200	:17.89	88	LottaToro,AnEsyWinner,FrenchDelt	10

```
1Jly90-2Rui    400 :20.06 ft tw   4    120    2no 2no  Dolphus S A 5   4000 :20.07 92  Dark Jay, An EasyWinner,EaglesPatti  9
17Jun90-1Rui   350 :18.07 ft hw  3¾    118    3¹  1¹   Dolphus S A 1   5000 :18.07 83  An Easy Winner,DashNBreeze,Sistex   10
   17Jun90—Bore out start
25May90-5Rui   350 :17.93 ft hw   6    120    3nk 41   Hart K 8        3200 :18.07 90  AJSNtiveSmok,SilksTxsKid,PrlsAngl   10
12Aug89-17BnD  350 :18.09 ft hw        122 2  1nk 1½ 4 Bard R 8      AlwTRL :18.09 84  AnEasyWinner,DriftArray,SmshedSlly   8
   ↓12Aug89—Dead Heat
30Jly89-21BnD  350 :17.91 ft           122 4¾ 41  41½  Bard R8       Aw18966 :18.16 82  Pl3]ProperFul,HopkinsPriri,MrPiMn   10
   30Jly89—Sharp effort
23Jly89-11BnD  350 :17.92 ft           122 7²½ 6² 42½  Bard R 9       AlwTRL :18.32 78  Mr Pie Man, Proper Fuel,HighOnJack   9
   23Jly89—Best of others
25Jun89-7BnD   350 :17.88 ft cw        118 4¾ 41¾ 3¾   Wilson N 9    Fnl16896 :18.01 87  SeniorDinero,MkItMov,AnEsyWinnr   10
   25Jun89—Third best


MARTIN J D                                                          Life  9 1 1 1   $12,078
Feel Like Streakin
                          Ser. g. 3, by Streakin Six—Feeling Right, by Dash for Cash
                          Br.—Moore Robert W (Okla)          1990   1 0 0 0
Own.—Irvine T E Jr    116  Tr.—Brooks Jack W      $3,200     1989   8 1 1 1   $12,078
17May90-10Rui  400 :19.90 ft cw   17   120    9²½ 94¾  Martin J D 6   Dby Trl :20.54 79  MghtyEsyPss,MyMxdEmtns,MnsHgh   9
13Oct89-10BRD  400 :20.36 ft cw   3½   120 6  9²½ 94¼  MartinJcky4    @Futtrl :21.03 68  ZevisLegnd,DustyToro,GlimmrofHop  10
30Sep89-9RP    400 :20.14 ft      3¼   120 4  7³¾ 51¾  MrtnJcky5  BClsscsFut :20.41 91  Footprinc,BlushingStrkr,ProfitPolcy  12
20Sep89-1RP    400 :20.76 ft hw        120 7  51¾ 3½   MartinJcky2    @FutTrl :20.87 80  BlushingStreker,StnsPly,FelLikStrkin   7
23Aug89-13Rui  440 :21.95 ft hw   9½   120    8²½ 9²¾  Martin J D 3   Fut Trl :22.32 75  LeTusk,NtiveGypsyJet,EsyBginning  10
10Aug89-2Rui   440 :21.78 ft hw    4   120    3²  22¼  Martin J D 1   Fut Trl :22.01 83  HighlyTund,FlLikStrkin,LightOnCsh  10
   10Aug89—Bumped start
14Apr89-12Sun  350 :17.65 ft    *2-3   120    9³  73½  Martin J D 6   Fut Trl :18.17 84  Do No Wrong,SatinsEasyJet,RateMe  10
19Mar89-10Sun  330 :16.61 ft tw *6-5   120   103¾ 93¼  MrtnJD 10  W Tex Fut1 :17.06 92  JohnnysNight,Gabrdine,RentAWreck  10
   19Mar89—Stumbled start
3Mar89-9Sun    330 :16.72 ft      2¼   120    72¼ 1½   Martin J D 9   Fut Trl :16.71 104  FlLikStrkin,ThHookingBull,RlBrForth   9
```

The first bit of noise occurs with the fact that Dandy Danny Boy and Miss Julie Lark were scratched, moving all of the horses behind them forward in post position, and An Easy Winner into the 9 hole and Lotta Toro into the 10—the reverse of the order they are listed in the "Also Eligibles." Many times you will have no way of knowing this until you reach the track or offtrack facility and get your hands on a program.

The selection of past performances for speed figures is fairly straightforward, except for Working Class Man. His most recent race, on July 25, was run on a less-than-fast track, and he posted a 20.44 and 82 *Form* speed index. Now look at his second-last race. You don't need the method of calculating erroneous lengths-back placements given earlier to see that something is seriously amok. The winner of that race posted a 19.71. Working Class Man supposedly ran a 20.94, half a second slower than his most recent race, and yet he was given a speed index 12 points better. There is obviously a typo in the line somewhere and, since the winner's time and this horse's speed index seem to jibe, the time should probably read 19.94. Sometimes mistakes are less obvious, and to check you can try the Thoroughbred method of calculating losers' times from the lengths-back placement. In this case, it was a 400-yard race, which is 150 lengths, so the winner's average time per length was 0.1314. Working Class Man finished 1.5 lengths back, so his real time was

approximately 19.9—or, more likely, since it was published as 20.94, someone among the half-dozen hands, employed by two or three companies, that
record and type the numbers before they reach the printed *Form* simply
misthought a second. Plug in 19.94 and, even with the tail wind, you get a
very different picture of the potential outcome of the race.

No.	Horse	Dist.	Speed	Time
10	Lotta Toro	350	970	17.73
9	An Easy Winner	350	963	17.87
4	Working Class Man	400	960	19.98
5	Torch Run	350	959	17.95
3	Dash N Breeze	350	956	18.00
7	Leave Em Lonely	400	944	20.32
1	Simon Six	400	944	20.32
2	Shoot Em Up Linde	400	938	20.46
6	Bar One Lil	400	936	20.5
8	Jets Special Dude	350	926	18.59

Notice the effect of wind on time and the resulting speed figures. With the
dividend for head wind, Lotta Toro's speed figure jumps off the scale. But
since that was the fastest she has ever run in her life, I would bet that the
wind was not exactly ripping that day.

The crowd didn't miss An Easy Winner's 89, 88, and 92 published figures
and sent him off as the 2-to-1 favorite. Trainer Carlos Lucero didn't miss
them either and claimed him for the $3,200 price.

Since Lotta Toro has such a standout speed figure, the temptation might
be a win bet, or wheeling An Easy Winner and Working Class Man behind

her in exactas and trifectas. In this case, you would have all three finishers—
at *super* odds—and would lose every penny you bet. To avoid being a losing
winner, there is one more critical step.

SEVENTH RACE

Ruidoso
AUGUST 11, 1990

350 Yards. (:17.24) Quarter Horses. CLAIMING. Purse $2,800. 3-year-olds. Weight, 120 lbs. Non-winners of a race since July 10 allowed 2 lbs.; a race since May 9, 4 lbs. Claiming price $3,200. (Claiming races for $2,500 or less not considered.)

Value of race $2,800; value to winner $1,680; second $616; third $280; fourth $112; fifth $56. Mutuel pool $22,111.
Exacta pl $4,360. Quinella pl $10,900. Trifecta pl $17,837.

Last Raced	Horse	M/Eqt.A.Wt	PP	Str	Fin	Time	Jockey	Cl'g Pr	Odds $1
26Jly90 2Rui4	Working Class Man	Lb 3 120	4	3$1\frac{1}{2}$	1hd	0:17.82	Koyle K	3200	9.10
3Aug90 8Rui6	Lotta Toro	Lb 3 120	9	1hd	2$\frac{1}{2}$	0:17.84	Yoakum J	3200	4.40
5Aug90 1Rui5	An Easy Winner	b 3 118	10	2no	3$2\frac{1}{2}$	0:17.91	Dolphus S A	3200	2.00
23Jly90 8Rui6	Torch Run	b 3 120	5	4no	4no	0:18.18	Sumpter G	3200	6.60
26Jly90 2Rui5	Simon Six	Lb 3 120	1	5no	5hd	0:18.19	Hart K	3200	5.30
2Aug90 6Rui7	Dash N Breeze	b 3 117	3	6no	6no	0:18.21	Summerow D	3200	14.30
11Jly90 5RP3	Jets Special Dude	Lb 3 116	8	82	7nk	0:18.22	Payne L D	3200	17.70
22Jly90 2Rui4	Shoot Em Up Linde	Lb 3 120	2	7no	8$1\frac{3}{4}$	0:18.27	Brooks R	3200	21.70
30Jun90 9SFe9	Bar One Lil	b 3 120	6	9hd	9	0:18.48	Fuller S	3200	29.30
14Jly90 5Rui9	Leave Em Lonely	Lb 3 116	7	10	—	0:00.00	Martinez A J	3200	6.30

Leave Em Lonely, Eased.

OFF AT 3:49. Start good. Won driving. Time, :17.82 (Cross Wind). Track fast.

$2 Mutuel Prices:

4-WORKING CLASS MAN	20.20	8.40	4.40
10-LOTTA TORO		7.60	4.40
9-AN EASY WINNER			3.00

$2 EXACTA 4-10 PD $118.60. $2 QUINELLA 4-10 PD $65.80. $2 TRIFECTA 4-10-9 PD $189.60.

11

BETTING IN THE MONEY

"Racetrack! Well, what am I doin' *here?*"

—GROUCHO MARX
in the movie
A Day at the Races

Picking Losers

For one of the best handicappers I know, a winning day at the track would be an accident. Luckily, the track pays him to be there—to provide his picks to the public, among other things—and his bets don't exceed a rational percentage of his salary, so he has a relatively happy and productive career. The only thing that continually rocks his boat are the winning picks he gives away and the losing bets he makes.

Every day, an hour before post time, a small crowd of about fifty gathers in a corner of the grandstand for his handicapping seminar—to listen to him run down the day's races. Some are brand-new to racing and come out of curiosity and for help, but most are devoted followers of this man, who knows the horses and studies their trips with as much precision as anyone in the industry. Top-notch handicappers come to listen to him for his insights into horses, trainers, and jockeys, which puts the polish on their own methods. Ten minutes before the bugle sounds, they move back to their seats— some to be strong winners based on his handicapping—and he moves back to his office to quietly lose (his office is relatively soundproof) the $30 "amusement money" he allots himself each day.

Because his job requires him to cover every race for the crowd, he picks winners, like most good handicappers, about 30 percent of the time. Like most handicappers, too, he would not dream of betting every race, and in the races he considers his prime bets his average is far better. Although he breaks even or shows a small profit over a season, he loses many more races than he wins, because he holds to the romantic tradition of picking winners. When he wins, he wins big enough to carry himself over the losses and satisfy both the rationale of accepting nothing less than good odds and the sensation of being right.

He would probably deny every word of this, except maybe the part about being a great handicapper. And, in his own view of his betting, he would be right. He does not bet strictly win bets. He backs his win bets with place and show hedges, and he bets the exotics regularly. But his *focus* is in picking horses that will win their races, and his betting, both consciously and subconsciously, follows.

Good handicappers and good bettors are rarely combined in the same person. The actual difference in placing bets is minor, and the difference in thought process is subtle, but the difference in results is profound.

When you have handicapped a standout selection and bet it to win, with backup bets in the place and show pools, your place and show bets are scared money. If the horse fails to win, but pays on your place ticket, it may return your total investment on the race, or a little more or less, depending on the odds and the size of your backup bets—but you *lost* the race. Scared money rarely wins—at best, it helps you break even. The quickest way to scare all your money is to focus on picking winners.

If you shift your focus from picking winners to picking horses in the money, accept chaos as a fact of horse racing, and restructure your betting accordingly, very similar bets in the same race start winning.

No matter how good you are, a substantial percentage of the horses you pick to win are not going to win. On the other hand, if you are good, an extremely high percentage of the horses that you pick to be in the money will be. If you restructure your primary bets to make use of your skill in picking the top few horses, the onus of scared money disappears and a success or loss in picking the winner becomes simply the result of an accepted gamble.

There are as many systems for placing bets as there are systems for handicapping races. Many good bettors are poor handicappers and many superior handicappers are hopeless bettors because each tends to see the other side of the equation as a complete and unfathomable mystery. The most complicated betting methods may be devised by odds players and other nonhandicappers, but the most rigid are often the result of handicappers' resolutions over their losses.

Although there are hundreds of betting systems and variations, they all boil down to two general strategies for structuring bets. One addresses individual races, the other links bets over several. There is some subliminal encouragement for linking bets over races by the tracks supplying daily doubles, triples, and pick sixes, but there is no rational analogy in personal betting.

The classic bet-linking strategy is the straight parlay. The "parlay" is the most time-honored and widely known strategy both inside and outside of racing for increasing your winnings or status. It is also the most idiotic. With it, you place a bet and rebet your total winnings, continuously, until you reach an established goal, the day's racing ends—or you lose. With a parlay, you are not betting on horse racing. You are betting on the pure chance that the established goal or last race will bring an end to the madness before a total loss occurs—like calling the police before you sit down to play Russian roulette.

Parlays are fun, and often quite profitable, so long as they are not "straight." At one of my favorite tracks there is a group of college kids who hold summer jobs typing race results, bussing tables, and generally horsing around. A few of them have been around racing all their lives, know all the trainers by name, and provide the rest of their pals with inside information. None of them handicap. They all run $5-a-day show parlays. Once in a blue moon one makes it through the day, comes out $200 to $500 ahead, and buys pizza and beer for the whole crew. They place great status on having the guts to stay with the parlay of "the track's money" and mercilessly harass anyone who doesn't. They have great fun. Maybe it's best, since they show so little avarice that they don't realize they could have a lot more fun—and maybe pay their way through college—if they viewed their parlays as a business investment and took out profits for capital improvements. Winnings at the track are not a profit until you spend them somewhere else.

Profit taking is not a disgrace, it is the purpose of the game. I frequently run a parlay in parallel with other betting, but never as a test of machismo. As soon as the amount won exceeds what I would rationally risk on the next race, I take my profit and bet—perhaps a little more than what I would have if it were "my money," but with the profit in my pocket. In that sense, every bet is a parlay. When you play with a winning ticket, it is not the track's money—it is *your* money.

Each horse race is a separate and distinct occurrence, and money carried over between races constitutes a tool, not a strategy. It does not change your selection in the next race or call for riskier or even necessarily bigger bets. Money changes nothing in a race that hasn't happened, including bets that are linked by the track in daily doubles, triples, and pick sixes.

Each race should be viewed, *after* it is handicapped, in terms of its range of betting opportunities. This will result in far fewer betting mistakes than if you start with the objective of winning a trifecta—or picking the winner—and then force the results into a bet. The first step is in recognizing races where your methods are most likely to work; the next is handicapping; the last is deciding on bets. It is best not to do them backwards.

Betting in the Money

I know a number of good handicappers and not one of them has a problem predicting at least one, usually two, and often all three horses in the money. Some have a major problem, though, making money. The most important transition a handicapper can make is away from the rut of win-focus betting and losing money while winning bets.

If you use the method of objective speed analysis and subjective handicapping suggested here, or any other method that regularly predicts in-the-money horses, the challenge remains of selecting bets that convert knowledge into dollars.

At most tracks, the per capita daily betting average is about $100. Since some bet in the thousands, there are many who bet $20 or $30. In the following examples we will assume $2 base bets and you can add as many zeros as you like. We will look at the speed results from tracks around the country and how various results can be translated into bets.

Poppiano is a son of Fappiano, bred and owned by Mrs. Frances Genter, breeder and owner of Smile, the Eclipse Award winner and Champion Sprinter of 1986—not to mention owner of Unbridled, Fappiano's star son of 1990. Poppiano is Unbridled's half brother through his sire (the term is usually reserved to designate horses from the same mare); he is a full brother to Tappiano, a Grade I mare, and is Smile's nephew through his In Reality dam. Even breeding at this ethereal level can mean nothing in itself if the individual isn't a runner—but Mrs. Genter is not only the most photogenic breeder/owner in horse racing, she is also a force to be reckoned with in sprint racing. I would take a second look at any horse she enters. With good quality horses, such as this field, second looks at a mile for comparison with 7- and 6.5-furlong races are much safer than in the lower ranks.

Dramaturgo's last race was almost a year ago in Argentina and, even though he has a decent workout of 59:1 at 5 furlongs from the gate, his Argentine times are nothing like any other horse's in the field. I would pass him and hope that Argentine tracks are not that much slower than our own.

You have to stretch for Heady Days' speed. If he did not show some promise, I would not even try it. But the Paul Mellon-bred horse has done very well in three races, winning the last in allowance company comparable to today with a slow time on a muddy track. His third-last race was some time ago, but it is at today's distance, and these are good horses, so I would try it.

Horse	Distance	Speed
1 Poppiano	6.5 furlongs	963 ⎤
1 Poppiano	8 furlongs	962 ⎟
4 Silent Harmony	6 furlongs	962 ⎦
7 Postal Strike	6.5 furlongs	958
6 Heady Days	7 furlongs	952 ⎤
3 Square Ruler	7 furlongs	952 ⎦
2 Two The Twist	8 furlongs	931

Silent Harmony's speed figure equals Poppiano's in his mile run and essentially matches it in his most recent sprint. With the advantage of

8 BELMONT

7 FURLONGS. (1.20⅖) ALLOWANCE. Purse $28,000. 3-year-olds and upward which have never won two races other than Maiden, Claiming or Starter. Weights, 3-year-olds 116 lbs. Older 122 lbs. Non-winners of a race other than Maiden or Claiming since June 15 allowed 3 lbs. Of such a race since June 1, 5 lbs.

Poppiano

B. c. 3(Mar), by Fappiano—Taminette, by In Reality
Br.—F A Genter Stable Inc (Fla)
Tr.—Schulhofer Flint S
Own.—Genter F A
111
Lifetime 5 2 1 2 $39,770
1990 5 2 1 2 $39,770
1989 0 M 0 0

→29Jun90- 8Bel	fst	1	:46⅕	1:10⅕	1:35⅕	3↑Alw 31000	2	3	32½	32½	33	34¾	Santos J A	112	6.50	88-14	LeVoyageur1194¾AnyMinuteMan112hdPoppino112¾ Lckd rally	6
→15Jun90- 8Bel	fst	6½f	:22	:45⅕	1:16	3↑Alw 28000	6	4	43	2hd	21½	23	Santos J A	114	*.70	94-14	HrtofHro1173Poppino114¾EppingForst1172 Not good enough	8
30May90- 5Bel	gd	6f	:22⅗	:45⅘	1:10⅕	3↑Alw 27000	3	6	52½	32	1½	15	Santos J A	113	*.80	88-19	Poppino1135VictoryTost1191SilknSbr1122½ Steadied,hand rid	6
23Feb90- 7GP	fst	6f	:21	:44⅕	1:11⅘	Alw 22500	3	10	814	514	56½	33¾	Vasquez J	122	*.80	82-20	Wonkie'sBst1101¾EnsignG.1172Poppino1221½ Off slowly, brus	10
30Jan90- 5GP	fst	6f	:22⅖	:46⅕	1:11⅘	Md Sp Wt	2	11	21	11½	15	18¾	Vasquez J	122	2.60	86-19	Poppino1228¾SilvrTowr1225½T'sProspct122no Slow start, drvg	11

Speed Index: Last Race: +8.0 3–Race Avg.: +5.6 4–Race Avg.: +5.5 Overall Avg.: +4.8
LATEST WORKOUTS Jun 23 Bel 4f fst :50 B Jun 12 Bel 3f fst :36⅗ B Jun 7 Bel 4f fst :49⅘ B May 29 Bel tr.t 3f fst :38 B

Two the Twist

B. g. 3(Apr), by Two's a Plenty—Tiffiney Twist, by Gleaming
Br.—Dr. Stephen V.J. Dia (Fla)
Tr.—Shapoff Stanley R
Own.—Sasco Creek Stable
111
Lifetime 7 3 2 0 $22,731
1990 7 3 2 0 $22,731
1989 0 M 0 0
Turf 1 0 1 0 $2,900

9Jun90- 5AP	fm	1⅛	Ⓣ:49	1:14	1:51⅕	Clm 35000	3	3	45	44	33	2¾	Day P	113	3.00	87-08	InFullSl1173¾TwothTwst113nkDvnConncton1131½ Strong finish	6
→27May90- 3CD	fst	1	:47⅖	1:13⅕	1:39	Clm 25000	6	5	63¾	31	3nk	12½	Lopez R D	115	3.90	82-16	Two the Twist 1152½ Wild Ruler 1142¼ State Law1205 Driving	6
5May90-11Det	fst	1	:48⅕	1:13⅖	1:40⅖	Southfield	2	6	611	614	59	58½	Spieth S	114	9.10	76-17	Mc'sJohnny1155UptheTempo122½SilverVigors1142 Even rally	6
8Apr90-10Det	fst	6f	:22⅖	:46⅖	1:13⅗	3↑Alw 7600	7	3	56½	47½	34½	1nk	Morgan M R	114	*.70	80-14	Two the Twist 114nk Proxi'sJigger1144½C.W.'SObcession116½	8
28Mar90- 3Det	fst	5f	:23	:49⅗	1:01⅘	3↑Md Sp Wt	5	7	65¼	45	44	12	Aristone M	114	*.80	81-14	TwotheTwist1142NscoPendenc1121OurBnqut1224 Std'd often	7
3Mar90-10Tam	fst	1 1/16	:47⅕	1:12⅗	1:46	Sam F Davis	5	7	107½	99¼	712	712¼	Stroud R S	113	152.20	75-18	Fiery Best 1202¾ Thames 113½ Slew of Angels 1225 Outrun	10
24Feb90- 3Tam	gd	6f	:23⅕	:47⅘	1:13⅖	Md Sp Wt	3	8	74¾	43½	23½	24	Puckett H	118	21.00	75-22	OneTon1184TwotheTwist11814½BlushingRomn1181¼ No match	9

Speed Index: Last Race: –6.0 3–Race Avg.: –4.6 3–Race Avg.: –4.6 Overall Avg.: –5.0
LATEST WORKOUTS Jun 29 Bel tr.t 5f fst 1:02⅗ H Jun 24 Bel tr.t 4f fst :49⅕ B May 25 CD 3f fst :36⅘ B

Square Ruler

Ch. c. 4, by Majesty's Prince—Four Angles, by Quadrangle
Br.—Cantey & Cress (Ky)
Tr.—Peitz Dan C
Own.—Cantey J B
117
Lifetime 24 2 5 9 $97,420
1990 5 1 0 1 $25,620
1989 14 1 5 6 $66,160
Turf 7 1 2 2 $35,140

10Jun90- 5Bel	fm	1 1/16	Ⓣ:45⅘	1:09⅗	1:40⅕	3↑Alw 31000	8	7	84¼	44	26	47¾	Bailey J D		117	3.40	92-03	CurrentlyRed1174½PrivteTlk1171MinZmn1172¼ Steadied early	12
→20May90- 7Bel	fst	7f	:22⅖	:45	1:23⅖	3↑Alw 30000	3	6	41½	41½	2½	11	Bailey J D		119	15.80	87-20	SqureRuler1191SilkenSbr1121½SvnLords119nk Altered course	8
18Feb90- 6Aqu	fst	170	[•]:49⅖	1:14⅗	1:44⅗	Alw 32000	1	9	1011	95¼	54½	37½	Bruin J E	b	117	7.20	75-31	Injun 1175 Little Priority 1172½ Square Ruler 1171½ Fin well	10
29Jan90- 8Aqu	fst	1⅛	[•]:48⅗	1:14	1:51	Alw 32000	5	4	43	41½	47	513¾	Santos J A		117	2.50	73-21	Any Minute Man 1173½ Skyflash 1173¾MeanStreak1172¾ Tired	7
17Jan90- 7Aqu	fst	1 1/16	[•]:47⅘	1:13⅖	1:46	Alw 32000	6	10	810	63¾	43	46¼	Chavez J F		117	8.10	72-30	Miner'sEcho110nkAnyMinuteMn1174MyDelivr1172 Rough trip	10
28Dec89- 7Aqu	fst	1 1/16	[•]:47⅘	1:14⅖	1:49⅘	3↑Alw 32000	8	3	37	33	1½	3nk	Chavez J F		115	3.60	60-41	LostOpportnty115hdSprkfWr115nkSqrRlr1154½ Bid, weakened	10
7Dec89- 8Aqu	fst	1 1/16	[•]:49⅖	1:14⅗	1:46⅗	3↑Alw 32000	3	4	32	21½	31½	35½	Bailey J D		115	*1.40	70-37	Armaged 1151½ Indian Navy 1174 SquareRuler1152 Weakened	6
22Nov89- 5Aqu	fst	1⅛	:49	1:13⅘	1:52⅘	3↑Alw 32000	6	3	1hd	1hd	3½	56¼	Bailey J D		115	*1.90	66-31	Hrperstown1153[DH]Armgd115[DH]SocilAccntnc1151¼ Weakened	8
1Nov89- 7Aqu	fst	1⅛	:48	1:12	1:49⅘	3↑Alw 32000	2	2	2½	2½	1½	2nk	Bailey J D		115	*1.90	87-25	Hierarchy 115nk Square Ruler 1151¼ Sasquash1156 Just failed	6
11Oct89- 6Bel	gd	1¼	[T]:48	1:38	2:02⅘	3↑Alw 32000	3	3	44	51½	2½	78¼	Bailey J D		116	*3.00	72-19	Dan's Nephew 1171½ Armaged 1141 Emtor 119hd Tired	12

Speed Index: Last Race: +7.0 1–Race Avg.: +7.0 1–Race Avg.: +7.0 Overall Avg.: +1.2
LATEST WORKOUTS Jun 28 Bel [T] 4f fm :47⅘ H (d) Jun 3 Bel 4f fst :49⅖ B May 16 Bel 4f gd :50 B May 10 Bel 5f gd 1:01 H

Silent Harmony B. g. 4, by Seattle Song—Together, by Great Sun
Br.—North Ridge Fm-Jackson L-Johnson T (Ky)
Own.—Twilite Tee Stable Tr.—Widmer Wayne
112 5
Lifetime 11 2 0 2 $52,875
1990 8 1 0 2 $34,600
1989 3 1 0 0 $18,275
Turf 2 0 0 0 $2,850

→ 28Jun90- 3Bel fst 6f :23⅕ :45⅘ 1:09⅖ Clm 50000 2 5 55½ 55¾ 44 33¼ Toscano P R5 112 2.60 89-18 RelAccount1153Fugie113nkSilentHrmony1122 Wide, wild rally 7
25May90- 2Bel fst 7f :23 :45⅘ 1:23⅗ Clm c-50000 2 10 2½ 1hd 105½ 1013½ Vasquez J 117 6.60 72-21 Weak Knees Willie109½Wargod113½IrishChili1131¼ Gave way 10
11May90- 8Bel fst 6f :22⅘ :45⅗ 1:09⅕ 3↑Alw 31000 1 6 44 31½ 47 411 Vasquez J 119 2.60 82-17 Eternal Flight 110no Carson City 1125 Earnhardt 1166 Tired 6
25Mar90- 5SA fm *6½f Ⓣ:21 :43⅕ 1:13⅘ Alw 38000 4 8 99½ 89 86 82¾ Baze R A 119 3.60 89-08 Wonder Dancer1171¼Bashayer117½Pete'sPocketful117no Wide 10
15Mar90- 7SA fst 6½f :22 :44⅘ 1:15⅖ Alw 38000 2 5 42 31½ 43½ 44 Baze R A 119 *2.50 89-12 FiestDelSol117nkProudIrish1192½JustDeds1171¼ Troubled trip 7
12Feb90- 7SA fm *6½f Ⓣ:21⅗ :44⅕ 1:13⅘ Alw 38000 7 4 53¼ 41¼ 41¼ 42¾ Solis A 118 3.50 89-08 Santa Tecla 116½ Sam McGee 119hd Stylish Stud 1182¼ 8
31Jan90- 7SA fst 6f :21⅗ :44⅗ 1:10 Alw 38000 5 8 63½ 62¾ 52¾ 32¾ Solis A 120 2.70 83-23 ArYMyCsy1191OvrThPl1161¾SlntHrmn1201¾ Wide into stretc 9
5Jan90- 7SA fst 6f :21⅗ :44⅖ 1:08⅘ Alw 34000 3 7 1½ 1½ 11½ 14 Solis A 119 7.50 92-12 Silent Harmony 1194 Por D. J. 111½ Holy Smoly 1191¾ 8
24Dec89- 3Hol fst 6½f :22 :44⅗ 1:15 3↑Alw 27000 2 6 55 55 44½ 49¼ Solis A 118 9.40 91-09 Forli Light 1184½ Are You My Casey 1174 Sun Streak 118¾ 8
13Nov89- 6SA fst 7f :22⅗ :45⅖ 1:23 3↑Md Sp Wt 4 5 11 11½ 11 1hd Solis A 118 5.30 89-10 SilentHrmony118hdLuckyLuckyYou1184½VigorousGreen118hd 10

Speed Index: Last Race: +7.0 3–Race Avg.: –0.3 8–Race Avg.: +1.1 Overall Avg.: +0.3
LATEST WORKOUTS ●Jun 23 Bel 4f fst :47 H ●Jun 18 Bel tr.t 5f fst 1:01 H May 21 Bel 6f gd 1:18⅗ B

***Dramaturgo** Ch. c. 4, by Mariache—Dama Nortena, by Majestic Prince
Br.—Haras Vacacion (Arg)
Own.—Clark S C Jr Tr.—Watters Sidney Jr
117
Lifetime 4 2 0 1 $1,944
1989 4 2 0 1 $1,944
1988 0 M 0 0
Turf 2 1 0 0 $806

3Sep89♦8Hipodromo(Arg) fst*1 1:36⅖ Polla dePotrillos(Gr1) 33¼ Valdivieso J 123 *1.20 — — Royal Heroe 123nk Mat Day 1233 Dramaturgo123hd Prom, led 15
29Jly89♦9SanIsidro(Arg) sf*1 1:36⅖ Ⓣ GranPremio2000Guineas(Gr1 43 Garcia M 123 *1.70 — — Speed Boy 123hd Lazy Lord1232 Intrepide1231 Prom thruout 16
5Jly89♦3SanIsidro(Arg) fm*1 1:35⅖ Ⓣ Premio Tagore(Alw) 11½ Valdivieso J 123 *1.50 — — Dramaturgo 1231½ Autentico 1232 Cacao 123no Led thruout 12
17Jun89♦4Hipodromo(Arg) fst*7f 1:25 Premio Solyluz(Mdn) 16 Garcia L 121 *1.35 — — Dramaturgo1216 IndioSeductor121½ Kalnow1215 Led thruout 9

Speed Index: Last Race: (—) 3–Race Avg.: (—) 12–Race Avg.: (—) Overall Avg.: (—)
LATEST WORKOUTS ●Jun 30 Bel 5f fst :59⅕ Hg Jun 23 Bel 5f fst 1:01⅘ H Jun 18 Bel 4f fst :48⅘ H Jun 13 Bel 4f fst :48⅗ H

Heady Days B. c. 3(Mar), by Fit to Fight—Wild Applause, by Northern Dancer
Br.—Paul Mellon (Va)
Own.—Rokeby Stable Tr.—Miller Mack
113
Lifetime 3 2 1 0 $36,540
1990 3 2 1 0 $36,540
1989 0 M 0 0

9Jun90- 3Bel my 6½f :22⅖ :45⅘ 1:17⅘ 3↑Alw 27000 10 12 52½ 3½ 12½ 1nk Bailey J D 114 *3.00 88-12 HedyDys114nkIslndMusic1112½SilkenSber1172 Good handling 13
31May90- 7Bel fst 6f :22⅗ :46⅗ 1:11 3↑Md Sp Wt 5 5 41½ 41 1hd 1½ Bailey J D 115 *.40 84-15 HedyDys115½PnnisMkBucks11510½SrtogCt1151¼ Blocked turn 8
→ 19May90- 7Bel fst 7f :23 :46 1:23⅖ 3↑Md Sp Wt 8 1 31½ 11 11 2no Bailey J D 115 2.60 87-15 All Silver 115no Heady Days 1151¾ Figure 1158½ Just missed 9

Speed Index: Last Race: 0.0 3–Race Avg.: +0.3 3–Race Avg.: +0.3 Overall Avg.: +0.3
LATEST WORKOUTS ●Jly 3 Bel 3f fst :35 B Jun 26 Bel 4f fst :48 H Jun 21 Bel 4f fst :49⅘ B Jun 15 Bel 3f fst :35⅗ H

Postal Strike B. g. 4, by Strike The Anvil—Tour En Voiture, by Large As Life
Br.—Pilcher Docia & Mr-Mrs H (Fla)
Own.—Jakubovitz J R Tr.—Hushion Michael
117
Lifetime 25 3 6 6 $82,260
1990 12 2 2 4 $58,180
1989 13 1 4 2 $24,080
Turf 1 0 0 0

→ 15Jun90- 8Bel fst 6½f :22 :45⅕ 1:16 3↑Alw 28000 2 6 812 88¼ 55½ 45¾ Migliore R b 117 7.40 91-14 HertofHero1173Poppino114¾EppingForst1172 Wide, lckd rally 8
1Jun90- 8Bel fst 6f :22⅖ :46⅕ 1:11⅘ 3↑Alw 28000 5 5 611 69 64¼ 2nk Migliore R b 119 5.60 80-21 Agittor114nkPostlStrike119½KentuckyHope109½ Wide,fin. fast 6
14May90- 5Bel fst 6f :22⅗ :45⅗ 1:09⅘ Clm 45000 8 7 87 85 64 33¼ Smith M E b 115 5.90 87-11 VgorousRply1133Kt'sNoblst115nkPostlStrk1151¼ Belated rally 8
29Apr90- 6Aqu fst 7f :22⅘ :46⅕ 1:23⅗ 3↑Alw 31000 5 4 76 77¾ 46½ 47 Migliore R b 124 6.10 77-23 Barkada 1196½ Wargod 119½ Earnhardt 119no Mild gain 7
19Apr90- 8Aqu fst 6f :22⅖ :45⅖ 1:11⅕ 3↑Alw 30000 5 5 87½ 75 32 12 Smith M E b 119 3.20 84-20 Postal Strike 1192 River Patriot 114nk Icy Glow 1193 Driving 8
10Apr90- 7Aqu fst 7f :22⅗ :45⅕ 1:23⅖ 3↑Alw 30000 6 9 96¾ 64 21 33 Smith M E b 119 6.90 82-19 Earnhardt 1141¾ Washingtonian 1211½PostalStrike1191½ Wide 10
21Mar90- 7Aqu fst 7f :22⅗ :45⅗ 1:22⅘ Alw 30000 8 4 76½ 42 2½ 32¼ Smith M E b 117 6.40 88-19 CraftyJimbo1172RiverPatriot112nkPostalStrike1171¾ Fin. well 9
3Mar90- 7Aqu fst 6f ⊡:22⅗ :46⅕ 1:12⅕ Alw 30000 6 11 1012 1014 65½ 22½ Thibeau R J Jr b 117 *2.50 82-11 SamSm1172½PostlStrike1171½DncingMinstrel117nk Slow start 11
23Feb90- 5Aqu fst 6f ⊡:22⅕ :45⅗ 1:10⅗ Clm 20000 9 11 67¼ 44 11 13 Thibeau R J Jr b 113 6.40 93-14 PostlStrik1133DncngMnstrl1191¾SwornIn1177 Poor st., steadi 11
16Feb90- 1Aqu fst 6f ⊡:22⅘ :46⅘ 1:12 Clm 20000 9 8 74¾ 73¾ 31½ 34½ Thibeau R J Jr b 113 12.90 81-14 So Private 1174½ Super Chap113noPostalStrike113¾ Five wide 12

Speed Index: Last Race: +5.0 3–Race Avg.: +1.3 10–Race Avg.: +1.1 Overall Avg.: +1.1
LATEST WORKOUTS Jun 28 Bel Ⓣ 3f fm :38 B (d)

hindsight, it is easy to say that Silent Harmony's past performances do not come close to Poppiano's. But there is no way you can push his figure down past the natural speed gap, and there is no way you can pull Heady Days' up, even though his past performances show a touch of class that may carry in this field—and even though the headline in that day's *Form* read: "Poppiano vs. Heady Days At Belmont."

In my heart I know that Silent Harmony is not going to beat Poppiano and that Heady Days has a much better chance in this race than Square Ruler, who has equaled his speed in the past. In my own betting I would use these subjective notions, but in these cases will make the decisions as objectively as possible to show conservative approaches to the figures.

The race offers win, place, show, and exacta betting. There are three horses above a major break in the speed figures and a 2-length gap between the top two horses and Postal Strike, then 3 lengths to Heady Days. How do you bet the race?

If your focus is win-betting, you would bet both top horses to win or each across the board, plus the two boxed in an exacta. Unless Poppiano falls down, he is going to show in this race, so an across-the-board bet ought to return something. Suppose you decide on $2 bets across the board ($2 win, $2 place, $2 show) on both horses and the two boxed in the exacta. The eight bets will cost $16, which is a comfortable betting amount.

If your focus is in-the-money betting, three horses above a speed gap, without a strong win pattern, calls for a simple three-horse exacta box costing $12. Poppiano is the standout in this race, so you might back the primary exacta bet with an acknowledged-gamble win bet or, more conservatively, with a place or show bet. I *really* like this horse, but I'm not sure if it's because of him or Mrs. Genter, who is not running today, and this is to be conservative, so I'll make it a place bet for $4 to match the $16 total.

The crowd at Belmont must have read the article, because Poppiano and Heady Days went off as almost equal favorites, with Postal Strike as a 14-to-1 longshot. Poppiano ran away with the race, but Heady Days finished right where he belonged, 3.5 lengths behind Postal Strike.

Win-focus betting on the speed figures of this race would have paid $10.20 on the across-the-board bet on Poppiano but lost the rest for a minus $5.80, which is better than minus $16, but a typical case of winning a bet while losing the race.

In-the-money betting would lose on *four* bets tied to Silent Harmony—*but* win the exacta for $39—and the two place bets on Poppiano would bring an additional $6.40, for $45.40 total. Although five of the six bets boxed in the exacta lost, the objective of winning it was accomplished, and even if the side bet had been lost, the net return would still be $35 and the original bet would be doubled. Bets were lost, but the race was won.

On January 31, 1990, a group of $25,000 claimers was set to run 7 furlongs

EIGHTH RACE
Belmont
JULY 5, 1990

7 FURLONGS. (1.20$\frac{2}{5}$) ALLOWANCE. Purse $28,000. 3–year–olds and upward which have never won two races other than Maiden, Claiming or Starter. Weights, 3–year–olds 116 lbs. Older 122 lbs. Non–winners of a race other than Maiden or Claiming since June 15 allowed 3 lbs. Of such a race since June 1, 5 lbs.

Value of race $28,000; value to winner $16,800; second $6,160; third $3,360; fourth $1,680. Mutuel pool $200,760. Exacta Pool $358,612

Last Raced	Horse	M/Eqt.	A.Wt	PP	St	¼	½	Str	Fin	Jockey	Odds $1
29Jun90 8Bel3	Poppiano		3 112	1	5	1^{1}	1^{3}	1^{7}	1^{12}	Santos J A	1.40
15Jun90 8Bel4	Postal Strike	b	4 117	7	7	7	7	$3^{1\frac{1}{2}}$	$2^{3\frac{1}{2}}$	Migliore R	14.20
9Jun90 3Bel1	Heady Days	b	3 113	6	4	6^{7}	$3^{\frac{1}{2}}$	2^{2}	$3^{2\frac{1}{2}}$	Bailey J D	1.70
28Jun90 3Bel3	Silent Harmony		4 112	4	6	$5^{1\frac{1}{2}}$	$6^{2\frac{1}{2}}$	$5^{1\frac{1}{2}}$	$4^{1\frac{1}{2}}$	Toscano P R5	9.30
9Jun90 5AP2	Two the Twist		3 111	2	3	$4^{\frac{1}{2}}$	$5^{\frac{1}{2}}$	6^{4}	5^{3}	Rogers K L	54.80
10Jun90 5Bel4	Square Ruler		4 117	3	1	3^{hd}	4^{5}	$4^{\frac{1}{2}}$	$6^{6\frac{1}{2}}$	Cordero A Jr	6.50
3Sep89 8Arg3	Dramaturgo		4 117	5	2	$2^{\frac{1}{2}}$	$2^{\frac{1}{2}}$	7	7	Antley C W	6.70

OFF AT 4:23 Start good, Won ridden out. Time, :22$\frac{4}{5}$, :45$\frac{3}{5}$, 1:09$\frac{3}{5}$, 1:22 Track fast.

$2 Mutuel Prices:			
1–(A)–POPPIANO	4.80	3.20	2.20
7–(G)–POSTAL STRIKE		6.60	3.20
6–(F)–HEADY DAYS			2.40

$2 EXACTA 1–7 PAID $39.00

B. c, (Mar), by Fappiano—Taminette, by In Reality. Trainer Schulhofer Flint S. Bred by F A Genter Stable Inc (Fla).

POPPIANO showed good early foot, remained well out from the rail into the stretch and drew off under a hand ride. POSTAL STRIKE, badly outrun early, finished well while racing wide to best the others. HEADY DAYS rallied from the outside approaching the stretch but tired during the drive. SILENT HARMONY was checked sharply along the inside at the turn. TWO THE TWIST was finished early. SQUARE RULER tired badly. DRAMATURGO gave way suddenly approaching the stretch.

in the third race at Gulfstream. Three horses could be dismissed out of hand: Irish Kris had not run since the previous July and August at Rockingham Park and Suffolk Downs, where he had never gone further than 5.5 furlongs; Distinctive Hooch had shown nothing; and China Pleasure had shown only a little more, at times well behind this field. The remaining horses sorted like this:

Horse	Distance	Speed
1 Shrewd Prospector	7 furlongs	928
6 Sailaroo	6 furlongs	921]
4 Atomic Splash	7 furlongs	921]
2 Buddy Breezin	6 furlongs	920]
8 Allover Alex	6 furlongs	913

According to the *Form*'s published speed indexes, all of Buddy Breezin's three most recent past performances at 6 furlongs at Caulder Race Course were *five to seven points better* than Shrewd Prospector's 7-furlong race, which received a 77 at Gulfstream.

Atomic Splash's 1:26:1 loss by a head at 7 furlongs at Caulder was given an 84 speed index—again over Shrewd Prospector's 77 for 1:25:3 by a nose at Gulfstream—which, by my figures, was actually 7 points, or about 3 1/2 lengths *faster* than Atomic Splash. When you make your own figures, these are the races you live for.

The 7-furlong, 84 speed index was apparently what made Atomic Splash the crowd's favorite at $1.40-to-$1.

The race offered win, place, show, perfecta, and trifecta betting. Shrewd Prospector's speed is almost enough of a standout to justify wheeling but, unlike Poppiano, he has not produced a pattern to support it and it is still a horse race, with two identical figures not far behind. Allover Alex's speed figure is poor, but he is an erratic horse that either leaps to the lead and stays in the money, or lags far behind and loses. He, or one of the discounted horses, could be a spoiler in this race, which would make me very leery of the trifecta. A four-horse perfecta box on the top four is probably a safer bet than even a show bet on Shrewd Prospector, who might succumb to chaos. The $24 bet is justified by the odds produced by the misleading published figures. A side bet on Shrewd Prospector to win, place, or show would satisfy my urge to gamble.

With the race run, it is easy to see that a $1 five-horse trifecta box costing $60 or a $120 full box would have turned a healthy profit, not to mention a wheel around Shrewd Prospector, which would have cost only $24 and returned $417. But Shrewd Prospector had nothing to back up his speed figure except the fact that it was a recent effort on today's track to justify a wheel. I like to see at least two consistent and recent speed figures to support wheeling and win betting. The speed pattern is not clear enough to ensure much more than running in the money. Other horses, like Irish Kris, racing for the first time this year after very decent two-year-old performances, might have been ringers after their long layoff. With the safe $24 perfecta

THIRD RACE
Gulfstream
JANUARY 31, 1990

7 FURLONGS. (1.20⅘) CLAIMING. Purse $11,000 (Plus $1,500 FOA). 3-year-olds, weights, 122 lbs. Non-winners of two races since December 31, allowed 3 lbs. Of a race since then, 5 lbs. Claiming price $25,000 for each $2,500 to $20,000 2 lbs. (Races when entered to be claimed for $18,000 or less not considered). Registered Florida breds preferred.

Value of race $12,500; value to winner $8,100; second $2,090; third $1,320; fourth $550; balance of starters $110 each. Mutuel pool $53,735. Perfecta Pool $52,367. Trifecta Pool $42,246.

Last Raced	Horse	Eqt.	A.	Wt	PP	St	¼	½	Str	Fin	Jockey	Cl'g Pr	Odds $1
23Jan90 $^{3}GP^{2}$	Shrewd Prospector	b	3	117	1	6	$4^{\frac{1}{2}}$	3^{2}	$1^{2\frac{1}{2}}$	$1^{8\frac{1}{4}}$	Suckie M C	25000	6.30
24Jan90 $^{3}GP^{1}$	Sailaroo		3	117	6	3	2^{1}	2^{1}	3^{3}	2^{2}	Hunter M T	22500	3.80
19Jan90 $^{5}GP^{2}$	Allover Alex		3	117	8	1	1^{1}	1^{1}	2^{1}	$3^{1\frac{1}{4}}$	Penna D	25000	4.50
9Jan90 $^{6}Crc^{3}$	Buddy Breezin	b	3	117	2	8	$6^{\frac{1}{2}}$	$6^{\frac{1}{2}}$	4^{1}	4no	Ramos W S	25000	12.90
30Dec89 $^{7}Crc^{2}$	Atomic Splash		3	117	4	7	7^{1}	7^{7}	5^{6}	$5^{5\frac{1}{2}}$	Bailey J D	25000	1.40
19Jan90 $^{5}GP^{4}$	China Pleasure	b	3	117	7	2	3^{hd}	4^{1}	$6^{1\frac{1}{2}}$	6^{3}	Dos Ramos R A	25000	16.00
12Dec89 $^{6}Crc^{8}$	Distinctive Hooch		3	117	5	4	5^{2}	5^{hd}	7^{12}	$7^{17\frac{3}{4}}$	Douglas R R	25000	26.60
18Aug89 $^{6}Suf^{6}$	Irish Kris	b	3	114	3	5	8	8	8	8	Saumell L	20000	7.00

OFF AT 1:58. Start good. Won driving. Time, :22⅗, :46, 1:11⅘, 1:24⅗ Track fast.

$2 Mutuel Prices:

1–SHREWD PROSPECTOR	14.60	7.20	4.60
6–SAILAROO		4.60	2.80
8–ALLOVER ALEX			3.60

$2 PERFECTA 1–6 PAID $95.40. $2 TRIFECTA 1–6–8 PAID $417.00.

box, you would collect $95.40, plus whatever gamble was made on Shrewd Prospector. (For an alternative view of four-horse boxes and some great betting strategies, see Mitchell 1995.)

Naked Races

It may sound a little lurid, but there is a small movement in the management of various tracks to reverse the trend toward exotics and return to win, place, and show betting. They call them "naked races" and talk about scattering them throughout the race card in the same, mildly conspiratorial way their predecessors introduced exotics. Since track managers do few things without an economic objective, there must be one; but I have listened to what they say and I miss it every time. The only thing that does come through is their belief that the public wants to return to the glory of win betting.

In-the-money betting is at its most powerful when the results of handicapping suggest quinella and exacta boxes. As long as you watch the exacta odds in the closing minutes before the race, you can frequently find odds that justify the risk of the compound bet and avoid losing money on a winning ticket. It also has applications in trifectas, but requires much more care, both in handicapping chaos horses and in ensuring that the odds in compound bets do not drop below the accepted risk.

The first race at many tracks is essentially a naked race for in-the-money betting, since it usually comprises the first half of the daily double, which is a double-whammy win bet, especially if the races are purposely loaded to raise the double odds.

The first race at Ruidoso on July 23, 1990, was typical of this type of race, although it had a better field than you often might find, of well-bred, but lightly raced two-year-old maiden quarter horses. Two in the field showed no past performances, but the rest showed from one to five, some of which were very respectable. Sometimes horses will startle the field in their very first out, but usually not when the rest have the experience of good races, so these two could be fairly confidently disregarded. The rest of the field sorted like this (all past performances were at 350 yards):

Horse	Speed
5 Cash Stride	964
8 Mr Cash It	956
3 Im Made In USA	952
7 Jet Beduino	946 ⎤
1 Easy As She Goes	945 ⎦
2 Mayolas Yeller Moon	940
4 Okeydokey Dandy	937

Cash Stride stands 8 speed points, or about a length (on the quarter horse scale), over Mr Cash It, but in a field of well-bred, lightly raced two-year-old quarter horses, a spoiler on a win bet is more than just a possibility. With the major speed break between Im Made In USA and Jet Beduino, a three-horse exacta box would be the preferred bet, but it is not offered on this race.

In this type of field the question shifts from which horse is most likely to win—which is any in the top three—to which horse is most likely to finish in the money, and that is Cash Stride. Show is the safest bet in this field, although I would be willing to back it strongly (on the $2 scale we are using) with a $10 bet and play it further with a gamble of about half the primary amount to place.

Just as well, because Im Made In USA ran the 350 yards faster than he or any other horse in the field ever had in their young lives (17.72), nipping Cash Stride and Mr Cash It, who paid a whopping $9.80 to *show*. Cash Stride paid only $3.20 to both place and show, but the bet returns $24 for about a 40 percent profit.

With the excellent $9.80 show payoff for Mr Cash It, considerably more could be made with a show bet on him than even the win bet on Im Made In USA, which paid only $6.20. And with this distribution of speed figures, if you were at Ruidoso and watching the mutuel pools (as I happened to be that day), then stretching for the odds for Mr Cash It to show would be a rational bet, with about the same risk factor as the place bet on Cash Stride. This type of stretch for odds is acceptable, because it remains within the framework of the handicapping results.

One of the more bizarre twists of win-focus betting is that many of those who practice it find themselves continually at odds with the odds. They handicap a standout winner and when they find, during the post parade, that they weren't the only one—the crowd is making it a favorite—they search frantically in the last moments for better odds on the tote board and bet their second or third choice to *win*—or a long shot, which they hadn't even considered, to place or show.

Whether it is explicit and formalized or vague and intuitive, every handicapper has a worry zone that is a function of odds, which looks something like Figure 11.1.

The lower curve represents the handicapper's skill and confidence in the outcome of a particular race. The area of the vertical wall behind it represents the degree of worry interaction between skill and the crowd's odds. Almost everyone has a blunt end on confidence that creates the small triangular worry zone on the right, where bets will not be made, no matter how strong the results of handicapping. The drop to zero may come at 2-to-1, 1-to-1, 3-to-5, or some other arbitrary point. The most confident bets are made in the narrow zone where confidence and potential payback are parallel. For many people, the confidence curve might look more like an escargot, with a high rise on the right where their confidence meets or

FIGURE 11.1

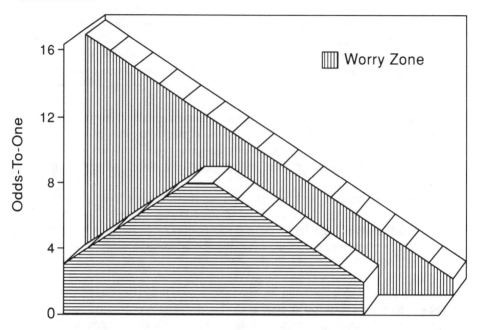

exceeds the odds, but the gap represents the fact that it is always a horse race. Confidence builds with the odds to about 8-to-1, where many make their favorite bets, then drops as the odds get larger, expanding the worry zone. Bets are still made at high odds, but maybe with white knuckles. Every bettor has a personal confidence curve, which should change shape with every race. Rigid curves, set by betting systems, fail to adjust as the variables of handicapping move around them.

Odds must be watched constantly before betting to prevent losing on winning bets, but odds do nothing to alter the results of handicapping. Any time that a bet moves too far out into the worry zone, whether it drops like a marble into the right triangle because of unacceptably low odds at the last minute or wobbles high on the left because of unclear handicapping, changing to a worse bet solves nothing. The area between the two curves could also be called "gambling," and each person has to decide how far he will wander into it before it is time to pass.

Tough Speed

In-the-money betting uses analysis of patterns of past speed that can be translated into a pattern of bets for each specific race. Certain tracks, like Aqueduct and Hawthorne, are tough tracks for speed and would produce false patterns for analysis, unless track constants are applied. They, and a few others, would be tough tracks for *anything*, if for no other reason than that they frequently offer huge fields with the maximum number of "Also Eligibles," so unless you have the track program, you will have to be prepared—with sixteen to twenty horses analyzed—which would cover two races at many other tracks. Yet the odds and payoffs at both tracks are not much different from others around the country, so the home crowd has learned to bet them the way a good fisherman learns a stream.

Hawthorne is a slow track in comparison with others from which it draws horses and, although it is a bullring, even its one-turn races are usually a full second or two slower than one-turn sprints at Arlington Park. This can be seen by simply glancing down the past performances of individual horses early in the meeting. Claimers that have regularly run 6 furlongs in 1:12+ at Arlington, drop to 1:14+ at Hawthorne; 1:10's become 1:12's.

This is in direct contrast with the *Form*'s speed index baseline, set at the fastest times of the past three years. Notice in the fastest times table in chapter 7 that Arlington is 2/5 faster at 5 furlongs; equal at 5.5; 1 1/5 seconds *slower* at 6 furlongs—and a huge 2 1/5 seconds slower at 6.5 furlongs.

Hawthorne calls for the development of track constants to adjust times before converting to speed. The best source of the constants would be a very large sample of one- or preferably two years' charts from Hawthorne, Arlington, and any other tracks required for comparison, so that an average speed can be established for each distance. The large sample will dampen the effect of extremes in class and wild fliers, while it is the wild fliers themselves that are used for the published speed index for the crowd. Comparison of the averages should provide the constants and show if they are uniform across racing distances. You would then set one track equal to zero, or "par," and add or subtract the constants from the others before you enter the times for comparison with the universal baseline.

To see how this works, we'll try a Hawthorne race using an unrefined guess at a constant. The eighth race on November 10, 1990, was a 6-furlong allowance for three-year-old and up Illinois-bred horses with a $14,800 purse. It was a twelve-horse field, with four "also eligibles" and two sets of couplings, involving four horses, so the sequential, post-position numbering was completely scrambled in terms of the actual betting numbers. All of the "also eligibles" were scratched, and four of the field could be dismissed, leaving eight horses to be handicapped with times mixed between Hawthorne and Arlington Park.

The Arlington times for the same horses are almost universally faster, so whenever a past performance is selected from an Arlington race, one second will be added for comparison with Hawthorn. Thus, if the Arlington time was 1:12:2, it will be entered as 1:13:2, and so on.

If these are your tracks and you research the constant, you may find that it is really 4/5 of a second, or 1 2/5, and you may want to build it into your program or simply make the change as you enter it, as I did, with the following results:

Post	Horse	Speed
12	Maram	921
7	Francis Paul	919
3	Sulemark	916
10	Opal Klaus	914
8	Intraflux	908
2	It's The Natural	908
9	Grand Rea	906
4	Riplass Due	904

This is not exactly a hot field on any track, but they produce a nice speed gap, with only four horses above it. There are no tight clusters above the line, so this is more a weak four-horse cluster than a division of power, but it is small enough to box an exacta (a perfecta at Hawthorne) for twenty-four bucks.

Speed Gaps, Lines, and Clusters

When the results of speed analysis are sorted from fastest to slowest, they will often form, by themselves, the natural speed gaps that separate the contenders from those out for the air. Both above and below the gap, the horses will often cluster according to speed.

EIGHTH RACE
Hawthorne
NOVEMBER 10, 1990

6 FURLONGS. (1.08⅕) ALLOWANCE. Purse $14,800 (includes $1,350 IBF). 3-year-olds and upward, non-winners of a race other than maiden or claiming, Illinois registered, conceived and/or foaled. Weight, 3-year-olds, 118 lbs.; older, 122 lbs. Non-winners since September 30 allowed 3 lbs.; August 30, 5 lbs.; a race in 1990, 8 lbs. (Claiming races not considered.)

Value of race $14,850; value to winner $8,910; second $2,970; third $1,634; fourth $891; fifth $445. Mutuel pool $144,119. Perfcta pool $127,697.

Last Raced	Horse	M/Eqt.	A.	Wt	PP	St	¼	½	Str	Fin	Jockey	Odds $1
27Oct90 ^{7}Haw^{8}	Sulemark		3	113	3	6	$2^{1\frac{1}{2}}$	$2^{2\frac{1}{2}}$	$1^{2\frac{1}{2}}$	$1^{2\frac{1}{2}}$	Silva C H	7.90
6Oct90 ^{3}AP^{1}	Maram	L	4	114	12	1	6^{4}	$4^{\frac{1}{2}}$	2^{3}	$2^{4\frac{1}{4}}$	Sellers S J	5.80
20Oct90 ^{7}Haw^{2}	Opal Klaus	Lb	4	109	10	4	9^{8}	$7^{\frac{1}{2}}$	$4^{\frac{1}{2}}$	$3^{\frac{3}{4}}$	Mahorney W TJr^{5}	3.10
27Oct90 ^{7}Haw^{7}	Poppy's Kids	Lb	4	119	1	7	4^{1}	5^{1}	$3^{1\frac{1}{2}}$	$4^{\frac{1}{2}}$	Baird E T	67.30
13Oct90 ^{10}Haw^{2}	Francis Paul		3	113	7	8	5^{hd}	$6^{\frac{1}{2}}$	5^{hd}	$5^{3\frac{1}{2}}$	Fires E	3.50
20Oct90 ^{2}Haw^{1}	It's the Natural		3	118	2	10	7^{hd}	8^{3}	$7^{\frac{1}{2}}$	$6^{1\frac{1}{4}}$	Patin K C	24.20
27Oct90 ^{7}Haw^{2}	Intraflux	Lb	4	122	8	9	$8^{2\frac{1}{2}}$	9^{8}	$8^{1\frac{1}{2}}$	7^{nk}	Gabriel R E	4.90
27Oct90 ^{7}Haw^{4}	Riplass Due	L	3	115	4	5	3^{1}	$3^{\frac{1}{2}}$	$6^{\frac{1}{2}}$	8^{hd}	Meier R†	b-10.60
20Oct90 ^{7}Haw^{6}	Em Em Iron	L	4	122	5	11	10^{1}	11^{4}	10^{4}	9^{4}	Schaefer G A†	b-10.60
25Aug90 ^{7}AP^{3}	Grand Rea	b	3	109	9	3	$1^{2\frac{1}{2}}$	$1^{1\frac{1}{2}}$	9^{1}	10^{1}	Hernandez B J^{5}	5.70
7May90 ^{6}Spt^{8}	Boss Clay		3	113	6	2	12	12	11^{3}	11^{5}	Lasala J	46.50
27Oct90 ^{4}Haw^{8}	Pursue Me	L	7	109	11	12	11^{1}	$10^{\frac{1}{2}}$	12	12	Jocson G J^{5}	99.90

b-Coupled: Riplass Due and Em Em Iron.

OFF AT 4:10. Start good. Won driving. Time, :21⅕, :45⅘, :58⅕, 1:11⅕ Track fast.

$2 Mutuel Prices:

4-SULEMARK	17.80	8.80	5.60
11-MARAM		7.40	5.60
9-OPAL KLAUS			3.40

$2 PERFECTA (4-11) PAID $171.60.

In the previous race, Sulemark and Francis Paul stepped out from behind their speed figures in opposite directions to win and place out of the money, which in a four-horse cluster one horse obviously must do. Maram's speed figure places him 3.5 lengths ahead of Opal Klaus; he actually ran 4.25. The matched pair below the line (Intraflux and It's The Natural) didn't form a betting cluster, but are interesting because, as you can see, they ran most of the race together. Chaos occurred in the race, but speed held the money.

In the second race at Churchill Downs on November 11, 1990, there was a gap, a cluster, and an arbitrary bet-cutoff line. This was a 6-furlong race for $5,000 claiming fillies and mares, with a nice purse for the price of $6,650. Seven horses in the twelve-horse field didn't stand a prayer and were dismissed before making figures. The five remaining horses sorted like this:

Horse	Speed
7 Liv Metro	931
11 Miss Leslie M.	928 ⎤
1 Crossed Flags	928 ⎥
1 Crossed Flags	927 ⎦
5 Ridan Miss	926
4 Pritch's Princess	865

The embarrassing time for Pritch's Princess was marked in the past performances and tried, simply because when I came to it I hadn't yet formed a picture of what a 6.5-furlong time should look like for this field and it is less time-consuming to simply put it in than search around the fine print. She quickly became the eighth horse with no prayer.

Crossed Flags was the only horse with similar enough times to try two, and her 1:12:0 loss in her most recent 6-furlong race turned out to be almost exactly the same performance as her 1:12:2 closer loss in the race immediately before that. When this kind of consistency is competitive with more erratic (toward slow) past speed of the other contenders, you have a solid in-the-money horse.

Although the gigantic, natural speed gap occurs after Ridan Miss's 926 (there are seven horses *worse* than Pritch's Princess), there are three closely matched horses a length ahead of Ridan Miss, and for a conservative exacta bet, the line is drawn above her. A different kind of conservatism might include her in a four-horse box, but that would cost twice as much at $24, while picking two out of three of the top horses for $12 is an acceptable risk with this particular pattern. Crossed Flags is the best in-the-money gamble for a place or show ticket.

Notice that this race comprised the second half of the daily double, which paid barely over a half of the exacta on this race. Speed in this race produced

SECOND RACE **6 FURLONGS. (1.08⅗) CLAIMING. Purse $6,650. Fillies and mares. 3–year–olds and upward. Weight, 3–year–olds, 119 lbs.; older, 121 lbs. Non–winners of three races since July 29 allowed 3 lbs.; two races since September 2, 6 lbs.; a race since October 7, 9 ls. Claiming price $5,000.**

Churchill

NOVEMBER 11, 1990

Value of race $6,650; value to winner $4,323; second $1,330; third $665; fourth $332. Mutuel pool $75,107. Exacta pool $75,729.

Last Raced	Horse	M/Eqt.	A.	Wt	PP	St	¼	½	Str	Fin	Jockey	Cl'g Pr	Odds $1
22Oct90 ^{9}RD^{4}	Miss Leslie M.	LB	5	112	11	4	4^{1}	$3^{\frac{1}{2}}$	$1^{2\frac{1}{2}}$	1^{2}	Cooksey P J	5000	2.70
29Oct90 ^{7}RD^{2}	Crossed Flags	LB	6	112	1	3	$3^{1\frac{1}{2}}$	4^{hd}	3^{hd}	$2^{\frac{3}{4}}$	Neff S	5000	4.80
22Oct90 ^{9}RD^{2}	Liv Metro	LB	5	114	7	5	7^{hd}	6^{1}	2^{hd}	3^{4}	Griffin J W Jr	5000	3.90
20May90 ^{5}CD^{1}	Trend	LB	6	112	8	10	$5^{\frac{1}{2}}$	5^{hd}	6^{2}	$4^{\frac{1}{2}}$	Deegan J C	5000	14.90
3Oct90 ^{2}TP^{6}	Shimi's Flower	LBb	4	112	2	11	10^{2}	8^{2}	7^{1}	$5^{\frac{1}{2}}$	Troilo W D	5000	70.30
28Oct90 ^{7}RD^{8}	Della Belle	LB	5	113	3	2	1^{hd}	2^{hd}	$5^{1\frac{1}{2}}$	6^{nk}	Sexton R D	5000	24.30
13Oct90 ^{4}Kee^{6}	Ridan Miss	Bb	3	114	5	1	2^{hd}	1^{hd}	4^{hd}	7^{2}	Bruin J E	5000	3.90
5Oct90 ^{6}TP^{12}	Down the Apalachee	LB	4	112	6	7	6^{hd}	7^{1}	$8^{\frac{1}{2}}$	$8^{\frac{1}{2}}$	Bryan M W	5000	60.20
17Oct90 ^{9}RD^{7}	Ask and Run	B	3	113	10	6	$11^{\frac{1}{2}}$	$10^{1\frac{1}{2}}$	9^{hd}	$9^{2\frac{1}{2}}$	Moss R	5000	45.80
15Oct90 ^{2}RD^{8}	Changing Tide	LBb	5	107	9	8	9^{hd}	$9^{1\frac{1}{2}}$	10^{4}	$10^{2\frac{1}{4}}$	RodriguezAF^{5}	5000	78.30
10Jly90 ^{4}EIP^{3}	Pritch's Princess	LB	7	110	4	9	12	11^{10}	11	11	Leeds D L^{5}	5000	24.20
29Jly90 ^{6}EIP^{2}	Green Green	LB	5	112	12	12	8^{1}	12	—	—	Woods C R Jr	5000	5.90

Green Green, Eased.

OFF AT 1:32. Start good. Won driving. Time, :22⅕, :47⅖, 1:13⅘ Track fast.

$2 Mutuel Prices:				
	11–MISS LESLIE M.	7.40	5.20	3.20
	1–CROSSED FLAGS		6.00	3.80
	7–LIV METRO			2.80

$2 EXACTA (11–1) PAID $43.20.

Ch. m, by Raise a Bid—Miss Vernor, by Vertex. Trainer Ackerman D Kelly. Bred by Gettys L & Birds B J (La).

MISS LESLIE M., in hand while outside the leaders and stalking the pace, moved to the fore leaving the turn, then was under mild urging to prevail. CROSSED FLAGS, close up early, was steadied at the half-mile ground along the inside, continued on to have clear aim at the winner in the drive and wasn't good enough. LIV METRO, never far back, moved up outside the winner in upper stretch and flattened out. SHIMI'S FLOWER made a mild late gain. DELLA BELLE dueled for the lead to the stretch and weakened. RIDAN MISS dueled for the lead with DELLA BELLE and tired. DOWN THE APALACHEE had no rally. ASK AND RUN was outrun. CHANGING TIDE was never a factor. PRITCH'S PRINCESS was outrun. GREEN GREEN reared at the start, was outrun, then eased in the lane.

Owners— 1, Ackerman D Kelly; 2, Crone Nancy; 3, Hagen Patrick & Kathy; 4, Woodrum Thomas; 5, Robertson John; 6, Vaught Joseph C; 7, Mills S; 8, Lucky Trio Stable; 9, Vaught J L; 10, Brummett & Burton; 11, Bluegrass Creek Farms Inc; 12, Raymond Terry.

Trainers— 1, Ackerman D Kelly; 2, Horrell Donald G; 3, Hagen Kathy; 4, Banks David P; 5, Robertson John; 6, Barker James R; 7, Brown Bruce; 8, Walcott Charles A Jr; 9, Faust Steve; 10, Burton Phillip G; 11, Elliott Raymond M; 12, Romans Dale.

Overweight: Liv Metro 2 pounds; Della Belle 1; Ridan Miss 4; Ask and Run 3; Pritch's Princess 3.

Scratched—Double The Count (2Nov90 ^{2}CD^{2}); Escalation (2Nov90 ^{2}CD^{1}); Dance Student (2Nov90 ^{2}CD^{6}); Besetting (2Nov90 ^{9}CD^{5}).

$2 Daily Double (11–11) Paid $26.40. Daily Double Pool $108,820.

all of the in-the-money horses, but not in winning order, so even if you had only two strong contenders in the first half of the daily double, it would take two three-horse wheels to wrap the three contenders in this one. This is about the maximum that can be productively bet on a daily double at low to moderate odds. It would cost $12, which is as low as the payoff may sometimes drop; double or triple your bet and the proportion remains the same—until your bet gets big enough to drop your own odds.

The more horses that are included in wheels and boxes, the closer you have to watch the odds and the more likely that low odds may sneak in, since you can't know who else may be placing a heavy bet at the same moment that you are. In most exacta bets, however, the natural gaps and clusters help avoid extensive boxing.

The sixth race at Los Alamitos on May 11, 1990, is an example of a cluster and arbitrary gap. It was a 350-yard claiming race for $3,200 three-year-old fillies with a ten-horse field.

A filly named Speeding Again had not raced since the previous November, and although her past times were competitive, she would probably need a race to remember just how fast these things are supposed to be. Oh Baby Me's times were not in the class. None of the other eight could be discounted at first glance.

Horse	Speed
3 Ima Merrigold	955
7 Egos Prospect	952 ⎤
6 Holly Speed Doll	951
8 Port Of Leisure	950 ⎦
9 Very Merry	948
10 Romany Waltz	946
4 Shes Everyonesdream	944
2 Summer Spice	923

Ima Merrigold's top time was against a field of $2,500 claiming fillies nine days earlier, and it was the fastest race of her life, so it is not likely to hold up against this field, some of which are dropping to enter at this level. She cannot be discounted, but the setting of her past speed doesn't warrant a side bet. The three below her are clustered around 951 and can't be separated further. The speed gap between Port Of Leisure and Very Merry is narrow and might seem arbitrary, but by the time you get to Very Merry you have four contenders and about a length's difference from the top speed, which is often plenty in a quarter horse race.

There are also two points' difference between Egos Prospect and Port Of Leisure, which is the same as the small gap where the line is drawn but, for clustering, the figures are almost always linked downward and quarter horses linked by one point will often be found together in the race. When they are running from neighboring gates, they frequently link up, literally, to form one of the centers of energy that moves across the track.

With three clustered horses and one questionable standout, a four-horse exacta box will take care of it, with no side bet to stretch for odds. Too bad, because Egos Prospect paid nicely, but to pick her out of the four would have been simply a roll of the dice.

Occasionally, the right set of past performances come together to form a strong win-bet pattern. You may see it twice a day and then not again for a week. The sixth race at Golden Gate Fields on May 23, 1990, was one. It was

SIXTH RACE 350 Yards. (:17.28) Quarter Horses. CLAIMING. Purse $3,300. Fillies. 3-year-olds, which have not won two races since September 11. Weight, 122 lbs. Claiming price $3,200. (Maiden races not considered).

Los Alamitos
MAY 11, 1990

Value of race $3,300; value to winner $1,815; second $742; third $413; fourth $247; fifth $83. Mutuel pool $49,764. Exacta pool $78,574.

Last Raced	Horse	Eqt.A.Wt PP	1	2	Fin	Time	Jockey	Cl'g Pr	Odds $1
2May90 11LA2	Ego Prospect	b 3 122 7	1½	11½	11½	0:17.87	Creager J	3200	11.40
3May90 11LA4	Port Of Leisure	b 3 122 8	4no	3hd	2nk	0:18.11	Garcia E	3200	2.20
3May90 4LA5	ShesEveryonesDream	b 3 122 4	6hd	5no	3nk	0:18.15	Didericksen K	3200	7.10
24Apr90 7LA2	Holly Speed Doll	b 3 122 6	2½	2hd	4hd	0:18.18	Cardoza D	3200	3.20
24Apr90 7LA7	Oh Baby Me	b 3 122 5	5no	6hd	5no	0:18.20	Aguilar C	3200	32.30
2May90 11LA1	Ima Merrigold	b 3 122 3	3no	4no	6½	0:18.21	Meier J	3200	5.20
27Apr90 1LA1	Romany Waltz	b 3 122 10	7hd	7nk	7½	0:18.30	Seville R	3200	39.70
3Mar90 2Sun6	Very Merry	b 3 122 9	8nk	81	8½	0:18.41	Figueroa R	3200	5.70
14Apr90 3BM1	Summer Spice	b 3 122 2	9no	9nk	9½	0:18.49	Brossette A	3200	63.10
15Nov89 1LA4	Speeding Again	b 3 122 1	10	10	10	0:18.59	Pilkenton B	3200	16.80

OFF AT 9:32. Start good. Won handily. Time, :17.87 Track fast.

$2 Mutuel Prices:

7-EGO PROSPECT	....	24.80	9.40	6.80
8-PORT OF LEISURE			4.40	4.00
4-SHES EVERYONESDREAM				5.80

$2 EXACTA 7-8 PAID $76.00.

a $20,000 allowance race for good fillies and mares set to go 6 furlongs. It was also a naked race, or at least in a string bikini, since it formed the first race of a triple, on the sixth through ninth races, with no other exotics offered.

Icee Freeze was scratched, so all of those behind her moved up in post-position order. Kiss Me Quack was now the 3 horse, but showed no races this year. In the preceding race, we dropped a horse just like her from consideration without undue concern. They both show year-old performances within the range of their fields, but Kiss Me Quack showed something more. This is one of the rare times when the workouts deserve more than a passing glance.

Kiss Me Quack shows four nicely spaced workouts, with two bullets—which mean nothing except that her last was a well-designed, short blowout with a hot 35:3 *from the gates* after three long-distance runs. Allen Severinsen is serious about bringing this filly into form for her first race of the season. She may well be in the thick of it and she needs to be represented in the figures. Since she has two 6-furlong times to chose from, I would pass her one mile race, even though in this case it might produce a usable figure. The

Kiss Me Quack
B. f. 4, by Quack—Venetian Dancer, by Norcliffe
Br.—Gleis Josephine T (Ky)
Tr.—Severinsen Allen

CHAPMAN T M   **118**
Own.—Gleis Josephine T

1989	3 1 2 0		$16,200
1988	0 M 0 0		

Lifetime 3 1 2 0 $16,200

14Jun89-7GG	1 :453 1:102 1:371ft	*6-5 117	32 34 33½ 22	ChpmnTM5	⑩Aw21000	77-19 MoonltDsrt,KssMQuck,Mrgrt'sNtv 10
→21May89-5GG	6f :213 :441 1:104ft	*1 115	78½ 67½ 34½ 11½	Chapman T M9	⑩Mdn	85-16 KissMeQuck,DorothyKirstn,Scrod 11
7May89-5GG	6f :213 :442 1:092ft	11 115	44½ 24 23 21	Chapman T M3	⑩Mdn	91-14 My Future, Kiss Me Quack,Towaoc 8

Speed Index: Last Race: +1.0   2-Race Avg.: +3.0   2-Race Avg.: +3.0   Overall Avg.: +0.6
●May 19 GG 3f ft :353 Hg   May 15 GG 4f ft :473 H   ●May 9 GG 6f gd 1:162 H   May 2 GG 6f ft 1:162 H

first race of her life was a little too fast at 1:09:2 plus a length to think that she can duplicate it after a year, but her winning effort of 1:10:4 may place her in this field.

Horse	Speed
4 Boomer Lady	951
4 Boomer Lady	951
4 Boomer Lady	951
3 Kiss Me Quack	949
2 Symbolize	947
6 Just Rule	944
1 Fancy Girl	939
5 Miss Nells Alibhai	936

With three solid and identical speeds above the rest of the field, Boomer Lady is a respectable win bet. She is consistent and is racing in her normal class, while Kiss Me Quack is coming back well groomed but after a year layoff, and the next speed horse, Symbolize, is a length further behind. There is a natural speed gap between Symbolize and Just Rule, so this is one naked race to load up on.

I would take Boomer Lady for all but the gas money to get home and whatever place and show bets feel good on Kiss Me Quack and Symbolize.

Boomer Lady, Kiss Me Quack, and Symbolize finished not only in the order that their past speed suggested, but with the exact one-length separation of their proven past abilities. Chaos took a holiday.

SIXTH RACE
Golden Gate
MAY 23, 1990

6 FURLONGS. (1.07⅗) ALLOWANCE. Purse $20,000. Fillies and mares. 4–year–olds and upward. Non–winners of $3,000 other than maiden, claiming, starter or classified handicap. Weight, 121 lbs. Non–winners of a race other than claiming or classified handicap since March 15, allowed 3 lbs.

Value of race $20,000; value to winner $11,000; second $4,000; third $3,000; fourth $1,500; fifth $500. Mutuel pool $182,714.

Last Raced	Horse	Eqt.	A.	Wt	PP	St	¼	½	Str	Fin	Jockey	Odds $1
11May90 ^{8}GG^{2}	Boomer Lady		4	118	4	4	4^{1}	3^{2}	2^{2}	1^{1}	Frazier R L	3.20
14Jun89 ^{7}GG^{2}	Kiss Me Quack		4	118	3	5	$5^{1\frac{1}{2}}$	4^{1}	4^{4}	2^{1}	Chapman T M	3.00
11May90 ^{8}GG^{3}	Symbolize	b	4	118	2	1	2^{2}	$1^{1\frac{1}{2}}$	1^{hd}	3^{1}	Gonzalez R M	6.10
2May90 ^{5}GG^{1}	Fancy Girl		4	118	1	3	1^{hd}	$2^{\frac{1}{2}}$	$3^{\frac{1}{2}}$	4^{7}	Judice J C	5.60
4May90 ^{6}GG^{1}	Miss Nells Alibhai		4	121	5	6	6	6	5^{2}	5^{1}	Kaenel J L	11.00
19Apr90 ^{3}GG^{4}	Just Rule	b	4	118	6	2	3^{1}	5^{hd}	6	6	Hansen R D	2.00

OFF AT 3:28. Start good. Won driving. Time, :22⅖, :46⅗, :59⅘, 1:13⅕ Track slow.

$2 Mutuel Prices:				
	5–BOOMER LADY	8.40	3.40	2.40
	4–KISS ME QUACK		4.00	2.80
	3–SYMBOLIZE			3.00

Priceless Fun

Speed gaps, clusters, and lines can form innumerable natural patterns, and these are only a few of the most common. As you work with the figures, you will see patterns that recur regularly and will come to admire them, along with some of those that you see much more rarely.

Shrewd Prospector was the superior horse in his race, hidden behind misleading published speed ratings. You will find more and, once you do, it's seductive; you will always search for the next one.

Occasionally, you will find a series of figures from the same horse that will make you stop in awe. You might forget about betting—*almost*—just to watch a great animal run.

You may find, as I did this past summer, a race in which eight of the ten-horse field have precisely the same, excellent speed figure, with the other two just one point behind. It was the most competitive race I have ever seen—ten horses battling with the heart and conviction of Easy Goer and Sunday Silence in their electrifying stretch run. I enjoyed it more for watching undistracted and unworried; a bet would have been sacrilegious, not to mention dumb.

The track may appear a single entity, but it is actually a trading ground for hundreds of independent businesses, ranging from individual journeymen who sell their skills to corporations that may be bigger than the track itself. Jockeys, agents, two-horse trainers, and the giants of the industry gather there to conduct their business. Horse racing is a participatory sport, and when you handicap and place bets, you are just as much an essential part of it as the great breeding farms of Kentucky. You are not just a fan, you are one of the independents—an integral part of the sport and the economic system that supports it.

The true fun of horse racing is the inseparable duality of the magnificent competition of the animals on the track and the world of the betting windows. It is a rare kind of fun that can be enjoyed at no cost—and maybe even a profit.

BIBLIOGRAPHY

Ainslie, Tom. *Ainslie's Complete Guide to Thoroughbred Racing.* New York: Simon and Schuster, 1968.

Beyer, Andrew. *Picking Winners: A Horseplayer's Guide.* Boston: Houghton Mifflin, 1978.
Beyer on Speed: New Strategies for Racetrack Betting. Boston: Houghton Mifflin, 1993.

Brohamer, Tom. *Modern Pace Handicapping.* New York: William Morrow, 1991.

Davidowitz, Steven. *Betting Thoroughbreds: A Professional Guide for the Horseplayer.* New York: E.P. Dutton, 1977.

Gleick, James. *Chaos: Making a New Science.* New York: Viking Penguin, 1987.

Hambleton, Tom, Dick Schmidt, Michael Pizzolla, and Dr. Howard Sartin. *Pace Makes the Race.* Banning, California: O. Henry House Publishing, 1991.

Mahl, Huey. *The Race Is Pace.* Las Vegas: Gamblers' Book Club Press, 1983.

Meadow, Barry. *Money Secrets at the Racetrack.* Anaheim, California: TR Publishing, 1988.

Mitchell, Dick. *Commonsense Betting: Betting Strategies for the Racetrack.* New York: William Morrow, 1995.

Pine, Gordon. *1995 Par Times.* Studio City, California: Cynthia Publishing, 1995.

Quinn, James. *The Best of Thoroughbred Handicapping: Advice on Handicapping from the Experts.* New York: William Morrow, 1987.
Figure Handicapping: A Practical Guide to the Interpretation and Use of Speed and Pace Figures. New York: William Morrow, 1992.

Quirin, William L. *Winning at the Races: Computer Discoveries in Thoroughbred Handicapping.* New York: William Morrow, 1979.

Scott, William. *How Will Your Horse Run Today?* Baltimore: Amicus Press, 1984.

Ziemba, William T. and Donald B. Hausch. *Dr. Z's Beat the Racetrack.* New York: William Morrow, 1987.

Periodicals Cited

The American Racing Manual, 10 Lake Drive, Hightstown, NJ 08520 (annual, book format)

The Blood-Horse, Box 4038, Lexington, KY 40544 (weekly plus special issues)

Daily Racing Form, 10 Lake Drive, Hightstown, NJ 08520

The Quarter Racing Journal, American Quarter Horse Association, P.O. Box 32470, Amarillo, TX 79120 (monthly) http://www.aqha.com

Source for Books and Software

Gamblers' Book Club
630 South 11th St.
Las Vegas, NV 89101
(Free catalog: 1-800-634-6243)
Extensive mail order catalog; no
  purchasing commitment. An
  interesting place to visit in Las Vegas.
  http://www.gamblersbook.com

Desert Sea Publishing
Star Route 2, Box 84
Socorro, NM 87801
  desertc@desertsea.com
  http://www.desertsea.com

World Wide Web Handicapping Data Sources

Bloodstock Research Information Services, Inc.
  http://www.bris.com

Dark Horse http://members.aol.com/jojerr/index.html

Equibase Company http://www.equibase.com

International Thoroughbred Superhighway, Inc.
  http://www.itsdata.com

Thoroughbred Sports Network http://www.horseracinginfo.com

ACKNOWLEDGMENTS

A mong the many people who made the research for this book a pleasure were Eric Alwan, Henry and Linda Bowlan, Jack Brooks, Betsy Burroughs, Richard Chamberlain, Alex Chavez, Casey Darnell, Tom Dawson, Billy Fowler, Dwayne Gilbreath, Greg Huether, Jimmy Jones, Richard Lidberg, Randy Meche, Butch Murray, Harold Murray, Richard Neff, Oscar Steinley, and Phil Taylor.

Special thanks to my friend and debating partner, Tim Menicutch.

Thanks for the kind words and encouragement from Andrew Beyer, Ian Blair, Tom Brohamer, Paul Catania, David Fogel, Barry Meadow, Dick Mitchell, Gordon Pine, James Quinn, Howard Sartin, Howard Schwartz, and Joe Takach.

I am grateful to the Stewards of Ruidoso Downs, New Mexico, who granted permission to work in the gate area to do the timing and photography of quarter horse races, which had profound effects on ideas used in this book.

Special thanks to my long-time friend and literary agent, William B. R. Reiss, to Lilly Golden, editor of the revised edition, and to Peter Burford, for being willing to take a gamble.

Credits

Mr. William H. Williams, National General Manager of the *Daily Racing Form*, his staff, and the staffs of each of the regional editions, were helpful as I compiled the original data for this book, and gracious in granting permission for its use.

Photos were provided by The American Quarter Horse Association, *The Blood-Horse* magazine, Henry and Linda Bowlan, Bob Coglianese, Four-Footed Fotos, Orren Mixer, Sunland Park (photographer Bill Pitt Jr.), and Mr. Earl Holmes of Vessels Stallion Farm.

APPENDIX

SPEED HANDICAPPER™ Computer Program

DOS Version 2.0

Copyright Notice

Copyright 1984, 1991, 1996 by Charles H. Carroll. All rights reserved. This program is provided for the personal, noncommercial use of the readers of *Handicapping Speed: The Thoroughbred and Quarter Horse Sprinters*. No part of this program nor the output from it, may be reproduced in any form or by any means or stored in a database or retrieval system, except that of the individual reader and user, without prior written permission of the copyright owner. Making copies of any part of this program for any purpose other than your own personal use is a violation of the United States copyright laws.

This program is provided as a horse race handicapping tool for use within a broader handicapping strategy, the success of which is dependent upon the individual approach of the user. No further warranty is expressed or implied.

This listing of QBasic code provides the opportunity to type in and use the central portions of the Speed Handicapper program for DOS. To obtain this program or more advanced versions on disk for DOS or Microsoft Windows, write to Desert Sea Software, Star Route 2, Box 84, Socorro, NM 87801 (http://www.desertsea.com).

The following program accepts past performance data from the keyboard. It calculates parallel speed for the past performances, sorts the past performances according to several options, and displays the results on the screen or printer. The program is written in Microsoft QBasic, which is supplied with Microsoft DOS versions 5.0 and later. If you are not familiar with QBasic, or are uncertain if you have it, go to the DOS "C:\" prompt, type "cd dos" then at the "C:\DOS\" prompt, type "qbasic". QBasic should start with an introductory screen. You *must* have QBasic or a similar BASIC interpreter in order to run the program (earlier versions of BASIC lack some of the commands used and will not run). QBasic has a good screen editor, but if you are not familiar with it, you may be surprised when you type in some of the lines and it jumps to a secondary screen for a new "Sub" or "Function." When you finish the Sub and type "End Sub" or "End Function" as shown in the listing, the program automatically jumps back to the prior screen.

In the following listing, the ▶ symbol is used to indicate that the current line continues. When you reach that symbol, do not hit return, but continue typing on the same line. QBasic allows lines to be much wider than the printed page or computer screen. Any spaces (or absence of spaces) between double quotes (" " or "") are important. These spaces set up the screen and printer position of words and data when you view them (or await a key stroke), so if the outputs are misaligned, count the spaces and insert more or less to correct the problem. Text following single quotes (') are comments and are not essential.

When you have finished typing the program, save it in your C:\DOS directory (which will be automatic if you type in QBasic). Open it from QBasic and follow the menu to "Run" and "Start" it. Any typing errors will be identified with error messages. QBasic has a fairly good on-line HELP that will guide you in corrections.

To use the program simply follow the screens. "Track" should be the common abbreviation of the track you are handicapping. It can be left blank by hitting return. "Horse number" is generally the order in which the horses' past performances occur in the *Form*; you can use any other whole numbers that suit your purposes. For "Name" you can type some or all of the horse's name—or leave it blank by hitting return. "Distance" is the distance of the past race in furlongs for Thoroughbreds, or yards for quarter horses. For Thoroughbred races, type the decimal equivalent in furlongs (e.g., 6 1/2 furlongs = 6.5; one mile = 8; for 1 mile 40 yards and 1 mile 70 yards, type 8.4 or 8.7 respectively and the program will convert to the actual decimal equivalents to save typing—do not be concerned when the screen shows 8.2 and 8.3, which results from rounding of the output format). Enter Thoroughbred time in minutes, seconds, and fifths, with no spaces or punctuation, e.g., "1111" for one-minute-eleven-seconds-and-one-fifth, "0594" for fifty-nine-and-four-fifths-seconds. With the few exceptions of data that require letters, you can learn to input very rapidly using the numeric key pad.

Test the program by inputting the base point times for both breeds (pages 137 and 140), which should each return a speed of 1000 (except the extrapolated time for 1 mile 70 yards, which will be 999 or 1001 when entered to the nearest fifth).

The Thoroughbred Variant option is discussed in Chapter 4. To determine the "Zero Variant" take the average of recent *Daily Racing Form* variants separately for sprints and routes on fast tracks. Ten or twelve should suffice and can often be obtained from the recent past performances of horses entered in a single race. The same race may occur repeatedly in a group of past performances, so be sure to use it only once. For "Zero Variant" enter the average for sprints or routes depending upon the past performance that you are handicapping. For "Form Variant," enter the Daily Racing Form variant for the particular past performance. For example: Zero Variant : 16, Form Variant 22. This feature should be used only with great care and testing, as discussed in Chapter 4.

The text of the program follows:

```
DECLARE SUB LPrtHead (track AS STRING, month AS STRING, day AS STRING, ▶
year AS STRING, race AS STRING, breed AS INTEGER, variant AS INTEGER, ▶
Wind AS INTEGER, num AS INTEGER)
DECLARE SUB LScrPrint (breed AS INTEGER, Number() AS SINGLE, hname() AS ▶
STRING, dist() AS SINGLE, Speed() AS SINGLE, lenBack() AS SINGLE, sorted() ▶
AS INTEGER, ct AS INTEGER)
DECLARE SUB UpDown (dir AS INTEGER, sortR() AS SINGLE, ct AS INTEGER, ▶
sorted() AS INTEGER)
DECLARE SUB PrtHead (track AS STRING, month AS STRING, day AS STRING, ▶
year AS STRING, race AS STRING, breed AS INTEGER, variant AS INTEGER, ▶
Wind AS INTEGER, num AS INTEGER)
DECLARE SUB ScrPrint (breed AS INTEGER, Number() AS SINGLE, hname() AS ▶
STRING, dist() AS SINGLE, Speed() AS SINGLE, lenBack() AS SINGLE, sorted() ▶
AS INTEGER, ct AS INTEGER)
DECLARE SUB SortKey (sortCh AS INTEGER)
DECLARE FUNCTION Tbcalc% (tbTime AS STRING, dist AS SINGLE, variant AS ▶
INTEGER, adjust AS STRING, drfVar AS SINGLE, lenBack AS SINGLE)
DECLARE SUB GetTbpps (tbT AS STRING, lb AS SINGLE, variant AS INTEGER, ▶
zeroVar AS INTEGER, formVar AS INTEGER, drfVar AS SINGLE, adjust AS ▶
STRING)
DECLARE SUB GetQHpps (Wind AS INTEGER, rawTime AS SINGLE, windir AS ▶
INTEGER)
DECLARE FUNCTION QHcalc% (Wind AS INTEGER, windir AS INTEGER, ▶
rawTime AS SINGLE, dist AS SINGLE, Speed AS SINGLE)
DECLARE SUB GetVar (zeroVar AS INTEGER, formVar AS INTEGER, drfVar AS ▶
SINGLE, adjust AS STRING)
DECLARE FUNCTION MkDay$ (dy AS INTEGER)
DECLARE SUB Retry (check AS INTEGER)
DECLARE SUB Menu1 (breed AS INTEGER, variant AS INTEGER, Wind AS ▶
INTEGER)
DECLARE SUB GetTrack (track AS STRING, mon AS INTEGER, dy AS INTEGER, ▶
year AS STRING, race AS STRING)
DECLARE FUNCTION MkMonth$ (mon AS INTEGER)
DECLARE SUB center (text AS STRING, where AS INTEGER)
DECLARE SUB InitScreen ()
CONST MAX% = 50
CONST PROGNAME$ = " Speed Handicapper v2.0 Copyright 1996 by Charles ▶
Carroll "
CONST FORM1$ = " ##   \      \   ##.#   ##.##   ####"
CONST FORM2$ = " ##   \      \   ###   ####"
CONST PERROR$ = "Printer Not Ready –> Hit Any Key When Ready"
CONST prompt1$ = "<1> Print Hard Copy   <2> Sort Again   <3> Begin Next Race ▶
<4> Exit"
CONST PROMPT3$ = "Hit <0> to Handicap"
DIM Number(MAX%) AS SINGLE
```

```
DIM hname(MAX%) AS STRING
DIM dist(MAX%) AS SINGLE
DIM tbTime(MAX%) AS STRING
DIM lenBack(MAX%) AS SINGLE
DIM qhTime(MAX%) AS SINGLE
DIM sorted(MAX%) AS INTEGER
DIM Speed(MAX%) AS SINGLE
DIM rawTime AS SINGLE
DIM correct AS INTEGER
DIM windir AS INTEGER
DIM breed AS INTEGER
DIM variant AS INTEGER
DIM Wind AS INTEGER
DIM R AS INTEGER
DIM ct AS INTEGER
DIM sortCh AS INTEGER
DIM last AS INTEGER
DIM slect AS STRING
DIM SHARED CLRLIN AS STRING


correct% = 0
R% = 1
ct% = 0
CLRLIN$ = SPACE$(80)


InitScreen
VIEW PRINT 2 TO 24

DO
newrace:
CLS 2
Menu1 breed%, variant%, Wind%

correctFile:
CLS 2
GetTrack track$, mon%, dy%, year$, race$
Retry correct%
IF correct% = 1 THEN
EXIT DO
END IF
LOOP

month$ = MkMonth$(mon%)
day$ = MkDay$(dy%)

FOR R% = 1 TO MAX%
start:

CLS 2
center PROMPT3$, 3
LOCATE 7, 5
INPUT "Horse Number : ", Number!(R%)
IF R% = 1 AND Number!(R%) = 0 THEN
GOTO start
```

```
END IF
IF Number!(R%) = 0 THEN
center CLRLIN$, 3
center CLRLIN$, 7
EXIT FOR
END IF
center CLRLIN$, 3
LOCATE 10, 5
INPUT "Name : ", hname$(R%)
LOCATE 10, 35
INPUT "Distance : ", dist!(R%)
IF dist!(R%) = 8.4 THEN
dist!(R%) = 8.182
ELSEIF dist!(R%) = 8.7 THEN
dist!(R%) = 8.318
END IF
IF breed% = 1 THEN
GetTbpps tbTime$(R%), lenBack!(R%), variant%, zeroVar%, formVar%, drfVar!, ▶
adjust$
Retry correct%
IF correct% = 0 THEN
GOTO start
END IF
Speed!(R%) = Tbcalc%(tbTime$(R%), dist!(R%), variant%, adjust$, drfVar!, ▶
lenBack!(R%))
ELSEIF breed% = 2 THEN
GetQHpps Wind%, qhTime!(R%), windir%
Retry correct%
IF correct% = 0 THEN
GOTO start
END IF
Speed!(R%) = QHcalc%(Wind%, windir%, qhTime!(R%), dist!(R%), Speed!)
END IF
center CLRLIN$, 23
LOCATE 23, 5
PRINT "PP # : "; R%; " Parallel Speed : "; Speed!(R%)
SLEEP 1
ct% = ct% + 1
NEXT R%

Resort:
SortKey num%
SELECT CASE num%
CASE 1
dir% = 1
UpDown dir%, Speed!(), ct%, sorted%()
CASE 2
dir% = 2
UpDown dir%, Number!(), ct%, sorted%()
CASE 3
dir% = 2
UpDown dir%, dist!(), ct%, sorted%()
END SELECT
```

```
PrtHead track$, month$, day$, year$, race$, breed%, variant%, Wind%, num%
ScrPrint breed%, Number!(), hname$(), dist!(), Speed!(), lenBack!(), sorted%(), ct%

FinalOpt:
center prompt1$, 23
DO
slect$ = INKEY$
LOOP WHILE ((VAL(slect$) < 1) OR (VAL(slect$) > 4))
last% = VAL(slect$)
SELECT CASE last%
CASE 1
LPrtHead track$, month$, day$, year$, race$, breed%, variant%, Wind%, num%
LScrPrint breed%, Number!(), hname$(), dist!(), Speed!(), lenBack!(), sorted%(),
ct%
LPRINT
LPRINT STRING$(80, "+")
GOTO FinalOpt
CASE 2
GOTO Resort
CASE 3
CLEAR
GOTO newrace
CASE 4
CLS
END
END SELECT
END
PrintFix:
BEEP
center CLRLIN$, 25
center PERROR$, 25
DO WHILE INKEY$ = " "
LOOP
center CLRLIN$, 25
RESUME

SUB center (text AS STRING, where AS INTEGER)
DIM it AS STRING
it = LEFT$(text, 80)
LOCATE where%, 41 – LEN(it) / 2
PRINT it;
END SUB

SUB GetQHpps (Wind AS INTEGER, rawTime AS SINGLE, windir AS INTEGER)
LOCATE 13, 5
INPUT "Time, This Horse : ", rawTime!
IF Wind% = 1 THEN
LOCATE 16, 5
PRINT "Tail Wind = 1   No Wind = 2   Cross Wind = 3   Head Wind = 4"
DO
PRINT
LOCATE CSRLIN, 5
INPUT "Wind : ", windir%
```

```
LOOP WHILE (windir% < 1) OR (windir% > 4)
END IF
END SUB

SUB GetTbpps (tbT AS STRING, lb AS SINGLE, variant AS INTEGER, zeroVar AS ▶
INTEGER, formVar AS INTEGER, drfVar AS SINGLE, adjust AS STRING)
LOCATE 13, 5
INPUT "Winner's Time : ", tbT$
LOCATE 13, 35
INPUT "Lengths Back : ", lb!
IF variant% = 1 THEN
GetVar zeroVar%, formVar%, drfVar!, adjust$
ELSEIF variant% = 0 THEN
zeroVar% = 0
formVar% = 0
drfVar! = 0
adjust$ = "f"
END IF
END SUB

SUB GetTrack (track AS STRING, mon AS INTEGER, dy AS INTEGER, year AS ▶
STRING, race AS STRING)
LOCATE 10, 5
INPUT "Track : ", track$
DO
PRINT
LOCATE CSRLIN, 5
INPUT "Month : ", mon%
LOOP WHILE (mon% < 1 OR mon% > 12)

DO
LOCATE (CSRLIN – 1), 18
INPUT "Day : ", dy%
LOOP WHILE (dy% < 1 OR dy% > 31)
LOCATE (CSRLIN – 1), 30
INPUT "Year : ", year$
PRINT
LOCATE CSRLIN, 5
INPUT "Race : ", race$
END SUB

SUB GetVar (zeroVar AS INTEGER, formVar AS INTEGER, drfVar AS SINGLE, ▶
adjust AS STRING)
LOCATE 16, 5
INPUT "Zero Variant : ", zeroVar%
LOCATE 16, 35
INPUT "DRF Race Variant : ", formVar%
IF formVar% = zeroVar% OR formVar% = zeroVar% + 1 OR formVar% = zeroVar% ▶
– 1 THEN
drfVar! = 0
adjust$ = "f"
ELSEIF formVar% < zeroVar% – 5 THEN
drfVar! = 2 + ((zeroVar% – 5) – formVar%)
```

```
adjust$ = "f"
ELSEIF (formVar% < zeroVar% – 1) AND (formVar% >= zeroVar% – 5) THEN
drfVar! = ABS(((zeroVar% – 1) – formVar%) / 2)
adjust$ = "f"
ELSE
drfVar! = ABS((formVar% – (zeroVar% + 1)) / 2)
adjust$ = "s"
END IF
END SUB


SUB InitScreen
CLS
COLOR 7, 4
center PROGNAME$, 1
COLOR 7, 1
END SUB


SUB LPrtHead (track AS STRING, month AS STRING, day AS STRING, year AS ▶
STRING, race AS STRING, breed AS INTEGER, variant AS INTEGER, Wind AS ▶
INTEGER, num AS INTEGER)
ON ERROR GOTO PrintFix
LPRINT
LPRINT "Track : "; track$
LPRINT month$; " "; day$; ", 19"; year$; " Race: "; race$
SELECT CASE breed%
CASE 1
SELECT CASE variant%
CASE 0
LPRINT "Tbred Without Variant"
CASE 1
LPRINT "Tbred With Variant"
END SELECT
CASE 2
SELECT CASE Wind%
CASE 0
LPRINT "Quarter Horse Without Wind"
CASE 1
LPRINT "Quarter Horse With Wind"
END SELECT
END SELECT
SELECT CASE num%
CASE 1
LPRINT "Sorted by Speed"
CASE 2
LPRINT "Sorted by Horse Number"
CASE 3
LPRINT "Sorted by Distance"
END SELECT
ON ERROR GOTO 0
END SUB
SUB LScrPrint (breed AS INTEGER, Number() AS SINGLE, hname() AS STRING, ▶
dist() AS SINGLE, Speed() AS SINGLE, lenBack() AS SINGLE, sorted() AS ▶
```

```
INTEGER, ct AS INTEGER)
DIM pass AS INTEGER
LPRINT
SELECT CASE breed%
CASE 1
LPRINT "Horse No.";  "  Name          ";  "   Dist ";  " (LensBack)  Speed"
CASE 2
LPRINT "Horse No.";  "  Name          ";  "   Dist ";  "  Speed"
END SELECT
FOR pass% = 1 TO ct%
SELECT CASE breed%
CASE 1
LPRINT USING FORM1$; Number!(sorted%(pass%)); hname$(sorted%(pass%)); ▶
dist!(sorted%(pass%));lenBack!(sorted%(pass%)); Speed!(sorted%(pass%))
CASE 2
LPRINT USING FORM2$; Number!(sorted%(pass%)); hname$(sorted% ▶
(pass%)); dist!(sorted%(pass%)); Speed!(sorted%(pass%))
END SELECT
NEXT pass%
END SUB


SUB Menu1 (breed AS INTEGER, variant AS INTEGER, Wind AS INTEGER)
DIM clect AS STRING
DIM choice AS INTEGER
DO
LOCATE 7, 5
PRINT "Type of Race:"
LOCATE 9, 10: PRINT "1  Thoroughbreds Without Variant"
LOCATE 10, 10: PRINT "2  Thoroughbreds With DRF-Based Variant"
LOCATE 11, 10: PRINT "3  Quarter Horses Without Wind"
LOCATE 12, 10: PRINT "4  Quarter Horses With Wind"
LOCATE 13, 10: PRINT "5  Exit"
LOCATE 15, 5
INPUT "Select (1 – 5) : ", clect$
LOOP WHILE ((VAL(clect$) < 1) OR (VAL(clect$) > 5))
choice% = VAL(clect$)
SELECT CASE choice%
CASE 1
breed% = 1
variant% = 0
Wind% = 0
CASE 2
breed% = 1
variant% = 1
Wind% = 0
CASE 3
breed% = 2
variant% = 0
Wind% = 0
CASE 4
breed% = 2
variant% = 0
Wind% = 1
CASE 5
```

```
CLS
END
END SELECT
END SUB

FUNCTION MkDay$ (dy AS INTEGER)
IF dy% > 9 THEN
MkDay$ = LTRIM$(STR$(dy%))
ELSE
SELECT CASE dy%
CASE 1
MkDay$ = "01"
CASE 2
MkDay$ = "02"
CASE 3
MkDay$ = "03"
CASE 4
MkDay$ = "04"
CASE 5
MkDay$ = "05"
CASE 6
MkDay$ = "06"
CASE 7
MkDay$ = "07"
CASE 8
MkDay$ = "08"
CASE 9
MkDay$ = "09"
END SELECT
END IF
END FUNCTION

FUNCTION MkMonth$ (mon AS INTEGER)
SELECT CASE mon%
CASE 1
MkMonth$ = "Jan"
CASE 2
MkMonth$ = "Feb"
CASE 3
MkMonth$ = "Mar"
CASE 4
MkMonth$ = "Apr"
CASE 5
MkMonth$ = "May"
CASE 6
MkMonth$ = "Jun"
CASE 7
MkMonth$ = "Jul"
CASE 8
MkMonth$ = "Aug"
CASE 9
MkMonth$ = "Sep"
CASE 10
MkMonth$ = "Oct"
```

```
CASE 11
MkMonth$ = "Nov"
CASE 12
MkMonth$ = "Dec"
END SELECT
END FUNCTION


SUB PrtHead (track AS STRING, month AS STRING, day AS STRING, year AS ▶
STRING, race AS STRING, breed AS INTEGER, variant AS INTEGER, Wind AS ▶
INTEGER, num AS INTEGER)
CLS 2
PRINT "Track : "; track$
PRINT month$; " "; day$; ", 19"; year$; " Race: "; race$
SELECT CASE breed%
CASE 1
SELECT CASE variant%
CASE 0
PRINT "Tbred Without Variant"
CASE 1
PRINT "Tbred With Variant"
END SELECT
CASE 2
SELECT CASE Wind%
CASE 0
PRINT "Quarter Horse Without Wind"
CASE 1
PRINT "Quarter Horse With Wind"
END SELECT
END SELECT
SELECT CASE num%
CASE 1
PRINT "Sorted by Speed"
CASE 2
PRINT "Sorted by Horse Number"
CASE 3
PRINT "Sorted by Distance"
END SELECT
END SUB


FUNCTION QHcalc% (Wind AS INTEGER, windir AS INTEGER, rawTime AS ▶
SINGLE, dist AS SINGLE, Speed AS SINGLE)
DIM qhT AS SINGLE
DIM yards AS INTEGER
DIM feet AS INTEGER
DIM lenRun AS SINGLE
DIM timeLen AS SINGLE
IF Wind% = 1 THEN
SELECT CASE windir%
CASE 1
qhT! = rawTime! + .04
CASE 2
qhT! = rawTime!
CASE 3
qhT! = rawTime! - .06
CASE 4
```

```
qhT! = rawTime! − .13
END SELECT
ELSEIF Wind% = 0 THEN
qhT! = rawTime!
END IF
yards% = dist!
feet% = yards% * 3
lenRun! = feet% / 8
timeLen! = qhT! / lenRun!
IF dist! = 220 THEN
basePt! = .1408
ELSEIF dist! = 250 THEN
basePt! = .1378
ELSEIF dist! = 300 THEN
basePt! = .1339
ELSEIF dist! = 330 THEN
basePt! = .1328
ELSEIF dist! = 350 THEN
basePt! = .131
ELSEIF dist! = 400 THEN
basePt! = .1279
ELSEIF dist! = 440 THEN
basePt! = .1274
ELSEIF dist! = 550 THEN
basePt! = .1277
ELSEIF dist! = 660 THEN
basePt! = .132
ELSEIF dist! = 770 THEN
basePt! = .1369
ELSEIF dist! = 870 THEN
basePt! = .1348
ELSEIF dist! = 1000 THEN
basePt! = .1382
END IF
Speed! = basePt! / timeLen!
Speed! = (Speed! + .0005) * 1000
Speed! = INT(Speed!)
QHcalc% = Speed!
END FUNCTION

SUB Retry (check AS INTEGER)
DIM hit AS STRING
DIM prompt AS STRING
CLRLIN$ = SPACE$(80)
PRINT
PRINT
prompt$ = "<Space> Continue  <r> Replace"
center prompt$, 23
DO
hit$ = INKEY$
LOOP UNTIL ((hit$ = CHR$(32)) OR (LCASE$(hit$) = "r"))
IF (LCASE$(hit$) = "r") THEN
check% = 0
ELSEIF hit$ = CHR$(32) THEN
check% = 1
```

```
END IF
center CLRLIN$, 23
END SUB

SUB ScrPrint (breed AS INTEGER, Number() AS SINGLE, hname() AS STRING, ▶
dist() AS SINGLE, Speed() AS SINGLE, lenBack() AS SINGLE, sorted() AS ▶
INTEGER, ct AS INTEGER)
DIM pass AS INTEGER
DIM low AS INTEGER
DIM hi AS INTEGER
low% = 1
hi% = 12
PRINT
DO
SELECT CASE breed%
CASE 1
PRINT "Horse No.";  " Name          "; "  Dist  "; " (LensBack)  Speed"
CASE 2
PRINT "Horse No.";  " Name          "; "  Dist  "; " Speed"
END SELECT
FOR pass% = low% TO hi%
SELECT CASE breed%
CASE 1
PRINT USING FORM1$; Number!(sorted%(pass%)); hname$(sorted% ▶
(pass%)); dist!(sorted%(pass%)); lenBack!(sorted%(pass%)); Speed!(sorted%(pass%))
CASE 2
PRINT USING FORM2$; Number!(sorted%(pass%)); hname$(sorted%(pass%)); ▶
dist!(sorted%(pass%)); Speed!(sorted%(pass%))
END SELECT
SELECT CASE pass%
CASE IS = ct%
EXIT DO
CASE IS = hi%
PRINT
PRINT "Hit Any Key For Next Group"
DO WHILE INKEY$ = " "
LOOP
low% = low% + 12
hi% = hi% + 12
CLS 2
PRINT
PRINT
END SELECT
NEXT pass%
LOOP
END SUB

SUB SortKey (sortCh AS INTEGER)
DIM clect AS STRING
DIM prompt2 AS STRING
prompt2$ = "    Sort By:  <1> Speed   <2> Horse Number   <3> Distance      "
center prompt2$, 23
DO
clect$ = INKEY$
LOOP WHILE (VAL(clect$) < 1) OR (VAL(clect$) > 3)
```

```
sortCh% = VAL(clect$)
END SUB

FUNCTION Tbcalc% (tbTime AS STRING, dist AS SINGLE, variant AS INTEGER, ▶
adjust AS STRING, drfVar AS SINGLE, lenBack AS SINGLE)
DIM mins AS INTEGER
DIM secs AS INTEGER
DIM fifths AS SINGLE
DIM rawTime AS SINGLE
DIM feet AS SINGLE
DIM lenRun AS SINGLE
DIM timeLen AS SINGLE
DIM varTime AS SINGLE
DIM actTpl AS SINGLE
DIM actTime AS SINGLE
DIM realTpl AS SINGLE
DIM basePt AS SINGLE
DIM varSpeed AS SINGLE
mins% = VAL(LEFT$(tbTime$, 1)) * 60
secs% = VAL(MID$(tbTime$, 2, 2))
fifths! = VAL(RIGHT$(tbTime$, 1)) * .2
rawTime! = mins% + secs% + fifths! 'winner's raw time
feet! = (dist! / 8) * 5280
lenRun! = feet! / 8
timeLen! = rawTime! / lenRun! 'winner's time per length
IF variant% = 1 THEN
IF adjust$ = "f" THEN
actTime! = rawTime! + drfVar! * timeLen!
ELSEIF adjust$ = "s" THEN
actTime! = rawTime! – drfVar! * timeLen!
END IF
ELSEIF variant% = 0 THEN
actTime! = rawTime!
END IF
actTpl! = actTime! / lenRun! ' winner's adjusted time/length
IF lenBack! > 0 THEN
actTime! = actTime! + lenBack! * actTpl! 'loser's time
END IF
realTpl! = actTime! / lenRun!
IF dist! = 4 THEN
basePt! = .134
ELSEIF dist! = 4.5 THEN
basePt! = .1357
ELSEIF dist! = 5 THEN
basePt! = .1338
ELSEIF dist! = 5.5 THEN
basePt! = .1353
ELSEIF dist! = 6 THEN
basePt! = .1358
ELSEIF dist! = 6.5 THEN
basePt! = .1372
ELSEIF dist! = 7 THEN
basePt! = .1375
ELSEIF dist! = 8 THEN
basePt! = .1397
```

```
ELSEIF dist! = 8.182 THEN
basePt! = .1407
ELSEIF dist! = 8.318 THEN
basePt! = .1409
ELSEIF dist! = 8.5 THEN
basePt! = .1403
ELSEIF dist! = 9 THEN
basePt! = .1414
ELSEIF dist! = 9.5 THEN
basePt! = .1434
ELSEIF dist! = 10 THEN
basePt! = .1428
END IF
varSpeed! = basePt! / realTpl!
varSpeed! = (varSpeed! + .0005) * 1000
Tbcalc% = INT(varSpeed!)
END FUNCTION

SUB UpDown (dir AS INTEGER, sortR() AS SINGLE, ct AS INTEGER, sorted() AS ▶
INTEGER)
DIM A AS INTEGER
DIM B AS INTEGER
DIM Q AS INTEGER
FOR A% = 1 TO ct%
Q% = 1
FOR B% = 1 TO ct%
SELECT CASE dir%
CASE 1
IF sortR!(A%) < sortR!(B%) THEN
Q% = Q% + 1
END IF
CASE 2
IF sortR!(A%) > sortR!(B%) THEN
Q% = Q% + 1
END IF
END SELECT
IF sortR!(A%) = sortR!(B%) THEN
SELECT CASE dir%
CASE 1
IF A% < B% THEN
Q% = Q% + 1
END IF
CASE 2
IF A% > B% THEN
Q% = Q% + 1
END IF
END SELECT
END IF
NEXT B%
sorted%(Q%) = A%
NEXT A%
END SUB
```

INDEX

Aerobic exercise, 44, 135–36
Ainslie, Tom, 22–23, 27, 66, 123
*Ainslie's Complete Guide to
    Thoroughbred Racing* (Ainslie),
    22–23
All-American Futurity, 59, 70
Allowance races, 8–9, 70
American Quarter Horse, 48–49
American Quarter Horse Association
    (AQHA), 48–49
    MSTs, 125, 127–30
    Quarter Racing Journal, 159
Anaerobic/aerobic threshold, 135–36
Anaerobic exercise, 44, 58, 135–36
Aqueduct race track, 202–3
Assessing the field, examples of actual
    races, 172–90

Baselines
    quarter horse, 133–37
    Thoroughbred, 137–40
BASIC language, 155–58
Belmont Park, 46
Bets (betting)
    boxing, 37–38
    handicapping and, 192
    in-the-money, 197, 204–10
    show, 29, 30, 36
    takeout and breakage and, 32–33
    by trainers, 103–4
    wheeling, 38
    win, 193–94, 197, 201
Beyer, Andrew, 22, 24, 25, 27, 66, 75,
    103, 123
Beyer speed figures, 5, 76, 77, 124
Big T, 34
Blood cell volume, 58

Bloodstock Research Information
    Services, 159
Bookies, 27–28
Boxing a bet, 37–38
Breakage, 32–33
Breeding, 48–62
    handicapping and, 48, 50–51
    male vs. female lines, 50
    nicks and, 49–50
    phenotype and, 49, 50, 54
    prepotency and, 49
    quarter horse, 54, 58–59, 62
    runner genes and, 117–18
    speed and, 48, 71
    sprinters and, 52, 53
Breezing times, 104–5
Brohamer, Tom, 24, 78
Brooks, Jack, 29
Bull Dog, 51
Bullet horses, 102–3

Calculators, computing speed with,
    153–54
Caliente Race Track (Tijuana, Mex.),
    27–28
Calls, 93
Chaos, 109–10, 117–20
Charts, *Daily Racing Form*, 12–13, 159
chefs de race, 50–51, 118
Chinook Pass, 51, 52
Class. *See also* Racing classes
    handicapping, 74–78
    in horses, 71–75
Class par times, 123
    statistical programs and, 161–63
Clockers, 84–91, 104
Clusters, 204–10

Colts, 66

Combination bets. *See* Exotics; *and specific types of bets*

Computers, 108–10, 154–68
BASIC language and, 155–58
par times and, 77
quarter horse, 156–57
speed handicapping in, 5
spreadsheet prgrams and, 158–65
statistical programs, 161–68
Thoroughbred, 157–58

Computing speed, 153–68
with calculators, 153–54
with computers, 154–68

Condition books, 67

Conformation, 54

Coupling, 7

Cynthia Publishing, 78

Daily doubles, 34, 37

Daily Racing Form, 5–13
charts in, 12–13, 159
editions of, 6
"Experts' Selections" in, 6
finish times listed in, 88, 92–94
"Graded Handicaps" in, 6–7
morning-line odds in, 7
"Past Performances" in, 8–11
speed handicapping and, 25–27
speed indexes listed in, 124–31
workout times listed in, 102–4

Dark Horse, 159

Darnell, Casey, 113

Davidowitz, Steven, 66, 123

Dirt (racing surface), 94–100

Distances, running
correlation of racing times and, 111–17
quarter horse, 47–48

Dog racing, 42

Dominance, social, 71–74

Dosage analysis, 50–51

Downs, The (NM), 99–100

Dr. Fager, 25–26, 71

Dr. Z's Beat the Racetrack (Ziemba and Hausch), 29–30

Duck Butter, 144–46

Electric eye timers, 84

Endurance horses, 58

Equibase, 159

Exactas (perfectas), 34, 37, 38, 40, 200

Exotics, 36–42, 67, 200
losing winners and, 39–41

"Experts' Selections" *(Daily Racing Form)*, 6

Fast track, 97

Field, assessment using actual races, 172–90

Fillies, 66. *See also* Mares

Finishes, video replays of, 93

Finishing times. *See* Times

Flagman, 84

Flatterer, 51

Flying start, 80–82

Forego, 52–54

Fractures, leg, 119

Gamblers' Book Club, 13, 212

Gaps, speed, 204–10

Geldings, 66, 71, 72

Gender, handicapping and, 72–73

Genetics. *See* Breeding

Genotype, 49

Genter, Frances, 194

Gleick, James, 110

Good track, 97

"Graded Handicaps," *Daily Racing Form*, 6–7

Hambleton, Tom, 24

Handicappers, professional, 191–92

Handicapping. *See also* Speed handicapping
betting and, 192
breeding and, 48, 50–51
class, 74–78
computers and, 108–10
gender and, 72–73
mathematical equations and, 108–20
microtrip, 47
odds playing vs., 29–30
pace, 23–24, 26
time management and, 169–72

trifectas, 39
trip, 19–23, 26, 27
Handicap races, 70–71
Handily times, 104–5
Hand-timing, timing cameras vs., 115
Happy Idiot, 141–43
Hausch, Donald B., 29
Hawthorne, 202–3
Heavy track, 97
Hollywood Park, 46
Horses. *See also* Quarter horses;
    Thoroughbreds; *and other specific*
    topics
    bullet, 102–3
    class in, 71–75
    endurance, 58
    social dominance and, 71–74

Inertia, start-up times and, 113,
    115–16
Inertia/drag propulsion threshold, 116,
    131, 135, 136
International Thoroughbred
    Superhighway, 159
In-the-money betting, 197
    past performances and, 202–4
    speed gaps, lines, and clusters and,
        204–10

Jockeys
    sprint strategy, 44–45
    statistical programs and, 163–64
Junior Meyers, 132

Kansas Futurity (1990), 21
Kentucky Derby, dosage analysis and,
    50, 51
King Ranch, 58

Lane biases, 99
La Mesa Park (NM), 132
Layout of the race, 82–84
Leg fractures, 119
Lengths back
    quarter horse, 88–91
    Thoroughbred, 91–94
Li, Tien-Yien, 117–18
Lines, 204–10
Long races, 44

Lorenz, Edward N., 109–10
Los Alamitos, 11, 115, 177, 178, 184
Losing winners, 39–41
Lukas, D. Wayne, 66

McGaughey, Shug, 66
Mahl, Huey, 24, 42
Maidens, 66
Mares
    breeding and, 50
    quarter horse racing and, 73
    social dominance and, 71–72
    Thoroughbred racing and, 72
Mathematical equations, handicapping
    and, 108–20
    correlation of time and distance and,
        111–17
Meadow, Barry, 42
Menicutch, Tim, 77
Microtrip handicapping, 47
Minimum Standard Time (MST), 125,
    127–30
Minus pool, 36
Mitchell, Dick, 42, 78, 200
Morning line (probable odds), 7
Muddy track, 97
Mud runners, 98–99

Naked races, 200
National Charts Weekly, 13
Northern Dancer, 4

Odds (odds playing), 27–30, 34–36
    calculating the odds, 35
    exotics and, 36–42
    in-the-money betting and, 200–2
    at less than even money, 35
    losing winners and, 39–41
    pools and, 34–35
    probable, 7
    win betting and, 201
Old Sorrel, 58–59
Owners, claiming and, 8–9, 67–70

Pace handicapping, 23–24, 26
Pancho Villa, 52
Parallel speed, 123–24

calculating speed with computers
 and, 156–58
 quarter horse, 151, 156–57
 Thoroughbred, 146–49, 151, 157–58
Parimutuel racing and betting, 31–34
Parlays, 192–93
Par times, 66, 123
 racing classes and, 74–78, 123,
  161–63
Past performances, 8–11, 141–46
 calculating speed with computers
  and, 156–58
 in-the-money betting and, 202–4
Perfectas. *See* Exactas
Performance horses, 59
Phenotype, 49, 50, 54
Photo-finishes
 hand-timing vs., 115
 quarter horse racing and, 85–89
 Thoroughbred racing and, 79–80, 85
Picking Winners (Beyer), 24
Pick Six, 34
Piebyeu, 21
Pine, Gordon, 77
Pizzolla, Michael, 24
Place, 33
Pools, bet, 33–34
 minus, 36
 show, 36
Position listings, 12–13
Post position, 7
Pratt, George W., 95, 96, 115
Prepotency, 49
Probable odds (morning line), 7

QBasic, 155
Quarter horses, 46–48
 All-American Futurity, 59, 70
 American Quarter Horse, 48–49
 anaerobic/aerobic threshold and,
  135–36
 baselines for, 133–37
 blood cell volume of, 58
 breeding, 54, 58–59, 62
 calculating speed with computers
  and, 156–57
 class and, 73–74

inertia/drag propulsion threshold
 and, 131, 135, 136
lengths back, 88–91
organization of, 18–19
parallel speed, 151, 156–57
"Past Performances" listing in the
 Form, 11
performance, 59
photo finishes and, 85–89
running distances, 47–48
speed handicapping and, 26, 47–48
speed indexes, 125–31, 178
sprints, 43
start-up times and, 113, 115–16
times, 80–81, 85–91
wind direction in, 11
world records, 137
Quarter Racing Journal, The, 159
Quinella, 34
Quinn, James, 24
Quirin, William, 66, 123

Races
 allowance, 70
 claiming, 8–9, 67–70
 handicap, 70–71
Racing classes, 66–71
 par times and, 74–78
 statistical programs and, 161–63
Racing secretaries, 67
Racing surface (dirt), 94–100
Racing times. *See* Times
Registers of Merit (ROM), 125
Routes, 44
Ruidoso Downs (NM), 11, 29–30, 47,
 115, 164, 184
Runner genes, 117–18
Running distances
 correlation of racing times and,
  111–17
 quarter horse, 47–48
Rusido Downs (NM), 179

San Juan Downs (NM), 139
Sartin, Howard, 24, 78
Schmidt, Dick, 24

Scott, William, 78
Second law of thermodynamics,
    111–12
Secretariat, 52, 54, 93
Short horses. *See* Quarter horses
Show, 34
Show betting, 29, 30
Show pools, 36
Sloppy track, 97
Slow track, 97
Social dominance, 71–74
Speed. *See also* Computing speed;
    Parallel speed
    breeding and, 48, 71
Speed gaps, 204–10
Speed handicapping, 24–27, 46. *See
    also specific topics*
    assessing the field, examples of
        actual races, 172–90
    lengths back and, 88–91
    par times and, 74–78
    quarter horse racing, 47–48
    racing classes and, 66
    track conditions and, 94–100
    workouts and, 100–6
Speed indexes
    baselines and, 132–40
    quarter horse, 125–31, 133–37, 178
    Thoroughbred, 125, 129, 131, 133,
        137–40
    variables and, 131–33
Split times, 85
Spreadsheet programs, 158–68
    statistical programs and, 161–68
Sprinters, breeding and, 52, 53
Sprints, 43–62
    definition of, 44
    jockey's strategy, 44–45
    quarter horse, 43
    Thoroughbred, 43–46
    track and, 46
Stables, distribution of, 66
Stallions
    breeding, 49–50
    prepotent, 49
    social dominance and, 71
Starting position, 80–82

Start-up times, 113, 115–16
Statistical programs, 161–68
    class-par-time and, 161–63
    jockeys and, 163–64
    trainers and, 163–64
    wind and, 164–68
Steinley's Photochart Systems, 90–92
Straight parlays, 192–93
Strawberry Silk, 29–30, 59, 73
Superfectas, 34, 39–40

Takeout, 32–33
Thoroughbred Sports Network, 159
Thoroughbreds (Thoroughbred racing)
    baselines for, 137–40
    breeding of, 49–54
    calculating speed with computers
        and, 157–58
    flying start and, 80–82
    gender of, 72
    lengths back and, 91–94
    parallel speed, 146–49, 151, 157–58
    "Past Performances" listing in the
        Form, 8–11
    quarter horse breeding and, 58–59, 62
    speed indexes, 125, 129, 131, 133,
        137–40
    sprints, 43–46
    times, 80–85, 144–46
    world records, 136–37, 139
Time management, handicapper's
    169–72
Times (finishing times)
    clockers and, 84–91
    correlation of distance and, 111–17
    electric eye timers and, 84
    hand-timing vs., 115
    lengths-back, 88–94
    photo-finish and, 79–80, 85–89, 93,
        115
    quarter horse, 80–81, 85–91
    Steinley's Photochart Systems,
        90–92
    Thoroughbred, 80–85, 144–46
Track, 31–33
    balancing process and, 66–67
    condition of, 94–100

layout of, 82–84
par times and, 76–78
photo-finishes and, 79–80, 85–89,
  93
sprints and, 46
starting positions, 80–82
takeout and breakage and, 32–33
video replays, 93
world records and, 139–40
Track constants, 81–85, 203
  spreadsheet programs and, 159–61
Track variants, 76–78
  racing surface (dirt), 94–100
Trainers
  betting by, 103–4
  class and, 74
  statistical programs and, 163–64
Trifectas, 34, 37–38
  handicapping, 39
  twin, 34, 38–39
Trip handicapping, 19–23, 26, 27
Triple, 34
Triple Crown, 52, 67
Turf Paradise, 139, 140

Twin trifectas, 34, 38–39

Valid Proposal, 21
Video replays, 93

Wheeling, 38
Win, 33
Win betting, 193–94, 197
  odds and, 201
Wind (wind direction)
  quarter horse racing and, 11
  statistical programs and, 164–68
Winners
  losing, 39–41
Workout times, 100–6
World records
  quarter horse, 137
  Thoroughbred, 136–37, 139
  tracks and, 139–40

Yorke, James, 117–18

Zany Tactics, 139
Ziemba, W. T., 29